Information Sharing Handbook

INFORMATION SHARING HANDBOOK

Edited by Claire Bessant

Consultant Editor: Phil Tompkins

The Law Society

ISBN-13: 978-1-85328-589-9

Published in 2009 by the Law Society
113 Chancery Lane, London WC2A 1PL

Typeset by IDSUK (DataConnection) Ltd
Printed by CPI Antony Rowe, Chippenham, Wiltshire

FSC
Mixed Sources
Product group from well-managed forests and other controlled sources
Cert no. SGS-COC-2953
www.fsc.org
© 1996 Forest Stewardship Council

The paper used for the text pages of this book is FSC certified. FSC (the Forest Stewardship Council) is an international network to promote responsible management of the world's forests.

Contents

About the authors

Claire Bessant qualified as a solicitor in private practice in 1998, specialising in family law. She is now a Principal Lecturer at Northumbria University School of Law teaching child law at undergraduate level, and at postgraduate level teaching various courses relating to the law affecting children, including a module focusing on children and information sharing. Claire is one of the founder members of Northumbria University's Centre for Information Rights Law and Practice. She is also a member of the Law Society's Children Law Sub-Committee. Claire has previously written *Domestic Violence, Crime and Victims Act 2004: A Guide to the New Law* also published by Law Society Publishing. Claire's research and writing is now focused on children, family and information sharing issues.

Phil Tompkins is a director at Dickinson Dees LLP and his practice area includes information law and IT law. He advises various private and public sector clients on all aspects of information law including freedom of information, data protection, data security and compliance issues. Phil has provided advice in relation to freedom of information requests, refusal notices, data protection audits, advised on complex data subject access requests, advised businesses on the sale and use of databases and drafted data protection policies. He frequently advises organisations in relation to data sharing and data protection aspects of using third party processors, including in relation to outsourcing deals. Phil lectures on the LLM in information rights law at Northumbria University.

Liane Atkin is a senior lecturer in law at Northumbria University. She originally trained as a solicitor at Ward Hadaway solicitors, a commercial law firm in Newcastle, before qualifying as a solicitor in their employment department where she advised clients on various contentious and non-contentious employment law issues. Since joining Northumbria University Liane has taught commercial law and employment law to legal practice course students and employment law and information rights law to masters students.

Leanne Bell spent two years as a medical student at the University of Sheffield before transferring to Northumbria University to study law, where she was named best student in medical law by the North of England Medico-Legal Society. She trained with a large commercial law firm in Newcastle before qualifying as a solicitor, advising public and private organisations on the implementation of the Freedom of Information Act. After several years in private practice she became the in-house legal advisor to the North East England Stem Cell Institute, based jointly at the universities of Durham and Newcastle, where she dealt with the complexities of information sharing law and other regulatory issues as they apply to fertility treatment and stem cell research. She is now a senior lecturer at Northumbria University specialising in public and medical law.

Elisabeth Griffiths is a senior lecturer at Northumbria University. She is the Programme Leader for the Masters in Employment Law in Practice. She qualified into a large commercial firm in the North East of England in 1996 and has been a tutor at Northumbria since 1997. Elisabeth returned to practice in 2003 as a practice support lawyer for a leading team of national employment law solicitors and then returned to Northumbria in 2005. She has taught extensively in employment law on both undergraduate and postgraduate programmes. She has also supervised employment law 'firms' in the Student Law Office run at Northumbria University. She is currently teaching employment law on the BVC, LPC and LLM programmes.

Kevin Kerrigan is Associate Dean at Northumbria Law School responsible for undergraduate and clinical programmes. He is also a practising solicitor and Human Rights Act consultant with experience of conducting criminal and human rights cases in courts at all levels. His teaching and research interests are in the fields of criminal litigation, human rights and legal education. In particular, he has an active interest in clinical legal education and runs a criminal appeal clinic at Northumbria University's award winning Student Law Office. Kevin has written numerous articles and text books and delivered papers at academic conferences and training courses for professionals, including, police, lawyers, social workers, mental health professionals and court clerks.

Helen Kingston is a senior lecturer at Northumbria University School of Law where she specialises in medical and mental health law, as well as acting as Director of the School's Enterprise Unit. Helen qualified as a solicitor in 1992 and after a number of years in private practice, where she specialised in advising on mental health and health law matters, including issues relating to health information, joined the Law School in 2004. Helen has maintained a consultancy in private practice and is currently a consultant with Beachcroft LLP.

Helen Morris qualified as a solicitor in 1987 and worked in City commercial firms before joining the Law School at Northumbria University in 1993. Her main teaching and research interests are intellectual property and information rights law. Helen was involved in setting up the university's LLM programme in Information Rights Law and Practice, and has been programme leader since it began in 2006.

Dean Murray is an Associate within the EU and competition law team at Dickinson Dees LLP. He qualified in 2001 and has specialised in competition law since that time. Dean has acted for clients in a number of investigations, helping to achieve satisfactory outcomes for clients in high profile cases. He has undertaken compliance work across a number of industry sectors including branded goods, manufacturing, transport, energy utilities and chemicals. Dean provides competition law support to the corporate, commercial and litigation teams. His clients have included commercial businesses of all types, councils, local authorities, regional development agencies, universities and third sector bodies.

Andrew Watson is a former local authority solicitor for Sheffield City Council and has been a senior lecturer at Northumbria University since 2006. As a local authority lawyer he advised on social services matters and on issues such as information sharing with partner agencies and the treatment of adoption records. He has a particular interest in information rights and lectures on data protection and access to information. A member of the Centre for Information Rights Law and Practice at Northumbria University, Andrew continues to research and write on information rights issues.

Susan Wolf is Director of LLM Programmes at the University of Northumbria School of Law having taught there since 1992. She is Principal Lecturer teaching European Union law and environmental law at both postgraduate and undergraduate level. Susan was responsible, in conjunction with Claire Bessant and Helen Morris, for establishing the LLM in Information Rights Law and Practice at Northumbria University and is also one of the founder members of the University's Centre for Information Rights Law and Practice. In recent years Susan has specialised in the Environmental Information Regulations (EIR) 2004 and has given a number of conference and seminar papers on the EIR 2004. She is co-author of *Wolf & Stanley on Environmental Law* and is a regular contributor to the *Osborns Dictionary of Law* and is also now writing a book on the EIR 2004 to be published by Law Society Publishing.

Preface

The fact that information is held and shared, by government, business, schools, local authorities and others, is well recognised (see for example Surveillance Studies Network, 2006 *A Report on the Surveillance Society, for the Information Commissioner* by the Surveillance Studies Network and Home Affairs Select Committee, Fifth Report 2007–8 *A Surveillance Society* HC 58). Still greater information sharing is envisaged, both in the commercial sector and in order to 'protect and support individuals and society as a whole' (the Foreword to the Government's *Information Sharing Vision Statement* (HM Government, 2006)).

The reality, unfortunately, is that:

> Sharing data across and between organisations can be a complex process. As there is no single source of law regulating the collection, use and sharing of … information, these activities are governed by a range of express and implied statutory provisions and common-law rules. Yet despite, or more likely because of, this broad range of provisions, the legal basis setting out whether and how information can be shared in any given situation is often far from clear-cut.
>
> Thomas and Walport, *Data Sharing Review Report* (2008) para 31.

Important as it undoubtedly is to understand statutes such as the Data Protection Act 1998 and Freedom of Information Act 2000, knowledge of individual statutes is unlikely to be sufficient when you are determining whether a specific piece of information can be shared. In this handbook, we explore the wide range of sources that must be taken into account when an information sharing decision is taken, and their interactions. Through flow-charts and scenarios we provide practical guidance to help you to determine when information can be shared.

We believe that this handbook, written by solicitors and academics with expertise in teaching information rights law, is essential for anyone who regularly advises on sharing information.

The law is stated as at 20 April 2009.

Table of cases

Table of statutes

Table of statutory instruments

Table of international legislation

List of abbreviations

Articles 2, 3, 6, 8, 10	Articles 2, 3, 6, 8 and 10 of the European Convention for the Protection of Human Rights and Fundamental Freedoms
CA 1989	Children Act 1989
The Convention	European Convention for the Protection of Human Rights and Fundamental Freedoms
DPA 1998	Data Protection Act 1998
Data Protection Directive	Council Directive 95/46/EC on the protection of individuals with regard to the processing of personal data and on the free movement of such data.
EIR 2004	Environmental Information Regulations 2004, SI 2004/3991
FOIA 2000	Freedom of Information Act 2000
HRA 1998	Human Rights Act 1998
Public Contract Regulations	Public Contracts Regulations 2006, SI 2006/5
PII	Public Interest Immunity
Re-Use Regulations	Re-Use of Public Sector Information Regulations, SI 2005/1515

Introduction

Claire Bessant

INTRODUCTION

Decisions about whether to share information must be taken on a case-by-case basis. Before sharing information numerous legal and practical issues must be addressed.

What sources can assist us to identify these issues? First, several legal provisions may be relevant. They must be identified and correctly applied, taking account of the facts of the case, before information is shared. In addition to legal sources, an increasing number of documents are available which are relied upon to clarify whether information sharing can take place. Whilst this handbook focuses on the law, this introductory chapter identifies several important non-legal sources and highlights several practical issues raised by them.

Consent is not a prerequisite to information sharing. However, under several of the legal regimes considered in this handbook, the obtaining of valid consent permits information to be lawfully shared. It is included in this introductory chapter for that reason.

An understanding of the law, the content and status of non-legal sources and the doctrine of consent is fundamental to the holistic understanding of information sharing issues needed when anyone considers 'can I share this information?'

THE LAW

The complexity of the law relating to information sharing has recently been highlighted (Foreword to the *Data Sharing Review* (2008) Thomas and Walport). It is appropriate to begin by outlining the legal sources encountered in this handbook.

Key statutory and common law obligations

Part I of this handbook explains the key legal regimes relevant to anyone considering whether to share information. Many of the principles explored apply to public bodies, commercial organisations and individuals alike. Public authorities are, however, subject to additional obligations, covered in Chapter 1.

The primary statutory provisions in the information sharing context are often considered to be the Data Protection Act 1998 and the Human Rights Act 1998. Both statutes play important roles in regulating whether information is shared. However, the Freedom of Information Act 1998 and the Environmental Information Regulations 2004, SI 2004/3391 also enable individuals and companies to obtain information held by public, and some private bodies; when information is disclosed to these bodies, the discloser should be aware that the information may potentially be shared with others under this legislation.

Practitioners must also consider the duty of confidentiality, and less frequently encountered statutes and statutory instruments, which play important roles in determining whether information can be lawfully shared or should not be shared. Chapter 4 highlights some of these diverse provisions, relating to matters including national security, crime, health, education, council tax data, adoption and whistleblowing.

Decisions of the Information Commissioner, the Information Tribunal and the courts

This handbook refers throughout to decisions of the courts, the Information Commissioner and the Information Tribunal. The particular remit of the Information Commissioner (the ICO) is to ensure that data controllers comply with obligations imposed by the Data Protection Act 1998, the Freedom of Information Act 2000, the Environmental Information Regulations 2004 and the Privacy and Electronic Communications Regulations 2003. The Information Tribunal hears appeals from notices issued by the ICO under these regimes. Appeals from the tribunal, on points of law, lie to the High Court.

How the ICO, the Tribunal and the courts have dealt with a particular issue will be an important factor in determining whether, in similar situations, information should be shared. However, a different approach must be adopted when relying upon court decisions compared to decisions of the ICO and the Tribunal.

Every civil and criminal court is bound to follow decisions of courts above it. Generally, appeal courts are bound by previous decisions provided the facts of the second case are sufficiently similar to the original case. This principle of judicial precedent means that court judgments are useful in indicating how a similar issue might be dealt with in future. The ICO and the Information Tribunal are not, however, bound by the same rules:

> It is clear that, in law, each request for disclosure of information must be considered by the Commissioner on its merits, against the framework of the Act and that

> his decision in one case is not binding in another in any event. Neither is the decision of one tribunal, considering a particular request, binding on another tribunal, considering a different request. Of course, where the Commissioner or tribunals are considering requests which arise in similar circumstances, it may be expected that similar decisions will follow.
>
> *Kitchener* v. *Derby City Council* EA/2006/0044, para. 12

European law

Whilst our focus is English law, compliance with English law necessitates consideration of European Union law and the case law emanating from the European Court of Human Rights.

The Data Protection Act 1998, the Privacy and Electronic Communications (EC Drective) Regulations 2003, SI 2003/2426 and the Environmental Information Regulations 2004, SI 2004/3391 were all enacted to implement European Union Directives (Directive 95/46/EC on the protection of individuals with regard to the processing of personal data and on the free movement of such data, Directive 2002/58/EC concerning the processing of personal data and the protection of privacy in the electronic communications sector and Directive 2003/4/EC on public access to environmental information and repealing Council Directive 90/313/EEC). Where English legislation originates from European Union Directives, it must be interpreted to give effect to the underlying Directive. (Since other European Member States will implement the directives through their own legislation, organisations must potentially consider multiple laws when undertaking cross-European business).

Whilst UK courts may now determine an individual's complaint that his rights under the European Convention for the Protection of Human Rights and Fundamental Freedoms (the Convention) have been breached, decisions taken by the European Court of Human Rights still play an important role in guiding our own judges and shaping domestic law.

Practice point

Before relying upon a case as authority to share or withhold information:

1. Ensure that the facts of the case relied upon are sufficiently similar to the circumstances you are dealing with.
2. Check that no higher court has overturned or overruled the case.
3. Note that the Information Commissioner, the Information Tribunal and the European Court of Human Rights may, but will not necessarily, follow earlier decisions.

Applying the law

The complexity of the law is in part caused by the convoluted drafting of some statutes and the fact that detail may be hidden in secondary legislation. It is exacerbated by the fact that several legal provisions may be relevant, and seemingly contradict one another. No particular regime takes precedence or must be considered first. It is not the order in which the provisions are considered that is important, rather that all appropriate legal provisions are considered and correctly applied.

Part II of the handbook specifically addresses the law's application, considering the interaction of legal provisions detailed in Part I with relevant professional obligations, guidance, legislation and case law directly relevant to:

- employment;
- healthcare;
- children;
- criminal investigations and proceedings; and
- business and commerce.

NON-LEGAL SOURCES

Much guidance is offered, nationally and regionally, to enable practitioners to share information appropriately. Information sharing agreements and protocols, privacy impact assessments and codes of practice are increasingly being used by organisations to identify and address issues that arise when information is shared (they will obviously only be effective in improving an organisation's legal compliance if staff comply with them). Additionally, certain professions must adhere to codes and guidance which detail the application of the law to that profession.

This range of non-legal sources, considered below, play an important role in assisting practitioners to comply with legal obligations. However, care must be taken to ensure that such sources are not seen as an alternative or substitute for the law, or indeed as an authoritative source of law.

Guidance

Most published guidance is not statutory guidance and is not legally binding. Concerns have been expressed about its quality: 'much of it is piecemeal and outdated, . . . or apparently in conflict with other guidance' (Thomas and Walport, *Data Sharing Review* (2008) para. 8.29). Accordingly, caution should be taken when using guidance. It should never be used as a substitute for the law. However, these concerns notwithstanding, the Information Commissioner's website (**www.ico.gov.uk**) is a key source of advice upon the practical implications of the Data Protection Act 1998, the Freedom of Information Act 2000, the Privacy and Electronic Communications Regulations 2003 and the Environmental Information Regulations 2004.

Information sharing agreements and protocols

Information sharing agreements and protocols are designed to facilitate inter-agency information sharing. They are agreed between two or more agencies.

These agreements and protocols are not legally binding. They are not required before information can be shared about a specific case. They are not a substitute for compliance with the law. However, clear benefits are afforded by such protocols (Department for Constitutional Affairs *Public Sector Data Sharing – A Guide to Data Sharing Protocols* (November 2003)).

Why implement an information sharing agreement or protocol?

- To explain the process and types of information that may be exchanged.
- To detail reasons for data sharing.
- To specify common standards for information, collection, storage and disclosure.
- To clarify responsibilities within and between organisations.

Further guidance and precedents are available and merit consideration (see **www.crimereduction.homeoffice.gov.uk/infosharing21.htm** and **www.foi.gov.uk/sharing/toolkit/library.htm↑rt3**, and Appendix 11 to the Caldicott report).

Privacy impact assessments and privacy strategies

Privacy impact assessments (PIAs) and privacy strategies, considered in detail in the ICO 2009 *Privacy Assessment Handbook*, aim to ensure staff identify privacy issues (see **www.ico.gov.uk/for_organisations/topic_specific_guides/pia_handbook.aspx**).

Privacy strategies

A privacy strategy is an expressly articulated plan, aligned with the organisation's nature and mission, which, as a minimum, ensures compliance with privacy laws, including the Data Protection Act 1998, but which might extend further to deal with privacy of personal communications and behaviour (i.e. how and whether surveillance is undertaken). A privacy strategy is not a precursor to a PIA but will assist in its implementation.

PIAs

PIAs are used to manage risks posed by the development or introduction of technological or organisational systems, databases and schemes which either process personal information or may otherwise interfere with personal privacy. The ICO suggests that a screening process should be carried to determine the need for a PIA, recognising that PIAs are usually needed:

> where a project is of such wide scope, or will use personal information of such a nature, that there would be genuine risks to the privacy of the individual. PIA's will usually be recommended where new and intrusive technology is being used, or where private or sensitive information which was originally collected for a limited purpose is going to be reused in a new or unexpected way.
>
> ICO 2009 *Privacy Impact Assessment* Handbook: Top Tips for conducting a PIA

Ultimately, a PIA should provide a sound business case for sharing information by:

(a) identifying the intended benefits of sharing information, whether for society as a whole or for individuals directly affected;
(b) demonstrating that risks of intrusion into personal privacy or which threaten the integrity of personal data have been identified and addressed; and
(c) justifying sharing information on the basis that the benefits, supported by safeguards, clearly outweigh the risks and minimise any negative effects of information sharing.

See ICO 2007 *Sharing Personal Information: Our Approach.*

Framework Code of Practice for Sharing Personal Information

The ICO 2007 Framework Code of Practice (available at **www.ico.gov.uk**) aims to ensure all organisations who share personal information within the UK (whether internally or with other organisations) meet legal requirements and adopt good practice. It is a useful tool whether used to develop an organisation's own code of practice, as a stand-alone document, or to enhance or evaluate existing policies, and whether or not protocols or PIAs exist.

The Framework Code recommends that organisations address eight elements:

1. Deciding to share personal information

Consider your objective. Why is information being shared? What are the benefits? Can the objectives be achieved without sharing? How much information is involved? Is it sensitive? How will sharing affect individuals? What is the legal basis for sharing? Is consent needed?

2. Fairness and transparency

Do you have a fair processing notice? Is it clear and accessible? Does it explain how information will be shared? Is it updated? Does it identify when information might be shared without consent or notice? How are public enquiries or requests for further information dealt with?

3. Information standards

Is the information checked regularly to ensure it is of good enough quality to meet your objectives? Is the information accessible? Is information shared relevant and not excessive to meet your objectives? How are problems or inaccuracies dealt with by the receiving organisation?

4. Retention of shared information

Detail retention periods for all information provided, not just broad classes, and detail measures to ensure procedures are implemented. Review those periods regularly. Identify legal or professional requirements. Identify out of date information. Identify information to be returned to the provider.

5. Security of shared information

Identify the level of security required for the information shared. Specify technical and organisational arrangements to protect the information.

6. Access to personal information

Detail the alternative ways that individuals can access their information. Describe how a person can access all information about themselves. Offer guidance on how to advise the public how their information is used, where it is from and who it is provided to. Offer guidance so that practitioners understand when information is exempt from disclosure.

7. Freedom of information

Incorporate policies on information sharing into publication schemes (where provided). Consider how assistance can be provided to individuals who request personal and non-personal data.

8. Review

Check your information sharing continues to meet your objectives. Are fair processing notices up to date and accurate? Are your procedures for ensuring accuracy of information effective? Are retention periods appropriate and complied with? Is security adequate? Are individuals able to access information they are entitled to?

Caldicott

In 1997 it was recommended that each health organisation should nominate a senior person, preferably a health professional, to act as a guardian, responsible for safeguarding the confidentiality of patient information (*Review of Patient-Identifiable Information* (the *Caldicott Report*) Department of Health (December 1997) Recommendation 3). The Caldicott Guardian, and the Caldicott principles, considered further in **Chapter 5**, play important roles in ensuring appropriate use of personal information within health and social care.

Professional obligations

Finally, professional obligations; their role is often misunderstood. They are not legally binding. They do not take precedence over the law. There may be serious consequences, however, if practitioners do not follow their professional code or guidance.

Solicitors, social workers, doctors, nurses, midwives, health visitors, teachers and the police are all subject to professional obligations of confidentiality. However, the guidance explaining what the duty entails varies greatly. Despite government promotion of the benefits of information sharing, there are relatively few consequences professionally for not sharing information, whilst there are potentially penalties for breaching confidentiality.

The fact that various professions follow dissimilar pieces of guidance inevitably affects how different professionals interpret and apply the same legal provisions. Professional obligations therefore play an important role in determining whether information is shared. (See **Chapter 5** for further consideration of the professional codes and guidance on confidentiality.)

CONSENT

Whilst until now we have considered the sources we use to determine whether information can be shared, as the introduction notes, an understanding of consent is essential to many subsequent chapters, and therefore appropriately completes this introductory chapter.

What is valid consent

Certain requirements must be satisfied before consent can be relied upon. Valid consent is:

1. Voluntary consent: the consent giver should have a genuine free choice whether to consent and should not be placed under unfair or undue pressure to do so. Where the consent giver cannot refuse without suffering detriment consent may not be valid (ICO (2007) *Sharing Personal Information: Our Approach*).
2. Informed consent: if consent to share information is sought, the person to whom the information relates must be appraised of all relevant infor-

mation; what information needs to be shared, who will use it, how it will be used, the purpose of the information sharing, what will happen if consent is not given and the likely outcome if information is not shared.

3. Given by someone with capacity: the consent giver's capacity to consent to this particular matter must be assessed.

Implied and explicit (express) consent

Distinctions are made in practice between implied and explicit consent.

Explicit consent does not mean written consent. It merely requires the terms of the consent to be clear. Directive 95/46/EC on the protection of individuals with regard to the processing of personal data and on the free movement of such data OJ L 281 23.11.95 ('the Data Protection Directive') defines consent as:

> any freely given specific and informed indication of his wishes by which the data subject signifies his agreement to personal data relating to him being processed
>
> Article 2, paragraph (h)

Under the Directive, therefore, it seems that consent should be explicit. Explicit consent should address details such as: the information type or specific information to be shared, the purposes of sharing information, with whom information will be shared, and duration of the consent.

Implied consent is consent implied by the information giver's conduct. For example, it is implied that if a patient tells a doctor certain facts for the purposes of medical treatment, that information will be shared with medical colleagues for those purposes. Use of implied consent recognises that it may not be practical to obtain explicit consent whenever information is shared. Whilst implied consent enables the NHS to function without compromising patient care, it is rather a fallacy to assume that patients appreciate the number of people within the NHS that can access their confidential information.

Given the potential pitfalls posed by reliance on implied consent, organisations should, where possible, obtain explicit consent. Do not infer consent from a failure to respond to a request for consent. The ICO clearly indicates that, at least for the purposes of the Data Protection Act 1998 and the Directive, the individual should be in no doubt that they are giving their consent. This means there must be 'active communication between the parties' (ICO 2006 *Data Protection Act 1998 Legal Guidance*).

Practice point

If there is likely to be any question as to whether consent was provided it is advisable to ensure that consent is explicit, recorded in writing, and signed by the information provider. If this is not possible, consider whether another legal foundation for information sharing applies.

Duration of consent

Consent can be sought to cover continuing foreseeable circumstances, but do not assume that consent lasts forever. Individuals can, and should be allowed to withdraw consent at any time. If information may need to be shared on several occasions discuss this with the consent giver. A balanced approach ensures individuals can withdraw consent, but that they are not 'badgered' to provide consent for identical reasons.

From whom should consent be obtained?

Commonly, consent is given by the information giver. However, they may not always be the appropriate person to provide consent. Where information relates to a business, careful consideration should be given to who has requisite authority to consent to information sharing (although the recipient of the information need only be satisfied that the information giver ostensibly has authority). Where information sharing will disclose information about a third person, that third person may need to provide consent. What if the individual lacks capacity to consent?

Capacity

An assessment of an individual's capacity to consent must be made with regard to the particular decision to be taken. Since the legal principles that apply when assessing the capacity of adults and minors differ, they are both considered below.

Adults

It is presumed that individuals aged 16 and above have decision-making capacity (Mental Capacity Act 2005 (MCA 2005), s.1(2)).

However, if a person, at the time when consent is sought, and in relation to that specific request, is unable to decide whether to consent because of impairment of or disturbance in the functioning of their mind or brain, they will be considered to lack capacity to take that particular decision (MCA 2005, s.2(1)). It does not matter whether the situation is a permanent one or temporary (MCA 2005, s.2(2)).

A person is unable to make a decision, if they cannot (MCA 2005, s.3):

- understand relevant information, including information about the likely consequences of taking a particular decision;
- retain that information (even for a short period);
- use or weigh up that information; and
- communicate their decision.

Since the MCA 2005 aims to maximise individuals' ability to participate in decision making, appropriate practical steps should be taken to help a person decide whether to consent, whether by using simple language, visual aids or non-verbal communication or asking someone else to help with communication. (MCA 2005, s.1(3) and MCA Code of Practice, para. 2.7).

If an individual lacks capacity to consent, information can only be disclosed if consent is provided on that individual's behalf by someone appointed under a Lasting Power of Attorney or by a Court Deputy appointed by the Court of Protection, or if it is in the individual's best interests, taking account of all relevant circumstances (see MCA 2005, s.4).

Steps taken to assess capacity and any decision to share information in the individual's best interests should be carefully recorded to demonstrate the practitioner's objectivity. Only that information which is absolutely necessary should be disclosed.

If a person lacks capacity, for reasons other than an impairment or disturbance of the mind or brain, they will not lack capacity under the MCA 2005. Common law rules will apply. The assessment of capacity is, however, very similar to that under the MCA.

Children

The MCA 2005 treats children aged 16 and 17 in a similar way to adults, presuming they have decision-making capacity. If they lack capacity, then the MCA 2005 applies as to adults. It seems that the ability of someone with parental responsibility to take decisions on behalf of an incapable 16 or 17 year old coexists with the MCA 2005, thus parents may also consent on the child's behalf.

No presumption of capacity applies to children aged below 16. Any child aged 15 or below, must demonstrate sufficient understanding to provide consent. Sufficient understanding is a developmental concept, dependent upon the child's maturity and understanding, rather than their age, requiring the child to understand the consequences of providing or refusing consent (*Gillick* v. *West Norfolk and Wisbech Area Health Authority* [1985] 3 WLR 830). The child's understanding must be assessed in relation to the specific decision.

If a child aged 15 or below lacks sufficient understanding a decision must be taken whether to seek consent from a third party with parental responsibility, or to seek an alternative basis for information sharing.

Under the common law, anyone with parental responsibility can take decisions, including to consent to information sharing, on behalf of a child aged 15 or below, notwithstanding that the information sharing legislation considered in this handbook does not expressly authorise this.

Practice point: obtaining consent from a parent

Do not assume that a parent is the appropriate person to act upon behalf of a child.

1. Consider who holds parental responsibility. All married parents and mothers (whether married or unmarried) automatically obtain parental responsibility. Unmarried fathers, other relatives, step-parents, the local authority and others will need to acquire parental responsibility, usually by court order.
2. What relationship does the child have with the parent/other individual who holds parental responsibility? Has the child said he does not want his parent to be consulted or information discussed with them? Is the parent alleged to have caused harm to the child, and would it be inappropriate to consult them? A parent has no legal duty to act in the best interests of their child.
3. Consider whether a third party who has acquired parental responsibility is the more appropriate person to consult.

CONCLUSION

A wealth of legal and practical issues must clearly be considered before practitioners decide to share information.

Can I share information?

Consider:

(a) the information to be shared;
(b) the means by which, or basis on which information was acquired;
(c) the purpose and thus the benefits of the information sharing;
(d) the amount of information to be shared; no more and no less than necessary;
(e) the person or bodies with whom information will be shared, and what they will do with the information;
(f) the legal power which authorises information sharing;
(g) whether any legal provision restricts or prevents information sharing;
(h) technical factors which may prevent safe, secure information sharing;
(i) risks (including risks of breaching the law) posed by sharing or failing to share information, and safeguards to counter the risks (such as a scheme under which information is marked as restricted or confidential).

Although it is crucial to understand the bigger picture, as explored in this chapter, the importance of understanding the nitty-gritty of the law explored in the remainder of this handbook cannot be underestimated.

PART I

Legal regimes

CHAPTER 1

Public authorities and disclosure of information

Leanne Bell and Claire Bessant

1.1 INTRODUCTION

All organisations and individuals whether in the private or public sector must, when sharing information, comply with various legal provisions, including the Data Protection Act 1998 (DPA 1998) and the duty of confidentiality. Public bodies must also comply with administrative law requirements.

A basic principle of administrative law is that public bodies must act in accordance with the law. This may mean that they have a legal obligation to share information, or that they are prohibited from doing so. As we will see, many of the bodies which share information about individuals on a daily basis are public bodies. It is fundamental, therefore, that we understand how and when they can share information, and what can be done if they share information or fail to share information, contrary to the law.

The Freedom of Information Act 2000, the Environmental Information Regulations 2004 and the Human Rights Act 1998 all play an important role in relation to disclosure of information. These pieces of legislation have specific application to certain public bodies. Whether a public body is bound by this legislation depends upon whether it falls within the definition of public authority for the purposes of the legislation. We, therefore, briefly consider the relevance of the Human Rights Act 1998, the Environmental Information Regulations 2004 and the Freedom of Information Act 2000, although these regimes are explained in detail in **Chapters 3** and **6.**

1.2 PUBLIC BODIES AND BODIES SUBJECT TO PUBLIC LAW CONTROLS

Numerous bodies exercise public and/or governmental functions and are, therefore, subject to public law controls. Whilst those who work for a public body should appreciate its status, an overview of different types of public bodies is provided to assist those who do not work within the public sector, or who need to know whether a particular organisation is a public body.

Most people will recognise that central government departments headed by a crown minister or secretary of state are public bodies. Examples include the

Ministry of Justice, the Home Office, the Department for Children, Schools and Families and the Department of Health. Subordinate to ministerial departments are executive agencies, which have some autonomy in operational functions but report to a government department which set the agency's funding and strategic policy (for example, the Child Maintenance and Enforcement Commission, responsible to the Department for Work and Pensions). Non-ministerial central government departments or sub-departments, created by statute, headed by senior civil servants, and covering matters for which direct political oversight is judged unnecessary or inappropriate are also included (for example, the Crown Prosecution Service, HM Revenue and Customs, and the Office of Fair Trading). The term public body also encompasses crown organs controlled by government such as the police, the armed forces and local authorities and their members or servants.

In addition, there are three further categories of public bodies, most of which have been created by separate Acts of Parliament, which exercise public/governmental functions:

1. **Public corporations:** these semi-autonomous public corporations responsible for providing or managing a public service are subject to public law controls, at least to the extent that they are carrying out public functions. Examples include the two remaining nationalised industries, British Nuclear Fuels plc and British Shipbuilders, as well as bodies such as the Royal Mail, the British Broadcasting Corporation and the Civil Aviation Authority.
2. **National Health Service bodies:** this term includes not only NHS Trusts but also organisations such as the National Blood Authority and National Institute for Clinical Excellence (NICE).
3. **Non-departmental public bodies:** these are entrusted with certain activities to reduce the possibility of direct political control and interference and to enable discretionary decisions to be taken without consideration of short-term political issues. These include:

    (a) executive bodies, which deliver a particular public service, are overseen by a board rather than ministers, employ their own staff and are allocated their own budgets (examples include the Advisory and Arbitration Service (ACAS) and the Higher Education Funding Council);

    (b) advisory bodies, which advise ministers on particular policy areas and are often supported by a small secretariat and expenses from the parent department (for example, the Advisory Committee on the Safety of Medicines and the Fuel Poverty Advisory Group);

    (c) tribunals, which are coordinated by the Tribunals Service, an executive agency of the Ministry of Justice.

Some private persons or corporations also exercise functions of a public or governmental nature and will be subject to public law controls (for example, the Law Society and the General Medical Council perform some public or governmental functions and are subject to judicial review in respect of those, yet they are not public authorities).

1.3 LEGAL POWERS AFFORDED TO PUBLIC BODIES

The source of a public body's powers depends upon its type, and how it was established. The majority of public bodies, including government departments established by statute, may only take actions they are expressly or impliedly permitted to do so by statute. Government departments headed by a crown minister, additionally derive power to act from prerogative and common law powers. A public body must only share information if its powers expressly or impliedly permit such sharing.

Good practice

It is important to carefully identify the powers that are afforded to a public body whether you are acting on behalf of that body or when you are seeking to challenge its actions. If a public body goes outside its powers in obtaining, holding or sharing information it will be acting unlawfully. This is the *ultra vires* rule.

Consider also:

- The first principle of the DPA 1998, which requires information to be lawfully processed. If information constitutes personal data and the public body acts outside its powers in sharing such information, then the First Data Protection Principle may also be breached.
- European Convention for the Protection of Human Rights and Fundamental Freedoms, Art. 8, which requires a public authority to act in accordance with the law when interfering with the right to respect for privacy.

1.3.1 Express statutory provisions permitting information sharing

Express statutory powers fall into two categories: permissive and mandatory.

- Permissive powers, such as Crime and Disorder Act 1998, s.115 or DPA 1998, s.29, permit information to be shared. However, where a permissive power applies, a public body is not obliged to share information and indeed may be perfectly justified in refusing to share information (for example, because it would breach the duty of confidentiality).
- Mandatory statutory provisions require information to be disclosed. For example, Criminal Appeal Act 1995, s.17 requires a public body to provide information to the Criminal Cases Review Commission about exercise of its functions, when requested.

Even where express statutory powers authorise information sharing, care should be taken to ensure that powers provided are not exceeded, by sharing more information than permitted or required. Where information is obtained by virtue of statutory powers, care should also be taken to clarify what use may be made of that information. For example, it was made clear in *Morris* v. *Director S.F.O.* [1993] Ch 372, that whilst the Serious Fraud Office was able to obtain documents under the criminal investigative powers of Criminal Justice Act 1987, s.3(5), this did not entitle them to subsequently disclose those documents, without notifying the owners or previous holders of those documents of their intentions.

It is important, finally, to be aware that circumstances may arise where one statute requires information to be disclosed, whilst another statute may specifically prohibit information sharing. No clear guidance exists clarifying how to resolve such a conflict. You should also note that where action is prohibited by statute (and illegal), consent to disclosure will not make such action legal unless this is expressly provided in the statute.

1.3.2 Implied powers to share information

Many activities undertaken by statutory bodies are carried out under implied statutory powers. In *Attorney General* v. *Great Eastern Railway Company* (1880) 5 App Cas 473, Lord Selborne justified the use of such implied powers stating that 'whatever may fairly be regarded as incidental to, or consequential upon, those things which the Legislature has authorised, ought not (unless expressly prohibited) to be held, by judicial construction, to be *ultra vires*'.

In practical terms an implied power is a power granted to a public body to take such action as is reasonably necessary to carry out its primary functions.

Practice point

There is no general statutory power to disclose data, just as there is no general power to obtain, hold or process data. If you are employed by a public body and wish to share information in order to undertake the functions for which the body was established you should consider the legislation that relates to the body or the specific policy or service for which you work. You should:

- Identify any express powers to share information.
- If no express powers exist, consider whether permission to share information may be implied from the terms of the legislation.

Any decision as to whether the public body has power to share data must be taken on the specific facts of each case. You should specifically consider who will benefit from sharing information, the specific benefits that will be afforded and risks posed.

1.3.3 Prerogative and common law powers

Government departments headed by a minister of the crown may, where there is no express or implied statutory power to share information, rely upon common law or prerogative powers to do so.

Prerogative powers are unique to the crown. Examples include powers in relation to foreign affairs, defence and mercy.

Common law powers grant the crown legal capacity to take any action which an ordinary person has capacity to take, provided such action is not prohibited expressly or implicitly by statute. The use of the crown's common law powers to obtain and share information was expressly considered in relation to the Consultancy Service Index, the precursor to the statutory list implemented under the Protection of Children Act 1999. In *R* v. *Secretary of State for Health*, ex parte *C* [2000] 1 FLR 627 Lady Justice Hale commented that:

> The powers of public authorities are . . . essentially different from those of private persons. A man making a will may, subject to any rights of his dependants, dispose of his property just as he may wish . . . This is unfettered discretion. But a public body may do none of these things unless it acts reasonably and in good faith and on lawful and relevant grounds of public interest . . . The whole conception of an unfettered discretion is inappropriate to a public authority, which possesses powers solely in order that it may use them for the public good.

Notwithstanding its recognition of the limitations imposed upon public bodies, the court concluded that the operation of the list, compiled after seeking the views of those to be included, and made available to childcare employers only once a decision to offer employment had been made, was both lawful and reasonable.

R v. *Chief Constable of the North Wales Police*, ex parte *AB* [1998] 3 All ER 310 equally confirms that implied and/or common law powers may be relied upon when it is necessary to share information in order to perform public duties (in this case, the court confirmed it was lawful to disclose information to individuals living in a particular area about paedophiles that posed a risk). *Woolgar* v. *Chief Constable of Sussex Police* [2000] 1 WLR 25 confirms that where there is a strong public interest for disclosing information to a regulatory body for the purposes of an inquiry, the police has power to make such disclosures.

1.3.4 Specific statutory powers which permit information sharing

A wide range of legal provisions are influential in determining when and whether information can be shared. The Local Government Acts 1972 and 2000, for example, grant wide-ranging powers to local authorities to take actions necessary to exercise their functions. **Chapter 4** highlights some of the more commonly encountered provisions which authorise or prohibit information sharing. A detailed breakdown is not provided in this chapter, although an example is provided below.

Practical example: information sharing powers

Angela, aged 51, was recently badly injured in a car accident and suffered brain damage. She is unable to walk unaided and is struggling to accomplish everyday tasks.

National Health Service and Community Care Act 1990, s.47, requires a local authority, where it appears necessary to do so, to carry out an assessment of an individual's needs for community care services. Where housing or health provision may be required, section 47 requires the local authority social services department to contact and, where appropriate, seek assistance from a housing authority, primary care trust or health authority in undertaking the assessment. In determining the services to be provided, the local authority must take into account any services likely to be made available by these housing and health authorities. In order to undertake a holistic assessment of Angela's disability, and determine support available from social services, health or housing, information needs to be shared by relevant agencies. Section 47 clearly implies that health and housing will share information about services they might offer and implies power for the local authority to share information with these authorities for the purposes of completing the assessment. As a matter of good practice, the information to be shared, with whom it will be shared and reasons for sharing information should be discussed with Angela. Ideally her explicit consent to sharing the information would be obtained and recorded, to comply with DPA 1998, Scheds. 2 and 3.

1.4 ACCOUNTABILITY

> Public law is not at base about rights, even though abuses of power may and often do invade private rights; it is about wrongs – that is to say, misuses of public power. . .
>
> per Sedley J in *R* v. *Somerset CC and Arc Southern Limited* ex parte *Dixon* (1998) 75 P & CR 175 para. 183

This section considers how the law holds to account those who misuse public power.

When an individual shares or proposes to share information received from another individual, for example when confidential information is shared without the confider's consent, an injunction may be sought to restrain disclosure, or remedies for breach (damages) may be pursued by the aggrieved individual before the civil courts. If disclosure breaches the criminal law, prosecution may follow. Other remedies are afforded by the DPA 1998.

Slightly different issues arise where the person who has shared information in breach of the law is a public body or employed by a public body and action has been taken in the course of public duties. Where a public body shares information contrary to the law, the issue of whether that body can be sanctioned or restrained through the courts, will depend in large part upon the body's legal status. The process by which a public body may be held accountable for a decision to share information, for example, may be very different to the manner in which a private individual is held accountable for the same action.

Under the principle of ministerial responsibility, the minister responsible for each central government department takes personal responsibility for activities ongoing in his department (the convention of ministerial responsibility). However, ministerial responsibility provides no real recourse for aggrieved individuals. Most public bodies, while they may officially be linked to a government department or have a minister to whom they have notional accountability, essentially operate as independent organisations and in fact, actively try to distance themselves from political issues and from central government. Whilst a public body's action may come up for debate, for example at question time in the House of Commons, a lack of parliamentary time available for debate, and the party political nature of question time, mean that true accountability may not be possible. The resignation of a government minister is unlikely to be an effective remedy for someone whose personal confidential information has either been disclosed without their consent or lost.

There may be indirect accountability where ministers select the members of public bodies and may ultimately legislate to change their nature or composition if things go wrong. However, the main vehicle for accountability to the public is now the process of judicial review (considered at **1.5**).

Not all public bodies are, however, susceptible to judicial review. The crown benefits from certain privileges and immunities. It is not bound by statute law, unless this is expressly stated or implied. The normal position is that central government departments headed by a crown minister benefit from crown privileges and immunities. For other public bodies to benefit from crown immunity the public body or its employees must be crown servants. The statutory definition of a public body's rights, duties and obligations and the degree of control which ministers can exercise over the public body in the performance of their duties is key to determining whether crown immunity applies (see *Bank voor Handel en Scheepvaart NV* v. *Administrator of Hungarian Property* [1954] AC 584, 616 and *BBC* v. *Johns* [1965] Ch 32). Where a public body has substantial independent discretion, even if its members are appointed by a minister and may be required to give him information, they are unlikely to be crown servants (*Tamlin* v. *Hannaford* [1950] 1 KB 18).

In order to make things clearer, it is now common practice for the statute that creates a public body to specifically address the issue of its legal status. We therefore know that some public bodies are able to take advantage of crown immunity (the Health and Safety Executive, Health and Safety at Work, etc. Act 1974, s.10). On the contrary, the National Health Service and Community Care Act 1990, s.60 largely stripped away the National Health Service's crown immunities. Again, therefore, whenever information is shared by a public body, the statutory provisions which established that body are relevant.

1.5 JUDICIAL REVIEW

1.5.1 What is judicial review?

The High Court exercises a supervisory jurisdiction over bodies exercising public law functions (*R* v. *City Panel on Take-Overs and Mergers*, ex parte *Datafin plc* [1987] QB 815) through the process of judicial review.

If any person is aggrieved at the actions of a public body or its employees exercising their public functions (for example where the body has disclosed information that the person wished to keep confidential) a challenge to this decision may be brought by invoking the inherent jurisdiction of the High Court. However, judicial review is a discretionary remedy and will normally only be granted where there is no alternative remedy, such as a complaints procedure (*R* v. *Birmingham City Council,* ex parte *Ferrero Ltd* [1993] 1 All ER 530). Where the ICO provides an adequate alternative remedy judicial review will be inappropriate. Even if the matter does raise an issue of public law, the courts may refuse to intervene on the grounds that the matter is not justiciable (*Council of Civil Service Unions* v. *Minister for the Civil Service* [1985] AC 374).

The starting point for the courts in matters of judicial review is that the powers of public bodies are not and should not be absolute – there must be adequate control. The court's powers are based on the traditional doctrine of *ultra vires*; that the actions taken by a public body in excess of its powers are invalid. The doctrine cannot be used to question an Act of Parliament, but it serves to control those who exceed the powers given by statute, defined widely to include powers not expressly conferred by statute but which are reasonably incidental to those expressly conferred (see *R* v. *Richmond upon Thames Council,* ex parte *McCarthy and Stone Ltd* [1992] 2 AC 48). When a public body is challenged, the court will focus on the statute which is the source of the power. However, it is often the case that the Act is drafted so broadly that mere exercise of statutory interpretation is not sufficient to resolve the case. More intricate rules of judicial review have therefore developed, which also now take account of the Human Rights Act 1998, and as a result, the scope of judicial review has widened considerably.

It should be emphasised that in reviewing a decision, the court is not hearing an appeal against the decision. Nor is it considering its merits, whether it is right or wrong or indeed, whether it would have reached the same conclusion. These are matters for the public body itself, subject to any right of appeal given by statute. Instead, the court is concerned with whether the decision was within the jurisdiction of the body in question and whether it was a power it was entitled to exercise (*R* v. *Human Fertilisation and Embryology Authority,* ex parte *(1) Assisted Reproduction and Gynaecology Centre (2) H* [2002] EWCA Civ 20).

1.5.2 Procedure

If an individual wishes the High Court to judicially review a decision, he must apply to the Administrative Court, within three months of the decision, unless there are exceptional circumstances (Supreme Court Act 1981, s.31, Civil Procedure Rules 2003, SI 2003/1236, Part 54).

To be granted permission to bring judicial review proceedings, a person or organisation must first establish to the court that they have 'standing' to bring the claim. This requires them to demonstrate that they have 'sufficient interest in the matter to which the application relates'. (Supreme Court Act 1981, s.31(3)). In *Inland Revenue Commissioners,* ex parte *National Federation of Self Employed and Small Business Ltd* [1982] AC 617, the court stated that the applicant must show:

(a) what the interest is and that he or she has an arguable case; and
(b) his or her individual relationship to the matter.

It is generally considered to be easier for individuals to demonstrate they have a relationship to the matter than it is for organisations (see for example *R* v. *Secretary of State Foreign and Commonwealth Affairs,* ex parte *Rees-Mogg* [1994] QB 552). When it comes to organisations, the court tends to require rather more by way of evidence of their interest in the matter. Well known, national organisations representing the wider public interest such as Greenpeace and World Development Movement tend to do better than smaller, niche organisations. That said, the court has suggested it will take a flexible approach to standing where the matter is important (*R* v. *Secretary of State for Foreign and Commonwealth Affairs,* ex parte *World Development Movement* [1995] 1 WLR 386).

The procedure for applying for judicial review involves two stages. The claimant asks permission to apply and must satisfy the court it has standing. The claim, accompanied by an affidavit containing all basic factual material, is served on the defendant and any interested party. Whilst the application for permission operates as a significant filter, no uniform approach or criteria is apparent at this stage. The claim itself is heard in the Administrative Court before two judges (or three if the matter is of great importance or complexity). The principle source of evidence is the written affidavit. The court may order oral evidence and cross examination, but this is unusual. Any person (including pressure groups or government ministers) may intervene by filing evidence and making representations.

1.5.3 The substantive rules of judicial review

The grounds upon which a judicial review claim may succeed are considered in some detail here, since they establish the circumstances in which information sharing is likely to be unlawful. They suggest, therefore, what actions might alternatively be lawful.

There are traditionally three grounds upon which a person affected may bring an action for judicial review of a decision by a public body to disclose information:

- illegality;
- irrationality; and
- procedural impropriety.

See *Council of Civil Service Unions* v. *Minister for the Civil Service* [1985] AC 374 (the CCSU case), Lord Diplock, p. 410.

Three further grounds are increasingly being argued:

- legitimate expectations;
- breach of European Union law; and
- breach of diversity duties.

Lord Diplock also referred to proportionality as a possible ground of challenge, discussed in **1.6.2**.

Illegality

Lord Diplock explained in the CCSU case at page 410 that: 'By illegality as a ground for review I mean that the decision maker must understand correctly the law that regulates his decision making power and must give effect to it.' Immediately we can see how important it is that the law contained in subsequent chapters of this book regarding common law confidentiality, data protection, freedom of information and the Human Rights Act 1998 are fully understood and complied with by public bodies.

One of the most common grounds of challenge under the illegality head is that the decision was taken by the wrong person (see *Allingham* v. *Minister of Agriculture* [1948] 1 All ER 780 where a direction was wrongly given by an executive officer not the Agricultural Executive Committee, who alone had power to issue such directions). There are exceptions, such as where the statute gives an express power to delegate or where such a power of delegation can reasonably be implied considering the nature of the person (*R* v. *Croydon JJ*, ex parte *WH Smith, The Times,* November 22, 2000) and the nature of the functions being performed (*Vine* v. *National Dock Labour Board* [1957] AC 488). It is, however, crucial that public bodies have the correct procedures in place to ensure that decisions regarding confidential information and processing of personal data are taken by the correct people within the organisation.

Irrationality

Irrationality encompasses any decision 'so outrageous in its defiance of logic or of accepted moral standards that no sensible person who had applied his mind to the question to be decided could have arrived at it' (the CCSU case,

p. 410). It includes grounds such as unreasonableness, irrelevant considerations and improper motive. These are not discreet categories as such and there is significant overlap in the case law.

The concept of unreasonableness was first examined and defined in *Associated Provincial Picture Houses Ltd* v. *Wednesbury Corporation* [1948] 1 KB 223 where Lord Greene used it essentially as a synonym for abuse of power. This is often referred to as the Wednesbury principle. To emphasise the fact that the courts were not substituting their view on the merits of the decision for that of the decision maker, the courts have indicated they will only intervene where a decision was manifestly unreasonable, for example where the decision was 'so unreasonable it would jump off the page at you' (*R* v. *Lord Chancellor,* ex parte *Maxwell* [1996] 4 All ER 751).

The concept of irrationality also includes the concept of irrelevant considerations. This includes outright refusals to consider relevant matters, taking into account wholly irrelevant or extraneous consideration or wholly omitting to take into account relevant considerations (*Padfield* v. *Minister for Agriculture, Fisheries and Food* [1968] AC 997).

Importantly, a failure by a public body to give reasons for its decision may in itself imply that the decision was unreasonable as it may be evidence that there is no good reason.

Procedural impropriety

This head includes things such as failure to deal with express procedural requirements, failure to comply with the rules of natural justice (in circumstances where this can be inferred) and failure to comply with other rules of procedural fairness.

A statute will sometimes specify actions such as public consultation or laying of an instrument before parliament as preconditions of power being given to a body. For example, NHS Trusts may hold and process personal data about patients but they must have appointed a Caldicott Guardian in order to safeguard that information. Since it is rare for statutes to provide clear guidance on the effect of non-compliance with procedural requirements, the court must determine the consequences of breach of procedural requirements. While a court must start by assessing the importance of a particular procedural requirement, in deciding the effect of the breach it must consider all the circumstances of the case (*Coney* v. *Choyce* [1975] 1 WLR 422, *London & Clydesdale Estates Ltd* v. *Aberdeen District Council* [1979] 3 All ER 876).

Historically, the rules of natural justice also play a part in deciding whether a public body has complied with all requirements in making its decision. The two main rules are the *nemo judex* rule (the right to an unbiased judge) and *the audi alteram partem* rule (the right to a fair hearing). There is also an implied duty of fairness attached to all administrative acts (see the CCSU case and *Doody* v. *Secretary of State for the Home Department* [1993] 3 All ER 92).

The right to a fair hearing will apply where the decision being taken affects an individual's rights or where the decision was taken by a body which had a duty to act judicially (this need not be a court-like body, see *Ridge* v. *Baldwin* [1964] AC 40). It may therefore apply to decisions taken regarding information sharing. Factors the court will take into account include whether the person concerned has a legitimate expectation of being heard, whether the consequences of the decision are serious and whether a statutory procedure applies.

It is not easy to clarify what constitutes a fair hearing, in such situations, however, as a bare minimum, public bodies must ensure that the person affected has an adequate opportunity to present his case, although not necessarily orally (*Local Government Board* v. *Arlidge* [1915] AC 120) and has reasonable time to prepare his arguments.

A mere suspicion of bias is sufficient to claim contravention of the right to an unbiased judge (i.e. decision maker). Therefore, where a close connection between the person who discloses information and the person who receives it suggests bias, it may be enough to render the decision unfair.

Legitimate expectations

A claim on this basis may be brought upon the basis that a particular procedure will be adopted before a decision is made (a procedural legitimate expectation) or that a certain outcome will or will not occur (substantive legitimate expectation). In the latter case it is likely that the claimant will need to show that they have suffered or will suffer detriment (*R* v. *North and East Devon Health Authority,* ex parte *Coughlan* [2001] QB 213 where a promise not to move the claimant from her nursing home gave rise to a legitimate expectation). Legitimate expectation claims are likely to succeed only in exceptional situations.

Breach of European Union law

Domestic legislation, such as the DPA 1998, introduced to implement European Union law is amenable to judicial review where it is argued that the domestic legislation fails to implement the European Union legislation correctly. It is also possible to judicially review an act or omission (including a failure to legislate or adequately enforce) which is contrary to an obligation imposed by the European Union Treaty or Community secondary legislation, such as procurement directives.

Breach of diversity duties

Race Relations Act 1976, ss.71–71E, Disability Discrimination Act 1995, ss. 49A–49F and Sex Discrimination Act 1975, ss.76A–76E impose requirements on public bodies specified in the legislation to eliminate discrimination and promote equality of opportunity (and where race relations are concerned, to promote good relations). A failure to conduct a diversity assessment when formulating a new policy, or a total failure to consider these legislative requirements will found a claim for judicial review (see *Secretary of State for Defence* v. *Elias* [2006] EWCA Civ 1293).

Practice point

- All relevant circumstances should be taken into account and given appropriate weight before a decision is made.
- If, by virtue of a business or family relationship, an inference of bias is possible against the decision maker, consider whether anyone else within the organisation could take the decision.
- Record all decisions to share or to withhold information together with reasons for the decision. Retain relevant supporting evidence or documentation. If an explanation is being given to an individual, for example, for refusing to provide information, sufficient explanation should be given to the individual to enable her to understand the decision.
- Where information relates to a specific individual, consider consulting that individual, before a decision to share or withhold information is taken. This will be particularly important where the decision maker is specifically required to consult certain individuals before taking a decision. For example, the Data Protection (Subject Access Modification) Health Order 2000, SI 2000/413 requires, subject to certain exceptions, a data controller who is not a health professional to consult the person who appears to be the appropriate health professional before withholding information sought under DPA 1998, s.7.
- Consider whether, as a result of a policy or other statement, a legitimate expectation of consultation arises.

1.5.4 Remedies

Although judicial review provides an aggrieved individual with direct means to challenge a public body, the individual may consider the outcome less than satisfactory, since judicial review affords limited remedies:

- Mandatory Order: an order of the court requiring the decision maker to do something, such as reconsider the decision.
- Prohibiting Order: where the court prohibits the body from doing something, such as enforcing or acting on the decision until it has been reconsidered.
- Quashing Order: quashing the original decision.
- Declaration: a statement by the court regarding the legal position, such as that the public body has acted beyond its powers or the decision or action taken is or was invalid.
- Injunction: a court order preventing or requiring certain actions.

Very rarely, and only in exceptional circumstances, where they would have been available in a private action, nominal damages may be awarded.

The problem with all of these remedies in the sphere of information sharing is that very often, the action is brought after information has been shared, the damage is done and none of these remedies put the victim back in the position they were in before the breach. Even where the original decision is quashed, there is no guarantee that the public body will take a different decision when it reconsiders the matter. If it follows the proper decision-making process, no further means of redress will be available.

1.6 THE HUMAN RIGHTS ACT 1998

The protection of human rights in England and Wales is primarily governed by the European Convention for the Protection of Human Rights and Fundamental Freedoms (the Convention), an international treaty which details certain fundamental human rights which should be protected by law in signatory countries.

The Convention (considered further in **Chapter 6**) allows challenges to the acts of public bodies to be brought before the European Court of Human Rights in Strasbourg, even if they are in accordance with national law. Until the Human Rights Act 1998 (the HRA 1998) came into force in October 2000 individuals had no way of directly enforcing the Convention in UK courts. The HRA 1998 is important for public authorities and individuals for several reasons.

1.6.1 Specific obligations imposed upon public authorities

HRA 1998, s.6 makes it unlawful for public authorities, including courts and tribunals, to act in a way which is incompatible with Convention rights.

Although there is no definitive test for what a public authority is, section 6 confirms that a public authority will include a person 'certain of whose functions are functions of a public nature'. It would certainly include central government departments, the police, armed forces, health authorities and primary care trusts, but the status of, for example, foundation NHS Trusts that have opted out of government control would be uncertain. It applies to non-governmental bodies carrying out public functions, but if a body is essentially private in nature, its private functions fall outside section 6.

Section 7 permits individuals to bring proceedings against public authorities for an alleged breach of a Convention right, or to rely on Convention rights as a defence in legal proceedings in UK courts. In particular, the potential victim may apply for judicial review of the public authority's decision (s.7(3) and 7(4)).

1.6.2 The European Convention and judicial review

Article 13 of the Convention requires domestic legal systems to provide an effective remedy to those who allege a breach of these Convention rights. The

European Court of Human Rights has found in several instances that judicial review may not provide such a remedy because it cannot investigate the merits of the decision (see, for example, *Lustig-Prean and Beckett* v. *UK* Apps 31417/96 and 32377/96, although note these decisions pre-date the HRA 1998). However, in recent years, where human rights issues have been raised, the court's attitude to judicial review has altered.

The requirement of Art. 6 of the Convention to provide a 'fair and public hearing within a reasonable time by an independent and impartial tribunal' must be considered. In *R* v. *Home Secretary* ex parte *Isiko* [2001] 1 FLR 930, the Court of Appeal emphasised this did not mean the court could substitute its own view of the merits of the decision. However, where fundamental human rights were involved, the burden of proof fell on the decision maker to show rights had not been violated. The more fundamental the right, the higher the standard of proof.

Whilst a more intrusive mode of judicial supervision comes into being when human rights are concerned, the court's function remains one of judging whether the decision maker had exceeded his discretion.

In *R (Daly)* v. *Secretary of State for the Home Department* [2001] 2 AC 532, p. 547, Lord Steyn suggests that when a qualified Convention right is interfered with:

> The starting point is that there is an overlap between the traditional grounds of review and the approach of proportionality. Most cases would be decided in the same way whichever approach is adopted. But the intensity of the review is somewhat greater under the proportionality approach. . . . First, the doctrine of proportionality may require the reviewing court to assess the balance which the decision maker has struck, not merely whether it is within the range of rational or reasonable decisions. Secondly, the proportionality test may go further than the traditional grounds of review in as much as it may require attention to be directed to the relative weight accorded to interests and considerations. Thirdly, even the heightened scrutiny test developed in *R* v. *Ministry of Defence,* ex parte *Smith* [1996] QB 517, 554 is not necessarily appropriate to the protection of human rights. . . . [T]he intensity of the review, in similar cases, is guaranteed by the twin requirements that the limitation of the right was necessary in a democratic society, in the sense of meeting a pressing social need, and the question whether the interference was really proportionate to the legitimate aim being pursued.

An individual who believes that information may have been shared in breach of her Convention rights and in breach of the powers afforded to a public body may potentially bring judicial review proceedings under the heading of proportionality, or any of the more traditional grounds.

1.7 FREEDOM OF INFORMATION LEGISLATION

Under the Freedom of Information Act 2000 a person who makes a written request for information from a public body will be entitled, subject to certain exemptions, first, to be told whether the public body has the information that was requested and second, to have that information communicated to him. Unlike the HRA 1998, which leaves the concept of public authority very vague and allows the courts to interpret it flexibly, the Freedom of Information Act 2000 specifies clearly which bodies will be classed as public bodies for the purposes of the Act (see ss.3, 6 and Sched. 1).

The Environmental Information Regulations 2004, SI 2004/3391 (EIR 2004) apply where environmental information is sought from a public authority, widely defined to include certain private bodies exercising public functions (reg. 2). The EIR 2004 impose a duty upon public authorities to make environmental information available upon request, subject to certain exceptions.

Central government departments, local authorities, the police and other emergency services, armed forces and NHS Trusts will be subject to both regimes.

Since both regimes also require public authorities to proactively disseminate information, they clearly play an important role in requiring public authorities to share information with the public (although there are limits to these duties, particularly where information is confidential or subject to the DPA 1998). Chapter 3 provides a detailed analysis of the extensive duties imposed by the Freedom of Information Act 2000 and the EIR 2004, and the implications for public authorities of holding information shared with them by third parties.

1.8 CONCLUSION

As we have seen, whilst public bodies are provided with extensive powers to share information, they are also subject to onerous duties and responsibilities. They must ensure that they comply with their general duties as well as the specific rules on information sharing. Above all, they must act fairly within the powers conferred by statute and in compliance with the Convention. This can require difficult decisions to be taken, particularly where two legal regimes apparently conflict.

Although often criticised for not being adequately accountable to government or to the public, public bodies are under a great deal of scrutiny. Their decisions are susceptible to challenge by the courts and by the Information Commissioner on numerous grounds. A detailed understanding of the legal regimes, and the practical implications of the law is clearly essential if public bodies are to act lawfully, and avoid challenge.

CHAPTER 2

Information sharing and data protection

Andrew Watson and Claire Bessant

2.1 INTRODUCTION

The Data Protection Act 1998 (DPA 1998) was introduced to comply with the Data Protection Directive (Council Directive 95/46/EC on the protection of individuals with regard to the processing of personal data and on the free movement of such data). Although understanding the DPA 1998 is key to understanding whether you can share personal information (the DPA 1998 applies only to personal information), it is a complex statute, supplemented by numerous regulations and orders. This chapter aims to demystify the DPA 1998, clarifying when it applies, what it obliges certain individuals or organisations to do, and the remedies afforded to individuals when the DPA 1998 is breached.

2.1.1 What the DPA 1998 does

The DPA 1998 requires persons who hold or share personal information to comply with eight principles of good information handling and to demonstrate that certain schedule conditions are satisfied before information is shared. Individuals whose information is being processed must also be afforded certain rights (including a right to access their information). In specified circumstances, those who process personal data may rely on exemptions, which relieve them from the obligations to provide information to the individual or from complying with part or all of the principles.

2.1.2 Regulation

Individuals can enforce their rights (s.7 and ss.10–14) through the county court, and seek compensation (s.13) for damage and distress suffered. However, the Information Commissioner (ICO) is the primary regulator of rights and obligations under the DPA 1998.

Individuals are entitled to ask the ICO to investigate whether their personal data is being handled appropriately (s.42). If the ICO decides to undertake an assessment, the ICO may request information from a person processing (holding, sharing, etc.) information. If information is not provided voluntarily, the ICO may serve an Information Notice requiring production. The ICO may also obtain warrants for entry and inspection of premises where there are reasonable grounds for suspecting that a data controller has or is breaching the eight principles or where an offence under the DPA 1998 has been or is being committed.

Following an assessment, the ICO may make various recommendations for change. If these are not followed, the ICO may issue an Enforcement Notice requiring specified steps to be taken. The use of Information and Enforcement Notices (breach of which is a criminal offence) is relatively rare. Much of the ICO's regulatory work is settled through informal resolution or the giving of undertakings by data controllers. Appeals against Information and Enforcement Notices lie to the Information Tribunal, and they do not have effect until the appeal is concluded.

The ICO does not merely act to identify and stop bad practice. Importantly, he is under a statutory duty to promote good practice (s.51) and provides an important source of guidance on the DPA 1998 and information sharing (see ICO 2007 *Sharing Personal Information: Our Approach*, the ICO 2007 *Framework Code of Practice for Sharing Personal Information* and the *Privacy Assessment Handbook*, all available at **www.ico.gov.uk**). An understanding of the contents of *Sharing Personal Information*, aimed primarily at public bodies but containing advice relevant to all sectors, is key to sharing personal information in accordance with the DPA 1998.

Summary: The ICO's approach to sharing personal information

- When considering whether to share personal information organisations should balance the benefits to the individual or society of sharing information against the likely risk or effect on the individual and the reasonable expectations of the individual. The more sensitive the information, the greater detriment to the individual or the greater the impact on a person's privacy, the greater justification will be needed to permit the sharing.
- Even where there is a strong justification for sharing information, organisations should adopt a privacy friendly approach.
- Before sharing information consideration should be given to whether goals can be accomplished without information sharing. If not, then only the minimum amount of personal data should be shared.
- Organisations must have sufficient safeguards in place to ensure that information shared is accurate and secure (see **2.5**).
- Organisations must apply their minds to these issues (using a privacy impact assessment where appropriate) at the outset of a project. Information sharing cannot be justified after the event.

2.2 WHO DOES THE DATA PROTECTION ACT APPLY TO?

The DPA 1998 only applies to individuals or organisations who process data. Processing is defined extremely widely and covers almost anything you can do with data; including obtaining it, holding it and sharing it (whether internally or externally).

There are three key groups which the DPA 1998 applies to data controllers, data processors and data subjects (DPA 1998, s.1).

2.2.1 The data controller

The data controller decides how and why data is processed. The main obligations under the DPA 1998 are imposed on the data controller. Data can be processed by more than one data controller (unless processing is undertaken to comply with a statutory obligation).

2.2.2 The data processor

A data processor is not employed by the data controller but processes information on their behalf. It remains the data controller's duty to comply with the DPA 1998. The data processor need only comply with the DPA 1998 if required to do so by a contract. Contractual arrangements will therefore need to be agreed with the data processor for the data controller to ensure DPA 1998 compliance.

2.2.3 The data subject

The data subject is the person who is the subject of the data. They are afforded a number of rights under DPA 1998, Part 2, considered at **2.7**.

2.3 DATA

The DPA 1998 only applies to information which is data. Data does not mean documents. Data can take many different forms, but it must be recorded in some way. Know-how, opinions, beliefs and ideas do not fall within the DPA 1998 unless they have been recorded (for guidance on the DPA 1998 and professional opinions, see ICO 2006 *Data Protection Good Practice Note: How does the Data Protection Act apply to professional opinions*).

If the information to be shared is not data, the DPA 1998 does not apply.

Definition

Data means information which:

(a) is being processed by equipment operating automatically in response to instructions given for that purpose;
(b) is recorded with the intention that it should be processed by means of such equipment;
(c) is recorded as part of a relevant filing system or with the intention that it should form part of a relevant filing system;
(d) does not fall within (a), (b) or (c) but forms part of an accessible record as defined by DPA 1998, s.68;
(e) is recorded information held by a public authority and does not fall within any of paragraphs (a) to (d) (DPA 1998, s.1).

These five categories are explained below.

2.3.1 Electronic information

Paragraphs (a) and (b) of the definition deal essentially with electronic information. Anything held on computer (e-mails, spreadsheets, databases and other electronic formats), mobile phone, memory sticks, digital cameras, Blackberries, etc. will be covered as will anything which is recorded with the intention that it will be transferred to such an electronic system.

2.3.2 Structured manual filing systems

Paragraph (c) covers manual information. A relevant filing system is:

> any set of information relating to individuals to the extent that, although the information is not processed by means of equipment operating automatically in response to instructions given for that purpose, the set is structured, either by reference to individuals or by reference to criteria relating to individuals, in such a way that specific information relating to a particular individual is readily accessible
>
> section 1(1)

A relevant filing system need not be files per se. The information and the ease with which it can be located must be assessed, rather than whether it is in itself a file or filing system (*Data Protection Act 1998, Legal Guidance*, p. 9). In *Durant* v. *Financial Services Authority* [2003] EWCA Civ 1746 the Court of Appeal concluded that a relevant filing system is one which has a level of sophistication equivalent to that of a computerised file. It should be clear when commencing a search whether specific information about an individual is held and if so, such a system should be structured to enable it to be easily located.

The ICO suggests that 'the key consideration is not the time and effort involved but whether there is a system in place that allows the organisation to find information, applying a standard search procedure, without searching through every item in a set of information' and that as 'long as specific information within the set is readily accessible the set of information will be data in a relevant filing system' (ICO 2009 *Determining what information is 'data' for the purposes of the DPA*).

2.3.3 Accessible records

Paragraph (d) covers accessible records, but only applies when paragraphs (a) to (c) do not.

Accessible records, defined in section 68, include health, education or accessible public records.

- Health records are records created by or on behalf of a health professional dealing with the individual's care, which contain information about a person's mental or physical health or condition (s.68).
- Educational records primarily cover information held by teachers and governing bodies of schools (Sched. 11).
- Accessible public records essentially cover information relating to local authority tenancies and information relating to social services functions (Sched. 12).

2.3.4 Unstructured manual records

Paragraph (e) covers manual records not already covered in the preceding paragraphs but held by a public authority (as defined in the Freedom of Information Act 2000, Sched. 1). All recorded information held by those public authorities, is data, no matter how or where it is held. Such data is subject to various exemptions (see s.33A and **2.8.8** below). Practitioners must therefore properly identify which category the information to be shared falls into.

2.4 PERSONAL DATA

The DPA 1998 only applies if the data is personal data (s.1(1)). The data must relate to a living, identifiable individual, as defined further below. The importance of establishing whether personal data is also of a sensitive nature is also considered.

2.4.1 Identifiable living individual

Data is only personal if you can identify a living person from it. The DPA 1998 does not cover information about businesses, clubs, societies or deceased individuals.

For an individual to be identifiable it must be possible to locate data about them either from data you hold or which is likely to come into your possession.

The most common way an individual might be identifiable is by name. However, the lack of a name does not mean an individual cannot be identified. Addresses, telephone numbers, customer numbers, order number or referencing systems may still allow you to identify an individual.

Where it is not clear that an individual can be identified, all the means likely reasonably to be used either by the controller or by any other person to identify the individual must be considered (Data Protection Directive, Recital 26). The ICO suggests practitioners approach identification in the manner likely to be used by a determined person such as an investigative journalist rather than those available to the ordinary person in the street (ICO 2007 *Data Protection Technical Guidance: Determining What is Personal Data*).

To determine whether an individual is identifiable consider:

(a) how might the individual be identified;
(b) how accessible are those methods;
(c) how feasible are the methods of identification;
(d) how cost effective are the methods of identification.

If data can truly be anonymised then the DPA 1998 will not apply. However, the fact that information has been anonymised does not mean an individual will not be identifiable. By applying the factors above a judgement can be made whether an individual can nonetheless be identified from the information.

2.4.2 Relates to

Data relates to a person if it affects their privacy, either in their personal or family life, business or professional capacity (*Durant* v. *Financial Services Authority* [2003] EWCA Civ 1746). Two notions may assist practitioners to make this decision:

1. Biographical information: it is not enough that the data simply records a person's involvement in an event. That event must have some impact upon their personal life such that their privacy can be said to have been compromised.
2. Focus: the data should have the individual as its focus. Records of events in which a person is a marginal figure or has only a limited interest do not affect their privacy.

The Information Commissioner's guidance (ICO 2007 *Data Protection Technical Guidance: Determining What is Personal Data*) suggests that data will relate to an individual where it is obviously about them, or otherwise where:

(a) it can be used to learn, record or decide something about an individual;
(b) an incidental consequence of using the information allows you to learn or record something about an individual or could have an impact on or affect them.

Summary

Data is likely to relate to an individual when it:

(a) is linked to an individual such that you can obtain information about them;
(b) can be used to inform or influence actions or decisions about the individual;
(c) has biographical significance to the individual;
(d) focuses on the individual;
(e) might impact on an individual whether in their family, personal, business or professional life.

2.4.3 Sensitive personal data

Some types of personal data, by virtue of their greater sensitivity, gain greater protection under the DPA 1998 (see **2.6**). This sensitive personal data is personal data consisting of information about the data subject's (DPA 1998, s.2):

(a) racial or ethnic origin;
(b) political opinions;
(c) religious beliefs or beliefs of a similar nature;
(d) membership of a trade union;
(e) physical or mental health or condition;
(f) sexual life;
(g) involvement in the commission or alleged commission of a criminal offence; or
(h) involvement in criminal proceedings, their disposal or sentence.

2.5 THE DATA PROTECTION PRINCIPLES

The DPA 1998 requires data controllers to comply with eight rules on data processing called the Data Protection Principles (DPA 1998, s.4(4) and Sched. 1).

2.5.1 The first principle

This principle requires personal data to be processed fairly and lawfully and, in particular, not to be processed unless:

(a) at least one of the conditions in Schedule 2 is met; and
(b) in the case of sensitive personal data, at least one of the conditions in Schedule 3 is also met.

This principle has three elements:

- fairness;
- lawfulness; and
- compliance with the Schedule conditions.

Each separate element must be satisfied for processing to comply with the DPA 1998. Compliance with a Schedule 2 or 3 condition does not automatically make processing fair or lawful.

Since an understanding of how the Schedule conditions can be met is essential whenever you consider whether to share personal information, the conditions are detailed at **2.6**. The remaining elements of the first principle are considered below.

Fairness

It is presumed that information has been processed fairly where it is obtained from someone authorised or required by statute to provide it (DPA 1998, Sched. 1, Part II). In all other instances, to determine whether information sharing is fair we must consider:

1. How was the information obtained?
2. Was the individual deceived or misled about why the information was obtained and the likelihood it would be shared?
3. Was the individual provided with fair processing information? A fair processing notice is important to demonstrate processing is fair.

Fair Processing notices (DPA 1998, Sched. 1, Part II)	
Data obtained from the data subject	**Data obtained from a third party**
As far as practicable, when information is obtained from and about an individual they should, upon providing information, be provided with a written 'fair processing notice' or otherwise be informed: (a) of the identity of the data controller or their representative; (b) what will be done with the information, including whether and with whom information will be shared; and (c) of other information needed to make the processing fair.	When information is obtained from another person, the fair processing notice need not be provided upon obtaining information, but should, where practicable, be provided the first time information is processed. If the intention is to share information with another third party within 'a reasonable period' the 'fair processing notice' should be made available to the individual either: when the data is first disclosed; if it is unlikely to be disclosed, when you become aware of that fact, or at the end of that reasonable period.

There is no requirement to provide a fair processing notice where:

(a) provision of the notice would require disproportionate effort. Whilst the DPA 1998 does not define disproportionate effort, it is suggested that it is a question of fact to be determined in each individual case, taking account of the nature of the data; the time and cost involved in providing the notice; prejudice to the data subject; and the data subject's own knowledge (ICO 2004 *Data Protection Act 1998, Legal Guidance*, p. 34).

A data subject may still request the fair processing information and if so, it must be provided even if it requires disproportionate effort. It may, therefore, make sense to have one available in any event (see Data Protection (Conditions under Paragraph 3 of Part II of Schedule 1) Order 2000, SI 2000/185); or

(b) data is obtained from a third party and the recording or disclosure of the information is necessary to comply with a legal obligation (other than one imposed by contract). Data controllers cannot rely on this exception simply because they have obtained the data from a third party.

Lawfulness

The DPA 1998 does not define lawfulness. Unlawful has, however, been defined as 'something which is contrary to some law or enactment or is done without lawful justification or excuse' (*R* v. *R* [1991] 4 ALL ER 481). Several areas of law may help to determine lawfulness:

(a) legitimate expectations;
(b) the *ultra vires* rule (that a public authority may only do what it is permitted to do by law);
(c) breach of confidence;
(d) Article 8, the right to respect for private and family life.

Points (a) and (b) were dealt with at **1.5** whilst (c) and (d) are considered in **Chapters 5 and 6**.

Summary

The first principle – before sharing information:

- What power authorises the proposed sharing (relevant primarily to public authorities)? If practitioners cannot identify a statutory, common law or prerogative power to share information, sharing will be ultra vires and will breach the first principle.
- Does any legislation prohibit sharing?
- Is there any legal obligation or requirement to share the information?
- Is the information sensitive personal data?
- What was the data subject told would happen with the information when it was collected?
- What are the individual's reasonable expectations?
- What risks of harm to the data subject are posed by sharing information?
- Is there a relevant Schedule 2 and/or 3 condition (see **2.6**)?

2.5.2 The second principle

The second principle has two limbs:

- The initial collection of personal data must be for specified, lawful purposes (these must either be notified to the data subject in a fair processing

notice or notified to the ICO when the data controller registers with the ICO under DPA 1998, s.16(1)).
- Subsequent use of data must be for purposes which are not incompatible with the original purposes.

If a data controller complies with its notification and fair processing requirements the first limb of the principle will be met, provided processing is not unlawful.

Under the second limb, however, problems may arise when information sharing is proposed. Information obtained by one professional should only be shared with another professional if the information sharing is not incompatible with the original purpose of collection. Importantly, regard must be paid to the purposes for which personal data will be used by the person to whom they are disclosed, to determine whether that disclosure is compatible with the purposes for which the data were obtained (DPA 1998, Sched. 1, Part II, para. 6). The ICO takes a strict view of compatibility. A decision whether subsequent use by a third party is compatible with the original purpose for collection cannot be made retrospectively (ICO *Data Protection Act 1998: Legal Guidance*, p. 36).

Summary

The second principle – before sharing information:

- Why was data initially collected?
- What do you now intend to do with it?
- Are you covered by your notification to the ICO?
- Have you told the data subject what you now propose to do with the information?
- If you have not told them, would it fall within their reasonable expectations?
- What will the recipient of the data do with it – would that fall within the data subject's reasonable expectations?

2.5.3 The third principle

This principle requires data controllers to ensure data is adequate, relevant and not excessive, having regard to the purpose of processing. Whether information is shared between organisations or within an organisation, no more information than strictly necessary and relevant to the purpose of sharing should be shared. Information should not be shared on the basis that it might be useful in the future.

2.5.4 The fourth principle

Personal data must be accurate and, where necessary, kept up to date.

Personal data must be accurate

Data controllers must take reasonable steps to ensure information held and shared is accurate. What is reasonable depends upon circumstances but relevant factors include; the nature of the data, the feasibility of keeping it accurate, the cost and the potential impact on the data subject of inaccurate data.

Inaccuracy of personal data does not, however, breach the fourth principle if the data accurately portrays the information obtained by the data controller from the data subject or a third party and:

(a) having regard to the purpose(s) for which the data were obtained and further processed, the data controller has taken reasonable steps to ensure the accuracy of the data; or

(b) if the data subject has notified the data controller that they consider the data are inaccurate, the data indicate that fact. (Note there is no automatic requirement to correct data which the data subject considers inaccurate. The data controller and data subject may have different views on the data's accuracy. The data subject can request the court to order data is corrected or removed if a dispute arises (DPA 1998, s.14). The data controller should record the objections of the data subject alongside the data to ensure the full picture is available anyway.)

Data must be up to date

The requirement to keep data up to date applies where necessary. This is a question of fact, depending on circumstances. Most historical information is unlikely to need to be updated, whilst information which is continually used to make decisions about the data subject needs regular updating.

2.5.5 The fifth principle

Personal data must not be kept for longer than necessary for the purpose for which it is processed.

The DPA 1998 does not specify how long any particular type of personal data can be retained for. That question must be answered by each organisation and differs for different types of data. Some data will have a retention period specified by statute. Other retention periods will be determined by business need or risk analysis (for example information may need to be kept for a short period after an employee leaves to defend potential court claims). Data which is held for historical or archival purposes may never be destroyed.

2.5.6 The sixth principle

The sixth principle will be breached if the data controller breaches any of the rights given to the data subject under DPA 1998, ss.7, 10, 11, 12 or 12A. These rights are discussed in greater detail at **2.7**.

2.5.7 The seventh principle

This principle requires data controllers to take appropriate technical and organisational measures to prevent unauthorised or unlawful processing of personal data and accidental loss, destruction, or damage to personal data. The measures to be taken to afford appropriate security and care to personal data will vary but the following factors will be relevant:

(a) the state of available technology (this requires a regular review of technological and other developments);
(b) the cost of implementing security measures;
(c) the harm which might result from the unauthorised or unlawful use of the data or its accidental loss, destruction or damage;
(d) the nature of the data to be protected.

This principle must be considered when security systems or information sharing protocols are designed. Currently technological measures include options such as encryption, passwords and virus protection. Organisational measures cover physical security of data, access to buildings, storage areas, monitoring and review of practices and disaster recovery. Data controllers must take reasonable steps to ensure the reliability of any employee who has access to the personal data (DPA 1998, Sched. 1, Part II, para. 10). If a data controller uses a data processor (see **2.2.2**) he must ensure that the processor provides and complies with appropriate security guarantees, by means of a written contract requiring the processor to act only on instructions from the controller and requiring the processor to comply with conditions equivalent to the seventh principle (DPA 1998, Sched. 1, Part II, para. 12).

Summary: security measures

At organisational level

- Is there a policy, backed by senior management for information security?
- Is the person or department responsible for information security clearly identified, particularly where a data processor is used?
- Do inter-agency information sharing protocols appropriately address information security?
- If you use a data processor do contractual obligations imposed upon the processor ensure adequate security?
- Are sufficient resources and facilities available to provide effective security in accordance with organisational policies and inter-agency protocols?
- Is access to information properly controlled, i.e. with locked doors, passwords?
- Is there adequate protection from events such as theft, corruption or disaster?
- Is there a proper regime of staff selection and training and is knowledge kept up to date?
- Are there adequate provisions for detecting and dealing with security breaches?

At practitioner level

- What procedure exists to authenticate the identity of a person to whom personal data may be disclosed over the telephone?
- How will you ensure information shared can only be accessed and used by those who need to access it?
- If information is particularly sensitive or might have a significant impact on an individual's privacy have more stringent safeguards been considered?

2.5.8 The eighth principle

The eighth principle prohibits the transfer of personal data to a country outside the European Economic Area (EEA) unless that country ensures an adequate level of protection for data subjects' rights and freedoms in relation to processing of personal data. It does not prevent information sharing within the EEA.

The principle applies to information shared with corporate partners overseas, or with other overseas public organisations, such as the police. It does not apply where information is merely moved through a non-EEA country by an e-mail which is sent via servers outside of the EEA to a country within it. The fact that a webpage is viewable from anywhere in the world does not necessarily involve transfer of data. A transfer will occur when the information is accessed or uploaded by the data controller with the intention it should be accessed outside of the EEA (ICO 2008 *The Data Protection Act 1998, The Eighth Data Protection Principle and International Data Transfers*, p. 5).

Where information is to be shared outside the EEA, information may be shared, but only where:

- The destination country provides adequate protection. The European Commission considers several countries to have an adequate level of protection based on their national laws, including Argentina, Canada, Switzerland, the Isle of Man, Guernsey and Jersey. The level of protection afforded by other countries must be assessed.
- The information is transferred to a company in the United States, which has signed up to a Safe Harbor Scheme. (The European Commission considers that generally the USA provides inadequate protection. It presumes, however, that once a US company registers a Safe Harbor scheme with the Federal Trade Commission, which incorporates principles similar to those in the DPA 1998, that organisation will provide adequate protection.)
- One of the exemptions in DPA 1998, Sched. 4 which deals with consent, performance of contracts, substantial public interest, legal proceedings and public registers applies. Many of these conditions are similar to conditions for processing personal data in Schedules 2 and 3 and the Regulations. Since there will be no assessment of adequacy and the level of protection afforded to the data subject's rights may therefore be weaker, the ICO recommends that these exemptions are construed narrowly

(ICO 2008 *The Data Protection Act 1998, The Eighth Data Protection Principle and International Data Transfers*, p. 22).
- The recipient is bound by a contract which contains the standard contractual terms approved by the ICO as ensuring adequate safeguards and which, where incorporated in a larger contract are not amended or contradicted by other clauses.
- The recipient is bound by contract terms which, whilst different to the standard terms approved by the ICO, nevertheless contain appropriate safeguards. In contracts involving multiple data controllers (for example in a large outsourcing agreement involving different parts of the same overall group of companies located in different EU countries) it may be sensible to use the standard approved clauses.
- The recipient is subject to binding corporate rules which have been approved by the ICO (these have only been approved in relation to Phillips and the General Electric Company and are not considered further).

Practice point: determining whether a non-EEA country offers adequate protection

Issues of general adequacy

A data controller must consider the nature of the information, reasons for transfer and processing, security arrangements provided, data subjects' expectations and the origin and destination of the data. General adequacy considerations focus on the nature and extent of risks to the data subject's rights from the transfer and subsequent processing. If the risk is low an exhaustive assessment of the legal issues may not be necessary. However, if the information is sensitive, if its misuse, loss or release could cause harm to the individual or if it will be processed overseas for a long period of time, more detailed legal analysis is required.

Issues of legal adequacy

This requires consideration of the law, international obligations and relevant codes of conduct or enforceable rules in place in the destination country. The data controller must consider risks to the data subject, prejudice they may suffer and the levels of protection offered by the law of the destination country.

DPA 1998, Sched. 1, Part II, para. 13 and ICO 2008 *The Data Protection Act 1998, The Eighth Data Protection Principle and International Data Transfers*, pp. 9–10.

2.6 SCHEDULE 2 AND 3 CONDITIONS

We identified in **2.5.1** that the first principle requires anyone who shares (or otherwise processes) non-sensitive personal data to identify a Schedule 2 condition which legitimises the processing. A Schedule 2 and a Schedule 3 condition must be satisfied to share sensitive personal data.

Since many conditions refer to processing being necessary we must define necessary before we consider the Schedules themselves. Necessary has the same meaning as it has under the Convention, that is, 'while necessary . . . is not synonymous with indispensable, neither has it the flexibility of such expressions as admissible, ordinary, reasonable or desirable . . . it implies the existence of a pressing social need' (Corporate Officer of the House of Commons (*Corporate Officer of the House of Commons* v. *The Information Commissioner and others* [2008] EWHC 1084 (Admin)) and *The Sunday Times* v. *United Kingdom* (1979) 2 EHRR 245).

Three indicators that information sharing is necessary are:

(a) the reasons for sharing data are valid;
(b) the goal can be achieved only by sharing;
(c) the information sharing is proportionate to the proposed aim.

2.6.1 Schedule 2: conditions for processing sensitive and non sensitive personal data

The data subject has given his consent to the processing (para. 1)

Individuals do not like the concept of their information being shared without their explicit consent, even where to do so may bring them advantages. However, it is not a requirement of fair processing that the data subject consents to processing. Although it may be good practice to seek consent, it is often not the best Schedule 2 condition to rely on, for practical reasons.

Consent does not last forever. Consent may have been provided to cover a particular transaction. It may not survive the ending of the relationship between data subject and data controller. A data subject can also withdraw consent at any time.

Not all individuals have capacity to give valid legal consent. Data controllers who process information about children or the mentally ill must be particularly careful. A child should not be assumed incapable to consent. Their age and understanding must be considered. A mentally unwell adult may be capable of consenting. If parents or carers apply for personal data on behalf of children or partners the data controller must satisfy itself that they can legally act on their behalf.

Unless written consent is provided, or at worst a contemporaneous note made, difficulties may arise in the event of a complaint from the data subject.

The individual must understand exactly what they are consenting to. (Detailed consideration of consent is provided in the **Introduction**.)

Contractual obligations (para. 2)

This condition requires:

(a) a contractual relationship to exist between the data subject and another; processing must be necessary to perform the contract; or

(b) that the data subject has initiated steps to enter into a contract; processing is for that purpose.

The contract does not have to be between the data subject and the data controller.

Legal obligations (para. 3)

Processing must be necessary in order for the data controller to comply with a legal obligation to which it is subject, save for obligations imposed by contract (for example a statutory requirement to share information).

Vital interests (para. 4)

'The processing is necessary in order to protect the vital interests of the data subject.' The DPA 1998 does not define vital interests, but the Information Commissioner suggests that the condition applies where it is a matter of life or death, for example, disclosure of a person's medical history to an A&E department treating the data subject for serious injuries (ICO *Data Protection Act 1998: Legal Guidance*, p. 20).

Administration of justice (para. 5)

This surprisingly wide condition applies when processing is necessary:

(a) for the administration of justice (this will generally cover courts and tribunals);
(aa) for the exercise of any functions of either Houses of Parliament;
(b) for the exercise of any functions conferred on any person by or under any enactment;
(c) for the exercise of any functions of the crown, a minister of the crown or a government department; or
(d) for the exercise of any other functions of a public nature (including public functions exercised by a private company) exercised in the public interest by any person. The DPA 1998 does not define public interest and the ICO has not issued guidance on the subject. It is likely that it involves similar issues to those found in human rights legislation, including proportionality. Thus data controllers must balance the nature of the function and the public good to be achieved against the harm to the rights and freedoms of the individual.

Points (aa), (b) and (c) will apply to central and local government, but also to a wide range of other public, and some private bodies, who are provided with statutory powers to obtain or share information.

Legitimate interests (para. 6)

The processing is necessary for the purposes of legitimate interests pursued by the data controller or by the third party or parties to whom the data are disclosed, except where the processing is unwarranted in any particular case by reason of prejudice to the rights and freedoms or legitimate interests of the data subject.

Example

A journalist requests a local authority to disclose a detailed account of the expenses claimed by its elected members under the Freedom of Information Act 2000 (FOIA 2000). FOIA 2000 contains an exemption where the information is personal data and its release would breach one of the principles. The expenses details clearly contain personal data. Does their release breach the first principle?

Consider:

- What is the legitimate interest pursued by the data controller or third party?
  In this case there is a legitimate interest in the request. The accountability of public figures who are responsible for spending large sums of public money imposes an obligation of transparency and openness.
- Is the processing unwarranted because it prejudices the rights, freedoms or interests of the data subject?
  The Information Tribunal and courts have distinguished between personal information which is private and that which is public, i.e. relating to activities as a public servant. The expectation of privacy for such information is generally lower and the justification for disclosure more pressing. Note that the ICO takes a wide view of this condition (ICO *Data Protection Act 1998: Legal Guidance*, p. 20). It seems Schedule 2 paragraph 6 may be satisfied.

2.6.2 Schedule 3: conditions for processing sensitive personal data

Because of the nature of sensitive personal data, Schedule 3 conditions (including additional conditions detailed in three statutory instruments enacted under Schedule 3, paragraph 10) tend to be more restrictive than the Schedule 2 conditions (one of which must also be satisfied if sensitive data is shared).

Consent (para. 1)

Consent under Schedule 3 is similar to consent under Schedule 2 with two significant differences. First, consent must be explicit. There must be no doubt that the data subject has given unambiguous, informed consent. The data controller must therefore provide clear, accessible information to the data subject about why information is being collected and what will be done with it.

Second, since reference is made to 'the processing of the personal data' not 'the processing' (Schedule 2), this suggests that consent obtained under Schedule 3 is more limited than consent obtained to legitimise processing under Schedule 2.

Employment obligations (para. 2)

This condition provides for processing which is required by employment law (including legal obligations and rights imposed by statute, statutory instrument, courts or tribunals). See **Chapter 9** (employment).

Vital interests (para. 3)

Processing must be necessary in order to protect the vital interests (life and limb) of the data subject or of a third person (note this is wider than Sched. 2, para. 4 which refers only to the data subject). However it applies only:

(a) where consent cannot be given by or on behalf of the data subject, or the data controller cannot reasonably be expected to obtain the consent of the data subject; or
(b) where the vital interests of another person are concerned where consent by or on behalf of the data subject has been unreasonably withheld.

Example

A social worker is told by a client with a history of mental health difficulties that he intends to burn down his ex-wife's flat because she is seeing someone else. The social worker is concerned because the client has a history of violence towards his ex-wife. The DPA 1998 would not prevent the social worker from notifying the police of his concerns.

Political, philosophical, religious and trade union organisations (para. 4)

This condition applies in narrow circumstances, where information is shared by a non-profit making body or association which exists for political, philosophical, religious or trade-union purposes, in the course of its legitimate activities. Appropriate safeguards must be afforded to data subjects' rights and freedoms. Information must relate to individuals who are members of the body or association or have regular contact with it in connection with its purposes. Personal data must not be disclosed to a third party without the data subject's consent.

Information made public by the data subject (para. 5)

This condition applies when data has been made public because of steps taken deliberately by the data subject. The section does not seem to require the data subject to be the person making information public. Disclosure to a journalist for future publication is likely to be caught.

Legal proceedings (para. 6)

Processing must be necessary:

(a) for the purpose of, or in connection with, any legal proceedings including prospective legal proceedings;
(b) for the purpose of obtaining legal advice; or
(c) for the purposes of establishing, exercising or defending legal rights.

In relation to point (a) no guidance is provided on how likely proceedings must be. Point (c) should be construed narrowly (ICO *Data Protection Act 1998: Legal Guidance*, p. 22).

This condition is relevant to lawyers, investigative and prosecuting authorities, but also to individuals involved in ongoing and prospective legal proceedings (including cases before civil and criminal courts, tribunals, inquiries and other judicial bodies).

Administration of justice (para. 7)

This condition, which allows processing for the administration of justice, and exercise of statutory or government functions, is identical to Schedule 2, paragraph 5, save that it omits the wider provision for processing in the public interest.

Fraud prevention (para. 7A)

This condition applies where sensitive personal data is disclosed or processed by a member of an anti-fraud organisation or in accordance with arrangements made by them; or is processed by the person to whom they have disclosed data. Disclosure must be necessary in order to prevent fraud or a particular kind of fraud. An anti-fraud organisation is an organisation which enables or facilitates information sharing in order to prevent fraud or which has fraud prevention as one of its purposes.

Since the condition authorises the actual disclosure of the information and the subsequent use of the information disclosed, it seems that the condition can be used to authorise disclosures relating to a specific investigation and for more general fraud prevention measures.

Medical purposes (para. 8)

Processing must both be necessary for medical purposes and undertaken either by a health professional, or a person who, in the circumstances, owes a duty of confidentiality equivalent to a health professional.

This condition is widely drafted to permit processing of sensitive data in many different medical settings. The non-exhaustive definition of medical purposes includes, but is not limited to; purposes of preventative medicine, medical diagnosis, medical research, the provision of care and treatment and the management of healthcare services. Health professionals include doctors, nurses, pharmacists, dentists, opticians and many others (DPA 1998, s.69).

Equality monitoring (para. 9)

This condition permits collection, retention and use of information about individuals' racial and ethnic origins but only where necessary to identify or review equal opportunity issues, with a view to promoting or maintaining equal opportunities. If such monitoring occurs then appropriate safeguards must be provided to protect data subjects' rights and freedoms (this could include issues such as maintaining confidentiality, respecting human rights and meeting other DPA 1998 obligations). It should be read in conjunction with the Schedule to the Data Protection (Processing of Sensitive Data) Order 2000, SI 2000/417 (the 2000 Order). This Order details numerous further conditions for processing sensitive personal data. Paragraph 7 authorises processing of sensitive data relating to religious belief and physical and mental health, for the purposes of monitoring equal opportunities afforded to those with different religious beliefs, or disability. No information may be processed to determine matters relating to a specific individual, without that individual's explicit consent. No processing may be undertaken which will or is likely to cause substantial damage or distress to the data subject.

Processing for detection or prevention of crime (2000 Order, Sched., para. 1)

This condition is relevant, during the course of a criminal investigation, to the police and other organisations which have responsibility for investigating or preventing criminal activity. Processing must be necessary for the specified purposes and in the substantial public interest. Seeking explicit consent must prejudice those purposes. It seems unlikely it could be used for general crime reduction strategies, the particular difficulty being to demonstrate that seeking explicit consent would prejudice those purposes.

Although substantial public interest remains undefined, the need for substantial public interest suggests that a high greater degree of justification is needed to process data under this condition.

See also para. 10 of the Schedule to the 2000 Order, Processing necessary to enable police constables to exercise functions conferred by law.

Processing to protect the public from improper conduct, etc. (2000 Order, Sched., para. 2)

The condition applies where processing is necessary, in the substantial public interest, to discharge functions which aim to protect the public from a person's dishonest or seriously improper conduct, their unfitness or incompetence or the administrative mismanagement of an organisation, and where seeking explicit consent would prejudice those purposes. It will apply to various organisations involved in regulatory or monitoring activities or which have public protection functions (e.g., the General Medical Council).

Disclosures of improper conduct, etc. (2000 Order, Sched., para. 3)

This condition authorises disclosure of information relating to the commission or alleged commission of an unlawful act or omission; a person's dishonesty or seriously improper conduct, unfitness or incompetence; administrative mismanagement of an organisation where the disclosure is made for literary, artistic or journalistic purposes or with a view to publication in the public interest. It allows the media to investigate alleged wrongdoing in the public interest. There must be a reasonable belief that the information will be published and that such publication is in the public interest. Since processing must be in the substantial public interest, journalists must consider carefully the balance between the public interest and the level of interference in private life. Unsupported allegations, even salacious ones, are unlikely to be sufficient justification for invasion of an individual's privacy (*Max Mosley* v. *News Group Newspapers Limited* [2008] EWHC 1777 (QB)).

Processing necessary for the provision of confidential advice, counselling or support (2000 Order, Sched., para. 4)

This condition, which allows processing in the substantial public interest, where explicit consent either cannot be given, is not reasonable to obtain or would prejudice the provision of the support recognises that an individual who seeks confidential advice or counselling may be unable to consent to information being recorded or shared due to physical or mental circumstances, and this should not necessarily prevent information being shared.

Processing for purposes of insurance (life, annuity, health, accident and sickness) and occupational pensions (2000 Order, Sched., paras. 5 and 6)

This is of limited relevance to the majority of readers. These conditions are noted for completeness.

Processing of political opinions by registered political parties (2000 Order, Sched., para. 8)

Such processing may only be undertaken if it does not or is not likely to cause substantial damage or distress to the data subject.

Processing necessary for research purposes (2000 Order, Sched., para. 9)

This provision allows for research in a wide variety of fields, provided it is in the substantial public interest, and does not relate to decisions or measures affecting the data subject (unless they explicitly consent) and does not cause or is not likely to cause substantial damage or distress to the data subject or another. Research purposes is undefined, but includes both statistical and historical research (DPA 1998, s.33).

Elected representatives (Data Protection (Processing of Sensitive Data)(Elected Representatives) Order 2002, SI 2002/2905)

This order permits sensitive personal data to be processed by:

(a) Members of Parliament, Members of the European Parliament, elected local authority members and elected mayors (the representative) acting on behalf of the data subject's request at the data subject's request;
(b) the representative, following a third-party request to act on the data subject's behalf and where the representative cannot gain, or it would be unreasonable to gain the data subject's explicit consent or where consent has been unreasonably withheld;
(c) a data controller, who discloses information to a representative, who is acting at the data subject's request; and
(d) by a data controller, who discloses information to a representative, without the data subject's explicit consent.

Criminal Information (Data Protection (Processing of Sensitive Data) Order 2006, SI 2006/2068)

This condition enables information about criminal convictions or cautions (for certain offences relating to indecent photographs of children) to be disclosed in order to manage or cancel the account linked to the payment card which was used in committing the offence.

Sharing sensitive personal data: key points

- No personal data, whether sensitive or not, may be shared unless the eight principles are complied with (or an exemption applies).
- Sensitive personal data is accorded greater protection under the DPA 1998 given the greater harm likely to be caused by its loss or misuse and the fact data subjects may have greater expectations of privacy in relation to their sensitive personal data.
- When sharing sensitive personal data, at least one Schedule 2 and at least one Schedule 3/Order condition must be satisfied (or the first principle is breached).

- Not all data which people consider sensitive falls within DPA 1998, s.2, for example, an individual's national insurance number or his financial and banking information is not caught.

2.7 RIGHTS OF THE DATA SUBJECT

DPA 1998, Part II grants data subjects several rights. We consider those of greatest relevance: access to personal data, preventing processing likely to cause distress, correcting or removing inaccurate data, and compensation.

2.7.1 Subject access (s.7)

Unless an exemption applies, the DPA 1998 requires any data controller who holds personal data about an individual to provide that data to the individual, on request, together with information about:

(a) why the data is being processed;
(b) who the data has been or may be disclosed to;
(c) any information about the source of the data.

A number of practical issues are raised by section 7. The request must be made in writing. Data controllers are entitled to charge a fee which can vary by sector. While electronic methods of communication (e-mail, text, fax) may satisfy the requirement that requests are in writing (DPA 1998, s.64(2)), some difficulties remain in accepting these forms of communication. The data controller is still entitled to charge a fee; how and when will this be paid?

The data controller must satisfy itself that the person making the request is the data subject or is authorised to act on her behalf. E-mail addresses are easy to set up and the use of a person's name in an e-mail does not mean the e-mail is from that person. Disclosing an individual's personal data to someone other than them may well involve a breach of the principles one, two and seven.

While section 7 does not require practitioners to keep specific records, record keeping is crucial for section 7 compliance and useful for demonstrating compliance with the principles. Unless a record is kept of why, when and with whom information was shared (and from whom it was obtained) it will cause later difficulties if a section 7 request is received or a decision to share information needs justifying retrospectively.

If the data subject's information cannot be separated from information about other individuals, consideration should be given to redaction/removal of third-party information from the document. However, if the personal data released cannot be understood without the third-party information, you may not be able to comply with section 7 (recognising that disclosure of third-party information may breach the DPA 1998, or the duty of confidence).

Section 7(4) states that in such situations, information cannot be disclosed unless the third party consents or it is reasonable to disclose without their consent. What is reasonable will vary but a number of factors are relevant:

- Whether there is a duty of confidentiality. The relationship between the organisation and the third party, the circumstances in which the information was obtained and the third party's expectations must be considered.
- Whether the third party is capable of giving consent and the steps taken by the data controller to obtain it. If the third party expressly refuses consent it is unlikely to be reasonable to disclose.

The consequence of non-compliance with a section 7 request is potentially breach of the sixth data protection principle. A data subject who is unhappy with the way their request has been handled can ask the county court to order that section 7 is complied with. The court will consider the disputed information and retains discretion as to whether or not to order disclosure.

Dealing with a request for a data subject's personal data

1. Who is the person seeking the information?
2. If the request is made under section 7, how can you be sure the data subject is the requester?
3. If a request is made on the data subject's behalf, what documentation has been provided (where appropriate) to establish authority to act?
4. If the requester is a third party who is not acting on the data subject's behalf, why do they want the data and what do they intend to do with it? Can you provide the information without breaching the principles? (Although see also **Chapter 3** regarding third-party requests under FOIA 2000 and EIR 2004)
5. Should you contact the data subject to seek their consent to disclosure?
6. Does the data include information about a third party?
7. Can information about a third party be redacted?
8. If the information cannot be redacted is it nevertheless reasonable to disclose the information?
9. Where should this information request and decision be recorded?
10. What information should be recorded, and for how long should it be retained?

2.7.2 Preventing processing likely to cause damage or distress (s.10)

A data subject can, by notice, require a data controller to stop or not to begin sharing or otherwise processing his personal data, where it is likely to cause unwarranted and substantial damage or distress. The data controller has 21 days to reply, confirming that the notice has been or will be complied with or explaining why it will not be complied with (and why they consider the notice to be unjustified). It is possible to agree to partial compliance with a notice.

A data controller does not have to comply with a section 10 notice if the processing is undertaken in accordance with the following Schedule 2 conditions: consent, performance of contracts, legal obligations and vital interests.

However, where consent to processing has previously been given, it is arguable that the notice constitutes withdrawal of that consent.

2.7.3 Rectification, blocking, erasure and destruction (s.14)

Where personal data is inaccurate the data subject can apply to court for the data, together with any expression of opinion which is based on the inaccurate data, to be rectified, erased, blocked or destroyed. This section applies even where data has been received from a third party.

Where the data has been shared with others, the court may order that the recipients of the inaccurate data are notified of the order, taking account of the practicalities of such notification, and in particular how many notifications would be required.

The court can also make an order where the data subject can show that they have suffered damage which would entitle them to compensation under section 13 and there is a substantial risk of further breaches of the DPA 1998.

2.7.4 Compensation (s.13)

Section 13 entitles data subjects to obtain compensation in the county court, where they have suffered damage as a result of breach of the DPA 1998. Any claim that the data subject has suffered from distress may only be brought if they have also suffered damage or the breach relates to processing for the special purposes (art, literature and journalism). Few compensation claims have been brought and damages have been relatively low.

A data controller will have a defence to an action if it took reasonable care in the circumstances to comply with the particular DPA 1998 provision.

2.8 THE EXEMPTIONS

2.8.1 Types of exemption (s.27)

The DPA 1998 and associated regulations include numerous exemptions. Whilst there are two primary types: exemptions from the subject information provisions and exemptions from the non-disclosure provisions, wider, and narrower, exemptions do apply to certain types of information.

The non-disclosure provisions are particularly relevant when considering sharing information. However, they do not provide an automatic gateway to information sharing. Once established that an exemption applies it is necessary to consider the exempted provisions individually to decide if they can be dispensed with because their application is inconsistent with sharing information. They should only be disapplied to the extent of dealing with that inconsistency.

The ICO warns that data controllers should exercise caution when relying on the non disclosure provisions exemptions (ICO *Data Protection Act 1998: Legal Guidance*, p. 61). None of the exemptions require a data controller to disclose information. The application of an exemption allows the data controller to process information without breaching the DPA 1998. It is important to remember that even if a DPA 1998 exemption applies, human rights, confidentiality or statutory bars may prevent information sharing.

The non-disclosure provisions	The 'subject information provisions'
(a) The First Data Protection Principle (fair and lawful processing) except for the requirement to comply with a condition in Schedule 2 or 3 (b) The Second (specified purposes), Third (adequacy), Fourth (accuracy) and Fifth (retention) Data Protection Principles (c) Section 10 (processing causing distress) and section 14(1) to (3) (rectification, erasure and destruction)	(a) The 'fair processing notice' requirement of the First Data Protection Principle (b) Section 7 (subject access)

The various exemptions are considered below. We first consider exemptions relating to specific types of information (different exemptions may apply depending upon the person or purpose of processing). We then consider exemptions which apply specifically to section 7 (subject access) and finally exemptions purely from the subject information provisions.

2.8.2 National security (s.28)

Personal data is exempt from most of the DPA 1998 (the principles in their entirety, the provisions affording data subjects rights, those requiring notification to the ICO, and those relating to enforcement) if exemption is required in order to safeguard national security. A minister must sign a certificate confirming the exemption applies. The certificate is conclusive evidence of that fact. If any individual is directly affected by the issuing of such a certificate then they can appeal against it to the National Security Appeals Panel, a separate section of the Information Tribunal.

2.8.3 Crime and taxation (s.29)

Section 29 creates four separate exemptions. The first three cover personal data which is processed for crime and taxation purposes. These are to:

(a) prevent or detect crime;
(b) apprehend or detect offenders; or
(c) assess or collect a tax, duty or similar imposition.

The first exemption (s.29(1)) exempts from section 7 and the first principle (except for the requirement to comply with a Sched. 2 and/or Sched. 3 condition) where compliance with those provisions would be likely to prejudice one of the crime and taxation purposes above. Likely to prejudice has been held to mean 'more significant than merely fanciful, a significant and weighty chance of prejudice such that there may very well be prejudice to the interests even if the risk is not so high as more probably than not' (*R (on the application of Alan Lord)* v. *Secretary of State for the Home Department* [2003] EWHC 2073).

The second exemption (s.29(2)) is to the subject information provisions. It applies where processing is to discharge a statutory function, information was obtained from someone who held it for a crime and taxation purpose, and compliance with a subject information provision would be likely to prejudice the crime and taxation purposes.

The third exemption (s.29(3)) is to the non-disclosure provisions where disclosure is for a crime and taxation purpose and applying the provisions would be likely to prejudice any of those purposes.

The final exemption (s.29(4)), exempting data from section 7 disclosure, can only be relied upon by government departments, local authorities or an authority administering housing or council tax benefit. It applies where a risk assessment, in relation to tax and fraudulent criminal claims against the public purse, has been undertaken.

Section 29 in practice

A GP has received a request from the police to disclose personal, including health, information about Mr Bloggs. It states that section 29 applies.

Practitioners cannot simply accept an assertion that section 29 applies. It is the data controller who must decide whether an exemption applies and the data controller who may be liable if that assessment is not made or is made wrongly. If in doubt, always ask the requestor to explain why section 29 applies.

It is necessary also to identify exactly which section 29 exemption applies, and why, if appropriate, the crime or taxation purposes would be likely to be prejudiced by non disclosure.

If section 29(1) or (3) apply, a Schedule 2 and/or Schedule 3 condition must still be satisfied. However, under section 29(3) practitioners are exempted from the second principle (and will not breach the DPA 1998 for using information for a different purpose to that for which it was collected), and the fair processing requirement (to have told Mr Bloggs that you will be sharing his information with the police).

Even if section 29 applies, the data controller retains discretion whether to disclose. Section 29 does not exempt data controllers from complying with obligations of confidentiality. It may still be inappropriate to disclose.

2.8.4 Health, social work and education (s.30)

Health, social work and education data are subject to various exemptions detailed in the Data Protection (Subject Access Modification)(Health) Order 2000, SI 2000/413, the Data Protection (Subject Access Modification) (Education) Order 2000, SI 2000/414 and the Data Protection (Subject Access Modification)(Social Work) Order 2000, SI 2000/415 (see **Chapters 8 and 10**).

2.8.5 Regulatory activities (s.31)

A number of regulatory activities are exempt from the subject information provisions where processing would be likely to prejudice those activities (the same definition of likely to prejudice applies as under s.29). Section 31 applies when public functions are exercised:

- to protect the public against financial loss arising from improper conduct in the provision of financial, banking, insurance, investment services or of corporations, or misconduct of other professionals;
- to protect charities;
- to ensure health and safety;
- by various Ombudsmen, Financial Services regulators, the Office of Fair Trading and the Legal Services Board;
- in relation to complaints about health and social care;
- by local authority monitoring and ethical standards officers in relation to the conduct of local authority members or employees.

2.8.6 Journalism, literature and art (s.32)

Section 32 provides wide exemptions (from all of the data protection principles except the seventh, and data subject rights under ss.7, 10, 12 and 14(1) to (3)). To rely on the exemption, processing must be undertaken with a view to publishing journalistic, literary or artistic material. The data controller must reasonably believe (having regard to the importance of freedom of expression and any relevant codes of practice) that publication is in the public interest and that complying with the particular provision in question is incompatible with the special purposes of journalism, literature or art.

2.8.7 Research, history and statistics (s.33)

Where it can be shown that personal data is being processed for research purposes (which can include disclosure to another person), that the data is not being used to support measures or provisions with respect to a particular person and that data processing will not or is not likely to cause substantial damage or substantial distress to an individual, then exemptions from:

(a) the second principle applies, the data can be used for research purposes regardless of the reason it was initially collected;
(b) the fifth principle applies, the data may be kept indefinitely;
(c) section 7 applies, provided the research results or statistics do not identify any data subject.

2.8.8 Manual data (s.33A)

In **2.3** we noted that all recorded information held by a public authority is subject to the DPA 1998, regardless of how information is recorded or held, and that the last category of personal data, unstructured manual data, is subject to special exemptions. The exemptions are from:

(a) the first, second, third, fifth, seventh and eight principles;
(b) the sixth principle except for the rights under section 7 and section 14;
(c) sections 10 to 12;
(d) section 13;
(e) Part III (Notification); and
(f) section 55 (certain criminal offences).

In addition, unstructured manual data relating to pay, discipline, superannuation or other personnel matters in relation to service in the armed forces or employment by the Crown or any public authority is exempt from the remaining principles and all sections of Part II (rights of the data subject).

2.8.9 Publicly available information (s.34)

Personal data are exempt from the non-disclosure provisions, the subject information provisions, the fourth principle and section 14 where the data must be made available to the public under any statute or secondary legislation (other than under the Freedom of Information Act 2000), whether by publication, inspection or otherwise. This provision enables disclosure of information by means of numerous public registers (see **Chapter 4**).

2.8.10 Disclosures required by law (s.35)

An exemption from the non-disclosure provisions applies:

(a) where disclosure is required by statute or secondary legislation, rule of law or court order; or
(b) where disclosure is necessary for the purpose of, or in connection with, any legal proceedings (including prospective proceedings), or for the purpose of providing legal advice; or
(c) is otherwise necessary for the purposes of establishing, defending or exercising legal rights.

Note that compliance with Schedule 2 (and 3) is still required. However, it should not be difficult to identify an appropriate condition where disclosure is required by law or court order (see Sched. 2, para. 3 and Sched. 3, para. 6). Where the exemption applies, but where information is required in connection with legal proceedings or is shared for the purpose of legal advice, a discretion to disclose remains (although not where statute or court order obliges disclosure).

2.8.11 Parliamentary privilege (s.35A)

Personal data are exempt from the first principle (except compliance with Sched. 2 and 3 conditions), second, third, fourth and fifth principles, section 7 (subject access), section 10 (preventing processing likely to cause damage or distress) and section 14 (rectification, destruction, erasure and blocking) if it is required to avoid infringing the privileges of either of the Houses of Parliament.

2.8.12 Domestic purposes (s.36)

Where information is processed by an individual for personal, family, household and recreation purposes it is exempt from the data protection principles, DPA 1998, Parts II and III.

2.8.13 Exemptions from section 7 subject access requests (Sched. 7)

Exemptions from section 7 apply where:

- A reference was given in confidence by the data controller for purposes of education, training, employment, appointment to any office or provision by the data subject of any service. It is worth noting that the exemption applies to the data controller who provides the reference but no mirror provision protects the recipient of the reference. A data subject could theoretically obtain it through a subject access request to the recipient, provided no other exemption applied (para. 1).
- The personal data consists of marks or information recorded by the data controller marking an academic, professional or other examination, or which has been processed as a result. This exemption does not prevent disclosure, merely delays it until a suitable time after formal announcement of marks (para. 8).
- The personal data was recorded in an examination script by the data subject during an academic, professional or other examination (para. 9).
- Compliance would reveal evidence of the commission of an offence (other than an offence under the DPA 1998) (para. 11). Note paragraph 11 also clarifies that information disclosed under section 7 may not be used in proceedings for an offence under the DPA 1998.

2.8.14 Exemptions from the subject information provisions (Sched. 7)

Personal data is exempt from the subject information provisions if:

- The provisions would be likely to prejudice the combat effectiveness of any of the armed forces (para. 2).
- It is processed to assess the suitability of any person for judicial office or the position of Queen's Counsel or in relation to conferring an honour or dignity (para. 3).
- It is processed for management forecasting or planning in connection with a business or activity, provided application of the provisions would be likely to prejudice the conduct of the business or other activity (para. 5).
- It is processed in connection with corporate finance services and the application of the provisions could or the data controller reasonably believes they could affect the price of a financial instrument (securities, options, futures, swaps, derivative contracts, etc.) or exemption is otherwise required to safeguard an important economic or financial interest of the UK (para. 6).
- It is records of the data controller's intentions in relation to any negotiations with the data subject and where application of the provisions would be likely to prejudice the negotiations (para. 7).
- It is protected by legal professional privilege (para. 10, see **Chapter 7**).

Exemptions: points to note

- Exemptions do not remove all DPA 1998 obligations. Be clear which exemption applies and which provisions it provides an exemption to.
- Exemptions apply to information, not documents.
- The data controller must be satisfied the exemption applies. When asked to disclose information, consider requesting more information about why an exemption applies.
- Exemptions do not create an obligation to disclose, they simply allow non-compliance with sections of the DPA 1998.
- Exemptions do not relieve data controllers from compliance with other legislation, confidentiality or human rights.

2.9 CONCLUSION

Before sharing any information, an assessment must be made whether information is personal and whether it is also sensitive personal data. If so, compliance with the eight principles is required, and a Schedule 2 and possibly a Schedule 3 condition must be satisfied, unless an exemption applies. The practice checklist below at **2.10** provides a basic structure for approaching information sharing, in all situations, in a way which complies with the DPA 1998 and associated guidance.

The DPA 1998 also requires information to be provided to data subjects about proposed information sharing (first principle). To comply with section 7 the data subject who requests their own personal information should be told when, why and with whom information has been shared.

The DPA 1998 clearly underpins lawful information sharing. Whilst this chapter outlines the essential elements of the DPA 1998, its practical application, when in apparent conflict with other legal regimes, is particularly difficult. We are now equipped, in future chapters, to consider the application and interaction of the DPA 1998 with other legal regimes (see **Chapters 3** (Freedom of Information legislation), **5** (confidentiality), **7** (court proceedings), **8** (health), **9** (employment), **10** (children) and **12** (criminal)).

2.10 PRACTICE CHECKLIST

Question 1: Have you considered the privacy implications of sharing the data and whether or not a Privacy Impact Assessment is required?

Yes – Go to Question 2	No – Do so before moving on to Question 2

Question 2: Is the information data under DPA 1998, s.1?

Yes – Go to Question 3	No – The DPA 1998 does not apply

Question 3: Is the data personal?

Yes – consider the test in *Durant* and the ICO Guidance – Go to Question 4	No – The DPA 1998 does not apply

Question 4: If the information is data, is it unstructured manual data (category e data) under section 1?

Yes – The DPA 1998 only applies if you are a public authority. Even if you are a public authority there are numerous exemptions under s33A	No – Go to question 5

Question 5: Do you have express or implied legal power to share the information?

Yes – Go to Question 6	No – the sharing will be unlawful and will breach the DPA 1998

Question 6: Have you given the data subject a fair processing notice?

Yes – Go to Question 7	No – consider if it is practicable to do so

Question 7: Do you meet a condition in Schedule 2 or, for sensitive personal data, Schedules 2 and 3 to justify your processing?

Yes – Go to Question 8	No – Your sharing will breach the DPA 1998

Question 8: Is the information being shared for a different purpose from which it was collected?

Yes – consider if the new purpose is incompatible with the original before sharing	No – Go to Question 9

Question 9: Are you only sharing as much information as is necessary to meet your objectives?

Yes – Go to Question 10	No – review how much of the data needs to be shared and whether it can be anonymised.

Question 10: Is the information you are sharing accurate and up to date?

Yes – Go to Question 11	No – amend the data so that it is accurate and update it if necessary

Question 11: Does the transfer afford adequate security provisions?

Yes – Go to Question 12	No – update your security arrangements to a level appropriate to the sensitivity of the data and the risk involved

Question 12: Is the transfer of data outside of the EEA?

Yes – Comply with the eighth principle by use of Binding Corporate Rules, Model Clauses, other contractual provisions requiring the data processor to comply with the DPA 1998 or other assessment of adequacy	No – Go to Question 13

Question 13: Is the transfer to a data processor?

Yes – ensure there is a contract in place dealing with the transfer and how the processor handles the data	No – Go to Question 14

Question 14: Is there a relevant exemption covering the data or the reasons for sharing it?

Yes – consider what information the exemption applies to. Go to Question 15	No – Ensure the Data Protection Principles are complied with. Go to Question 15

Question 15: is there some other law which prevents you from sharing such as confidentiality, human rights or express statutory provision?

Yes – do not share the information, doing so will also breach the DPA 1998	No – Go to Question 16

Question 16: Is the information sharing to be on an ongoing or regular basis?

Yes – consider putting in place a code of practice or information sharing protocol	No – make sure you record this decision and your reasons

CHAPTER 3

Freedom of Information Act 2000 and Environmental Information Regulations 2004

Phil Tompkins and Susan Wolf

3.1 INTRODUCTION

The Freedom of Information Act 2004 (FOIA 2000) and the Environmental Information Regulations 2004, SI 2004/3991 (EIR 2004 or the Regulations), unlike most other legislation discussed in this book, actively encourage disclosure of information to the public, either proactively through publication schemes and disclosure logs, or reactively in response to requests. The underlying rationale is that public authorities, acting in the public interest, hold information that should be available to the public to ensure transparency and accountability or to facilitate public participation in decision making. A presumption runs through FOIA 2000 and the EIR 2004 that openness and disclosure of information are themselves in the public interest (ICO 2007 *Freedom of Information Awareness Guidance: The Public Interest Test (AG3)*). To that extent the provisions promote information sharing.

However, both regimes also recognise that disclosing all information held by public authorities is not necessarily in the public interest. Public authorities hold a wide range of information, including information about individuals, information provided by third parties in confidence, and information about highly sensitive policy formulation or international relations. Disclosure could, in relation to living individuals, breach the DPA 1998, or could adversely affect other interests such as commercial confidentiality or national security. Hence both regimes allow public authorities to withhold information on specified grounds.

One of the most significant features of both regimes is that, unlike other legislation, such as the DPA 1998, where information is provided solely to the applicant, information disclosed under FOIA 2000 and the EIR 2004 is considered to be within the public domain. It can be accessed and used subsequently by any other person. Similarly both regimes are applicant and motive blind. The public authority receiving a request for information should not be influenced by who is seeking the information or why they want the information. This is because the regimes are concerned with disclosure to the public in the public interest.

Their other notable feature, for information sharing purposes, is that whilst they impose obligations on public authorities, they are capable of catching information supplied to public authorities by individuals and companies. This clearly raises issues regarding information which individuals and organisations have provided to public authorities which could now be disclosed but which the providers never contemplated would be allowed to enter the public domain.

3.2 WHICH REGIME?

Both FOIA 2000 and the EIR 2004 enable anybody, whatever their nationality or country of residence, whether an individual, business or non-governmental organisation to request information. The person making the request need not specify which information rights regime they are seeking the information under. They may not be aware of the differences between the regimes nor specifically mind which regime is applied, providing the information requested is provided promptly. From a practical point of view, providing the information is disclosed to the applicant, it makes little real difference whether information is supplied under FOIA 2000 or EIR 2004 since a satisfied applicant is unlikely to challenge the basis of the disclosure. However, the Information Tribunal has ruled that:

> What is important is that if the information comes within the scope of the EIR 2004 then . . . it is exempt information under FOIA 2000 (pursuant to section 39), and the public authority is obliged to deal with the request under the EIR 2004.
>
> *Archer* v. *Information Commissioner and Salisbury District Council*, 09/05/07, EA/2006/0037

It is essential also, that public authorities understand their obligations under each regime and know which regime to apply to the information request, since there are substantive differences between the regimes. Where a public authority fails to recognise that it is subject to the EIR 2004 or fails to recognise that a request is for environmental information, the applicant could potentially be wrongly refused the information requested. A critical determinative factor is whether the information requested is environmental information (in which case it must be dealt with under the EIR 2004). Whilst admittedly undesirable and inconvenient, it may be necessary for a public authority to go through the minutia of documents applying FOIA 2000 and EIR 2004 respectively to different parts of the document.

Practical example: the misapplication of FOIA 2000

The misapplication of FOIA 2000 to a request for environmental information could result in prejudice to the applicant where:

- A public authority fails to respond to a request made orally on the basis that it should have been submitted in writing. Whilst FOIA 2000 requires an applicant to provide a name and address (an e-mail address will suffice), a request for environmental information under the EIR 2004 may be made orally.

- A body refuses to disclose environmental information on the basis that it is not subject to FOIA 2000 but where it is in fact subject to the EIR 2004 (for example, a private waste contractor may fall within the EIR 2004 but clearly has no responsibilities under FOIA 2000; see ICO Decision FS50114241).
- A public authority refuses to disclose the information on the grounds that the request exceeds the cost limits under FOIA 2000, where no such cost limit exists under the EIR 2004.
- A public authority applies an exemption under FOIA 2000 to an EIR 2004 request. This could potentially result in a refusal to disclose in circumstances where the information should have been disclosed under the EIR 2004 (because there are fewer exceptions under the EIR 2004 and they are all (with the exception of the personal data exception) subject to the public interest test).

3.3 BODIES SUBJECT TO FOIA 2000 AND THE EIR 2004

Whilst both FOIA 2000 and the EIR 2004 apply to public authorities, what constitutes a public authority differs between the two regimes, with the definition much wider under the EIR 2004. Consequently some bodies will escape obligations under FOIA 2000 but are still under a duty to disclose any environmental information that they hold. (For example, see ICO Decision FER0090259, 07/06/2006 in which Environmental Resources Management Ltd was held to be a public authority in respect of an environmental report it had prepared on behalf of the Regional Assembly for the North of England.)

3.3.1 Bodies subject to FOIA 2000

FOIA 2000 provides a right of access to all information held by or on behalf of a public authority. This means those public bodies listed in FOIA 2000, Sched. 1, certain authorities designated by order of the Lord Chancellor and publicly-owned companies (FOIA 2000, s.3(1)). Currently FOIA 2000 covers around 130,000 public authorities.

FOIA 2000, Sched. 1, Part I contains the core public authorities such as government departments. Part II contains a list of local government authorities. Part III covers the NHS including Health Authorities, NHS Trusts and individuals providing public medical, dental, ophthalmic and pharmaceutical services. Part IV includes schools and institutions providing further and higher education. Part V covers the police, and Parts VI and VII list miscellaneous public authorities and executive agencies such as the British Museum, the Coal Authority and the Commission for Racial Equality.

Schedule 1 makes clear that certain authorities are only partially subject to FOIA 2000. For example, the BBC is covered by FOIA 2000 for information held '. . . for purposes other than those of journalism, art or literature'.

Publicly-owned companies are covered by FOIA 2000 (s.6) if they are wholly owned either by the crown or by a public authority listed in Schedule 1, unless they are either a government department or are owned by an authority which is listed as a public authority in relation to certain specified information only (e.g. the BBC). The fact that they must be wholly owned by a single public authority leads to an anomaly: a company owned by a single public authority is covered by FOIA 2000, one jointly owned by two public authorities is not.

Not all bodies generally considered to be public authorities are covered by FOIA 2000. Certain bodies which receive either the whole or the majority of their funding from the state are nevertheless not subject to FOIA 2000 (for example, school academies). However, this position may be rectified in time, since FOIA 2000 affords the Secretary of State power to designate further bodies as public authorities for the purposes of FOIA 2000. This power can be exercised where the body appears to be exercising functions of a public nature or is contracted to provide services to a public authority and that service is a function of that public authority (i.e. outsourcing services). There may be some overlap between these two aspects.

If a body, which is not covered by FOIA 2000, receives an information request, it is not required to answer it, unless it is subject to the EIR 2004 and the request is for environmental information.

3.3.2 Bodies subject to the EIR 2004

Public authorities are defined in regulation 2(2) (reg. 3 specifically excludes any public authority to the extent that it is acting in a judicial or legislative capacity; and either House of Parliament to the extent required for the purpose of avoiding an infringement of the privileges of either House).

The term public authority is initially defined by giving it the meaning that it has under the FOIA 2000; it includes government departments and any other public authority as defined in FOIA 2000, s.3. However the EIR 2004 also includes (by disregarding the exception in FOIA 2000, Sched. 1, para. 6) the special forces and any unit or part of a unit which is for the time being required by the Secretary of State to assist the Government Communications Headquarters in exercising its functions. In contrast those bodies which are subject to FOIA 2000 but only in relation to the information specified in Schedule 1 (such as the Bank of England, or the BBC) are excluded from this part of the definition (although they may fall within other parts of the EIR 2004 definition). Similarly any person designated by Order under FOIA 2000, s.5 is excluded from the definition of public authorities in regulation 2(2)(b).

Unlike FOIA 2000, the EIR 2004 have their origins in international and European law and give effect to the UK's obligations under the Aarhus Convention (The UNECE Convention on Access to Information, Public Participation in Decision-making and Access to Justice in Environmental

Matters 1998) and EC Directive 2003/4 (Directive 2003/4/EC of the European Parliament and of the Council of 28 January 2003 on public access to environmental information). The Aarhus Convention specifically recognises that a broad range of services which were traditionally in the public domain, have recently been privatised and that such privatised solutions should not take public services out of the realm of public involvement, information and participation. To provide the broad coverage required by the Convention and Directive, the EIR 2004 includes two further categories of bodies that fall within the definition of public authorities.

The first is any other body or other person that carries out functions of public administration (reg. 2(2)(c)). These functions need not relate to the environment, however they must be administrative functions (*Network Rail* v. *Information Commissioner*, 17/07/07, EA/2006/0061, EA/2006/0062). A private body may carry out functions of public administration, for example where it is contracted to perform a function normally performed by governmental authorities. Additionally a body could carry out public administration functions at the same time as carrying out private functions. In practice most authorities that fall within this description are likely to already be subject to FOIA 2000.

The final, and perhaps most difficult, part of the definition, in regulation 2(2)(d), covers any other body or other person that is under the control of a person falling within sub paragraphs 2(2)(a)–(c) and:

(a) has public responsibilities relating to the environment;
(b) exercises functions of a public nature relating to the environment; or
(c) provides public services relating to the environment.

Essentially this involves a two-stage test. First, does the person/body fall under the control of a public authority and second, does the body demonstrate at least one of the responsibilities relating to the environment? The Tribunal and Commissioner have found no difficulty in holding that private sector companies that are carrying out statutory duties on behalf of a public authority fall under this limb. For example, South Downs Waste Services Ltd, a private waste company, was held to be a public authority by virtue of the integrated waste management contract it had entered into with two councils (ICO Decision FS50114241, 18/03/08). This clearly has important implications for private sector providers who enter into contracts to carry out the statutory responsibilities of public authorities. Authorities who put such contracts out to tender should make companies aware of their potential obligations under the EIR 2004. Figure 3.1 shows which bodies and persons are subject to the EIR 2004.

3.4 PROACTIVE DISSEMINATION OF INFORMATION

Both FOIA 2000 and the EIR 2004 promote information sharing through the proactive publication of information. FOIA 2000 requires public authorities

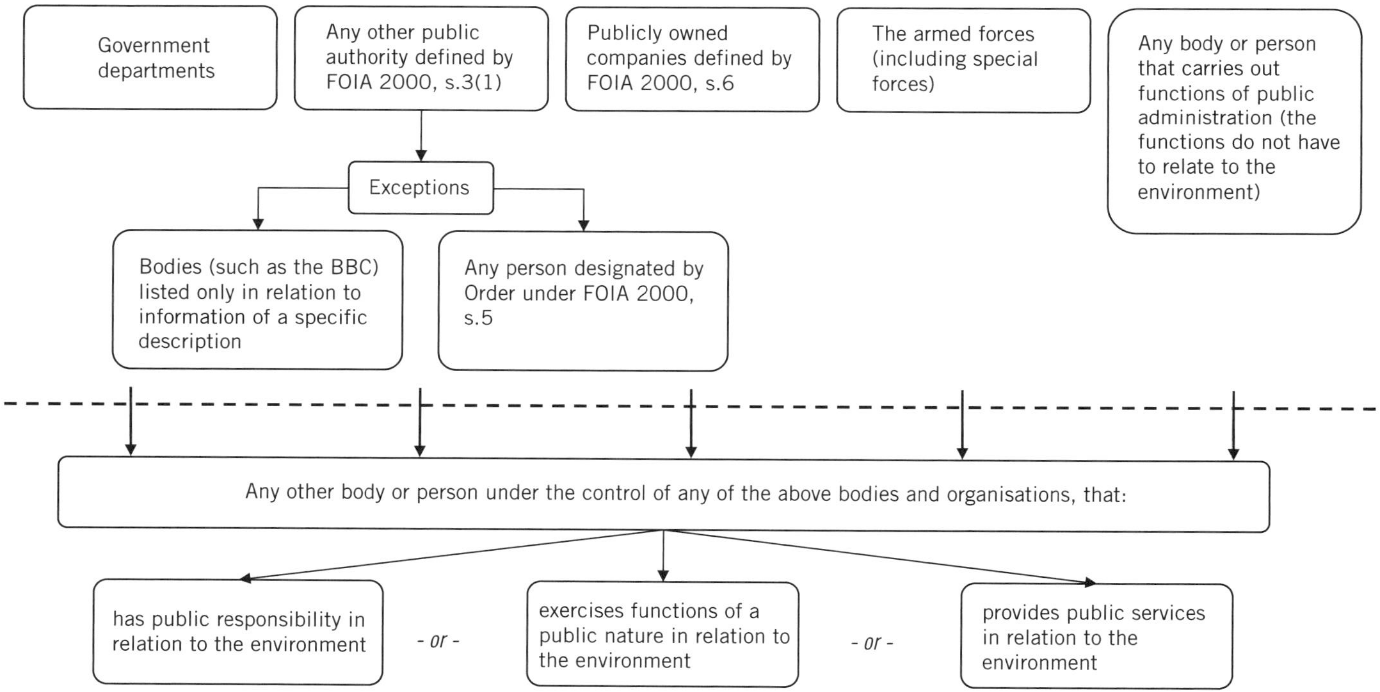

Figure 3.1 Bodies/persons subject to the EIR 2004

to maintain publication schemes. The EIR 2004 require public authorities to progressively make information available to the public by electronic means. The logic is that by proactively making information readily available, the resources needed for dealing with individual requests can be reduced.

3.4.1 Publication schemes

FOIA 2000, s.19 requires all public authorities to adopt, maintain and review a publication scheme, either developed by the public authority themselves (in which case the scheme must be approved by the ICO) or using model schemes (modifications to an approved scheme must also be approved by the ICO). Publication schemes must specify:

(a) the classes of information the public authority intends to publish (this should focus on the key areas of accountability of the public authority);
(b) the manner in which information in each class is, or is intended to be published; and
(c) whether the information is or is intended to be made available free of charge or if a fee will be paid.

The publication scheme is a guide to the information which public authorities routinely publish, as opposed to a list of all information available from or published by the public authority. Publication schemes give access to much important information and are important tools in making information held by public authorities easily available. Although there is no statutory requirement as to how such schemes must be published, good publication schemes facilitate access by different means.

The publication scheme overlaps with the Information Asset Register (IAR), which is meant to contain all information held by government departments and other crown bodies, although its focus is unpublished information (see *The Future Management of Crown Copyright*, Cabinet Office, (1999)). The publication scheme should also be considered alongside the Re-Use of Public Sector Information Regulations 2005, SI 2005/1515, which authorise re-use of information where the document has been identified by the public sector body as available for re-use (in other words where it has been included on the Information Asset Register) or where the document has been accessed or is accessible by virtue of FOIA 2000/the EIR 2004 (see further **Chapter 11**).

3.4.2 Disclosure logs and simultaneous releases

Any discussion about publication schemes would be incomplete without mention of disclosure logs and simultaneous release. Many public authorities have collated the information released in response to information requests into disclosure logs. The disclosure log is an online tool, usually found on the public authority's website, which lists information disclosed. It ensures information supplied as a result of an information request is made instantly, easily, available to as wide an audience as is possible. Whilst there is no legal requirement for public authorities to have disclosure logs, they promote public access to information, promote the aims of FOIA 2000, and can compliment publication schemes.

Disclosure logs vary in format from those which contain all information which has been disclosed in response to information requests, to those which only deal with the most interesting or high profile information. They often contain information which is proactively released in response to anticipated demand for that information.

Often information sought by an applicant may be of wider public interest. Since applicants are only entitled to information which any member of the public would be entitled to by making the same request, where information is of wider interest, the public authority should consider whether or not to simultaneously release the information to the public, perhaps by disclosure log. When considering simultaneous release the public authority should:

(a) ensure the simultaneous release does not reveal information relating to the original applicant;
(b) ensure the information released does not contain material which was not released to the original applicant;
(c) consider whether or not to charge the original applicant for the information; it is unlikely a public authority can justify charging for information which is released simultaneously;
(d) consider informing the applicant that it is simultaneously releasing the information and explain why it is doing so.

Certain information should not be contained on the disclosure log, for example, personal data and confidential information released on a discretionary basis.

3.4.3 The EIR 2004 and progressive dissemination of information

EIR 2004, reg. 4 requires public authorities to progressively make the environmental information they hold available to the public by electronic means. Such means should be easily accessible. Additionally, regulation 4 requires public authorities to take reasonable steps to organise the information relevant to its functions with a view to its active and systematic dissemination to the public. (These requirements do not apply to information otherwise exempt under the EIR 2004, or information collected before 1 January 2005 by non-electronic means.)

Environmental Information Regulations 2004 – Detailed Guidance, Defra, 2005 (the Defra Guidance), para. 5.7 suggests public authorities, in fulfilling this obligation, should prioritise the identification and dissemination of information which is most likely to be of interest to the public, such as information on emissions and waste streams. Regulation 4 prescribes, as a minimum, that information disseminated must include certain information referred to in the

Directive, art. 7(2) (for example, relevant international treaties, etc., policies, plans and programmes relating to the environment, reports on the state of the environment, monitoring results, environmental impact assessments) and also the facts and analyses of facts which the public authority considers relevant and important in framing major environmental policy proposals.

Although the EIR 2004 does not specifically require public authorities to maintain publication schemes, where organisations subject to FOIA 2000 produce a publication scheme which covers publication of environmental and non-environmental information, this should also satisfy regulation 4. The greater difficulty is for those bodies not subject to FOIA 2000 who must consider what steps they need to take to proactively disseminate the environmental information they hold, whether on websites, through annual reports or other literature.

3.5 INFORMATION COVERED

When a person makes a request for information to a public authority, they need not specify which access regime they are utilising or justify why they want the information. The responsibility for deciding the applicable regime rests with the public authority receiving the request. In practice, a public authority, on receipt of a request for information, should first ask itself whether the information requested falls within the scope of the EIR 2004, in other words, is it environmental information? If so, then the public authority should deal with the request under the EIR 2004, follow the EIR 2004 procedures and, where appropriate, apply the EIR 2004 exceptions.

FOIA 2000 applies to any other information.

3.5.1 What is environmental information?

The EIR 2004 provides a lengthy, very wide definition of what constitutes environmental information (reg. 2). Environmental information can take many forms, including information in written, visual, aural, electronic or any other material form. It includes, for example, information contained in documents such as decision letters, applications, inspection reports, concession agreements, contracts, tables, databases, spreadsheets, e-mails, photographs, sketches and handwritten notes or drawings and covers opinions and advice as well as facts. Information in raw and unprocessed form is capable of being environmental information.

However, environmental information must be information on one of the six limbs of the definition.

The first limb of the definition is central. It refers to the so-called elements of the environment. Rather than producing a finite and exhaustive list of these elements, the EIR 2004 provides a widely drafted illustrative list which contains the traditional media of air, water and land, but also includes landscape, natural sites, biological diversity and genetically modified organisms. Environmental information is defined in the first instance as any information on the state of the elements of the environment; a request concerning air quality clearly falls within this but so would a question to a highways authority about the state of the highway or footpaths.

The second limb includes any information on the factors affecting or likely to affect the elements of the environment. Such factors include traditional emissions or discharges or waste, which clearly impact upon air or water quality or biodiversity. Factors affecting the environment also include energy, noise and radiation. Although factors are defined widely the limb is qualified to the extent that the factors must affect or be likely to affect the elements of the environment (whether the effect is positive/negative, large scale or small). The Information Tribunal has shown marked reluctance to engage in any detailed scientific analysis of effect, preferring to give the definition its plain and ordinary meaning (see again *Ofcom* v. *Information Commissioner*, 04/09/07 EA/2006/0078).

The third limb refers to any information on measures (including administrative measures), such as policies, legislation, plans, programmes, environmental agreements, and activities affecting or likely to affect the elements and factors referred to above. Legal advice given to a public authority in respect of planning issues can constitute a measure likely to affect one of the elements of the environment (see *Kirkcaldie* v. *Information Commissioner and Thanet District Council*, 04/07/06, EA/2006/001). Similarly advice given to ministers by civil servants during policy formulation or decision making falls within this limb, as does information supplied by the public in questionnaire form during a process of consultation (see ICO Decision FS50079628, 29/11/06 Transport for London).

The final three limbs of the definition include reports on the implementation of environmental legislation; cost-benefit and other economic analyses and assumptions used within the framework of the measures and activities referred to above; and any information on the state of human health and safety, including the contamination of the food chain, where relevant, conditions of human life, cultural sites and built structures inasmuch as they are or may be affected by the state of the elements of the environment or through those elements by any of the factors or measures referred to.

In practice there are undoubtedly difficulties in identifying whether information sought is environmental information.

Practical example

A local authority is asked for correspondence about its social housing policy. The request specifically asks for information about housing density and assessments undertaken and actions proposed to ensure adequate parking, school and waste services are provided. In itself this may not appear to request environmental information. However, information about assessments of the need to increase waste services and actions in relation to waste collection is likely to be environmental information.

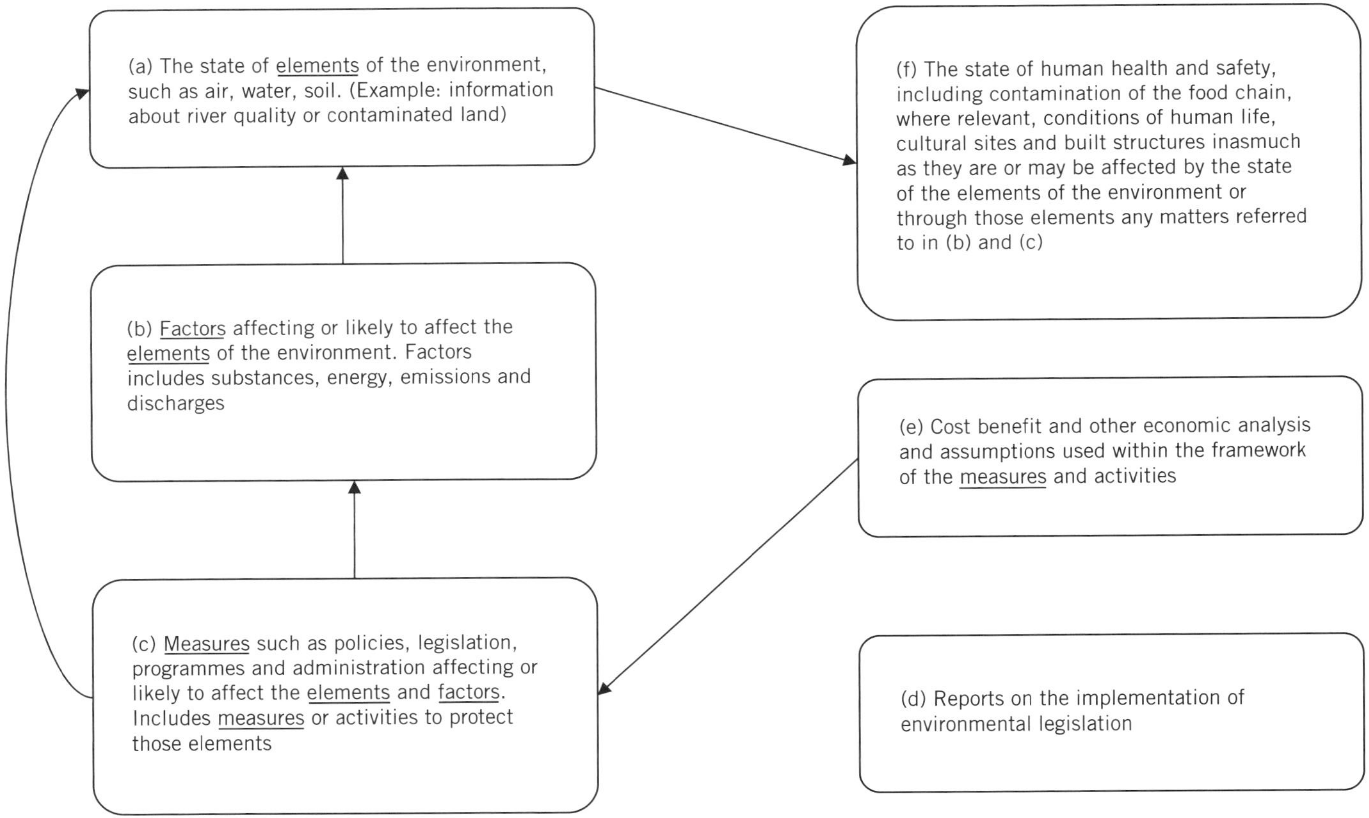

Figure 3.2 Is it environmental information?

Given the potential difficulties in practice of identifying whether FOIA 2000 or the EIR 2004 apply, Defra has produced useful guidance reflecting the increasing number of ICO and Tribunal decisions in this area. See Defra Guidance Chapter 3 'What is covered by the Regulations', and also 'How to decide whether a request is EIR 2004 or FOIA 2000' available from the Defra website. **Figure 3.2** is intended to provide further assistance, as a useful checklist as to whether information may be environmental.

3.6 RESPONDING TO REQUESTS FOR INFORMATION

3.6.1 Information requests under FOIA 2000

FOIA 2000 entitles anybody to make an information request. Provided that the information requested is not available through a publication scheme, the public authority must provide the information unless it is exempt or one of the procedural reasons for refusing a request applies.

On receipt of a valid information request made under FOIA 2000, a public authority must consider:

(a) does it hold the information; and, if so,
(b) is there any exemption or other reason why the information need not be disclosed.

What is a valid information request under FOIA 2000?

A request for information under FOIA 2000 must be in writing, legible and must include the name and address of the requester (FOIA 2000, s.8). There is no requirement to mention FOIA 2000. The request must include a clear description of the information requested. If the information sought is not obvious, the public authority can require the applicant to provide further information to clarify the request. The reason for the request is irrelevant. Public authorities are not permitted to ask the reason for the request.

Does the authority hold the information?

Public authorities only need to disclose information which they hold. Information is held by a public authority when:

(a) it is held by the authority otherwise than on behalf of another person; or
(b) it is held by another person on behalf of the authority.

INFORMATION HELD BY THE AUTHORITY

Most information held by a public authority will be covered by FOIA 2000, unless the information is held by the public authority on behalf of another person, for example where a public authority holds an archive on behalf of another for safekeeping. Other information, such as personal e-mails of the authority's staff, may also not be held (what constitutes a personal e-mail is of some debate).

INFORMATION HELD BY A THIRD PARTY ON THE AUTHORITY'S BEHALF

FOIA 2000 gives a right of access to information held on the authority's behalf by third parties, for example, where the public authority stores its information with a commercial storage company.

This provision also has wider implications, since it provides a right of access to information held by service providers on behalf of the public authority. One factor determining whether information is held on behalf of the public authority is whether the public authority has a contractual right to have access to that information, whether or not that right has been exercised (see *Leeds City Council and Swift Research Limited*, 27/05/08, FS50161274).

Whilst FOIA 2000 does not entitle applicants to make direct requests to third-party information holders, where information is held by a third party, the public authority must ensure it can access such information. The authority should ensure the third party is aware of its obligations to share information with the public authority, to enable the authority to provide the information to the requester. This can usually be achieved by means of contractual arrangements, requiring the third party to provide information within certain timescales pursuant to an information request. In the absence of any power to require the third party to provide the information it holds, the public authority may find itself in breach of FOIA 2000.

Where information held relates to an individual or another organisation, there is no statutory obligation to consult that third party before the information is provided to the requester. However, the Section 45 Code of Practice makes clear that the third party should be consulted prior to disclosure where (as a minimum):

(a) the views of the third party may assist the public authority to determine whether or not the information requested is exempt from disclosure;
(b) the views of the third party may assist the authority to determine where the balance of the public interest test applies.

Practice recommendations from the Information Commissioner have indicated that in some instances consultation with third parties is required (Department of Health Practice Recommendation 31 March 2008).

Form of the reply and time limits

If the information is not exempt and there is no procedural reason why the information cannot be provided, the public authority must inform the applicant that it holds the information and provide the information (FOIA 2000, s.1(1)).

The information must be provided promptly and in any event no later than 20 working days from the day following receipt of the information request (FOIA 2000, s.10). The applicant is entitled to either:

(a) a copy of the information;
(b) a reasonable opportunity to inspect a record containing the information; or
(c) a summary of the information (s.11(1)).

The right of access is to information only and not to the specific documents in which they are contained.

The 20 working day period can only be extended in very limited circumstances, for example, to consider the public interest test (and see Freedom of Information (Time for Compliance with Request) Regulations 2004, SI 2004/3364 in relation to information held by maintained schools, in archives, by members of the armed forces or outside the UK). In addition, the 20 day period stops if the public authority makes a request for fees, restarting once the fees are paid.

If the information request is refused, the public authority must provide the applicant with a refusal notice within the 20 working day period. The notice must state:

(a) that the request has been refused;
(b) when the request is refused in reliance on an exemption or limitation, the exemption or limitation relied on and the reasons why the authority believes the exemption or limitation applies;
(c) where the exemption is a qualified exemption, details of how the public interest test favours non-disclosure. If the qualified exemption is also a prejudice-based exemption the refusal notice should also show how disclosure would or would be likely to prejudice the public authority;
(d) details of the public authority's complaints procedure; and
(e) details of the applicant's right to appeal to the Information Commissioner about the decision.

3.6.2 Information requests under the Environmental Information Regulations

EIR 2004, reg. 5 specifies that (subject to certain conditions) a public authority that holds environmental information shall make the information available on request. The word *available* is emphasised here because of the interpretation placed upon it by the Information Tribunal in the *Rhondda Cynon Taff* Decision (05/12/07, EA/2006/0065).

Making information available

In the *Rhondda Cynon Taff* decision the Tribunal adopted a particularly literal approach to the interpretation of the EIR 2004, contrasting and distinguishing the wording of EIR 2004, reg. 5(1) with FOIA 2000, s.1(1). Under the EIR 2004 a public authority is only required to make the information available on request. In contrast, FOIA 2000, s.1(1) provides that an applicant is entitled to have that information communicated to him. According to the Tribunal this distinction is important. Whereas under FOIA 2000 an applicant has a right to receive the information, under the EIR 2004 the obligation is to provide access to the information and this 'may not mean physically providing an applicant with a copy of the information, i.e. there is no obligation to communicate it to the applicant'.

It is arguable that the Tribunal, in this instance, failed to adopt the wider purposive approach to interpretation generally regarded as essential when approaching the interpretation of national legislation that gives effect to Community law. An applicant has the right to ask that information is supplied in a particular form or format. Where this happens, the public authority is required (by reg. 6) to comply with the applicant's request, unless it is either reasonable for the authority to make the information available in another form or format (bearing in mind that some requesters may not be able to open electronic documents in certain formats) or the information is already publicly available and easily accessible in another form or format. If information is not provided in the requested format, the public authority must provide the applicant with an explanation why not (in writing if the applicant requests) as soon as possible or within 20 working days of the request.

Public authorities can make reasonable charges for making information available but if the applicant is invited and willing to examine the information at the offices of the public authority then no charge may be made. Authorities cannot charge for the time take to retrieve the information; they can only charge for actual, reasonable costs incurred (i.e. paper, printing, photocopying and postage costs). Since under the EIR 2004 there is no upper cost limit beyond which a public authority can refuse to disclose the information (as with FOIA 2000), if an applicant is willing to meet the reasonable costs of providing the information, they cannot be refused, unless the exception of a manifestly unreasonable request is engaged (reg. 12(4)(b)).

What is a valid information request under the EIR 2004?

Uniquely, the EIR 2004 includes a requirement to respond to oral as well as written requests for information. In addition, there is no requirement in the EIR 2004 for an applicant to provide her name or address, although in practice the supply of a name and address may be necessary in order for the authority to provide the information. Where the information requested is personal data, clearly the applicant must provide her name and address. Staff must therefore be properly trained and systems put in place to deal with situations where anonymity will pose problems, and to allow requests to be recorded and tracked.

Where the public authority takes the view that the request has been formulated in too general a manner, it must ask the applicant (as soon as possible and within 20 working days) to provide more particulars in relation to the request. It should assist the applicant in providing these particulars (applicants and prospective applicants have the right to receive reasonable advice and assistance in the formulation of requests (reg. 9)). Regulation 9 can be particularly important for individuals and ad hoc pressure groups trying to find out about environmental issues where they lack the specific knowledge or expertise to identify exactly what information they require.

Does the authority hold the information?

The EIR 2004 only confers a right of access to environmental information held by a public authority. Environmental information is held by a public authority (reg. 3(2)) if the information:

(a) is in the authority's possession and has been produced or received by the authority; or
(b) is held by another person on behalf of the authority.

The definition of the holding requirement differs to that in FOIA 2000 since it includes information in the authority's possession (or held by another person on behalf of the authority) which has been received from a third party. This means that where a public authority receives information from a third party (such as a company or individual) and then stores it within the authority's building or elsewhere on its behalf, the information is held for the purposes of the request. Third parties may supply information to a public authority which then becomes potentially discloseable under the EIR 2004, unless such information can be withheld on one of the exceptions listed in regulation 12. (Note, documents or information belonging to staff, which is unrelated to the workings of the authority (for example, correspondence brought into work by a member of staff) are not considered to be in the authority's possession). Where information is received from another person or body, it will be appropriate to consult on whether the environmental information requested should be supplied, unless the outcome can be predicted with reasonable confidence.

Practical example

A local authority recently began a campaign promoting use of solar water heaters, as a means of limiting the negative impacts of fossil fuels on the environment. Subsequently, the chief executive of a company which installs solar water heaters visited the authority's offices. The company does not provide services to or for the authority and operates as an entirely private enterprise. The company left various documents providing general company information with the local authority, to be held on its behalf. The company did not intend such information to be made publicly available. Nonetheless such information is held by the local authority, and subject to any exceptions, is liable to be made available on request.

Form of the reply and time limits under EIR 2004

Unless the public authority intends to withhold the information requested, relying on an exception in regulation 12, it must make the information available as soon as possible and in any event within 20 working days after the date of the receipt of the request (reg. 5). The time period may be extended to 40 working days if the authority reasonably believes the complexity and volume of the information requested makes it impracticable either to comply with the request within 20 working days or to make a decision to refuse to do so.

Information made available to a requestor should be 'up to date, accurate and comparable, so far as the public authority reasonably believes'. (reg. 5(4)). Since information can include opinions, where this is the case the applicant should be made aware of this. Where information comes from third parties, its reliability should be assessed. Public authorities should consider whether to issue a disclaimer addressing issues to be taken into account by the public, for example in relation to the reliability, source and accuracy of the information.

Where a request for environmental information is refused by a public authority because the information falls within one of the exceptions, the public authority must issue a written Refusal Notice under regulation 14. The Refusal Notice must specify the public interest factors (both for and against disclosure) taken into account in reaching the decision, to enable an applicant to challenge the decision at a later stage if he wishes. The Refusal Notice must provide the applicant with clear details about the procedures for reconsideration and appeal.

3.7 WHAT INFORMATION CAN BE WITHHELD?

Under FOIA 2000 and the EIR 2004 information can be withheld for procedural reasons, or because an exemption (FOIA 2000) or an exception (EIR 2004) operates to remove the obligation to provide information. Since these exemptions/exceptions clearly can impede the process of sharing public authority information, they are outlined below. Exceptions and exemptions particularly relevant when sharing personal and commercial information are considered further in **3.8** (and in **Chapter 5** in relation to confidentiality, and in **Chapter 11** regarding disclosure in the commercial context).

3.7.1 Reasons to deny an information request under FOIA 2000

Procedural reasons not to disclose information

There are five procedural reasons why information need not be provided in response to an information request.

COST

Where the cost of answering an information request would exceed the appropriate limit (£600 for central government and £450 for other public authorities) the public authority can, but is not obliged to, refuse the request (FOIA 2000, s.12 and Freedom of Information and Data Protection (Appropriate Limit and Fees) Regulations 2004 SI 2004/3244). The fees are calculated on the basis of the number of hours (at a rate of £25/hour) it would take to answer the request. If the cost is less than £600/450 (as relevant) the public authority can only charge for disbursements and even then the ICO recommends these charges are waived if the disbursements are less than £10 in total.

Factors that can be taken into account in working out if the appropriate limit has been reached include:

(a) determining whether the public authority holds the information;
(b) locating the information or documents containing the information;
(c) retrieving such information or documents; and
(d) extracting the information from the document containing it (including editing but not redaction of the document; see *John Jenkins* v. *ICO and Defra* EA/2006/0067, 02/11/07).

The public authority cannot charge for: time spent checking the request meets FOIA 2000's requirements; considering whether the information is subject to an exemption (including any costs in legal advice on the application of the exemptions); considering whether an information request is vexatious or repeated; obtaining authorisation to send the information; the time taken to calculate fees; and providing advice and assistance to the applicant in accordance with the duty under section 16.

NON-PAYMENT OF FEES

If a decision to charge is made the public authority must allow the individual a period of three months in which to pay the charge. If no payment is made within that period the authority need not answer the information request (s.9(2)).

THE APPLICANT HAS NOT PROVIDED FURTHER INFORMATION REQUESTED

Any request for information must clearly identify the information being sought (FOIA 2000, s.1(3)). Where the public authority informs the applicant that the information request does not identify the information requested clearly and reasonably requests further information to assist it, the authority is not obliged to provide the information requested until that further information is provided.

VEXATIOUS REQUESTS

A public authority is not required to answer a vexatious information request (FOIA 2000, s.14(1)). Whether or not the request is vexatious depends on the request, not the applicant. Thus each application must be considered on its own merits without consideration of the past behaviour of the applicant. A request will be vexatious if it is aimed at disrupting the work of the public authority, harasses individuals within the authority, has no serious purpose or value or is obsessive or manifestly unreasonable.

REPEAT REQUESTS

A request which is identical or substantially similar to a previous request from the same applicant may be refused if a reasonable time has not elapsed since the original request was answered (FOIA 2000, s.14(2)). Although 'reasonable time' is not defined, it is suggested 'reasonableness' will depend on the nature of the information requested.

THE FOIA 2000 EXEMPTIONS

FOIA 2000 additionally details 23 exemptions to the right of access to public authority information. Exemptions are classified into two types: absolute exemptions and qualified exemptions – see **Table 3.1**.

If information sits within a category of absolute exemption there is no need to prove its release would cause harm, nor does it matter that its release would be in the public interest. If the information fits within the absolute exemption the public authority is under no obligation to disclose it.

The qualified exemptions are subject to a public interest test. In order for the requested information to fit within a qualified exemption the public authority must not only show that the information fits within that category but must weigh up the factors in the public interest for disclosure and those against. If those factors which favour disclosure outweigh those against then the information should be released. The public interest is not defined within FOIA 2000 but general factors favouring disclosure include:

(a) furthering the understanding of a public debate;
(b) promoting accountability and transparency of decision taking and the spending of public money; and
(c) allowing an understanding of decisions made by public authorities which affect the lives of individuals.

Table 3.1 Summary of FOIA exemptions

ABSOLUTE EXEMPTIONS (see s.2(3) FOIA)	QUALIFIED EXEMPTIONS	
	Class-Based Exemptions (Apply the Public Interest Test)	**Prejudice-Based Exemptions (Apply the Prejudice Test then the Public Interest Test)**
Information accessible by other means (s.21)	Information intended for future publication (s.22)	National security (s.24)
Information supplied by, or related to, bodies dealing with security matters (s.23)	International relations where it relates to information obtained from another state (s.27(2))	Defence (s.26)
Court records (s.32)	Investigations and proceedings conducted by public authorities (s.30)	International relations (s.27(1))
Parliamentary privilege (s.34)	Formulation of government policy (s.35)	Relations within the UK (s.28)
Prejudice to effective conduct of public affairs so far as it relates to information held by the House of Commons or the House of Lords (s.36)	Communications with Her Majesty (s.37)	The economy (s.29)
Personal information where the applicant is the data subject and in certain circumstances where it is a third party (s.40)	Environmental information (s.39)	Law enforcement (s.31)
Information provided in confidence (s.41)	Personal information (s.40 – only part of this exemption is qualified)	Audit functions (s.33)
Prohibitions on disclosure (s.44)	Legal professional privilege (s.42)	The effective conduct of public affairs (s.36)
	Commercial interests (trade secrets) (s.43(1))	Health and safety (s.38)
		Commercial interests (s.43(2))

The qualified exemptions can also be subdivided further into those which are subject to a prejudice test (the prejudice-based exemptions) and those which are not (the class-based exemptions). Where information is subject to the prejudice test the public authority must first show that the disclosure of the information would, or would be likely to cause harm, and once that is shown, go on to consider whether or not it is in the public interest to disclose.

3.7.2 Reasons to deny a request for environmental information under the EIR 2004

The exceptions to the duty to disclose environmental information, contained in EIR 2004, Part 3 (regs. 12–15), are in some respects similar to the FOIA 2000 exemptions, but there are key differences (see **Table 3.2**).

The exceptions may be categorised into three groups: refusals based upon procedural grounds; refusals because the information falls into one of three class-based exceptions; refusals where disclosure of the information would (not simply might or could) adversely affect one of the matters specified in regulation 12(5). In relation to this last group, refusal to disclose is only permitted to the extent of the adverse effect. The threshold for engaging these exceptions is higher than the prejudice-based exemptions under FOIA 2000 where it is sufficient to prove that disclosure 'would or would be likely' to prejudice the protected interest.

Unlike FOIA 2000 all of the grounds for exception within the EIR 2004 (with the singular exception of requests which involve personal data) are subject to the application of a public interest test. The fact that an exception removes the obligation to provide information does not mean the public authority cannot disclose if it wishes. The only exception to this arises where the information includes personal data of which the applicant is not the data subject.

In contrast to FOIA 2000, the EIR 2004 contain an expressly worded presumption in favour of disclosure (reg. 12(2)). Additionally, the Directive upon which the EIR 2004 is based explicitly states that the grounds for refusal shall be interpreted restrictively. In every case, the public interest served by disclosure must be weighed against the interest served by the refusal. A public authority may only refuse to disclose environmental information requested if an exception to disclosure applies under paragraphs (4) or (5); and in all the circumstances of the case, the public interest in maintaining the exception outweighs the public interest in disclosing the information.

3.8 THE REGIMES AND THEIR IMPLICATIONS FOR INFORMATION SHARING

The information sharing debate has, to a large extent, been driven by concerns about the potential invasion of personal privacy caused by public

Table 3.2 EIR exceptions

Refusals based upon procedural grounds (reg. 12(4)(a)–(c))	Refusals because the information falls into one of three class-based exceptions	Refusals where disclosure would adversely affect one of the following (reg. 12(5))
The authority does not hold the information when the request is received. (Where a public authority does not hold the requested information but believes another public authority does it may supply the applicant with the authority's name and address or transfer the request to the other public authority (ideally first seeking the applicant's permission)).	Information that includes the personal data of someone other than the applicant (reg. 12(3)). Regulation 13 permits disclosure of third-party personal data only if it would not result in a breach of the DPA principles or other conditions.	International relations, defence, national security or public safety. The course of justice, ability of a person to receive a fair trial or ability of a public authority to conduct a criminal or disciplinary inquiry. Intellectual property rights. The confidentiality or proceedings of any public authority where such confidentiality is protected by law.
The request for information is manifestly unreasonable, i.e. it would place a substantial and unreasonable burden on the public authority's resources, diverting resources from provision of essential public services. (For example, where the request involves extensive scans of historic files).	The request relates to material still in the course of completion, to unfinished documents or incomplete data (reg. 12(4)(d)). Disclosure cannot be refused simply because a document is 'draft'. Regulation 12(4)(d) should be considered alongside regulation 14(4)) which requires the authority to tell the applicant (if it knows) of any other public authority preparing the information and when it is likely to be completed or finished.	The confidentiality of commercial or industrial information where such confidentiality is provided by law to protect a legitimate economic interest. The interests of the person providing the information where that person: • was not under (and could not have been put under) a legal obligation to supply it to that or another public authority; • did not supply it in circumstances such that that or another public authority was entitled apart from under the EIR to disclose it; and • has not consented to its disclosure.
The request for information is formulated in too general a manner even after the public authority has provided advice and assistance to the applicant to enable it to clarify the information required (as required by reg. 9).	The request involves disclosure of internal communications (reg. 12(4)(e)). Drafted in broad terms the rationale behind this exception is that it is often in the public interest to allow public authorities to have space to think in private, for example when formulating new policies. It includes communications between government departments.	The protection of the environment to which the information relates.

authorities disclosing personal information shared with them. In this section we consider the interactions between FOIA 2000, EIR 2004 and the DPA 1998 in the context of access to personal data held by public authorities. We also consider how individuals and organisations may use FOIA 2000 and the EIR 2004 to obtain information provided by other organisations.

3.8.1 Access to personal data under FOIA 2000 and EIR 2004

Access to personal data is dealt with in FOIA 2000, s.40 and EIR 2004, regs. 5(3) and 12(2). The definition of personal data under DPA 1998, s.1(1) is key to these exemptions/exceptions (see **2.3** and **2.4**). If information is not personal data these exemptions/exceptions do not apply.

A practical example: requests for personal data under FOIA 2000

In *Harcup* v. *Information Commissioner and Yorkshire Forward*, 05/02/08, EA/2007/0058 a request was made for the details of individuals who had attended corporate hospitality events. The Information Tribunal considered the names of individuals were not personal data as the information was not, using the test set out in *Durant*, significant in a biographical sense. It also considered that, as the data related to a corporate hospitality event, the personal data was not the focus of the information. Significant here was the fact that the information about individuals attending the events could not be matched up to the businesses they represented as that would constitute personal data.

Requests for an individual's own personal data

Under FOIA 2000 and the EIR 2004 if the requester seeks his own personal data, the information is exempt. FOIA 2000, s.40(1) and EIR 2004, reg. 5(3) are both absolute exemption/exceptions which recognise that individuals have a right to obtain their personal data by way of a data subject access request under the DPA 1998 and that there is no need for a duplicate right to be set out in either FOIA 2000 or the EIR 2004.

Sharing third-party personal data

If the person making the request is asking for personal data about another person, that information will be exempt under FOIA 2000, s.40(2) (and under the almost identical EIR 2004, reg. 13) if:

(a) it would be a breach of any of the eight data protection principles to release the information (an absolute exemption);
(b) its disclosure would breach DPA 1998, s.10. An individual can serve notice under DPA 1998, s.10, requiring the data processor to cease or to not begin processing that person's personal data on the grounds that the processing would cause unwarranted damage or distress to him or another.

Those personal data subject to the notice will be exempt from disclosure unless it is in the public interest to disclose the information. It will require a particularly strong public interest to outweigh this exemption; or

(c) due to the operation of one of the DPA 1998 exemptions, the data subject has no right of access to that information under DPA 1998, s.7(1)(c). If a request for information relates to information which the third-party data subject could not get access to under DPA 1998, s.7 because one of the DPA 1998 exemptions applies (for example, because disclosure would be likely to cause serious harm to the physical or mental health of the data subject or any other person), then the requester will have no right of access to that information either. This part of the exemption/exception is also subject to a public interest test.

Determining whether disclosures of third-party personal data will breach the data protection principles

The vast majority of cases relating to disclosure of third-party data have involved an examination of whether or not disclosure will breach one of the eight data protection principles. In (*House of Commons* (22/02/06, FS5007119) the applicant requested 'A detailed breakdown of expenses by individual MPs of: car travel, rail travel, and air travel, for the past three years.' The House of Commons sought to rely on section 40(2), in particular arguing releasing the information would breach the first data protection principle, i.e. the duty to process data fairly and lawfully and in accordance with the conditions of Schedule 2 (and Sched. 3 where appropriate). The House contended that since it had advised MPs of the information which would be included in the publication scheme, releasing further information would be unfair. The Information Commissioner did not consider the disclosure unfair. It related to information about the MPs' official capacity and would not impinge upon their personal privacy.

This decision suggests that information which is personal data but which is about someone acting in their official or work capacity should be shared, unless there is a danger of harm occurring to the individual concerned. Although this part of section 40(2) is not itself subject to the public interest test, there is a strong public interest in how a public authority spends public money. Therefore information about salaries, particularly of senior staff, is likely to be discloseable, as is information about what expenses were incurred in the course of official business.

In the *Department for Business, Enterprise and Regulatory Reform* v. *Information Commissioner and Friends of the Earth* (29/04/08, EA/2007/0072) a number of decisions on the release of information relating to attendees at meetings were considered. The Tribunal confirmed that senior personnel and spokespersons (whatever their level) of public authorities or lobbyists could expect to have details of their attendance at events disclosed in response to an information request and to have their comments attributed to them. Junior staff on the other hand, whose role was not that of spokesperson, could expect their privacy to be maintained.

In *Calderdale Council* (24/11/05, FS50068973) the information request related to information about the names of council officers sent to Australia and New Zealand to recruit social workers and other information about the trip. Although the names of the council officers were personal data, the ICO considered disclosure of such names would not breach any data protection principle. Considering the first data protection principle, particularly the requirement to process (share) information fairly, the ICO considered that consent to disclosure was not required, but that the individual's legitimate, reasonable expectations about whether information would be shared were relevant. However, concluding that the request for information was a request for professional personal information, considering the nature of their public role, the cost of the trip and the level of responsibility they had, it was felt that the information should be released. (Note, that whilst the officers were acting in a public capacity they were not senior officials.)

Section 40 and regulation 13 essentially seek to ensure that the protection afforded to personal data by the DPA 1998 is maintained by FOIA 2000/EIR 2004. Whilst there are clearly tensions between the aims of the DPA 1998 and the FOIA 2000/EIR 2004; the former being fundamentally concerned with confidentiality and the protection of information, the latter being about openness and transparency, the Information Commissioner suggests the different aims can be 'reconciled in the sense that one area of regulation safeguards personal information and the other seeks greater transparency for official information. Section 40 FOIA 2000 dovetails and reconciles the two approaches.' (*Freedom of Information and Privacy – the Regulatory Role of the Information Commissioner*, January 9 2008.) However, the case law suggests that the Information Tribunal is keen to ensure that the rights set out in FOIA 2000 are afforded the greatest possible strength.

3.8.2 Information shared by other organisations

The rights of access conferred by the FOIA 2000 and EIR 2004 have undoubtedly resulted in public authorities disclosing information relating to private organisations, particularly relating to contracts with the private sector. The exemptions/exceptions within FOIA 2000 and the EIR 2004 again aim to balance the need to disclose information in the public interest, and the need to protect certain private interests (for the public good). FOIA 2000, ss.41 and 43 and regs. 12(5)(e) and (f) are the exemptions and exceptions of most direct application.

Section 41

Under section 41 information is exempt information if it was obtained by the public authority from any other person and the disclosure of that information would constitute an actionable breach of confidence.

In *Derry City Council* v. *Information Commissioner* (11/12/06, EA/2006/14) an applicant requested details of Derry City Council's agreement with Ryanair regarding the use of Derry City Airport. The council claimed that the contract was confidential and contained commercially sensitive information. The Tribunal considered that since the exemption requires disclosure to be an actionable breach of confidence, to be covered by this exemption the information must be truly confidential in nature (see **Chapter 5**). Disclosure must breach any obligation of confidence (disclosure in the public interest would not breach the duty). This case also confirms that the exemption does not apply to the public authority's own confidential information. This arguably discounts any information set out in a contract from being covered by the exemption as that contractual document will represent the public authority's own information. However, it could include information disclosed in a tender process or information supplied pursuant to a contract.

Is information confidential?

The ICO has accepted there is an inherent duty of confidentiality when tenders are submitted to councils in procurement exercises, the circumstances in which tenders are communicated usually creating an obligation of confidence (*East Riding of Yorkshire Council* (12/02/08, FER0066052)). However the information must also have the necessary quality of confidence and in assessing this consideration should be given to whether the information is trivial and also whether it is available from other sources. Although in the *Derry* case the Tribunal disagreed that confidentiality would wane over time as a matter of course, the duty may come to an end if the information has either passed into the public domain or has ceased to have commercial significance.

The inclusion of a confidentiality clause or a general implication of a duty of confidence does not mean that all of the information caught by such a clause should be or will be considered confidential. In a series of decisions concerning requests for information about contracts with independent waste contractors the ICO has examined each section of a contract in detail to determine which provisions should be disclosed or redacted. (See for example *East Riding of Yorkshire Council* (12/02/081, FER0066052)).

Is the information confidential if it forms part of a publicly available body of information but is in an encrypted form? The Tribunal addressed this point in the *Ofcom* case (04/09/07, EA/2007/0078, para. 65). Referring to the decision of Jacob J in *Mars* v. *Teknowledge* [2000] FSR 138 which suggested that information put into the public domain in encrypted form may have lost the quality of confidence if it was accessible by anyone with the necessary skill to de-crypt, the Tribunal ruled that the information requested had lost its necessary quality of confidence because it was possible to access the detailed data even though it would take an enormous amount of time and skill to do so. 'We do not believe that, because this information would be significantly easier to access if the requested information were to be disclosed, the less easily accessed form of it retains confidentiality.'

Section 43

Section 43 is in two sections. Section 43(1) states that information is exempt information if it constitutes a trade secret. Trade secrets are not defined by FOIA 2000 but will be:

(a) information used in a trade or business;
(b) information which, if disclosed to a competitor, would be liable to cause real or significant harm to the owner of the secret;

(c) information which the owner must limit the dissemination of or, at the very least, not encourage or permit its widespread publication.

Trade secrets can extend to names of customers or anything which gives a company its competitive edge.

Under section 43(2) information is exempt if its disclosure would, or would be likely to, prejudice someone's commercial interests (including the authority's own). Commercial in the context of this exemption means relating to an activity in the way of a business, trade or profession. The public interest factors for the section 43(1) exemption are broadly the same as those for the section 43(2) exemption.

Section 43(2) in practice

John Connor Press Associates (JCPA) requested the National Maritime Museum (NMM) to provide all documentation and correspondence relating to payments made to the artist Conrad Shawcross for the Continuum exhibition. The NMM provided a copy of the contract between NMM and Conrad Shawcross and various other documents. All financial information was redacted on the basis that (relying on s.43(2)) disclosure would be likely to prejudice the commercial interests of the NMM and Conrad Shawcross. Even with the financial information redacted, the documents disclosed substantial amounts of information about the transaction of relevance to another artist considering entering into a contract with the NMM.

The Information Tribunal decided that whilst the commercial interests of the public authority might be prejudiced if certain information in relation to a transaction were to become available to another party involved in subsequent negotiations, this situation did not apply here. The interpretation of the term 'likely to prejudice' was key. The Tribunal held that there must be a real and significant risk of prejudice occurring, not just a hypothetical or remote risk. It decided that such a risk did not exist in this instance because:

- the information already disclosed by the NMM would provide valuable information to an artist in negotiation with the NMM;
- the fact that the contract disclosed showed that the NMM would contribute to the artist's material costs rather than just a flat fee, materially reduced the value of the financial information;
- the works created by the other artists were so different that they could not be treated as true comparables.

This case illustrates that in considering whether section 43 applies, the particular facts of the case are of great significance. It also shows that public authorities must take great care when disclosing information to ensure that the information disclosed will not cause them difficulties when trying to rely on a particular exemption. In this instance, if some of the details of the contract which had a significant commercial value, such as the assumption of risk by the NMM, the issue of the contribution to materials and the ownership of copyright, had been redacted from the contract, the outcome may have been different.

John Connor Press Associates v. *The Information Commissioner* 25/01/06, EA/2005/0005

Regulation 12(5)(e)

Regulation 12(5)(e) permits information to be withheld where disclosure would adversely affect the confidentiality of commercial or industrial information and where such confidentiality is provided by law to protect a legitimate economic interest. The tests to be applied by a public authority are:

1. Is the information commercial or industrial in nature?
2. Is the information subject to a duty of confidence which is provided by law (see **Chapter 5** and discussion above regarding s.41)?
3. Is confidentiality required to protect a legitimate economic interest?
4. Would the confidentiality required to protect a legitimate economic interest be adversely affected by disclosure?

This exception is somewhat wider than FOIA 2000, s.41 since it is not limited to information obtained by the public authority from any other person nor does it require disclosure to result in an actionable breach of confidence. In general, confidentiality only applies to the legitimate economic interests of the confider, (i.e. a company that enters into a contract with a public authority), as that is the organisation to whom the duty of confidence is owed. However, this exception could also be used to protect the public authority in circumstances where it has been agreed that the confidential information agreed in the contract would be confidential to both parties. (For example, where each party agreed to hold the information in confidence and could not therefore disclose it as each would owe the other a duty of confidence to protect their respective economic interests.)

The Defra guidance suggests that when a supplier of information believes that its release would adversely affect its economic interests he should seek to protect that information, by identifying what information needs to be protected and by providing the public authority with evidence and justification for the need for protection. Generally the protection of information under this exception should be limited to the minimum time necessary to safeguard the commercial or industrial interest. Even if this exception is engaged, the public authority is obliged to weigh up the respective public interest in maintaining the exception against the public interest in disclosing the information.

Regulation 12(5)(f)

Information may be supplied to a public authority on an entirely voluntary basis, i.e. not as a result of tendering for a contract or under any statutory provision. In the context of environmental information such information could include information provided by a person about a pollution incident or as part of a voluntary consultation exercise, such as completing a questionnaire on a proposed development or submitting a written representation about a proposed planning application.

Regulation 12(5)(f) allows information to be withheld if disclosure would adversely affect the interests of the person who provided the information where that person:

(i) was not under, and could not have been put under, any legal obligation to supply it to that or any other public authority;
(ii) did not supply it in circumstances such that that, or any other public authority is entitled apart from these Regulations to disclose it; and
(iii) has not consented to its disclosure.

The purpose of this exception is to protect the free flow of information from volunteered sources in order to protect the environment; it does not cover information supplied as part of the negotiations leading up to a contract (*R* v. *The Secretary of State for the Environment, Transport and the Regions and Midland Expressway Limited*, ex parte *Alliance Against the Birmingham Northern Relief Road and Others* Case No: CO/4553/98, High Court of Justice Queens Bench Division).

Note, if the information requested is information on emissions into the environment then, in accordance with regulation 12(9) the above two exceptions are not available and the information should be released unless some exception other than those in regulation 12(5)(d)–(g) are engaged.

3.9 CONCLUSION

As statutory access regimes, FOIA 2000 and the EIR 2004 have led to the widespread dissemination (both proactive and reactive) of information held by public authorities. The EIR 2004 and FOIA 2000 have raised individuals' expectations of what information should be shared by public authorities and have vastly enriched the information sharing debate by showing that the release of information in to the public domain benefits society.

However, one of the consequences of FOIA 2000 and the EIR 2004 is that information is being disclosed by public authorities which individuals, organisations and businesses did not realise would be disclosed. Those who provide information to public authorities and particularly those who derive income from their relationship with public authorities must understand that the money they earn comes at a cost; that of transparency of their dealings with such authorities. When information is obtained from individuals they should also be clearly informed of all circumstances in which their personal information may be shared, including under FOIA 2000 and the EIR 2004 (as required, in any event, by the DPA 1998 first principle). A clear understanding of the effect of FOIA 2000 and the EIR 2004 is particularly important in the light of the case law emanating from the Tribunal and the ICO which indicates their desire to see that the rights afforded by FOIA 2000 and the EIR 2004 are given effect.

CHAPTER 4

Miscellany of legislative provisions

Claire Bessant

4.1 INTRODUCTION

When considering whether to share information, the focus for many practitioners is undoubtedly the DPA 1998, the duty of confidentiality, the Human Rights Act 1998 and, perhaps, FOIA 2000. In reality these legal provisions form a small part of the legal framework relevant to information sharing. The range of legislative provisions that restrict, require or enable information sharing is immense, reflecting the disparate types of information, the numerous purposes for which information is shared, and the different bodies and individuals that need to share or access information.

We identified in **Chapter 1** that all public authorities must act within their legal powers. Public authorities must understand which legal powers enable them to share information or prevent them from doing so. However, private bodies must equally be aware of the legislation relevant to their profession and services they provide. First, the DPA 1998 requires information sharing to be lawful (unless an exemption from the first principle applies). Private bodies cannot, therefore, share personal information where explicitly prohibited from doing so by statute (in many instances such actions would also result in criminal prosecution). Second, many statutes require private bodies (companies, credit reference agencies, etc.) and individuals to share information. Third, private bodies may benefit from many of the provisions which require information to be made publicly available, but need equally to be aware that information that they have provided to a public authority (for example for licensing purposes) may subsequently be made widely available, under FOIA 2000, the EIR 2004 or, for example, a public register.

It is not easy for practitioners to identify every relevant piece of legislation. Many statutes which restrict or authorise information sharing do not ostensibly have anything to do with information sharing (consider, for example, the Domestic Violence Crime and Victims Act 2004, which enables a victim to obtain information about an offender's licence conditions). Numerous pieces of legislation include, deep within them, requirements to make information, including personal and commercial information, freely, publicly available. Recognising the practical difficulties of identifying the relevant law, the following pages outline a wide range of statutes and statutory instruments, and attempt to highlight their relevance. Given the vast array of legislation that plays a role in determining whether information may be shared, we have not elaborated upon the full range of circumstances in which legislative provisions apply, or explored the difficult issues that may arise in practice. However, numerous provisions are explored further in the second part of this handbook (in the context of employment, health, children, crime and commercial matters). In such instances, this is highlighted.

4.2 IDENTIFYING THE RELEVANT LEGISLATIVE PROVISIONS

Given the sheer volume of legislation which may require, enable or restrict information sharing, and the fact that many of the relevant provisions are hidden away within the legislation, the following table lists the legislation by title, but the type of information affected is also indicated in the left hand column.

Information type	Statute	
Health	Abortion Regulations 1991 (made under Abortion Act 1967, s.2)	Regulation 4 requires extensive, sensitive health information to be disclosed to the Chief Medical Officer by secure means when a medical practitioner terminates a pregnancy. Regulation 5 prohibits further disclosure, save for statistical purposes, to investigate whether a criminal offence has been committed for the purpose of court proceedings, to the General Medical Council, to another medical practitioner (with patient consent) or to the patient themselves.
Health	Access to Health Records Act 1990	This Act enables a deceased patient's personal representative, and any person who may have a claim arising out of the patient's death and needs information from their records to fulfil that claim, to access the deceased's medical records (see Chapter 8).
Personal	Access to Justice Act 1999	Sections 20–21 prevent disclosure of information relating to an identifiable individual's public funding, by a court, the Legal Services Commission, or a legal representative, unless the individual consents or disclosure is needed for the functioning of the public funding system, for the purpose of investigating or prosecuting offending, or within certain court and disciplinary proceedings.

Information type	Statute	
		Schedule 3 additionally enables the Legal Services Commission to request information from the Secretary of State for Work and Pensions or HM Commissioners for Revenue and Customs to verify the accuracy of information provided by an applicant and to determine whether to grant or withdraw criminal funding.
Health	Access to Medical Reports Act 1988	Sections 1–5 detail the procedure by which an employer may seek a medical report regarding an employee or prospective employee, and provide for the individual to obtain copies of the report (unless the medical practitioner considers access to all or part of the report would be likely to cause serious harm to the individual's or another's physical or mental health, or where disclosure would be likely to reveal third-party information).
Adoption	Adoption and Children Act 2002 and related regulations	These provisions regulate disclosure of information relating to adoption proceedings and the adopted person (considered further in Chapter 10, Children).
Health	AIDS Control Act 1987	Section 1 obliges certain health bodies to provide statistical information to the Secretary of State for health (but not details) of individuals who have been diagnosed with AIDS or as HIV-antibody-positive.
Airports	Airports Act 1986	Section 74 prohibits disclosure about an airport operation's business, save where explicitly required by certain listed statutes or where the person operating the business consents. Section 73, conversely, provides the Civil Aviation Authority with extensive powers to require disclosure of information to enable it to perform its functions.
Confidential	Animals (Scientific Procedures) Act 1986	Section 24 prohibits anyone working for an organisation licensed to undertake specified scientific procedures on animals to disclose confidential information (or information they believe to be confidential) save for the purpose of their functions.
Military	Armed Forces Act 1976	Schedule 3 authorises a court to hear all or part of certain proceedings to be heard in private where information disclosed might be directly or indirectly useful to an enemy.
Military	Airforce Act 1955, Army Act 1995	Section 25 of these statutes (expected to be replaced by Armed Forces Act 2006, s.1) prohibit service personnel from sharing information with an enemy or failing to share information received from

		the enemy, whilst section 94 enables all or part of court-martial proceedings to be held in private to prevent disclosure of information which would or might be useful to an enemy.
Financial	Audit Commission Act 1998	The Audit Commission is provided with extensive rights to inspect and copy documents and to require information to be provided, in order to undertake its statutory duty to audit certain public authority's accounts (including among others, local authorities, certain health bodies, police and fire rescue authorities (s.6)). The public may inspect audited accounts and auditors' reports, although personal information must not be disclosed (ss.5 and 14). Bodies subject to audit, together with English best value authorities not otherwise subject to audit, may also be required to provide the Audit Commission with information to enable it to carry out data matching exercises, for the purpose of prevention and detection of fraud (Part II). Other bodies may voluntarily disclose information for data matching purposes (provided disclosure does not breach the DPA 1998 or Regulation of Investigatory Powers Act 2000, Part 1). Information obtained by the Commission for data matching purposes may only be disclosed for fraud prevention and detection purposes or to undertake statutory duties (with further restrictions imposed on patient data disclosures).
Financial	Bankers Books Evidence Act 1879	Section 7 enables any party to civil or criminal proceedings to apply for an order permitting inspection and copying of entries in a banker's book.
Health	Blood Safety and Quality Regulations 2005 SI 2005/50	Regulation 14 prohibits disclosure of information about blood stored by a hospital or blood establishment unless the information has been anonymised; or is being disclosed to comply with a court order or other legal obligation, to trace a donation; or for purposes of inspection by the Secretary of State for Health.
Personal	Care Standards Act 2000	Certain organisations that provide care for vulnerable adults must refer people to the Independent Safeguarding Authority (ISA), who are unsuitable to work with vulnerable adults by virtue of misconduct which has harmed or placed a vulnerable adult at risk of harm (ss.81, 82). The ISA maintains the Protection of Vulnerable Adults (POVA) list. An employer who provides care to vulnerable adults must confirm that an individual is not on the list before employing them (s.9). The POVA list will be replaced by the new Safeguarding Vulnerable Groups Act 2006 (the SVGA 2006) vetting scheme from October 2009.

Information type	Statute	
Personal	Census Act 1920	Section 8 prohibits disclosure of personal census information.
Personal	Child Support Information Regulations 2008 SI 2008/2551	Part 2 imposes duties upon various individuals (including parents, the non-resident parent's employer, and others with relevant information such as local authorities, credit reference agencies, utilities, bank, vehicle licensing and courts) to provide information in order to trace non-resident parents, and to calculate and recover child support. Information received by the Child Maintenance and Enforcement Commission may be disclosed to a court or tribunal for the purpose of certain child support and benefit proceedings, or to either parent to justify its decisions (Part 3).
Personal	Children Act 1989	Sections 27 and 47, in particular, provide implied power for information to be shared by health, social care, housing and education, to assess and provide services to children and to investigate allegations of abuse and neglect (see Chapter 10).
Personal	Children Act 2004	Sections 10, 11 and 12 imply powers to share information to improve or promote and safeguard children's welfare (see Chapter 10).
Personal	Children Act 2004 Information Database (England) Regulations 2007 SI 2007/2182	These regulations make detailed provisions for the operation of the information sharing database, ContactPoint (see Chapter 10).
Personal	Children and Young Persons Act 2008	Section 7 requires the Secretary of State for Children, Families and Schools to promote the wellbeing of children and to take appropriate action in relation to looked after children, and certain others aged under 25. As yet to be implemented: Sections 1–6 empower local authorities to arrange for social work providers to act on the local authority's behalf in exercising duties towards looked after children (implying power to share information for such purposes). Section 31 requires a Registrar of births and deaths to notify the relevant Local Safeguarding Children Board within 7 days of the particulars of any minor's death, and authorises information being shared with the Secretary of State about deceased children (with further sharing permitted for research purposes).

Aviation	Civil Aviation Act 1982	This Act regulates disclosure of information by and with the Civil Aviation Authority.
Emergency planning	Civil Contingencies Act 2004 and Civil Contingencies Act 2004 (Contingency Planning) Regulations 2005 SI 2005/2042	Local authorities, the emergency services, various health agencies, the Environment Agency, Natural England, the Home Secretary, electricity and gas providers, water and sewage undertakers, telecommunications companies, rail, harbour and airport authorities and the Health and Safety Executive are obliged to share certain information with each other for the purposes of dealing with emergencies likely to cause injury or damage to life, limb, the environment or national security (s.6 and the Regulations).
Court proceedings	Civil Evidence Act 1995	This Act governs the admissibility of certain types of evidence in court proceedings (particularly relevant is the admissibility of hearsay evidence – this enables facts which have been shared by an individual with the evidence giver to be admitted as evidence even when the original discloser does not give evidence).
Court proceedings	Civil Procedure Rules 1998 SI 1998/3132	These rules govern disclosure of information in certain civil proceedings (see further Chapter 7).
Environmental	Clean Air Act 1993	Under sections 34–36 a local authority can require an occupier to disclose information about air pollutant emissions, and may publish such information, provided that it does not disclose trade secrets without consent.
Environmental	Coal Industry Act 1994	Sections 35 and 56 require the coal authority to maintain public registers containing certain information relating to coal mining operations (exclusions from disclosure apply to confidential information about an individual or organisation, who has not consented to disclosure, where disclosure might seriously prejudice its interests and where the information is not relevant to public safety).
Environmental	Coal Mining Subsidence Act 1991	Section 47 requires local authorities to maintain public registers containing information about underground coal-mining operations which may result in subsidence in their area.
Personal	Commissioners for Revenue and Customs Act 2005	Section 17 permits HM Revenue and Customs (HMRC) to use information acquired for one function to exercise other functions (save where this is prohibited by statute or international obligation). Further disclosure of information acquired by HMRC (even for verification purposes) may only be made: for Revenue and Customs functions; for certain crime prevention and investigation purposes

Information type	Statute	
		(where disclosure is to a public authority, the police, National Criminal Intelligence Service, National Policing Improvement Agency); to enable a professional regulatory body to investigate misconduct; to a public authority for the purposes of public safety and public health functions; to the Director of Revenue and Customs Prosecutions for purposes of criminal proceedings or the recovery of proceeds of crime; for certain other civil and criminal proceedings; in accordance with a court order, for the purpose of certain investigations and complaints, or with the consent of each person to whom the information relates (s.18).
Land	Commons Registration Act 1965 (repealed in relation to certain pilot areas under the Commons Act 2006, which Act applies to the pilot areas)	Sections 1 and 3 of the 2006 Act require public registers of common land and town and village greens to be maintained.
Commercial	Companies Act 1985	This Act provides extensive powers for the purposes of investigating companies' affairs. Inspectors appointed by the Secretary of State for Business, Enterprise and Regulatory Reform (BERR) may require production of company documents (provided they are not protected by legal professional privilege), require attendance before them, and require such other assistance as is necessary (Part XIV). The Secretary of State may also direct production of information or documents (s.447). Such information may only be disclosed to the Treasury, Director of Public Prosecutions, Financial Services Authority, a constable, or certain specified investigators for further specified investigations (ss.449, 451A). Where voluntary disclosure is made to assist the Secretary of State, in good faith, and no more information than necessary is disclosed, that disclosure does not constitute a breach of confidence, unless the disclosure is prohibited by statute, or has been made by a banker or lawyer who owed a professional duty of confidence (s.448A).

Commercial	Companies Act 1989	Sections 82–83 enable information to be shared with an overseas regulatory authority undertaking certain investigations, and for such purposes the Secretary of State for BERR, may require documents and information to be produced (provided they are not protected by legal professional privilege). Information about a business, received from the overseas authority or through its investigations, which is not already in the public domain, may only be disclosed by the Secretary of State with the discloser's consent, for the purposes of legal proceedings, for various statutory functions relating to companies or insolvency, to the Treasury in the interests of investors or the public, in pursuance of a Community obligation or where information is anonymised.
Commercial	Companies Act 2006	This Act makes extensive provision for information to be provided to the Companies Registrar. For example, section 9 requires an application for registration of a company to be accompanied by documents and information including the memorandum of association, company name and registered office, status and liability. Certain information held by the Registrar, such as certificates of incorporation and of registration of charges, must then be made publicly available on the Companies Register, for inspection and copying (ss.1080 onwards), although information such as directors' residential addresses are excluded from disclosure. Part 15 provides for accounts and reports to be maintained, and circulated to company shareholders, etc.
Commercial	Competition Act 1998	Sections 25 and 26 empower the Office of Fair Trading (the OFT) to investigate anti-competitive practices and to require disclosure of information or documents (save documents protected by legal professional privilege) for those purposes.
Electronic	Computer Misuse Act 1990	Section 1 prohibits anyone from making or enabling unauthorised access to a computer program or data, whether or not it is intended to use that data to commit further criminal offences.
Personal, Financial	Consumer Credit Act 1974 and Consumer Credit (Credit Reference Agency) Regulations 2000 SI 2000/290, Consumer Credit (Disclosure of Information)	Part V, together with the 2004 Regulations (made under s.55, and extending the application of the Consumer Credit (Agreement) Regulations 1983 SI 1983/1553) require certain information to be provided to a debtor before she enters into a regulated consumer credit agreement or consumer hire agreement, save for distance agreements. Alternative disclosure provisions apply to various other types of agreements (Part VI).

Information type	Statute	
	Regulations 2004 SI 2004/1481	A debtor or hirer must also be provided, on request, with the name and address of any credit reference agency a creditor has consulted about the debtor's or hirer's financial standing (s.157, reg. 3). Section 158 enables individuals, unincorporated companies and certain partnerships to obtain information held on file by a credit agency. Any individual who makes a section 158 request (or a request for personal information under DPA 1998, s.7 which by virtue of DPA 1998, s.9(2) is presumed to be a request for personal data relevant only to the individual's financial standing) must be informed of their rights to rectification of incorrect, prejudicial information (reg. 3). Where a request relates to a business consumer, disclosure may be restricted where the Office of Fair Trading considers full disclosure would adversely affect the service provided by the agency to its customers and restricted disclosure will not prejudice the requester (s.160)
Environmental	Control of Pollution Act 1974	Section 64 requires public noise level registers to be maintained, providing information on noise level measurements for premises in noise abatement zones.
Health and safety	Control of Substances Hazardous to Health Regulations 2002	These Regulations (save where an exemption applies to the armed forces on grounds of national security) require employers to monitor and record exposure to hazardous substances, to monitor and keep records of employees' health and to make records available to the employee and the Health and Safety Executive (with records provided to the Health and Safety Executive when a business ceases trading (regs. 10,11).
Copyright	Copyright Designs and Patents Act 1988	This Act governs use of copyright material (see Chapter 11, Commercial Information).
Court proceedings	Courts Act 2003	Section 98 provides for a register of High Court and county court money judgments open to inspection for a fee.
Criminal	Crime and Disorder Act 1998	Various information sharing powers are provided to a range of public authorities, for the purposes of preventing youth offending (see Chapter 10).
Court proceedings	Criminal Appeal Act 1995	This Act provides extensive powers to the Criminal Cases Review Commission to enable it to investigate alleged miscarriages of justice. In particular it may require a public body to produce or provide access to documents, and to allow their copying (s.17). It may prohibit the destruction of documents. Interestingly,

		the section 17 duty is not affected by any obligation of secrecy, statutory or common law limitation on disclosure (i.e. DPA 1998, duty of confidentiality) which would otherwise prevent disclosure to the Commission (although specific limitations on disclosure do apply where a government department holds documents whilst consideration is being given to the exercise of the royal prerogative). Information obtained by the Commission may only be disclosed in limited circumstances: for the purposes of legal proceedings, for purposes of determining an application for compensation for a miscarriage of justice, to another Commission employee, member or investigating officer, in statements or reports published by the Commission, or where disclosure is necessary to exercise the Commission's functions. No information obtained under section 17 may be disclosed without consent if the discloser specified the document was not to be further disclosed without consent. Consent should not be unreasonably withheld (but may be withheld if disclosure would otherwise have been prevented by obligations of secrecy or other limitations on disclosure).
Personal and Commercial	Criminal Justice Act 1987	Section 2 empowers the Director of the Serious Fraud Office (the SFO) to require questions to be answered, information to be provided or documents produced by (a) any person who they are investigating or considering investigating in relation to an offence which appears on reasonable grounds to involve serious or complex fraud, or (b) any other person they believe to have relevant information. In the event of non-compliance a warrant to enter and search premises and seize documents may be obtained. Section 3 provides statutory powers for the SFO to disclose information to government departments or public bodies acting on behalf of the crown and to certain 'competent authorities' (including certain investigatory and regulatory bodies and the Official Receiver), and to disclose information for the purpose of criminal investigations and proceedings. (Information subject to obligations of secrecy is subject to further restrictions.) The Director of the SFO is also empowered to enter written agreements for the supply of information to or by him, subject to obligations not to disclose that information otherwise than for specified purposes.
Commercial	Criminal Justice Act 1993	Part V makes it a criminal offence to engage in insider dealing. This means disclosing (save in the proper performance of employment) specific or precise information relating to particular securities

Information type	Statute	
		which is not in the public domain and which, if made public, would be likely to have a significant effect on the price of securities.
Personal, Criminal	Criminal Justice Act 2003	Section 325 provides the statutory basis for Multi-Agency Public Protection Arrangements, which assess and manage risks posed by certain sexual and violent offenders or offenders who might cause serious harm to the public. Explicit information sharing powers are provided (see Chapter 12, Criminal).
Personal, Criminal	Criminal Justice and Court Services Act 2000	Section 1 of this Act (which currently applies to England and Wales save in pilot areas where the Offender Management Act 2007 applies) provide the statutory gateway by which local probation boards, and officers of local probation boards, may share information for purposes such as assisting the determination of criminal sentences, and for the supervision and rehabilitation of offenders.
Court proceedings	Criminal Procedure and Investigations Act 1996	Part 1 details the duties of disclosure imposed in criminal proceedings (see Chapter 7, Court Proceedings).
Court proceedings	Criminal Procedure Rules 2005 SI 2005/384	These court rules (particularly Parts 23–26) detail the practice and procedure to be followed by criminal courts, including in relation to disclosure (see Chapter 7).
Personal, Criminal	Domestic Violence Crime and Victims Act 2004	Sections 35 to 44 require local probation boards and probation service providers to ascertain whether victims of certain serious sexual and violent offences wish to receive information about conditions (such as not to contact the victim), licence conditions and supervision requirements which will apply when the offender is released or discharged from prison/hospital. The purpose of disclosure is to enable the victim to make representations about such conditions and requirements.
Personal, Education	Education (Information about Individual Pupils) (England) Regulations 2006 SI 2006/2601	The regulations require information about state school pupils to be shared with and by the relevant local education authority (see Chapter 10).
Personal, Education	Education (Pupil Information) (England) Regulations 2005 SI 2005/1437	These regulations oblige state schools and special schools to keep pupil records and to make certain disclosures from them (see Chapter 10).

Personal, Education	Education (Special Education Needs) (Consolidation) Regulations 2001 SI 2001/3455	These regulations enable information to be shared with a range of agencies, prior to and following assessment of a child's special educational needs (see Chapter 10).
Personal, Education	Education Act 1996 and Education (Pupil Registration) (England) Regulations 2006 SI 2006/1751	These regulations enable information to be shared with a local education authority about pupils missing school (see Chapter 10).
Personal, Education	Education Act 2002	Section 142 permits a direction to be made by the ISA (on grounds of unsuitability to work with children, misconduct, health or incompetence) prohibiting a person from working in schools or further education, or permitting such employment only in accordance with certain conditions. Before employing an individual in a childcare or education position employers must consult list 99 (the list of such barred individuals). List 99 will be replaced by the SVGA 2006 vetting scheme from October 2009. Sections 157 and 175 and the Education (Independent Schools Standards) Regulations 2003 SI 2003/1910 impose duties to safeguard and promote the welfare of school pupils and imply power to share information for those purposes (see Chapter 10).
Personal, Education	Education and Skills Act 2008	This Act affords information sharing powers to assist certain young people to participate in education and training (see Chapter 10).
Utilities	Electricity Act 1989	The Act enables OFGEM to make a referral to the Competition Commission asking it to undertake an investigation and to report to OFGEM and the Secretary of State for BERR, where it believes that an electricity supplier is acting against the public interest. Any report should not make disclosures which are contrary to the public interest, which would harm the legitimate interests of the relevant business or might harm an individual's interests (s.13).
Employment	Employment Rights Act 1996	The amendments made to this Act by the Public Interest Disclosure Act 1998 aim to protect employees who disclose information in the public interest (see Chapter 9, Employment).

Information type	Statute	
Commercial	Enterprise Act 2002	Where a company merger is likely to significantly decrease competition, or where a restriction or distortion of competition is suspected, Parts 3 and 4 authorise the OFT, the government and regulators such as OFCOM to make references to the Competition Commission, and for the OFT and the Commission to share information with the Secretary of State for BERR for the purpose of deciding whether a reference is appropriate. Explicit information sharing powers are also provided (ss.105, 152, 170). The Commission is provided with extensive investigative powers including powers to order production of documents and information (ss.38, 50, 109, 136, 142 and 176), as is the OFT (s.174). The OFT, the Secretary of State and the Commission should, so far as possible consult enterprises subject to a reference (ss.104, 169). The Commission must publish and provide investigation reports to the referrer, detailing its reasoning and information needed to understand its reasoning. OFCOM may also be required to investigate and report to the Secretary of State, and where so required, also has power to carry out such investigations as it considers appropriate (s.61A). Part 6 of the Act affords extensive powers to the OFT to require production of information and documents (save those protected by legal professional privilege and a banker's obligation of confidence) for the purpose of investigating the forming of cartels. Part 9 details extensive prohibitions on disclosure of information obtained under Parts 3, 4 and 6 relating to an individual's affairs or a business, save where information is public knowledge, consent is provided, disclosure is to comply with a European Community obligation or to facilitate specified public authorities' functions and for certain legal proceedings. Any decision by the OFT, Commission or Secretary of State to disclose personal or business information, whether in a report, or to another public authority, must balance the need to exclude from disclosure certain information (information which it would be contrary to the public interest to disclose, commercial information disclosure of which might significantly harm the business, personal information disclosure of which might harm the individual's interests) and the extent to which disclosure of commercial or personal information is needed to achieve the purpose of the disclosure (s.244).

Environmental Health and Safety	Environment and Safety Information Act 1988	The Act requires public registers of certain information to be maintained: (a) notices issued by a fire authority under the Regulatory Reform (Fire Safety) Order 2005 SI 2005/1541 to be maintained by the fire and rescue authority, Health and Safety Executive or local authority depending on the nature of the premises to which the notice applies (b) improvement and prohibition notices issued for the purposes of the Health and Safety at Work etc Act 1974, ss.21 and 22 to be maintained by local authorities (c) notices issued by a local authority under Safety of Sports Grounds Act 1975, s.10 to be kept by the local authority (d) notices issued under the Food and Environment Protection Act 1985, s.19 in relation to unlawful use, sale, supply, advertisement or importation of pesticides to be maintained by DEFRA, the Health and Safety Executive, the individual's employer or the Secretary of State. Individuals upon whom such notices are served may claim exemption from disclosure where an entry would disclose a trade secret or secret manufacturing process, but only within 14 days of service of the notice.
Environmental	Environmental Protection Act 1990	Under this Act public registers must be maintained by local authorities disclosing: – authorisations and notices relating to discharge of pollutants (s.20) licences for waste disposal and related matters (s.64) – remedial work to be done on contaminated land (s.78R) However, information must not be included if it is contrary to national security (ss.21, 65, 78S) or, in certain circumstances, if it is commercially confidential information relating to an individual or business who has not consented to disclosure (ss.22, 66, 78T). Local authorities (excluding county councils) must also maintain public registers containing information relating to litter control areas and litter control notices (s.95) and in relation to stray dogs, including where the dog is returned to the owner, details of their name and address (s.149). The Secretary of State for Environment, Food and Rural Affairs must also maintain a register relating to genetically modified organisms, with information

Information type	Statute	
		to be excluded only where disclosure would be contrary to national security, might damage the environment, or in certain circumstances where it is commercially confidential information relating to an individual or business (s.122).
Adoption, Court proceedings	Family Procedure (Adoption) Rules 2005 SI 2005/2795	These court rules regulate disclosure of court documents relating to adoption proceedings (see Chapter 10).
Court proceedings	Family Proceedings Courts (Children's Act 1989) Rules 1991 SI 1991/1395, and Family Proceedings Rules 1991 SI 1991/1247	These court rules confirm the confidentiality of documents (save court orders) relating to children proceedings held in private and prohibit disclosure of court documents save where ordered by the court or as prescribed (see Chapter 10).
Personal	Finance Act 1989	Section 182 prohibits HMRC from disclosing information about the tax, tax credits, child trust fund, social security contributions, statutory sick pay, statutory maternity pay, statutory paternity pay, or statutory adoption pay of an identifiable person unless: – the individual consents; – the information is publicly available; or – there is lawful authority for disclosure (this includes where disclosure does not contravene express prohibitions, and is undertaken by a crown servant or HMRC employee in the course of their duties, is in compliance with a court order or statutory provision, is in connection with proceedings instituted by HMRC Commissioners or Board, is by an HMRC employee in the course of his functions). A similar prohibition on disclosure is imposed upon the Comptroller and Auditor General, members of the National Audit Office and the Parliamentary Ombudsman where they have received information from HMRC.
Commercial	Financial Services and Markets Act 2000	In order for the Financial Services Authority (the FSA) to undertake its obligations to investigate and prosecute certain unauthorised financial activities, the FSA and its investigators may require suspected offenders to produce specified documents or information, to attend and produce documents to an investigator, to produce a report providing information, or to state where a document is

		(Sections 165, 166, 167–173, 175). A lawyer may be required to provide their client's name and address. A third party may also be required to produce documents they hold (s.175), save where the third party is subject to obligations of confidence, is not themselves subject to investigation and disclosure has not been otherwise authorised. Warrants to enter premises and to seize or copy documents may also be obtained (s.176). The FSA is prohibited from disclosing confidential information relating to a person's business or other affairs whether obtained voluntarily or by coercion (s.348), save where information is anonymised, consent is provided or where disclosure is authorised, for example between the Treasury, FSA and Secretary of State or for certain legal proceedings and investigations (see Financial Services and Markets Act 2000 (Disclosure of Confidential Information) Regulations 2001 SI 2001/2188).The FSA must also maintain public records of information such as those authorised to conduct regulated business (s.347).
Environment	Food and Environment Protection Act 1985	Section 14 requires a public register to be maintained providing information about licences authorising deposits into the sea and incineration at sea, convictions for discharging without a licence and including certain information supplied or obtained from the licensee.
Personal	Gender Recognition Act 2004	Where a person has applied for a gender recognition certificate this Act limits the circumstances in which information about the individual's previous gender and about the application itself may be disclosed. The Gender Recognition (Disclosure of Information) (England, Wales and Northern Ireland) (No. 2) Order 2005 SI 2005/916 details certain situations where disclosure is permitted.
Health and Safety	Health and Safety at Work etc. Act 1974	To fulfil statutory functions relating to public health, public safety and environmental protection, the Health and Safety Executive (HSE) may share information with local authorities (s.18), or require information to be provided to the HSE or a local authority, to be used solely for HSE functions (s.27). HMRC may share certain information with a local authority or health and safety inspector in order to assist them in exercising health and safety functions (s.27A). Information obtained under section 27 or 27A may be disclosed only in prescribed circumstances, including with the consent of the provider, where information is anonymised, or where disclosure is to prescribed public bodies or for legal proceedings or HSE investigations (s.28).

Information type	Statute	
Health	Health Service (Control of Patient Information) Regulations 2002 SI 2002/1438	The Regulations make extensive provision for processing confidential health information for a wide range of medical purposes, including for research or statistical purposes. Disclosures undertaken in accordance with the Regulations are assumed to be lawful, notwithstanding any obligation of confidence, provided that the person processing information is a health professional or in the circumstances owes a comparable duty of confidentiality (reg. 4).
Personal	Housing Act 1996	Section 213 provides implied power for housing and social services authorities to share information in certain circumstances. See also section 213A, considered in Chapter 10.
Personal	Human Fertilisation and Embryology Act 1990	This Act details the limited circumstances in which information may be disclosed revealing whether or not an individual was born following fertility treatment and in order to clarify matters of parenthood (see Chapter 10).
Personal	Immigration Act 1971	Part 1, Schedule 2 affords extensive powers to immigration officers to require information and documents (including a passport or identity document) to be provided by those arriving in the UK, and to search a person for such documents, to enter and search premises to obtain and copy documents, and to require a ship or aircraft (or their owner) to provide passenger information including information about the expected arrival of non-EEA nationals being transported by the carrier.
Personal	Immigration and Asylum Act 1999 and the Immigration (Supply of Information to the Secretary of State for Immigration Purposes) Order 2008 SI 2008/2077	Section 20 enables a chief police officer, the Serious Organised Crime Agency or those accommodating UK Border Agency supported asylum seekers to share information with the Home Secretary for various immigration control purposes. In addition, under the Order, certain information held by the Secretary of State for Transport (including information held by the Driver and Vehicle Licensing Agency and the Maritime and Coastguard Agency), by the Secretary of State for Work and Pensions for the purposes of functions relating to social security and by the British Transport Police Force may be shared with the Home Secretary, for limited immigration purposes. Information obtained by the Home Secretary for immigration purposes may subsequently be shared with the police, the Serious Organised Crime Agency and HM Customs and Excise for the

		purpose of various functions relating to crime and national security (s.21).
Commercial	Insolvency Act 1986	Where a company is in administration or liquidation, or where a winding up order has been made, sections 234–6 impose certain obligations of disclosure (primarily upon company employees and those holding company information) and empower the court to order disclosure to administrators/administrative receivers/liquidators or official receivers. The court may also summons certain individuals to provide information (not limited to company employees, but including those able to give information about the business, for example, the Serious Fraud Office).
National security	Intelligence Services Act 1994	This Act empowers the Secret Intelligence Service to obtain and provide information about the actions or intentions of foreign nationals, but only for the purposes of its functions, in the interests of national security; for the purpose of the prevention or detection of serious crime; or for the purpose of any criminal proceedings. Government Communications Headquarters (GCHQ), one of its functions being the protection of information, must also only obtain information needed to discharge its functions and must not disclose information other than as necessary for its functions or for the purpose of criminal proceedings. Section 5 empowers the Home or Foreign Secretary, as appropriate, to authorise the Security Service, Secret Intelligence Service and GCHQ, by warrant, to enter property or interfere with wireless telegraphy where necessary for and proportionate to their functions and provided that appropriate arrangements (as detailed above and at Security Services Act 1989, s.2(2)(a)) are in place to restrict disclosure of information. Consideration must be given to whether the aim could be achieved by alternative means. No warrant may be issued in respect of UK property unless it is to prevent, investigate, prosecute, etc. serious criminal conduct.
Land	Land Registration Act 2002	Section 66 enables the Official Copy of Registered Entries maintained by HM Land Registry (which details whether land is registered, the title history and cautions registered against the title) and related documents to be inspected and copied.
Personal	Legal Services Act 2007	This Act (when in force) will allow information sharing by the Office for Legal Complaints or Legal Services Ombudsman and the Solicitors Regulatory Authority or Bar Standards Board where misconduct is identified such that the regulator may need to consider taking action against a professional

Information type	Statute	
		(s.143). An ombudsman may oblige a party to a complaint to disclose information or documents for the purposes of investigations and may report a failure to provide information to a regulator (ss.147 and 148).The Legal Services Board may also require the regulators to provide information (s.55).
Local Government	Local Authorities (Members' Allowances) (England) Regulations 2003 SI 2003/1021	Regulations 15 and 16 require local authorities to record payments made to their members, make these records freely available for inspection, supply copies for a fee and publish details of total sums paid. Regulations 30 and 31 make similar provision for payments to parish council members.
Local Government	Local Government Finance Act 1992	For the purposes of collecting council tax, HMRC listing officers must undertake domestic property valuations and maintain lists detailing the relevant valuation band for each dwelling in a local authority area (ss.22 and 22B). The local authority must make suitable arrangements for notice to be given of the list. Local authorities and occupiers may be required to provide information about dwellings for these purposes (s.27).
Local Government	Local Government Act 1972 and Local Government (Access to Information) Act 1985	Section 111(1) grants a local authority 'power to do anything . . . which is calculated to facilitate, or is conducive or incidental to, the discharge of any of their statutory functions', thus providing implicit information sharing powers. Part VA provides for public and press access to certain local authority meetings, and for certain documents to be made publicly available before and after those meetings. This does not prevent the local authority excluding the public from certain meetings, or parts of meetings (for example to protect confidential information from disclosure), and denying access to the agendas, reports, background papers and minutes of in specified circumstances.
Local Government	Local Government Act 1974	Where the Commission for Local Administration undertakes investigations into alleged local authority maladministration or failures to provide services their report must be provided to any complainant or referrer, the relevant authority and any other person who is alleged to have acted in relation to the matter, unless remedial action is being or has been taken, in which case a statement of reasons should be provided (s.30). An annual report of the Commission's activities will also be disseminated to local authorities (s.23A), although

		restrictions on disclosure may be imposed by a minister in the public interest.
Local Government	Local Government Act 2000	Extensive implied information sharing powers are provided to local authorities in order to achieve 'the promotion of improvement of the economic well-being of their area; the promotion or improvement of the social well-being of their area; the promotion of improvement of the environmental well-being of their area', or when local authorities, in order to achieve such goals, enter into arrangements or agreements and cooperate with or exercise the functions of other bodies (s.2). In exercising their section 2 powers a local authority may not, however, do anything which it is prevented from doing by statute, i.e. the DPA 1998 (s.3). The Act also enables local authority information to be shared with the public (a) by providing public access to minutes of executive or executive committee meetings held in private (s.22), and (b) through a public register of members interests (s.81).
Local Government	Local Government Finance Act 1988	Under Part III rating lists for non-domestic properties must be compiled and maintained by HMRC valuation officers for district and London borough councils, with each local authority making suitable arrangements for notice to be given of the list (s.41).
Health	Mental Capacity Act 2005	This Act provides a test for assessing the decision-making capacity of adults and children aged 16 and 17, and enables action to be taken and information shared in their best interests (see **Introduction** and **Chapter 8**).
Health	Mental Health Act 1983	This Act provides for individuals to be admitted to hospital for treatment for mental disorder. It enables information to be shared by an approved mental health professional with the patient's nearest relative (s.11); by local authority social services with an approved mental health professionals where they consider hospital admission may be necessary (s.13); by a hospital with local authority social services where a person is admitted by their nearest relative (s.14); by a hospital required to report to a criminal courts upon an offender's mental condition (s.35); and with an independent mental health advocate for the purpose of assisting certain patients (s.130B).
Motor vehicles	Motor Vehicles (Third Party Risks) Regulations 1972 SI 1972/1217	Before a tax disc is renewed or a vehicle registered the Vehicle Excise and Registration Act 1994 requires proof of insurance to be provided, either by the vehicle owner producing their insurance certificate or using information disclosed from the Motor Insurance Database (as authorised by reg. 9(4)).

Information type	Statute	
Health	National Health Service (Venereal Diseases) Regulations 1974 SI 1974/29	Regulation 2 requires specified health bodies to take necessary steps to ensure information obtained by them which might identify that an individual has been examined or treated for a sexually transmitted disease is not disclosed, save to a medical practitioner or to a person specifically employed by a medical practitioner to treat or prevent the spread of such disease.
Health	National Health Service Act 2006	This Act makes extensive provision for information sharing. Section 39 provides for a publicly accessible register of NHS Foundation trusts. Section 72 imposes a duty upon NHS bodies to cooperate with each other in exercising their functions. Section 82 requires NHS bodies and local authorities to cooperate with one another in order to secure and advance the health and welfare of the people of England and Wales. Section 249 makes similar provision for NHS bodies and the prison service to cooperate with a view to securing and maintaining prisoners' health. Part 10 of the Act makes extensive provision for disclosure of documents and information, for the purpose of preventing, detecting, investigating and prosecuting criminal offences against the health service and its employers. Restrictions upon further disclosure are imposed, particularly for personal information. Section 242 and 242A provide for certain NHS bodies to consult service users where proposals for development, etc. would have an impact on the manner of delivery and range of services provided. Sections 244–6 together with the Local Authority (Overview and Scrutiny Committees Health Scrutiny Functions) Regulations 2002 SI 2002/3048 enable local authorities to form overview and scrutiny committees to scrutinise and report on the health service in the area. Schedule 17 specifies those items for committee discussion which are specifically excluded from disclosure to the public or from public discussion, in order to prevent disclosures in breach of confidence. Section 270 empowers the Registrar General to disclose information relating to a birth or death to the Secretary of State for Health.

		Section 250 establishes the National Information Governance Board as a statutory body providing guidance upon the processing of health and social care information and monitoring its implementation.
Health	National Health Service And Community Care Act 1990	Section 47 requires a local authority, where necessary, to assess an individual's needs for community care services; and having regard to that assessment to decide whether to provide services. Assistance may be sought from a housing authority, primary care trust or health authority (it being implied that information will be shared), where the individual is disabled or requires health or housing provision and those authorities can assist with the assessment.
Employment	National Minimum Wage Act 1998	An employee is entitled to access records maintained by employers to demonstrate that the national minimum wage is paid, specifically to determine their rate of pay (s.10). Enforcement officers may also require employers, and their employees and agents to produce and explain records kept (s.14).
Health	NHS Bodies and Local Authorities Partnership Arrangements Regulations 1990 SI 2000/617	These Regulations enable primary care trusts, NHS Trusts and NHS foundation trusts to make partnership arrangements with local authorities, for the purpose of exercising NHS functions and local authority health-related functions (regs. 5, 6). Such partnerships must be likely to improve the exercise of those functions and fulfil the objectives in the relevant primary care trust health improvement plan. It is implied that the partners will share information to fulfil these aims.
Criminal	Offender Management Act 2007	Explicit powers to share information are provided to the Secretary of State for Justice, probation service providers, others who have entered into arrangements to assist probation service providers, local authorities, the Youth Justice Board, the Parole Board, anyone contracted to run prison, young offender institute or secure training centre or to transport prisoners, the police and persons responsible for electronic monitoring (s.14). The powers may be exercised where information sharing is not prohibited by statute, and where it is necessary or expedient to share information for 'probation purposes' (which include assisting sentencing and cautioning decisions, supervising and rehabilitating offenders, giving information to the victims of criminal offending and offender management).
National Security	Official Secrets Act 1911	Section 1 prevents numerous activities provided such activities appear to have been taken with intent to prejudice the safety or interests of the state. Prohibited activities include making

Information type	Statute	
		representations and notes which might be directly or indirectly useful to the enemy and unlawfully obtaining, collecting, recording, publishing or communicating any secret official code or password, documents, plans, etc. which are or might be directly or indirectly useful to the enemy. It is an offence to refuse to disclose information about such a 'spy' (section 7). Section 9 affords power to the police to obtain authority to search for evidence that an offence has been or is about to be committed.
National Security	Official Secrets Act 1920	The prohibitions in this Act are widely drafted to apply to any individual. It is a criminal offence for an individual, acting in a manner that appears to be for a purpose which is prejudicial to the safety or interests of the state, to: – retain an official document which they have no right to retain – provide another person with an official document provided solely for their use – share a secret official code or password – acquire an official document, code or password to which they have no authority, and fail to return it to the appropriate person, or the police – unlawfully manufacture or sell an official stamp or seal (s.1). If an individual communicates or attempts to communicate with a foreign agent, it is presumed that they have committed an offence by sharing information of potential use to the enemy, for purposes contrary to the state's safety or interests (s.2). Where breach of Official Secrets Act 1989, s.1 is suspected, the Act provides for certain senior police officers to be authorised to seek information from an individual who is believed able to provide information about the offence or suspected offence (s.6).
National Security	Official Secrets Act 1989	This Act prohibits the unlawful or unauthorised disclosure of certain types of information by certain individuals. The primary non-disclosure obligations are imposed upon: Members and former members of the security and intelligence services and those working with them who have been made aware of their non-disclosure obligations (s.1(1)). No disclosure may be made of information obtained in the course of employment.

		Crown servants (ministers, the civil service, the armed services, the police and the Serious Organised Crime Agency, various other groups detailed in the Official Secrets Act 1989 (Prescription) Order 1990 SI 1990/200, including the Independent Police Complaints Commission, the Parliamentary Ombudsman, Comptroller and Auditor General and members of the National Audit office) and government contractors (those who provide or are employed to provide goods and services to crown servants). Such individuals are prohibited from making damaging disclosures of 'protected information' – information relating to security or intelligence, the armed forces, international relations, and information relating to criminal offending (see ss.1–4). It is a defence for these individuals to show they were unaware they were prohibited from disclosing the information or that disclosure would result in the alleged damage. Crown servants and government contractors are also prohibited from disclosing information which might allow another person to access 'protected information'. They must return documents containing protected information on request (s.8). Third-party recipients of information disclosed unlawfully in breach of sections 1–4, are subject to obligations not to disclose (s.5) and to keep safely and return documents received (s.8).
Government (central/local)	Parliamentary Commissioner Act 1967	The Parliamentary Ombudsman's extensive powers to investigate allegations of maladministration made against government departments and numerous other public authorities extend to requiring disclosure of relevant information or documents (save cabinet documents). The same powers are afforded to the Ombudsman as to the court in relation to production of documents, attendance and examination of witnesses. Those compelled to disclose information are unable to refuse disclosure on grounds of crown privilege, or upon the basis of obligations of secrecy. The results of investigations must be disclosed to the complainant's Member of Parliament for the complainant following investigations and may be disclosed to parliament where injustice resulting from maladministration will not be remedied. Information may not otherwise be disclosed, save for the purposes of these and certain other investigations, or for the purposes of specified criminal proceedings (s.11). It may be further restricted where disclosure of information would

Information type	Statute	
		prejudice the safety of the state or otherwise be contrary to public interest.
Commercial	Patents Act 1977	This Act provides for publication, disclosure and inspection of information relating to patent applications and publication of patent information through the public register of patents. Specific exclusions from publication apply where disclosure might prejudice public safety or national security.
Environmental	Planning (Hazardous Substances) Act 1990	Section 28 requires a public register to be kept by local authorities relating to consents to allow hazardous substances on or in land (s.28).
Criminal	Police Act 1997	Part V details the statutory scheme for standard and enhanced disclosure of criminal records relating to potential employees (see **Chapter 12**).
Criminal	Police and Criminal Evidence Act 1984 (PACE)	PACE provides the police with extensive powers to search individuals, enter and search property, and obtain information and evidence for the purpose of investigating and prosecuting criminal offenders.
Criminal	Prevention of Terrorism Act 2005	This Act provides for the making of control orders, imposing certain obligations and restrictions on individuals to protect the public from terrorism. The Act, together with Part 76 Civil Procedure Rules 1998 empowers the court to order that a party's identity be kept anonymous, that control order hearings be held in the absence of the individual without notice having been given to them (s.4), and to exclude a party and their legal representative from hearings in order to prevent disclosure of information contrary to the public interest (in which case a special advocate will be appointed).
Telecommunications	Privacy and Electronic Communications (EC Directive) Regulations 2003 SI 2003/2426	These regulations make detailed provision in relation to communications by telephone, fax and email, including in relation to security (reg. 5), use of cookies (reg. 6), restricting use of information obtained by a network about a communication without the subscriber's prior consent (reg. 7), limiting disclosure of information required to trace malicious and nuisance calls to those persons with a legitimate interest (reg. 15), providing for telephone directories to include subscribers' information only if the subscriber consents (reg. 18) and restricting use of telephone, fax and e-mail for direct marketing (regs. 19–26). An exemption from compliance with all or part of the regulations applies only where exemption is

		needed in order to safeguard national security (reg. 28).
Criminal, Financial	Proceeds of Crime Act 2002	Part 7 imposes various disclosure obligations for the purpose of preventing money laundering. Section 328 – prohibits actions which may facilitate money laundering unless the professional involved has disclosed money laundering suspicions, as required by section 338, and has been authorised to act. Sections 330–2 – require those employed in certain professions who, in the course of business have acquired information about actual or possible money laundering, to disclose that information to the Serious Organised Crime Agency unless they have a reasonable excuse for non-disclosure or in certain circumstances where legal privilege exists. Section 333A prevents 'tipping off' where it is likely to prejudice investigations. Tipping off means informing a person about a disclosure of money laundering suspicions or an ongoing investigation into money laundering. It does not prevent disclosures to another employee within that business, a professional legal adviser, another credit or financial institution, or the supervisory authorities detailed in Money Laundering Regulations 2007 SI 2007/2157, or disclosure by a legal adviser to dissuade a client from offending. Section 337 enables disclosures to be made even where they would otherwise breach a restriction on disclosure of information such as the duty of confidentiality or the DPA 1998, but only where disclosure relates to information acquired in the course of business, relates to suspicions or knowledge of money laundering, and disclosure is made to the police, customs or a money laundering reporting officer within the discloser's business. Disclosures to the police or customs must be disclosed to the Serious Organised Crime Agency as soon as practicable (s.339ZA). For purposes relating to money laundering, etc. the court may order or authorise production of non-legally privileged material (ss.345, 348), entry to premises (s.347), seizure of material (s.352), disclosure of information (ss.357–8), disclosure of specific information relating to a financial institution's customers (ss.363–5) and for a bank or building society account to be monitored (ss.370–1).
Personal	Protection of Children Act 1999	This Act (until October 2009, when it will be replaced by the SVGA 2006 scheme) requires a list

Information type	Statute	
		of individuals considered unsuitable to work with children to be maintained by the ISA (s.1). Information must be provided by childcare organisations (including children's health and social care services) where, for example, a person has been involved in misconduct that has harmed a child or placed them at risk of harm. Childcare organisations must not employ an individual in a childcare position until they have checked that the individual is not contained within this list or List 99 (see Education Act 2002, s.142).
Health	Public Health (Control of Disease) Act 1984	Part 2 (to be amended by the Health and Social Care Act 2008) currently requires medical practitioners to share patient information with the local authority where the patient has food poisoning or a notifiable disease (cholera, plague, typhus, smallpox). The owner of premises in which a person is or has been suffering from such illness must provide the local authority with information to prevent the spread of disease.
Public records	Public Records Act 1958	Numerous public bodies, including central government departments are required to consider whether their administrative and departmental records need to be permanently preserved (s.3 and Sched. 1). Most documents to be preserved must then be transferred to the National Archives for safekeeping and to afford the public access (under FOIA 2000) unless, for example, they need to be retained for administrative or other purposes.
Procurement	Public Contracts Regulations 2006 SI 2006/5	These regulations specify procedures to be followed by public bodies awarding public works, public supply and public services contracts, specifically addressing disclosure of information in such instances (see **Chapter 11**).
Environmental	Radioactive Substances Act 1993	This Act requires certain information relating to the use, measurement, investigation and release of radioactive substances to be made public, provided disclosure will not reveal matters of national security, or details of trade secrets and confidential processes.
Commercial	Registered Designs Act 1949	This Act enables a designer to register his product designs, to prevent copying and to license and sell the design. The register is publicly available (s.17), the design may be inspected at the Intellectual Property Office (s.22) and information about whether, when and by whom a design is registered, may also be obtained, upon payment of a fee

		(s.23). Publication may be prohibited or restricted for defence purposes (s.5).
Personal, Criminal	Regulation of Investigatory Powers Act 2000	Part 1 RIPA enables interceptions of post and telecommunications messages: – with consent; – where authorised by warrant, in which case certain safeguards in relation to the extent of disclosure apply (ss.15 and 16) and wide obligations of secrecy in relation to the making of that warrant are imposed (s.19); – without warrant where the interception is undertaken by certain security bodies in the course of authorised surveillance, or is undertaken in certain prison and high security psychiatric settings. Section 17 restricts disclosure in legal proceedings where disclosure might reveal the content of an intercept, or that an interception has taken place. Part II of the Act allows authorised covert or intrusive surveillance to be undertaken and covert human intelligence sources (using a personal relationship to obtain or disclose information) to be used (s.26), where authorised, necessary and proportionate for reasons of national security, prevention or detection of crime and disorder, the UK's economic well-being, public safety and public health, tax and revenue purposes (ss.28 and 29). A wide range of public authorities may authorise covert surveillance (Sched. 1 Parts 1 and 2), including the police, various government departments, local authorities, the armed forces, the intelligence services, HMRC and the Financial Services Authority, the Health and Safety Executive, Special Health Authorities, OFSTED, and the Information Commissioner. A more limited range of authorities may use covert human intelligence sources. Intrusive surveillance must be authorised, by the Home Secretary, certain senior members of the police, HM Revenue and Customs, the Serious Organised Crime Agency or the Chairman of the OFT; in the interests of national security; for the purpose of preventing or detecting serious crime; or in the interests of the UK's economic well-being. Where electronic data is protected by encryption, Part III enables investigative agencies to require disclosure of information enabling the data to be accessed, for purposes of national security, crime prevention and the UK's economic well-being.
Criminal	Rehabilitation of Offenders Act 1974 and	This Act enables offenders who have committed all but the most serious criminal offences to become rehabilitated. No disclosures that might reveal the

Information type	Statute	
	Rehabilitation of Offenders Act 1974 (Exceptions) Order 1975 SI 1975/1023	existence of a spent conviction or caution should be made from court, police or central and local government records save to the rehabilitated person or another person at their request (ss.9, 9A). A rehabilitated offender is not expected generally to disclose information about previous convictions or criminal conduct (s.4(2)). However, the Exceptions Order enables information about spent convictions to be disclosed in order to assess the offender's suitability for certain professions (including certain health and legal positions) and posts involving work with children, work for the crown or other agencies where spent convictions must be disclosed for national security purposes, and to assess their suitability to hold certain licences (such as firearms and taxi driver certificates).
Electoral	Representation of the People Act 1983 and Representation of the People (England and Wales) Regulations 2001 SI 2001/341	The Act and the Regulations provide local authority election register officers with powers to obtain information and inspect records in order to maintain the election register (s.9A, regs. 23, 35). More importantly, they regulate disclosure of information held on the full and edited registers (the latter does not include anonymously registered electors or those who have requested their name and address be omitted). The full register should be publicly available for inspection (but not for electronic search or copying, reg. 43). It may be supplied free of charge to various libraries locally and nationally (regs. 97, 109A), and may be provided free of charge for jury summoning purposes (reg. 95) for electoral, statistical and research purposes, for the purpose of local government functions and to a wide range of agencies for crime prevention and security purposes (regs. 44, 92–115) An edited copy of the register may be sold to registered credit reference agencies (reg.114), to government departments, the environment agency, the Financial Services Authority, any body which carries out national security vetting (not the police and security services who already receive the full register) (reg. 113), and others (reg. 110). Strict limitations are imposed upon further disclosure.
Public authority	Re-Use of Public Sector Information Regulations 2005	These Regulations enable a wide range of public authorities to benefit financially from licensing the re-use of commercially valuable information (see **Chapter 11**, Commercial Information).

Motor vehicles	Road Traffic Act 1988	Section 46A enables the computerised MOT Test Certificate Database to be cross-checked with vehicle registration and licensing records, and where appropriate to be amended. Where a vehicle is being driven, or is believed to have been involved in an accident or traffic offence, the police may require the driver's name, address, insurance and MOT certificates to be disclosed (s.165) To check a vehicle is insured, the police may require proof of insurance (s.171). Section 170 obliges a driver to disclose her, and the owner's name and address where an accident causes injury or damage, or to otherwise report the accident. Where a vehicle owner is alleged to have committed specified traffic offences, section 172 requires the car owner or any other person who can, to disclose details of the person who was driving the car to the police.
Motor vehicles	Road Traffic Regulation Act 1984	Where a vehicle owner is alleged to have committed specified traffic offences, section 112 requires the car owner or any other person who can, to disclose details of the person who was driving the car to the police.
Motor vehicles	Road Vehicles (Registration and Licensing) Regulations 2002 SI 2002/2742	Regulation 27 permits information about vehicle ownership to be disclosed to: local authorities for crime investigation and enforcement purposes, the police, HMRC or any person who can demonstrate reasonable cause for wanting the particulars (for example an individual or their insurer in connection with a traffic accident). Anonymised information derived from the register may also be sold (reg. 28).
Personal	Safeguarding Vulnerable Groups Act 2006	This Act provides a new legislative framework for vetting and barring individuals who propose to work with children or vulnerable adults. From October 2009, the Independent Safeguarding Authority (ISA) will maintain new lists of individuals who are registered to work with or are barred from working with children or vulnerable adults (s.1). Local authorities, regulated activity providers (see Sched. 4), personnel suppliers, those who maintain professional registers, the Care Standards Commission, and the Commission for Social Care Inspection may, or in specified circumstances must provide information they hold about a person to the ISA (see Safeguarding Vulnerable Groups Act 2006 (Prescribed Information) Regulations 2008 SI 2008/3265 for information to be provided). Providers of regulated activity (frequent/intensive contact with vulnerable groups) and controlled

Information type	Statute	
		activity (frequent/intensive support work, and access to certain sensitive records) must check the lists before employing someone.
National Security	Security Service Act 1989	This Act regulates disclosure to and by the Security Service. Information may only be obtained in order to protect national security (particularly from espionage, terrorism and sabotage, from the activities of agents of foreign powers and from actions intended to overthrow or undermine parliamentary democracy by political, industrial or violent means); to safeguard the UK's economic well-being against threats posed by foreign nationals, and to support the police, the Serious Organised Crime Agency and other law enforcement agencies in preventing and detecting serious crime. Information may be disclosed for the same purposes, or for crime prevention, detection or criminal proceedings. Information must not be used to determine whether a person should be employed in a particular post, without government approval (s.2(3)).
Criminal	Serious Crime Act 2007 and the Serious Crime Act 2007 (Specified Anti-Fraud Organisations) Order 2008 SI 2008/2353	Part 3 enables public authorities to share information, including confidential information, with a number of anti-fraud organisations, without breaching the duty of confidentiality or any other restriction on disclosure (save for the DPA 1998 and RIPA, which must be complied with). It prohibits further disclosure by such organisations save where disclosures are made internally, to another person acting for that organisation; for detection, investigation or prosecution of offending; with the public authority's consent; or in pursuance of a Community or statutory obligations. HMRC may also disclose confidential information to a public authority for the purpose of identifying proceeds of crime; to bring civil enforcement proceedings in relation to proceeds of crime; and for similar purposes (s.85). No further disclosure may be made without HMRC consent.
Criminal	Sexual Offences Act 2003	Part 2 requires individuals who have been found to have committed certain specified sexual offences to provide certain information to the police (see **Chapter 12**).
Health	Social Security (Medical Evidence) Regulations 1976 SI 1976/615	Regulation 2 enables a medical statement/ certificate to be provided by a doctor, where an individual claims benefits on the basis of incapacity for work, or where a woman claims maternity benefit.

Personal	Social Security Administration Act 1992	Part VII affords extensive powers for information sharing with and by HMRC and the Secretary of State for Work and Pensions, particularly for fraud prevention purposes. This includes power to share information with the Health and Safety Executive, the Government Actuary's Department, the Statistics Board, the Pensions Regulator, other government departments (for example in relation to immigration matters) and those administering certain social security benefits.
Statistical	Statistics and Registration Services Act 2007	This Act empowers various bodies (including the Registrar General, the Secretary of State for Health, HMRC) to disclose information to the Statistics Board for the purpose of its functions. Disclosures of information which would identify an individual or company may only be disclosed in prescribed circumstances, including where the person concerned consents, or to comply with court or other legal obligations (s.39).
Statistical	Statistics of Trade Act 1947	Under this Act various government departments may require persons carrying on a trade or business (including local authorities) to provide estimates and returns, for statistical purposes, to determine economic trends, and for the purpose of government departmental functions. Further disclosure is prohibited without consent, save to another government department, to the Environment agency, or for the purpose of legal proceedings (s.9).
Revenue and tax	Taxes Management Act 1970	Section 6 and Part 1, Schedule 1 require HMRC Commissioners not to disclose information received in executing their duties, save for the purposes of those duties or as required by law.
Telecommunications	Telecommunications Act 1984	Section 94 enables the government to require or prohibit OFCOM or any public electronic communications networks provider from acting contrary to national security interests or international relations (including by sharing information).
Land	Town and Country Planning Act 1990	This Act permits extensive dissemination of planning information. Each local planning authority must maintain a publicly available register containing every application for planning permission, information about how it was dealt with, applications for development, and information regarding enforcement action (s.69). A register of enforcement and stop notices must be maintained (s.188). Information about planning applications must be provided to parish councils, and made

Information type	Statute	
		publicly available on or near relevant land (Sched. 1, para. 8).
Environmental	Water Industry Act 1991	Part VII imposes various requirements upon water authorities and sewage operators to maintain publicly accessible registers of appointments, licences and directions to which they must conform, to maintain trade effluent registers, to maintain publicly accessible maps of water mains, etc. and to provide sewer maps to local authorities. However, information obtained under the Act about particular individuals or businesses should not be disclosed without consent, save in specified, albeit widely construed circumstances (s.206).
Environmental	Water Resources Act 1991	Part VIII makes extensive provision for the collation and dissemination of information about water demand and resources. The Environment Agency must, for example, make information available through registers relating to water abstraction and pollution, and maintain publicly accessible maps relating to rivers and waterworks (ss.192–5). The Environment Agency and the Secretary of State for the Environment, Food and Rural Affairs have extensive powers to require disclosure of information to enable them to exercise their water resource functions, but equally themselves have obligations to provide information to water undertakers and suppliers, for example, in relation to pollution (ss.201–3). Whilst section 204 restricts disclosure of information about living individuals and operational businesses without consent, information may still be disclosed for various purposes, including for the Environment Agency to fulfil its statutory functions.
Telecommunications	Wireless Telegraphy Act 2006	Section 48 prohibits a third party from using wireless telegraphy apparatus to obtain information about the contents, sender or addressee of a message and from disclosing that information, unless disclosure is made in the course of legal proceedings or for the purpose of a report of legal proceedings. However, this Act must be read in conjunction with RIPA, above.

CHAPTER 5

The duty of confidence

Leanne Bell and Claire Bessant

5.1 INTRODUCTION

The duty of confidentiality requires certain people, in certain situations, to keep information confidential.

Anyone who holds information subject to a duty of confidence must assess carefully, before sharing information, whether they can justify disclosure, and whether any third-party recipient would keep that information confidential. An understanding of the duty of confidence is also necessary to ensure information is shared in accordance with the DPA 1998 and the HRA 1998 (DPA 1998, first principle requires information sharing to be lawful, as does ECHR, Art. 8), and to ensure that appropriate exemptions/exceptions under FOIA 2000 and EIR 2004 are considered.

Although confidentiality is a legal concept, it is not a clear-cut area of law. As we will see, legal, ethical and moral duties, professional and contractual obligations play an important role in determining whether confidential information may be shared.

5.1.1 The legal framework

The legal framework is made up primarily of common law rules (see **5.2–5.5**), which are now influenced and informed by legislation. Increasingly the courts are recognising overlaps between the doctrine of confidentiality and the right to respect for privacy (see **5.6**). The interactions between the duty of confidentiality, the DPA 1998 and freedom of information legislation, are particularly important to professionals advising upon information sharing (see **5.7**).

5.1.2 Professional obligations

Understanding the interaction between the law and professional obligations is crucial to understanding the operation of the duty in practice. Whilst the same legal principles apply to everybody, the obligations and guidance applicable to different organisations vary. As we see in **5.5**, determining when disclosure is in the public interest is particularly difficult. Some professions accordingly err on the side of caution adopting a stringent approach to maintaining confidentiality. Knowledge of the obligations and guidance applicable to other practitioners can facilitate inter-agency discussion and thus information sharing. Reference is accordingly made throughout to some of the more stringent confidentiality obligations imposed by professional bodies.

It is fundamental to recognise that whilst professional guidance is helpful in drawing professionals' attention to confidentiality issues, it is not legally binding. Guidance, because it is written in non-legal language, can be misleading or open to different interpretations. The fact that a professional is bound by professional obligations of confidentiality does not necessarily mean that the professional fully understands the nature of their legal duties.

Professional obligations: examples

The Solicitors Code of Conduct, rule 4.01 requires **solicitors** to keep the affairs of former, current and sometimes prospective clients confidential except where disclosure is required or permitted by law or by the client. The duty extends to some information which might not ordinarily be considered confidential, and continues after the end of the retainer. The right to confidentiality passes to a deceased's personal representatives. A solicitor also owes a duty to disclose all information material to a client's matter of which a solicitor is aware, regardless of the source of the information. In practice, problems may arise where information obtained from one client is relevant and material to another client. The guidance stresses that if these duties conflict, the duty of confidentiality is paramount.

Registered doctors must comply with principles detailed in General Medical Council (GMC) 2006 *Good Medical Practice*, including: 'make the care of your patient your first concern', 'protect and promote the health of patients and the public' and 'respect patients' right to confidentiality'. Adherence to *Good Medical Practice* requires each principle to be carefully balanced. There is clear potential for doctors to reach different, yet justifiable, decisions by doing so. Paragraph 37 of *Good Medical Practice* also states 'Patients have a right to expect that information about them will be held in confidence by their doctors. You must treat information about patients as confidential, including after a patient has died. If you are considering disclosing confidential information without a patient's consent, you must follow the guidance in, GMC 2004 *Confidentiality: Protecting and Providing Information*. This guidance prohibits doctors from sharing confidential information with others unless the patient consents or disclosure can be justified' (the justifications are considered in **5.5**).

Social workers registered with the General Social Care Council, are subject to codes of practice, breach of which may result in removal from the register. In particular, a social care worker must:

- Protect the rights and promote the interests of service users and carers, including through respecting and maintaining privacy.
- Strive to establish and maintain the trust and confidence of service users and carers. Social workers must respect confidential information and clearly explain agency policies about confidentiality to service users and carers.
- Uphold public trust and confidence in social care services. In particular social care workers must not abuse the trust of service users and carers or the access given to their personal information.
- Respect the rights of service users whilst seeking to ensure that their behaviour does not harm themselves or others. Social workers must act to minimise risks posed by service users by ensuring that the results of risk assessments are shared with relevant colleagues and agencies (balancing this obligation against the obligations of confidentiality).

5.2 THE EXTENT OF THE DUTY

Confidentiality does not equate to secrecy. Information which is subject to the duty of confidentiality can be shared in prescribed circumstances. If confidential information is shared in other circumstances a breach of confidence action may be brought.

The requirements of a breach of confidence action were detailed in *Coco* v. *AN Clark Engineering Ltd* [1968] FSR 415, p. 419, Megarry LJ:

> three elements are normally required if, apart from contract, a case of breach of confidence is to succeed. First, the information itself, . . . must 'have the necessary quality of confidence about it'. Secondly, that information must have been imparted in circumstances importing an obligation of confidence. Thirdly, there must be an unauthorised use of that information to the detriment of the party communicating it.

Coco v. *Clark* has been reconsidered and approved in numerous cases (including leading Information Tribunal cases *Derry City Council* v. *Information Commissioner* (EA/2006/0014); *McTeggert* v. *Information Commissioner and Department of Culture, Arts and Leisure* (EA/2006/0084) and *S* v. *Information Commissioner and General Registry Office* (EA/2006/0030)). The circumstances in which the duty arises have been clarified. There has also been debate about whether 'detriment' to the confider must be shown. Indeed even in *Coco* v. *Clark* Megarry J commented (p. 421) that whilst at first sight detriment ought to be present if equity is to intervene:

> I can conceive of cases where a plaintiff might have substantial motives for seeking the aid of equity and yet suffer nothing which could fairly be called detriment to him, as when the confidential information shows him in a favourable light but gravely injures some relation or friend of his whom he wishes to protect.

Certainly detriment for the purposes of a duty of confidence does not need to be reflected in financial loss or potential financial loss, but could, for example, be proved by loss of reputation.

It appears that the duty extends beyond the death of the confider. Breach is actionable by the deceased's personal representatives. In *Bluck* v. *The Information Commissioner and Epsom and St Helier University NHS Trust* EA/2006/0090 the Information Tribunal concluded the duty lasts 'as any confidence does, until either the information passed into the public domain or the public interest in its disclosure came to outweigh the public interest in maintaining the confidence' (at para. 29). *Lewis* v. *The Secretary of State for Health* [2008] EWHC 2196 also confirms there are 'strong pointers towards the acceptance of the proposition that an obligation of confidence imposed on the conscience of the confidant does survive, or at least is capable of surviving, the death of the confider'.

5.3 DEFINING CONFIDENTIAL INFORMATION

A wide range of information may need to be protected by reason of confidentiality, including information about an individual's personal life, trade secrets, sensitive business details and government secrets.

Information may be recorded in writing, and by photographs and video recordings (*Campbell* v. *MGN Limited* [2004] UKHL 22; *TP and KM* v. *United Kingdom* Application No. 28945/95), although it need not be recorded at all. (If information is recorded it will be easier to prove breach.) Certain items (e.g. new product plans) if recorded in a copyright protected form may alternatively be protected through intellectual property law (see **Chapter 11**). It should be noted, however, that copyright protects the document or other form of recording, not necessarily its content.

5.3.1 The necessary quality of confidence

It is important to remember that at common law, the duty of confidentiality only applies to information deemed to be confidential in nature. This sounds obvious, but it is actually far from easy to define confidential information.

To be protected, information must be specific and must have some value, though not necessarily a financial value. Some types of information are always likely to be confidential (health information, information of significant commercial value not in the public domain, information relating to national security). *Saltman Engineering Company* v. *Campbell Engineering Company Limited* (1948) 65 RPC 203 suggests confidential information is any information which has 'the necessary quality of confidence about it, namely it must not be something which is public property and public knowledge'.

AG v. *Guardian Newspapers Ltd ('Spycatcher')* [1990] 1 AC 109 confirms that information is not confidential if it is:

(a) useless information or trivia;
(b) within the public domain and so easily accessible that it cannot be regarded as confidential.

However, these points are subject to some qualifications.

In *Saltman Engineering Company* v. *Campbell Engineering Company Limited* (1948) 65 RPC 215 Lord Greene made clear there are circumstances where information which has been in the public domain can possess the necessary characteristics of confidence 'where . . . something new and confidential may have been brought into being by the application of the skill and ingenuity of the human brain. Novelty depends on the thing itself, and not upon the quality of its constituent parts. Indeed, often the more striking the novelty, the more commonplace its components'.

Information which has had some restricted disclosure may still be regarded as subject to the obligation of confidence (*AG* v. *Guardian Newspapers Ltd*

[1990] 1 AC 109). Information widely known throughout an organisation, but not outside that organisation might be deemed confidential. Indeed, even where confidential papers are circulated to numerous private individuals, who are either subject to contractual duties of confidentiality or aware the papers are to be treated as confidential, they may be considered to retain their confidential nature (see *Associated Newspapers Limited* v. *HRH Prince of Wales* [2006] EWCA Civ 1776).

Information which is of a confidential nature may be rendered non-confidential where it has, for example, been published on a website (and is thus in the public domain).

5.3.2 Confidentiality clauses and contractual agreements

The absence of a confidentiality provision within a contract does not mean that the contract is not confidential nor that information supplied by one party to another in the course of performing the contractual obligations is not confidential. Provided the requisite tests are made out, the information will be confidential to whatever extent is warranted by the circumstances. The length of time since a contract was agreed or terminated may be relevant in determining whether information contained within it is confidential. In *Derry City Council* v. *Information Commissioner* (EA/2006/0014) disclosure of an agreement containing commercially sensitive information which was six years old, and where much information about the contract was public knowledge, was not considered likely to result in an actionable breach of confidentiality. In *Ms Cartlidge and the Scottish Executive* (Decision 028/2005), heard under the Freedom of Information Scotland Act 2002, s.36(2) (equivalent to FOIA 2000, s.41) the fact that the contract had terminated only eight months previously was considered relevant in limiting disclosure of commercially sensitive information.

Confidentiality clauses are frequently included in commercial contracts. The person who has disclosed confidential information may accordingly expect that the information will not be disclosed. The reality in this situation is that whilst the information may not have the requisite confidential nature to prevent disclosure at common law, an action for breach of the contractual requirement to maintain confidentiality may be brought. *Associated Newspapers Limited* v. *HRH Prince of Wales* [2006] EWCA Civ 1776 highlights the important public interest in ensuring employees who handle sensitive confidential information respect their contractual obligations of confidence.

Confidentiality clauses may, however, be unenforceable if:

- they prevent an employee from making use of acquired skills, or if the provision amounts to a restraint of trade;
- competition law renders the provision void;

- it is in the overriding public interest to publish the material;
- the confidentiality forms part of an illegal contract or is otherwise unlawful.

5.3.3 Protective marking

One might assume that correspondence marked confidential will be considered confidential information. However, the Information Commissioner advises against such assumptions of confidentiality

> . . . a duty of confidence does not necessarily arise just because a letter is marked 'confidential' . . .
>
> ICO 2000 *Data Protection Act 1998: Subject Access and Third Party Rights*, para. 9)

Marking a document confidential may be persuasive and can be important in highlighting the need to consider confidentiality. It is not conclusive. If an organisation routinely marks letters confidential the marking may itself defeat the intended object, particularly where information marked confidential has not been treated as confidential in practice, or where disclosures have been previously made without authorisation but no action for breach has subsequently been brought.

Similarly marking information as confidential will not convert non-confidential information (to which no duty of confidence can apply) into confidential information. As Lord Greene said in Saltman (p. 215) 'However confidential the circumstances of communication, there can be no breach of confidence in revealing to others something which is already common knowledge.' Deciding whether information is confidential is therefore crucial. If not, there is no need to consider the circumstances in which it was disclosed.

5.4 WHO OWES THE DUTY AND CIRCUMSTANCES IN WHICH IT ARISES

The first question, emphasised in *Stephens* v. *Avery and others* [1988] Ch 449, relates to the parties' relationship. Was the relationship such that the person divulging information would expect it to be kept confidential?

However, the relationship alone does not determine whether the duty arises. The circumstances in which the information was imparted are key. Was it clear from the circumstances that the person divulging the information expected it to remain confidential? Was the information accepted on the basis it be kept confidential? Where a person has notice or agrees information should remain confidential, he should be precluded from disclosing it.

***Attorney General* v. *Guardian Newspapers Ltd ('Spycatcher')* [1990] 1 AC 109 per Lord Goff at 281**

> I start with the broad general principle . . . that a duty of confidence arises when confidential information comes to the knowledge of a person (the confidant) in circumstances where he has notice, or is held to have agreed, that the information is confidential, with the effect that it would be just in all the circumstances that he should be precluded from disclosing the information to others. I have used the word 'notice' advisedly, in order to avoid the (here unnecessary) question of the extent to which actual knowledge is necessary; though I of course understand knowledge to include circumstances where the confidant has deliberately closed his eyes to the obvious . . . .
>
> . . . in the vast majority of cases, in particular those concerned with trade secrets, the duty of confidence will arise from a transaction or relationship between the parties – often a contract, in which event the duty may arise by reason of either an express or an implied term of that contract. It is in such cases as these that the expressions 'confider' and 'confidant' are perhaps most aptly employed. But it is well settled that a duty of confidence may arise in equity independently of such cases; and I have expressed the circumstances in which the duty arises in broad terms, not merely to embrace those cases where a third party receives information from a person who is under a duty of confidence in respect of it, knowing that it has been disclosed by that person to him in breach of his duty of confidence, but also to include certain situations . . . where an obviously confidential document . . . is dropped in a public place, and is then picked up by a passer-by.

5.4.1 Relationships giving rise to a duty

A duty may arise by virtue of a contract which expressly or impliedly imposes a duty upon one or both parties. Duties are imposed both upon employer and employee in the employment context. The employment contract may expressly, or impliedly, require certain information to be kept confidential (see **Chapter 9**).

It is also well-recognised that a duty arises in the solicitor/client relationship, in other fiduciary relationships such as bank/client, and in caring relationships such as those between teacher/pupil, counsellor/client or social worker/child. Private information disclosed within the context of a sexual relationship is subject to the duty (*Stephens* v. *Avery and others* [1988] Ch 449, *Max Mosley* v. *Newsgroup Newspapers Limited* [2008] EWHC 1777). *AG* v. *Guardian Newspapers Ltd* [1990] 1 AC 109 suggests members and former members of the Security Service owe a lifelong obligation of confidence to the crown. The duty applies to many health professionals (see **Chapter 8**).

5.4.2 Disclosure of confidential information to third parties

The range of individuals who Lord Goff considered in *Spycatcher* might owe a duty of confidence goes wider. The duty arises when a third party agrees or has notice that the information is subject to the duty, or deliberately closes their eyes to the duty.

The duty falls on those who have had information confided to them, and third parties who receive information from the person who owed the original duty. For example, where a child discloses abuse to his doctor and the doctor discloses this to a social worker, the doctor and social worker would be subject to the duty. In *Spycatcher*, the MI5 agent Peter Wright breached his duty of confidence in publishing his memoirs, the *Sunday Times* also breached the duty by publishing part of those memoirs.

More importantly, the doctrine of confidentiality is not in fact dependent upon any existing confidential relationship (*Spycatcher*, p. 281; *Campbell* v. *MGN Limited* [2004] UKHL 22, Lord Nicholls, para. 14). A duty of confidentiality may be imposed upon an individual with whom information is shared in error. It may also arise, when a photograph is taken without an individual's knowledge or consent.

Practical example

Gavin, a learning-disabled adult, is being provided with assistance by the council's adult services department. His file contains:

- records of conversations between the individual and social workers;
- descriptions of daily routines;
- information about family visits;
- medical reports and recommendations;
- opinions shared at professionals' meetings.

Some documents are marked confidential. However, this does not mean they are confidential. Most if not all information within medical records is covered by the obligation of confidence. Likewise, medical reports and recommendations are considered to be subject to the duty. Social workers and other professionals will owe a duty to respect the client's confidences. Other information within the files will be confidential to other people, for example, opinions shared at professionals' meetings (*Stevens* v. *Plymouth City Council* [2002] 1 WLR 2583).

Stevens suggests straightforward descriptions of everyday life, daily routines and family visits are not confidential. However, it is risky to assume that descriptions of family visits are never confidential. Disclosure to one family member that another individual has had contact with Gavin may have repercussions if there is family conflict. When information is filed a record should be made whether anyone would reasonably expect that information to be kept confidential. If no such record has been made, no disclosure of potentially sensitive personal information should be made before discussions with an individual who has detailed knowledge of the case and understands the ramifications of disclosure.

5.5 WHEN CONFIDENTIAL INFORMATION CAN BE DISCLOSED

Information subject to the duty of confidentiality may be disclosed in certain circumstances:

1. Where the person to whom the duty is owed consents to information sharing.

2. To comply with a court order or other legal obligation.
3. Where disclosure is in the overriding public interest.

Even where information is covered by an obligation of confidence, the breadth of that obligation depends upon the circumstances. If information was brought into existence for certain authorised purposes, then it can be disclosed for those purposes (*Stevens* v. *Plymouth City Council* (2002) 1 WLR 2583 para. 34 Hale LJ, in accordance with the second data protection principle). Therefore, if, for example, a social worker instructs a doctor to examine a child for evidence of child abuse the doctor's duty of confidence towards the child does not bar disclosure to the social worker who instructed him.

Further consideration is given below to points 1–3. Attention is first given to practical guidance available to some professionals to determine whether disclosure should take place.

The Caldicott principles

Whilst not legally binding, these principles provide a framework against which decisions whether to share confidential information can be tested by professionals. Applicable to health and social care they provide sound advice to all who share confidential information. Their potential overlap with the DPA 1998 principles is also noted:

- Justify purpose(s) for sharing confidential information (DPA 1998 principles 1 and 2).
- Only use the information when absolutely necessary (DPA 1998 principles 1 and 2).
- Use the minimum information required (DPA 1998 principles 1–3).
- Allow access on a strict need-to-know basis (DPA 1998 principles 6 and 7).
- Everyone must understand his responsibilities (DPA 1998 principles 1–8).
- Understand and comply with the law (DPA 1998 principle 1).

In the health and social care sector, advice on sharing confidential information may also be obtained from a Caldicott Guardian (a senior professional responsible for monitoring information flows within and outside the organisation, writing confidentiality policies and advising individuals, ethics committees and departments. See Department of Health December 1997 *The Review of Patient-Identifiable Information* (the Caldicott Report), Department of Health October 2006 *The Caldicott Guardian Manual* and 1999/012 Caldicott Guardians).

5.5.1 Consent

Confidential information may be disclosed with the explicit or implied consent of the person who provided such information. In practical terms it is advisable for written consent to be obtained and recorded. (The introductory chapter explores the issues of consent and capacity to consent.)

If consent cannot be obtained or is refused but an alternative legal basis for information sharing exists and it is justified to share information, you should still consider informing the confider of any proposed disclosure. This enables them to object through the courts if they wish.

5.5.2 Court orders and other legal obligations

Court order to disclose

Practitioners must take care not to confuse a court order to disclose with a mere request from a solicitor, police officer or officer of the court.

The courts have extensive powers to order disclosure of information in civil and criminal proceedings, including by witness summons, subpoena and warrants authorising seizure of confidential documents.

If any person considers that documents should not be disclosed on grounds of legal professional privilege or confidentiality, or considers that an order or warrant ought not to have been made or issued, an application can be made for non-disclosure on grounds of public interest immunity (PII) hearing. At such a PII hearing the relevant judge will consider objections to disclosure, any special circumstances, and whether it is really in the public interest for the document not to be disclosed (see **Chapter 7**).

Good practice

It is important that those receiving court orders for disclosure check that the order specifies the information sought, who it will be disclosed to, and for what purposes. It will rarely be appropriate to order disclosure of an entire file.

No more information should be disclosed than is strictly necessary to comply with the order. If the order appears to impose an excessive burden (and, where personal data is involved, requires disclosure of irrelevant material, contrary to the DPA 1998) consideration should be given to seeking an amendment to the terms of the order. Note that a court order to disclose information containing personal data should satisfy DPA 1998 Sched. 2, para. 3; Sched. 3, para. 6.

Consider whether third parties have provided information, which they expect to be kept confidential, and whether they might wish to claim public interest immunity or legal privilege.

Other legal obligation to disclose

If information is sought by a third party, the statutory power under which information is sought should be established and considered before any decision to disclose is made. Care must be taken not to confuse those statutory provisions which require disclosure with provisions which merely allow disclosure (for example, DPA 1998, s.29).

Certain statutes require information to be shared, notwithstanding that the information is confidential. Doctors, for example, are required to notify the local authority about infectious illnesses which pose a risk to public health and to provide information about the patient, including name, sex and address (Public Health (Control of Diseases) Act 1984 (provisions to be replaced upon implementation of the Health and Social Care Act 2008)). Again, no more information should be provided than is strictly required.

Whilst the Proceeds of Crime Act 2002 and the Money Laundering Regulations 2003 (SI 2003/3075) may override the duty of confidentiality, solicitors must consider whether information is additionally subject to legal professional privilege (see **Chapter 7**). Difficult judgements will still need to be made whether or not information should be shared with relevant authorities.

5.5.3 Public interest disclosures

Whilst individuals arguably have private interests/rights to confidentiality, there is also a strong public interest in maintaining confidentiality (*W* v. *Egdell* [1990] 1 All ER 835). However:

> although the basis of the law's protection of confidence is that there is a public interest that confidences should be preserved and protected by the law, nevertheless that public interest may be outweighed by some other countervailing public interest which favours disclosure. This limitation may apply . . . to all types of confidential information. It is this limiting principle which may require a court to carry out a balancing operation, weighing the public interest in maintaining confidence against a countervailing public interest favouring disclosure
>
> (*Attorney General* v. *Guardian Newspapers* [1990] 1 AC 109 Lord Goff of Chieveley, para. 282)

In order for confidential information to be disclosed in the public interest:

- there must be a public interest in disclosure; and
- the public interest in disclosure must be stronger than the public interest in maintaining confidentiality.

Determining whether disclosure is in the overriding public interest requires individuals to carry out a difficult balancing act. It will depend on the individual facts of each case. The value to the confider of maintaining confidentiality (whether financial, emotional or commercial) is relevant. As noted above, the courts recognise an important public interest in upholding contractual provisions obliging confidence). It is important to consider whether disclosure will, in reality, benefit the public. (If disclosing that an individual committed a criminal offence would not result in their prosecution due to age or illness, but will cause significant harm to the offender or others disclosure may not be in the public interest). The guiding principle will be proportionality.

Whilst it is a long-established principle that 'there is no confidence in iniquity', i.e. criminality, 'for a claimant's conduct to "trigger the public interest defence" a very high degree of misbehaviour must be demonstrated. Relatively trivial matters, even though falling short of the highest standards people might set for themselves, will not suffice' (*Associated Newspapers Limited* v. *HRH Prince of Wales* [2006] EWCA Civ 1776).

When might disclosure in the public interest be justified?

Guidance to the Law Society's Code of Conduct 2007 (as updated) (rule 4.01) suggests disclosure in the public interest *may* be justified:

- Where disclosure is necessary to prevent a client or a third party committing a criminal act that the solicitor reasonably believes likely to result in serious bodily harm.
- Where a child or adult client discloses abuse against a child but refuses to allow the solicitor to disclose, and the threat to the child's life or health, both mental and physical, is sufficiently serious to justify breaching the duty.
- Where it is reasonably necessary to disclose confidential information either to establish a defence to a criminal charge or civil claim brought by the client against the solicitor, or where the solicitor's conduct is being investigated or considered by the Solicitors Regulation Authority or Solicitors Disciplinary Tribunal.
- Where proceedings under the Children Act 1989 are ongoing and experts' reports are commissioned for the proceedings (they must be disclosed).
- In order to comply with a duty to report to the Legal Services Commission.

Guidance on disclosure of confidential information is also available to doctors registered with the General Medical Council. Some of the practical advice offered will be relevant to many professionals.

Adapted from General Medical Council (GMC) *Confidentiality: Protecting and Providing Information* April 2004

- Make sure that anyone to whom you disclose personal information understands it is given to them in confidence, which they must respect.
- Disclose information if ordered to do so by a court. Consider objecting to the court if attempts are made to compel you to disclose what appear to be irrelevant matters, for example matters relating to the patient's family members who are not party to proceedings.
- Before considering whether to disclose personal information 'in the public interest' satisfy yourself that identifiable data are necessary, or that it is not practicable to anonymise the data.
- Where there is a serious risk to the patient or others, disclosures may be justified even where patients have withheld consent to disclosure.
- Inform patients that a disclosure will be made, wherever practicable. You should document any steps taken to seek or obtain consent and reasons for disclosing information without consent, for example, because patients lack capacity to consent; records are of such age and/or number that reasonable efforts to trace patients are unlikely to be successful; the patient has been or may be violent or obtaining consent would undermine the purpose of the disclosure (e.g. disclosures in relation to crime); or action must be taken quickly (for example in the detection or control of outbreaks of some communicable diseases) and there is insufficient time to contact patients.
- If you decide to disclose confidential information be prepared to explain and justify your decision.

- When information relates to a deceased person the DPA 1998 will no longer apply but the duty of confidentiality continues to do so. If the patient asked for information to remain confidential, his or her views should be respected. If the patient did not indicate his expectations, consider (a) whether the disclosure of information may distress or benefit the patient's partner or family; (b) whether disclosure of patient information will in effect disclose information about the patient's family or others; (c) whether the information is already public knowledge or can be anonymised; and (d) the purpose of the disclosure.

5.6 THE HUMAN RIGHTS ACT 1998

In 2001 Lord Mustill recognised clear overlaps between the doctrine of confidentiality and Article 8 of the Convention (the right to respect for privacy) but concluded that:

> privacy and confidentiality are not the same. . . . the reading and copying of personal diaries, letters to relatives or lovers, poems and so on could ground not only an allegation of tortious conduct but also an additional complaint that the privacy of the writer and perhaps also of the recipient have been intruded upon. Such conduct is specially objectionable, not because legal rights have been infringed but because of the insult done to the person as a person. No such complaint would, I believe, be feasible when made by a company, not for the obvious reason that a corporation does not create documents of this kind, but because an intrusion into such matters has an extra dimension, in the shape of the damage done to the sensibilities of a human being by exposing to strangers the workings of his or her inward feelings, emotions, fears and beliefs—a damage which an artificial 'person', having no sensibilities, cannot be made to suffer. A company can have secrets, can have things which should be kept confidential, but I see this as different from the essentially human and personal concept of privacy.
>
> *R* v. *Broadcasting Standards Commission*, ex parte *BBC* [2001] QB 885 p. 900/para. 49

Since that decision, several cases dealing with privacy and confidentiality have reached the higher courts. Where personal information is concerned it seems that the gap between confidentiality and privacy has been narrowed. Lord Woolf suggested in *A* v. *B plc* [2003] QB 195 para. 4 that this was 'because, under section 6 of the Human Rights Act 1998, the court, as a public authority, is required not to act "in a way which is incompatible with a Convention right". The court is able to achieve this by absorbing the rights which Articles 8 and 10 protect into the long-established action for breach of confidence. This involves giving a new strength and breadth to the action so that it accommodates the requirements of those articles.' (See also Buxton LJ's comments in *McKennitt* v. *Ash* [2008] QB 73 para. 11 that the very rules of confidentiality are found in the jurisprudence of Articles 8 and 10.) Eady J also commented recently that:

> Although the law of 'old-fashioned breach of confidence' has been well established for many years, and derives historically from equitable principles, these have been

> extended in recent years under the stimulus of the Human Rights Act 1998 and the content of the convention itself. The law now affords protection to information in respect of which there is a reasonable expectation of privacy, even in circumstances where there is no pre-existing relationship giving rise of itself to an enforceable duty of confidence.
>
> *Mosley* v. *Newsgroup Newspapers Limited* [2008] EWHC 1777, para. 7

The relationship between confidentiality and privacy is undoubtedly complex, but the new approach to confidentiality may not in reality practically alter case outcomes. It will in cases involving a person's private life perhaps require a clearer articulation of arguments under the Convention and a change of language (information about an individual's private life might not be called 'confidential', but rather 'private' information with a claim instead brought for 'misuse of private information' *Campbell* v. *MGN Limited* [2004] UKHL 22, para. 14). The courts are, however, not averse to considering arguments as to breach of confidentiality and breach of Article 8 alongside each other (*Campbell* v. *MGN Limited* [2004] UKHL 22, *Mosley* v. *Newsgroup Newspapers Limited* [2008] EWHC 1777). This makes sense, since Article 8, for example, requires actions taken to be lawful. Breach of personal confidences by a public authority arguably automatically breaches Article 8.

The duty in practice

Donald has just learned that his boss, Edward, has been having a sexual relationship with their colleague Fallon. This is not common knowledge. Edward disclosed the information to Donald in confidence. Edward recently promoted Fallon. The decision to promote Fallon surprised many since George, who also applied for the promotion, was considered by all other employees to be the better person for the job. Donald is unclear whether he should disclose this information to Edward's superiors or to his colleagues.

It seems clear that the information is of a confidential type, and that it was disclosed in circumstances which gave rise to a duty. No disclosure should be made unless (a) Edward consents or (b) Donald can justify disclosure in the overriding public interest.

Mosley v. *Newsgroup Newspapers Limited* [2008] EWHC 1777 para. 20 acknowledges that there could be a genuine public interest in the disclosure of the existence of a sexual relationship in a situation giving rise to favouritism or advancement through corruption. Eady J warned, however, against disproportionate disclosures of unwarranted, salacious details. The Data Protection Act 1998 and the Public Interest Disclosure Act 1998 equally require consideration.

5.7 THE DPA 1998, FOIA 2000 AND THE EIR 2004

An understanding of the duty of confidentiality is essential to proper application of the FOIA 2000, the EIR 2004 and the DPA 1998.

5.7.1 The Freedom of Information Act 2000

The Freedom of Information Act 2000 requires a public authority (defined in FOIA 2000, Sched. 1) to make information it holds available to the public, unless an exemption applies.

Several exemptions may be relevant to confidential information. All relevant exemptions may be relied upon to justify withholding disclosure. However, even if an exemption applies, a public authority can choose to disclose the information held (see also **Chapter 3**).

Three absolute exemptions may potentially apply:

1. Section 41 applies specifically to confidential information.
2. Section 40 prohibits disclosure of personal data (which may also be confidential).
3. Section 44 prohibits disclosure of information if disclosure would constitute or be punishable as a contempt of court. It may apply if, for example, an injunction prohibits disclosure of the confidential information.

Two qualified exemptions may also be relevant, in both cases the public interest test must be applied to determine whether information is exempt:

1. Section 30 applies if the information was acquired by the public authority from a confidential source for the purposes of certain criminal and non-criminal investigations.
2. Section 43 applies if the confidential information is a 'trade secret' and its disclosure would, or would be likely to, prejudice the commercial interests of any person, including the authority.

FOIA 2000, s.41

Section 41 exempts a public authority from providing information, or confirming or denying it holds information obtained from another person, provided disclosure or confirmation whether information is held constitutes an actionable breach of confidence. The exemption does not apply to the authority's own confidential information, but will cover some information held about employees.

Since section 41 is an absolute exemption the authority need not consider the public interest test. In practice, however, a similar public interest balancing act is undertaken under the duty of confidentiality in order to determine whether disclosure is or is not in the overriding public interest (and thus whether disclosure would constitute an actionable breach of confidence).

Factors to consider include:

1. The general public interest in favour of maintaining appropriate confidentiality.
2. The public interest in ensuring public scrutiny of the activities of public authorities.
3. It is unlikely that it will be in the public interest to disclose information: where the duty of confidence arises out of a professional relationship; where disclosure would affect the continued supply of important information; where disclosure would cause risk to the public or personal safety; or where disclosure would damage public administration.

4. Due regard must be had to the interests of the person to whom the duty of confidence is owed.

No regard should be had to the identity of the information requester, or future use of that information. Since extensive further disclosures may be made by the requester it is clearly important to correctly identify when the duty of confidentiality arises. The fact that a contract between the public authority and a third party prohibits the local authority from disclosing information does not enable the local authority to rely on section 41, if the information in question is not of a confidential nature.

5.7.2 The Environmental Information Regulations 2004

The EIR 2004 apply a similar regime to that under FOIA 2000, in relation to environmental information held by public authorities. As with FOIA 2000, an absolute exception to disclosure of personal data applies. The other exceptions relevant to confidential information are:

- Where disclosure would adversely affect the confidentiality of the proceedings of that or any other public authority and such confidentiality is provided by law (reg. 13(5)(d)).
- Where disclosure would adversely affect the confidentiality of commercial or industrial information and such confidentiality is provided by law to protect a legitimate economic interest (reg. 13(5)(e)).
- Where disclosure would adversely affect the interests of the person who provided the information and that person (i) was not under, and could not have been put under, any legal obligation to supply it to that or any other public authority; (ii) did not supply it in circumstances such that that or any other public authority is entitled apart from these Regulations to disclose it; and (iii) has not consented to its disclosure (reg. 13(5)(f)).

Note, the absence of a provision within the EIR 2004 directly equivalent to FOIA 2000, s.41 means that information which might not be disclosed under FOIA 2000 may be disclosable under the EIR 2004. (See, for example, Decision Notice FS50126686, 21/07/06 where information held by the Health Protection Agency concerning investigations into legionnaires disease, was environmental information. The HPA were unable to rely on section 41, reg. 13(5)(e) was considered inapplicable, and in any event the ICO considered disclosure to be in the public interest.)

5.7.3 The Data Protection Act 1998

Whilst:

> the common law obligation to keep a confidence is conceptually quite different from the statutory obligation to process data in accordance with the data protection principles and from the right to respect for private life enshrined in

> Article 8(1) of the European Convention on Human Rights, ... there are overlaps.
>
> (*Stevens* v. *Plymouth City Council* [2002] 1 WLR 2583 para. 33 Hale LJ)

On many occasions the same information is private, confidential, and personal data.

Compliance with the DPA 1998 does not ensure compliance with the duty of confidentiality. The DPA 1998 does not apply to a deceased's personal data, whilst the duty of confidentiality is capable of surviving the death of the confider. However, it makes sense when sharing confidential information to consider the relevance of the DPA 1998 principles.

Compliance with the duty of confidentiality does not ensure compliance with the DPA 1998. Whilst sensible for professionals to check that confidential information is accurate and up to date, if the information is not personal data there will be no consequences for failing to do so. Breach of confidentiality will, however, result in breach of the DPA 1998 first principle.

Can it ever be sensible to consider the duty of confidentiality without considering the relevance of other legal regimes (and vice versa)?

Practical example

Decision Notice FS50153179 27 November 2007 *Trafford Metropolitan Borough Council*

Trafford Metropolitan Borough Council was asked to provide information from social services records about the applicant's deceased mother. The ICO determined that information, including sensitive personal data, relating to the deceased's carer, was exempt under section 40. Most of the remaining information related to the deceased, and had been obtained from medical professionals, the carer or the deceased. The Commissioner acknowledged that individuals accept social services care upon the basis that their information will be kept confidential and will not be disclosed without consent, accordingly a threat of further disclosure might inhibit clients from providing important information. The Commissioner recognised that the deceased's personal representatives would have a theoretical right to sue the Council for breach of such confidentiality. Note, however, that there was no discussion of disclosure in the public interest in this case, and there may be circumstances when disclosure in the public interest may be justified.

5.8 ENFORCING THE DUTY AND REMEDIES FOR BREACH

The issue of consequences and remedies for breach of confidentiality is a problematic one. Often the damage caused by an unauthorised disclosure is irreparable. No remedy after the information has been disclosed can truly compensate for that disclosure. It is for this reason that confidentiality clauses setting out a specific right to obtain an injunction to prevent information being disclosed are often included in commercial contracts, and why the pre-emptive strike of applying for an injunction has become so popular.

5.8.1 Preventing disclosure

In *Duchess of Argyll* v. *Duke of Argyll* [1967] Ch 302 Ungoed-Thomas J made clear that 'a breach of contract or trust or faith could arise independently of any right of property or contract'. The court, in the exercise of its equitable jurisdiction, would act to prevent a continuing breach (rather than to prevent the benefits afforded by breach). The court is more likely to award an injunction in relation to personal information than trade secrets (the harm in such a case being more easily assessed in financial terms, to award damages, see *Coco* v. *AN Clark (Engineers) Ltd* [1969] RPC 41).

An injunction can prevent disclosure to particular people or in a particular geographical location such as a particular country or group of countries, usually for a specific period of time. However, first, the person whose confidential information will be revealed must know before the event that disclosure will happen. In practice, this is rare. Second, it may be unclear against whom an injunction needs to be obtained. Third, an injunction, as an equitable remedy, will only be appropriate where it will provide benefit, for example, if it will prevent a breach, or will prevent further disclosures and thus further damage (see *Cream Holdings Ltd* v. *Bannerjee* [2005] 1 AC 253).

From the perspective of those wishing to disclose confidential information another concern arises. Injunctions can be extremely wide and very restrictive on those wishing to disclose information (in *Venables & Thompson* v. *News Group Newspapers and others* [2001] 1 All ER 908 an injunction was granted preventing media disclosure of information about the pair's whereabouts, in any country, indefinitely). However, the court will be cautious about granting a broad general injunction, with injunctions normally aimed at the prevention of some specific wrong by a specific person.

In order to obtain an interim injunction (particularly important where disclosure of confidential information is anticipated), the Court must consider whether there is a serious question to be tried, and balance the parties' competing interests and rights (*American Cyanamid Co* v. *Ethicon Ltd* [1975] AC 396; see **Chapter 6** for issues to consider when balancing ECHR, Arts. 8 and 10). Relevant factors include the nature of the case, the harm caused to either party by making or not making the injunction, the ability of the parties to pay compensation, whether damages would adequately compensate the claimant if the injunction were refused, whether damages would adequately compensate the defendant if the injunction were inappropriately granted, effects on any innocent third party, and whether publication of information is imminent (in which case an injunction is unlikely).

5.8.2 Damages for breach

AG v. *Guardian Newspapers Ltd* [1990] 1 AC 109 firmly established that a person could claim damages if their information was disclosed in breach of confidence. The extent of the damages available will depend on whether the action is brought in breach of contract or in tort.

When a contract exists between two business parties, the loss that is sustained by the confider may be calculated either by reference to the price that a willing buyer would be prepared to pay for the information, or if the information could be obtained by engaging a consultant, then damages equating to the fee chargeable by the consultant.

Certainly, unless actual financial loss can be established, damages paid for breach of contract are likely to be minimal (*Douglas* v. *Hello! Ltd and others* [2005] EWCA Civ 595) with no damages available for shock or mental distress (which in any event is difficult to prove). The costs of bringing a claim are often prohibitive.

A claim for an account of profit, if demonstrable, might be more likely to succeed. An account of profits is available to a claimant where the equitable right has been misused (that is, where no contract exists). It enables the claimant to claim the profits made by the defendant from the breach rather than compensation for damage (and as such it may be more valuable to the claimant). For example in *Spycatcher*, both Peter Wright and the *Sunday Times* committed a breach in publication of Peter Wright's memoirs. Both were called to account for their profits.

The question also arises as to who will pay damages. Whilst it will usually be an individual (a doctor, a social worker, a secretary) who discloses information, when an employee discloses information in breach of the duty, it is usual to sue the employer via the principle of vicarious liability for its employees. Practically a large employer is more likely to be able to pay damages from their own resources, or through insurance, than the individual.

Often, where the person disclosing the information is a professional such as a doctor, social worker, lawyer, etc., the best approach for a victim of wrongful disclosure is to make a formal complaint to that person's regulatory body. For example, the General Medical Council (GMC) is known to take such complaints extremely seriously and a finding of unauthorised disclosure can have a serious impact on a doctor's registration and future career. It is perhaps for this reason that in practice some professionals are particularly wary of disclosing confidential information.

5.8.3 Alternative remedies

In some cases, a search order to ascertain the location of material may be appropriate. At the discretion of the High Court, orders may also be made for delivery up and/or destruction of documents (or of articles made in breach of confidence). Delivery up may be ordered when the claimant owns the confidential documents, even if the defendant has added material to them (*Industrial Furnaces Ltd* v. *Reaves* [1970] RPC 605). Destruction may be ordered if documents, articles, machinery used to produce infringing articles

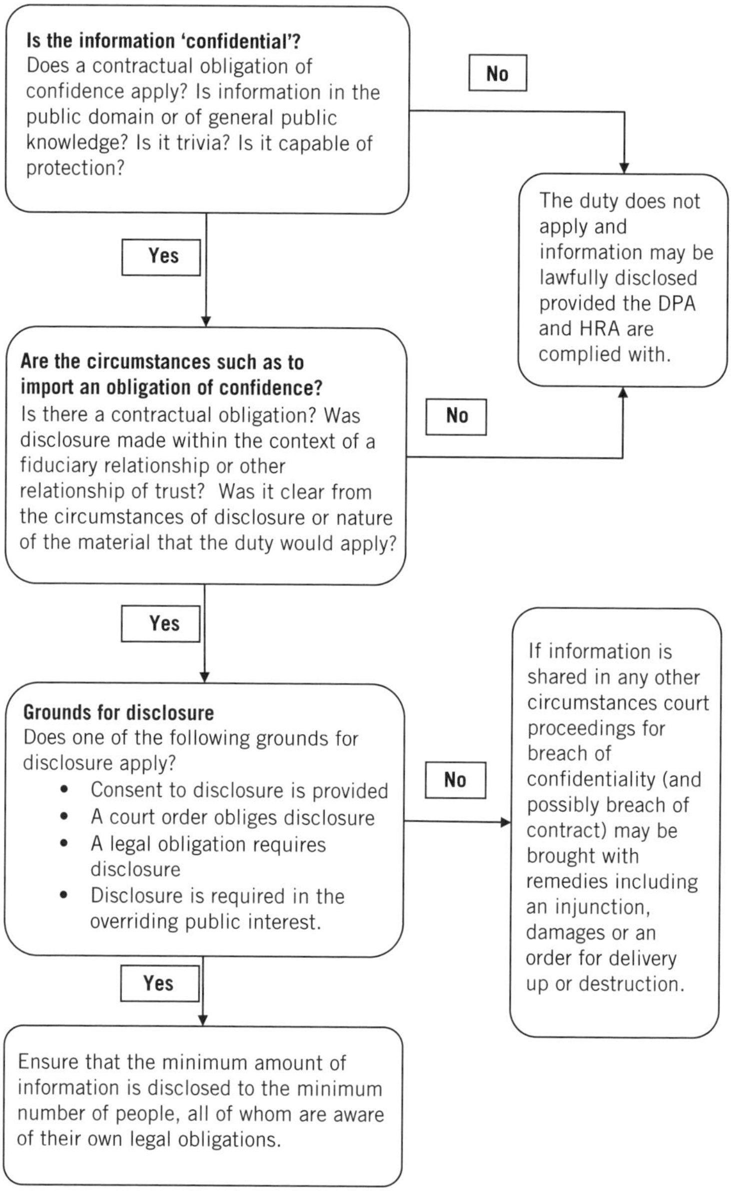

Figure 5.1 Summary of the duty of confidentiality

(for example, exact copies) are owned by the defendant, where the confidential information is important to continued breaches, and an award of damages will not suffice (*Reid & Sigrist Ltd* v. *Moss and Mechanism Ltd* (1932) 49 RPC 461).

If a court order prohibiting disclosure is flouted, a charge of contempt of court may be brought, and if proved can have serious consequences including prison.

5.9 SUMMARY

An understanding of whether information is confidential and can be lawfully disclosed is required whenever an information sharing decision is being taken, irrespective of whether the information is personal or commercial in nature, and whether disclosure aims to protect a child's health, to assist with a criminal investigation, or to determine whether to make information publicly available under FOIA 2000. By answering a number of key questions, it is much easier to determine (a) whether the duty applies and (b) whether information can nonetheless be disclosed (see **Figure 5.1**).

CHAPTER 6

The Human Rights Act 1998 and the European Convention

Claire Bessant

6.1 INTRODUCTION

In Chapters 1 and 5 we identified the increasing influence that the Human Rights Act 1998 (HRA 1998) is playing in relation to judicial review and the law of confidentiality. However, the influence of the HRA 1998, and the European Convention for the Protection of Human Rights and Fundamental Freedoms (the Convention), to which the HRA 1998 gives effect, is much wider. Several Convention articles afford rights either for information to be shared, or impose limits upon information sharing.

In this chapter we consider the application of the Convention and the HRA 1998, identify relevant Convention articles and highlight remedies afforded in relation to Convention breaches.

6.2 THE HUMAN RIGHTS ACT AND THE CONVENTION

The Convention, ratified by the UK in 1953, details certain fundamental rights and freedoms afforded to UK citizens. Prior to implementation of the HRA 1998, an individual claiming that a public authority/the UK Government had breached the Convention needed to take lengthy and costly proceedings to the European Court of Human Rights in Strasbourg (the European Court).

The HRA 1998 (in force since 2 October 2000), now enables individuals to challenge decisions which breach the Convention rights protected by the HRA 1998, before domestic courts. The HRA 1998 also imposes specific obligations upon public authorities, particularly courts.

6.2.1 Convention rights for the purposes of the HRA 1998

The Convention rights enforceable through the HRA 1998 are:

- Articles 2 to 12 and 14 of the Convention;
- Articles 1 to 3 of the First Protocol; and
- Article 1 of the Thirteenth Protocol (HRA 1998, s.1).

6.2.2 To whom does the HRA 1998 apply?

HRA 1998, s.6 requires public authorities to act in accordance with the Convention unless they are required to do otherwise by primary legislation which cannot be interpreted by the authority in another way.

Public authorities (s.6(3))

The term public authority includes courts and tribunals.

It covers organisations which are obviously public authorities, for example, local authorities, police and prison officers, government departments and NHS trusts (but not either House of Parliament exercising legislative functions). These public authorities must act in accordance with the Convention, whether or not actions involve exercise of functions of a private nature.

Other organisations which are essentially private in nature, must comply with the Convention when exercising public functions (s.6(3)(b)). This prevents the state from escaping liability by delegating public functions to private bodies (*Marcic* v. *Thames Water Utilities Ltd* [2002] QB 929). Where a private body exercises private and public functions, the crucial factor is whether the function performed is of a public nature, in other words is being done by or on behalf of the public (*Parochial Church Council of Aston Cantlow* v. *Wallbank* [2003] UKHL 37, para. 11). Their private functions are not subject to section 6.

Is a private organisation exercising public functions?

- Has the state assumed responsibility for the particular task?
- Absence of a statutory power or duty applying to the function may imply that the function is private in nature and unsuitable for public regulation.
- Does the state directly or indirectly, regulate, supervise and inspect performance of the function?
- Is the function one for which, whether directly or indirectly, the state pays?
- Is there an important public interest in having the task undertaken?
- What is the level of risk of violating the individual's Convention right provoked by improperly exercising the function?

(see *YL (by her litigation friend the Official Solicitor)* v. *Birmingham City Council and others* [2007] UKHL 27 paras. 6–11; 63–72).

Individuals

The Convention and the HRA 1998 primarily impose duties upon public authorities/the state, which are enforceable by the citizen. However, a court or tribunal determining disputes between individuals must, as a public authority, act compatibly with the Convention. Convention rights can, therefore, be used in disputes between individuals or an individual and a non-governmental body just as in disputes between individuals and public bodies. There is no logic for affording less protection against an individual than against the state, for example, in relation to dissemination of personal information (*Douglas* v. *Hello! Ltd* [2004] 2 AC 457 paras. 17–18, para. 50).

6.2.3 Specific duties imposed upon the courts

Domestic courts are required to interpret domestic law in accordance with the Convention and its case law.

Interpreting legislation in accordance with the Convention

The courts must read and give effect to statute and subordinate legislation (statutory instruments) in a way which is compatible with the Convention (HRA 1998, s.3).

The courts cannot rewrite legislation which is clearly incompatible, but may interpret their duty in a very broad manner, implying additional words to ensure compatibility, or limiting the scope of a broadly phrased provision (*R* v. *A* [2002] 1 AC 45 per Lord Steyn, para. 44). In *R (Morgan Grenfell & Co Ltd)* v. *Special Commissioner of Income Tax and another* [2002] UKHL 21 the House of Lords limited statutory disclosure powers which impliedly permitted disclosure of documents protected by legal professional privilege, recognising that legal professional privilege is considered a fundamental Convention right. In *R* v. *A* [2002] 1 AC 45 the House of Lords interpreted the Youth Justice and Criminal Evidence Act 1999, which placed strict limitations on admitting evidence of a rape complainant's sexual history, to admit such evidence where a failure to do so would deprive the accused of a fair trial under Article 6.

If primary or subordinate legislation cannot be interpreted compatibly the High Court, Court of Appeal, House of Lords and Privy Council may make a declaration of incompatibility. The declaration does not affect the provision's validity. It is not binding on the parties to the proceedings where it is made (HRA 1998, s.4). It therefore provides little real benefit to the complainant. However, it may provoke remedial action (s.10) – enactment of amending legislation.

Note HRA 1998, s.3 applies to legislation, not common law. However, where common law rules cannot be interpreted in accordance with the Convention, the HRA 1998 requires the courts to act compatibly with the Convention. Accordingly, as we saw in **Chapter 5**, Article 8 and Article 10 have been absorbed into the law of confidentiality.

Practical example

The police have asked a doctor to disclose his patient's confidential information. Both the police and the doctor must consider that individual's right to respect for privacy (Article 8). They must ensure interferences with that right are lawful, justified and proportionate. If the police ask the court to order disclosure, the court must comply with Article 8 and any other convention rights raised, unless it is impossible for them to do so in accordance with the legislation.

Interpreting legislation in accordance with Convention case law

To ensure compatibility with the Convention and the interpretation given to the Convention by the European Court and the Commission, domestic courts must take account of these bodies' case law and determinations (s.2).

This does not explicitly require courts to follow European decisions. Where a House of Lords or Court of Appeal decision is inconsistent with a later European Court decision, the domestic decision should be followed. This ensures certainty in the law and recognises that:

> the Strasbourg court accords a margin of appreciation, often generous, to the decisions of national authorities and attaches much importance to the peculiar facts of the case. Thus it is for national authorities, including national courts particularly, to decide in the first instance how the principles expounded in Strasbourg should be applied in the special context of national legislation, law, practice and social and other conditions.
>
> *Kaye and others* v. *Lambeth London Borough Council* [2006] 2 AC 465 HL, per Bingham LJ, para. 40–44).

However:

> In the absence of some special circumstances . . . the court should follow any clear and constant jurisprudence of the European Court of Human Rights. If it does not do so there is at least a possibility that the case will go to that court which is likely in the ordinary case to follow its own constant jurisprudence required to follow it.
>
> *R (on the application of Alconbury Developments Ltd)* v. *Secretary of State for the Environment, Transport and the Regions and other cases* [2001] UKHL 23 per Lord Slynn, para. 26

Relevant issues when deciding not to follow Strasbourg jurisprudence might be where the jurisprudence relates to a country with a civil law system, or different legal traditions.

6.2.4 Types of Convention rights

Absolute and qualified rights

Convention rights are characterised as absolute or qualified rights.

In principle, no interference with absolute rights is permissible. In practice, the European Court may limit their scope.

State interference in qualified rights is permissible if the interference is prescribed by law, in pursuit of a legitimate aim, necessary in a democratic society and proportionate. The European Court will accept no further limitation of such qualified rights, since the Convention article itself states the permissible qualifications (see *Golder* v. *UK* (1975) 1 EHRR 524, para. 44).

Positive and negative obligations

Convention rights often impose negative obligations, which prohibit public authorities from taking unjustified steps which violate Convention rights, for example, prohibiting sharing personal information contrary to the Article 8 right to respect for private life.

Where a Convention right imposes a positive obligation the state must take positive steps to ensure rights are not violated. A breach arises when there is a failure to act.

Practical example

In *Osman* v. *UK* (1998) 29 EHRR 245 the European Court held that Article 2 (which requires the right to life to be protected be law) expressly imposed positive obligations on the police to take reasonable steps to prevent foreseeable homicidal attacks. In reality, whether it is a negative or positive obligation being interfered with, similar principles apply; a fair balance must be struck between the competing interests of the individuals concerned and society as a whole.

6.2.5 Interpreting the Convention: key principles

Several key principles are used by the European Court when applying the Convention;

(a) the Convention's interpretation must afford effective, universal recognition to human rights;
(b) the Convention is a living instrument;
(c) Convention rights must be applied in a non-discriminatory manner;
(d) where qualified rights are raised, interference must be:

 (i) lawful;
 (ii) necessary; and
 (iii) proportionate.

Effective recognition

The principle of providing effective rights requires rights to be construed widely. Accordingly in *Niemitz* v. *Germany* (1992) 16 EHRR 97 the European Court considered the Article 8 right to respect for home and private life wide enough to cover business premises, activities and correspondence. Limitations or exceptions must be construed narrowly (see *Klass* v. *Germany* (1978) 2 EHRR 214).

In order to ensure rights are effective, the European Court may imply additional specific elements into Convention articles (for example implying a right to disclosure of unused prosecution material into the Article 6 right to a fair trial, see **6.6**).

A living instrument

The Convention must be interpreted in the light of present day conditions (*Tyrer* v. *UK* (1970–80) 2 EHRR 1, at para. 31), taking account of current moral standards and scientific expertise, and current opinions as to what is necessary in a democratic society.

This means that the European Court is not bound by its earlier decisions, although it requires good reasons to depart from earlier decisions, and evidence that a new social or legal standard is now accepted to such an extent that a new interpretation is required. In practice this imposes a difficult task for public authorities who must acknowledge developments in societal views whilst following existing domestic case law.

Non-discrimination

Article 14 states that:

> The enjoyment of the rights and freedoms set forth in this Convention shall be secured without discrimination on any ground such as sex, race, colour, language, religion, political or other opinion, national or social origin, association with a national minority, property, birth or other status (other status including sexual orientation and professional status).

To bring a successful Article 14 claim, an applicant must demonstrate an unjustified difference in treatment in the delivery of any convention article other than Article 14. The other Convention right need not be breached.

Practice guidance

To avoid breaching Article 14 consider:

- Is the individual being treated differently to others in a similar situation on the basis of their status?
- Is this in relation to the enjoyment of one of the rights of the Convention?
- Any difference in treatment must have an objective and reasonable justification.
- There must be a legitimate aim.

The means and the aim must be proportionate.

Lawful

Several articles refer to interference being lawful, in accordance with or prescribed by law. Essentially, this means that:

> Firstly the law must be adequately accessible: the citizens must be able to have an indication that it is adequate in the circumstances of the legal rules applicable to a given case. Secondly, a norm cannot be regarded as a 'law' unless it is formulated with sufficient precision to enable the citizen to regulate his conduct.
>
> *Sunday Times* v. *UK* (1979–80) EHRR 245, para. 49

Accordingly, any information sharing (which may engage both Articles 8 and 10, both qualified rights) must be authorised by statute, secondary legislation, European Community law, clear common law principles or measures which have their base in statute, such as a statutory code (*Sunday Times* v. *UK* (1979) 2 EHRR 245; *R (Munjaz)* v. *Mersey Care NHS Trust* [2005] UKHL 58). The scope of, and guidance on the exercise of discretionary rules should be clear (*Silver* v. *UK* (1983) 5 EHRR 347, *Olsson* v. *Sweden* (1988) 11 EHRR 259).

Practice point

Where an individual is subject to secret surveillance it is difficult for the individual to know whether his communications are likely to be intercepted and shared. In such instances the domestic law must clarify when such surveillance can occur, and provide adequate safeguards against abuse.

Necessity

Interferences with qualified rights must pursue one of the legitimate aims detailed in the relevant article (the aims varying depending on the article). In addition, any specific policy or action adopted must be demonstrably necessary in a democratic society to fulfil that aim. The more pressing the social need, the easier it will be to justify interference.

Proportionality

Where interference with a Convention right is necessary to achieve a particular aim, and a choice of measures is available, the least intrusive step possible should be taken, bearing in mind that a balance must be struck between the competing interests of the public as a whole and the individual whose rights are affected.

Proportionality is particularly relevant to lawful information sharing (see **6.7**).

In determining whether a state has acted proportionately, the court will allow a certain measure of discretion, known as the margin of appreciation. This allows domestic courts to take account of the social situation when considering the proportionality of interferences with Convention rights.

Article 3 provides an absolute prohibition on torture, inhuman or degrading treatment. There is little or no margin of appreciation available to the state if such a level of mistreatment is found. A significantly wider margin applies to interferences with Article 8, which permits public authorities to take certain steps which are necessary in a democratic society, but which interfere with that right. However, cogent reasons are needed to justify interference with intimate elements of private life (*Dudgeon* v. *UK* (1981) 4 EHRR 149), with legal professional privilege (*Silver* v. *UK* (1983) 5 EHRR 347) and with the right to freedom of expression (*Barthold* v. *Germany* (1985) 7 EHRR 383), interference on national security grounds is relatively easy to justify (*Leander* v. *Sweden* (1987) 9 EHRR 433). The state is also granted wide discretion to interfere to protect morals (see *Handyside* v. *UK* (1976) 1 EHRR 737), tax and economics. A very narrow margin applies where the European Court considers that across Europe proposed actions would not be accepted.

Any interference which restricts a right to such an extent that its very essence is impaired will be disproportionate. Accordingly if an obscene book is confiscated, but no consideration is given to allowing publication with the offensive pages removed, such action may be disproportionate (see *Handyside*).

Practical example

When devising information sharing policies consideration must be given both to the public policy objective, for example, protecting children from significant harm, and the means employed to achieve that objective. A policy which requires Connexions to share information with numerous other agencies whenever a child discloses they are having under-age intercourse, whether or not it was consensual and with another child of the same age, might not be a proportionate interference with the child's right to respect for privacy

6.3 RELEVANT CONVENTION RIGHTS

This chapter focuses upon Articles 2, 3, 6, 8 and 10. All are relevant to information sharing, the last two being of greatest importance.

Article 5 is also of limited relevance. Where an individual is arrested or detained, it requires them to be provided with certain information, as a minimum the essential legal and factual grounds for detention (*Fox, Campbell and Hartley* v. *UK* (1990) 13 EHRR 157). Article 5(1)(b) authorises detention for non-compliance with court orders, or to ensure compliance with a specific legal obligation which the individual has failed to comply with or which must now be fulfilled, provided there is no other practical alternative way to ensure compliance. Detention has been permitted where an obligation to provide information and documents was not complied with (*McVeigh, O'Neill and Evans* v. *UK* Apps Nos. 8025/77 and 8027/77; 25 DR 15).

6.3.1 Conflicts

In many situations more than one right may be engaged. For example, where a doctor suffers from a life-threatening medical condition, which might be transferred to patients in his care, the doctor's right to respect for privacy under Article 8 is engaged, but the patients' Article 2 right to life is also relevant.

Inherent 'in the whole of the Convention is a search for a fair balance between the demands of the general interests of the community and the requirement of the protection of the individual's fundamental rights' (*Soering* v. *UK* (1989) 11 EHRR 439, para. 89). Therefore, we must not only consider the legitimate justifications for interference afforded by specific articles, but must balance conflicting rights against each other. Wherever possible, we explore potential conflicts and the courts' approaches to resolving them.

6.4 ARTICLE 2

Article 2 protects the right to life. It prohibits public authorities from killing individuals, save in limited circumstances. It requires the state to make laws prohibiting killing, and to properly punish and properly investigate killings (in *Jordan* v. *UK* (2003) 37 EHRR 2 failures to disclose witness statements, and to provide security service evidence breached Article 2, thus proper investigation may imply some information sharing).

Article 2 also imposes implied obligations to protect individuals from threats to their lives posed by third parties and by themselves.

- In *Osman* v. *UK* (1990) 1 FLR 193, a headmaster shared information with the police and local education authority in respect of perceived threats to a child posed by a teacher. The teacher carried out various acts of vandalism but was not arrested. The teacher killed the child's father. The European Court recognised that the teacher's conduct in causing criminal damage did not suggest he would kill the father. Article 2 was not breached since it could not be shown that:

> The authorities knew or ought to have known at the time of the existence of a real and immediate risk to the life of an identified individual or individuals from the criminal acts of a third party and that they failed to take measures within the scope of their powers which, judged reasonably, might have been expected to avoid that risk' (para. 116). ('Measures' arguably encompasses inter-agency information sharing for public protection purposes).

- Article 2 also applies 'in the context of any activity, whether public or not, in which the right to life may be at stake, and . . . in the case of industrial activities, which by their very nature are dangerous, such as the operation of waste-collection sites.' (*Oneryildiz* v. *Turkey* App no. 48939/99 para. 71) In relation to such dangerous activities the European Court suggests the state should provide, through legislative and administrative means, for the:

  > licensing, setting up, operation, security and supervision of the activity and must make it compulsory for all those concerned to take practical measures to ensure the effective protection of citizens whose lives might be endangered by the inherent risks. Among these preventive measures, particular emphasis should be placed on the public's right to information (*Oneryildiz* para. 90).

  Public authorities have therefore been required to provide information about exposure to hazards, such as radiation, where such exposure engenders real risks to family members' health (*LCB* v. *UK* (1999) 27 EHRR 212, para. 38).

Conflicts between Article 2 and other rights have arisen.

Interferences with Article 10, the right to freedom of expression, have been justified in order to protect life (see *Venables* v. *News Group Newspapers Ltd* [2001] Fam 430 in which a worldwide injunction was granted protecting the claimants' identity and location, in order to protect them from risk of serious injury and death).

Where interferences with the Article 8 right to respect for privacy arise, the rights afforded by Articles 2 and 8 must be balanced against each other, recognising that whilst Article 2 provides an absolute right to life, the Article 8 right is qualified, and interference may be justified, for example to protect others' rights.

6.5 ARTICLE 3

Article 3 imposes an absolute prohibition on public authorities subjecting individuals to torture, inhuman or degrading treatment or punishment. (Techniques employed by the police, security services, etc. to elucidate information, or solitary confinement to prevent criminals collaborating or to prevent disclosure of sensitive information, may, depending upon the severity of the suffering, breach Article 3 (see *Krocher and Moller* v. *Austria* App no. 8463/78 34 DR 24; *Treholt* v. *Norway* App no. 14610/89 71 DR 168).

Public authorities must also take reasonable steps to prevent ill-treatment being inflicted by others.

States must take all reasonable steps to avoid real, immediate risks of ill-treatment posed by individuals, where the authorities have or ought to have had knowledge of those risks (*Z* v. *UK* [2001] 2 FLR 612).

Whilst Article 3 does not define 'ill-treatment', it must attain a minimum level of severity to fall within Article 3's scope, relevant factors to determine this including the circumstances of the case, the duration of the treatment, its physical or mental effects, and, in some cases, the sex, age and state of health of the victim (*Ireland* v. *UK* (1978) 2 EHRR 25).

In *E* v. *UK* App no. 33218/96 where an attacker had been convicted and imprisoned for sexual offences against his step-children, inadequate investigation, cooperation and communication by authorities upon his release meant further risks he posed were not adequately addressed. Article 3 was breached.

Independent, thorough investigations of incidents of abuse, torture, etc. must be taken speedily in order to learn lessons and prevent further breaches (as under Article 2 thorough investigation necessitates information sharing).

Conflicts inevitably arise between the Article 8 privacy rights of abusers and victims and the Article 3 rights of victims and potential victims. This very issue arose in *Z* v. *UK* (above). Both the Commission and European Court concluded that whilst the Article 8 rights of parents and other family members must be respected, where child abuse and neglect reaches the threshold of inhuman and degrading treatment, interference with Article 8 is justified.

6.6 ARTICLE 6

1. In the determination of his civil rights and obligations or of any criminal charge against him, everyone is entitled to a fair and public hearing within a reasonable time by an independent and impartial tribunal established by law. Judgement shall be pronounced publicly but the press and public may be excluded from all or part of the trial in the interests of morals, public order or national security in a democratic society, where the interests of juveniles or the protection of the private life of the parties so require, or to the extent strictly necessary in the opinion of the court in special circumstances where publicity would prejudice the interests of justice.
2. Everyone charged with a criminal offence shall be presumed innocent until proved guilty according to law.

3. Everyone charged with a criminal offence has the following minimum rights:
   (a) to be informed promptly, in a language which he understands and in detail, of the nature and cause of the accusation against him;
   (b) to have adequate time and facilities for the preparation of his own defence;
   (c) to defend himself in person or through legal assistance of his own choosing or, if he has not sufficient means to pay for legal assistance, to be given it free when the interests of justice so require;
   (d) to examine or have examined witnesses against him and to obtain the attendance and examination of witnesses on his behalf under the same conditions as witnesses against him;
   (e) to have the free assistance of an interpreter if he cannot understand or speak the language used in court.

Article 6 is relevant to information sharing because:

- It affords individuals certain rights to obtain information needed to achieve justice when decisions affecting them are taken.
- It promotes open access to decision making, and, subject to certain exclusions which protect individuals' rights, affords opportunities for third parties including the media, to attend court and obtain information.

The specific rights that an individual is afforded under Article 6 differ depending upon whether the matter relates to civil or criminal proceedings. Article 6(1) applies to civil and criminal proceedings. Ordinarily, Article 6(2) and (3) apply only to criminal proceedings. The European Court has concluded, however, that where the consequences of civil proceedings are particularly serious they should merit due process guarantees analogous to those provided to the defence in criminal proceedings (*Albert* v. *Belgium; Le Compte* v. *Belgium* (1983) 5 EHRR 533 concerning disciplinary proceedings against doctors. The same principles are reflected in case law concerning disciplinary proceedings of other professions regulated in the public interest, including lawyers).

6.6.1 Civil rights and obligations, and criminal charges

Article 6(1) applies to proceedings to determine a dispute, about civil rights and obligations of a genuine and serious nature. The dispute may concern the existence of the right, its scope or the way it is exercised. A civil right must be provided by domestic law, or under European Union law (for example, under the Data Protection Directive). It must generally be of personal, private or economic nature. A matter entirely within a public authority's discretion may not be a right.

Article 6(1) applies to, among others, family proceedings, proceedings relating to contracts between private individuals and the state (i.e. public works contracts), proceedings affecting commercial interests (i.e. relating to patent rights), and professional disciplinary proceedings where the individual's right to practise his or her profession is at stake.

Article 6(1)–(3) applies from when a person is charged with a criminal offence until any appeal is determined.

Article 6 rights are not, however, afforded to individuals:

- In certain proceedings relating to asylum, expulsion and nationality.
- Where proceedings relate to the employment or dismissal of public officials, civil servants, the armed forces or the police (*Pellegrin* v. *France* (2001) 31 EHRR 26).
- Where the issue relates to deprivation of liberty. In such cases Article 5 provides safeguards for court proceedings which determine the lawfulness of detention (see *R (Roberts)* v. *Parole Board* [2005] 2 AC 738 in which the use of a special advocate was approved as appropriate means for protecting an informant's rights whilst ensuring information could be scrutinised on the defendant's behalf).

Rights to access information and Article 6

In *Gaskin* v. *UK* (1989) 12 EHRR 36 the European Court concluded that Article 8 afforded a civil right to the applicant to obtain his personal data from a local authority.

Where the individual seeks information not personal to them it may not engage Article 6. In *Barry* v. *France* App No 14497/89 Dec 14.10.91 access to documents relating to political prisoners was requested by an organisation which defended such individuals. Denying access was not determinative of the applicant organisation's civil rights.

A decision not to disclose redacted portions of an applicant's police file (which would reveal the identity of members of security services) was also found not to determine the applicant's civil rights.

McGinley and Egan v. *UK* (1998) 27 EHRR 1 paras. 85–6 confirms, however, that if applicants are prevented from gaining access to documents, or if the existence of documents directly relating to the applicants is falsely denied when those documents could have assisted them in proceedings this would deny them a fair hearing, and violate Article 6(1).

6.6.2 Article 6(1)

Article 6(1) requires proceedings to be fair, public, conducted by an independent and impartial tribunal and for judgment to be pronounced publicly. It implies a right to access court. The elements of Article 6(1) particularly relevant to information sharing are considered below.

Fairness

Although the requirements inherent in the concept of fair hearing are not necessarily the same in civil and criminal cases:

> . . . it is clear that the requirement of 'equality of arms' in the sense of a fair balance between the parties, applies in principle to [civil]. . . as well as to criminal cases . . . as regards litigation involving opposing private interests, 'equality of arms' implies that each party must be afforded a reasonable opportunity to present his case – including his evidence – under conditions that do not place him at a substantial disadvantage vis-a-vis his opponent.
>
> *Dombo Beheer BV* v. *Netherlands* (1993) 18 EHRR 213, paras. 32–33

Importantly this implies a right to disclosure of the other party's evidence (*McMichael* v. *UK* (1995) 20 EHRR 205; *Feldbrugge* v. *The Netherlands* 8 EHRR 425). Parties should be able to comment on evidence adduced in order to influence the court's decision (*Ruiz-Mateos* v. *Spain* June 23 1993 Series A No. 262 para. 63, *Dowsett* v. *UK* (2004) 38 EHRR 41).

The right to disclosure is particularly important in criminal proceedings where the individual is prosecuted by the state. Prosecuting authorities must, subject only to some exceptions, disclose all material in their possession or which they could obtain, which may be used to exonerate the accused or reduce his sentence (*Jespers* v. *Belgium* App no. 8403/78 27 DR 61, and see **6.7.3**).

Although it is a fundamental right for a defendant to be present, to be able to hear and follow criminal proceedings, to be able to instruct lawyers, to give evidence and to understand the evidence and arguments (*T and V* v. *UK* (2000) 30 EHRR 121), Article 6(1) does not guarantee a right to be present in civil proceedings. This can impact upon litigants' ability to explain matters to the court and to challenge other parties' evidence. Therefore, in certain circumstances a right to attend proceedings determining civil rights is implied (for example, where the personal character and manner of life of the party is directly relevant to the court's opinion or when fairness can only be achieved with the presence and participation of a person; *Brabazon-Drenning* v. *UK Central Council for Nursing and Midwifery* [2001] HRLR 6).

Access to court

Access to court implies that access will be provided to a decision maker or court that provides all of the Article 6(1) guarantees (and in criminal proceedings those afforded by Article 6(2) and (3)). Where decisions are made by public bodies that do not themselves provide all of the Article 6 guarantees, Article 6(1) is not breached, provided there is a right of review or appeal procedure which overall ensures compliance. Although we highlighted in Chapter 1 that concerns have been raised regarding the effectiveness of judicial review, the current law does not breach Article 6(1) (*R (Alconbury Developments Limited)* v. *Secretary of State for the Environment, Transport and the Regions* [2003] 2 AC 295, para. 189). Where the decision maker is exercising delegated powers to take a policy decision or to determine the public interest, it is sufficient that the court of review is able to overturn decisions based on errors of fact or law (or made irrationally or in breach of principles of natural justice).

The right of access to court is clearly relevant where an individual is concerned that their personal or confidential information may be, or has been shared without consent. However, the right is not absolute. A requirement for a vexatious litigant to obtain judicial permission before proceeding with a claim is a lawful, proportionate means of assuring the proper administration of justice (*H* v. *UK* App no. 1159/85 45 DR 281).

Effective access to court additionally includes being able to effectively present one's case at court through legal representation, and arguably to be able to share information with one's legal representative for such purposes (*Golder* v. *UK* (1979–80) 1 EHRR 524).

Public hearing

Public and press access to proceedings is important to maintain public confidence in the administration of justice. Public hearings are also important to afford individuals their Article 10 rights to freedom of expression (which includes rights to receive and impart information).

However, this is subject to certain provisos. Press reporting must not overstep the bounds imposed in the interests of justice, for example through reporting statements which are likely to prejudice the chances of a person receiving a fair trial (*Worm* v. *Austria* (1997) 25 EHRR 454). Where conflicts arise, between the right to a public hearing and the privacy rights of children on trial (see *T and V* v. *UK* (1999) 30 EHRR 121), a public hearing may not be appropriate. Proceedings may be held in private if justified in the interests of morals, public order, national security, juveniles, the protection of the parties' private life or the interests of justice), with a proportionality test being applied to determine whether holding a hearing in private is strictly necessary, or whether a less restrictive measure could achieve the intended aim (*Handyside* v. *UK* (1976) 1 EHRR 737 para. 48; *Van Mechelen* v. *Netherlands* (1997) 25 EHRR 647, para. 59).

The European Court has acknowledged that without notice applications do not necessarily breach Article 6(1) (*Jasper* v. *UK* (2000) 30 EHRR 441). Proceedings in private have been considered acceptable in cases involving sexual offending against children, residence proceedings (*B* v. *UK*, *P* v. UK [2001] 2 FLR 261) and certain medical disciplinary proceedings (*X* v. *Austria* (1965) 2 Digest 438; *P* v. *BW* [2004] EWCA Civ 845; *Imberechts* v *Belgium* App no. 15561/89). Domestic case law has, to date, confirmed the legality of hearing proceedings under the Civil Procedure Rules 1998 in private where national security is raised (*R (on the application of A)* v. *Crown Court at the Central Criminal Court* [2006] EWCA Civ 884).

Public pronouncement

Pronouncing judgments publicly affords the public opportunity to obtain information to scrutinise decision making. However, whilst the right to public pronouncement is expressed in absolute terms, judgments need not be given orally in open court. The form of publicity may be determined nationally, taking into account the type of proceedings (for example, anonymised reports of residence proceedings together with court rules which permit individuals with sufficient interest to apply for court documents appropriately balance the public interest and the privacy rights of children involved; *B* v. *UK, P* v. *UK* [2001] 2 FLR 261).

6.6.3 Article 6(2) and (3)

Since, in criminal proceedings the state prosecutes the individual, it is particularly important that those individuals are afforded a fair trial; that they can obtain the information they need to defend themselves, can object to prosecution's use of information obtained unlawfully, and are not required to disclose information which might, for example, incriminate them. Article 6(2) and (3) therefore afford defendants numerous rights, crucial to the notion of a fair trial in criminal proceedings. (For example, Article 6(3) requires sufficient information about charges against him to be provided to the defendant in order to prepare an adequate defence.) Fairness may also require other conditions to be satisfied (*Deweer* v. *Belgium* (1980) 2 EHRR 439; *Jespers* v. *Belgium* App no. 8403/78, 27 DR 62).

Prosecution disclosure

In *Edwards* v. *UK* (1992) 15 EHRR 417 the court considered that fairness requires prosecution authorities to provide the defence with all material evidence for or against them. These strict disclosure obligations have, however, subsequently been limited.

Although Article 6 does not expressly consider victims' interests, *Doorson* v. *Netherlands* (1996) 22 EHRR 330, para. 70 confirms that the interests of the accused should be 'balanced against those of witnesses or victims called to testify', for example, where the victim would be endangered unless protective measures were taken (see articles 2 and 3). In *Doorson* the court concluded arrangements to preserve anonymity can be justified, providing adequate safeguards are provided. The Criminal Evidence (Witness Anonymity) Act 2008 aims to afford such safeguards to defendants when witnesses' identities are withheld from them.

In *Rowe and Davis* v. *UK* (1999) 30 EHRR 1 the European Court recognised (where the prosecution withheld information which would reveal the identity of, and place at risk, a police informant) that the prosecution may need to withhold information from the defence relating to national security, secret police investigative methods or vulnerable witnesses. The European Court made clear that any failure to disclose must be necessary. Procedural safeguards must be provided protecting the defendant's rights. *Edwards and Lewis* v. *UK* [2003] All ER (D) 368 suggests that without notice orders to withhold prosecution evidence on public interest grounds may not incorporate adequate safeguards to protect the defendant's interests (in this case the defendants were unable to establish whether evidence was obtained by entrapment and should therefore be excluded from court consideration). See **7.3** for further consideration of prosecution disclosure.

Non-incrimination and the right to silence

The right to a fair trial includes the right for the defendant not to incriminate themselves (by providing or not providing documents or giving oral evidence). However, this is not an absolute right (*Funke* v. *France* (1993) 16 EHRR 297 and *Heaney and McGuiness* v. *Ireland* (2003) 33 EHRR 12).

Article 6 does not prevent use of statutory powers to oblige disclosure of information during an investigation preceding criminal proceedings (*R* v. *Kearns* [2002] 1 WLR 2815).

Whilst it is inappropriate to base convictions solely or mainly on defendants' silence, refusals to answer questions, or to give evidence, the drawing of adverse inferences from an accused's silence, etc. does not automatically infringe Article 6. Where the law allows inferences to be drawn in regard to a refusal to answer police questions there is an implied right for suspects to normally have access to a lawyer (*John Murray* v. *UK* (1996) 22 EHRR 29 para. 63).

6.7 ARTICLE 8

Under Article 8(1) everyone has a right to respect for his private and family life, his home and his correspondence. Article 8 protects individuals from arbitrary interference by public authorities and requires public authorities to take measures to ensure respect for private/family life, etc. is afforded by one individual to another. This includes through courts acting to protect individuals' personal information from abuse (*Von Hannover* v. *Germany* [2005] 40 EHRR 1, para. 57).

However, interferences with Article 8(1) are permitted, in accordance with Article 8(2):

> There shall be no interference by a public authority with the exercise of this right except such as is in accordance with the law and is necessary in a democratic society in the interests of national security, public safety or the economic well-being of the country, for the prevention of disorder or crime, for the protection of health or morals, or for the protection of the rights and freedoms of others.

Whilst the focus of this section is private life, the four areas covered by Article 8(1) are not mutually exclusive. All have some relevance to information sharing.

6.7.1 Right to respect for private life

The notion of private life is broadly defined, although it extends only to individuals (*R* v. *Broadcasting Standards Commission* ex parte *BBC* [2000] HRLR 15).

Private life

Article 8(1) protects an individual's personal space (*R* v. *Broadcasting Standards Commission*, above). Accordingly, it protects social and sexual interactions with others (*Botta* v. *Italy* (1998) 26 EHRR 241, para. 32; *Von Hannover* v. *Germany* [2005] 40 EHRR 1, para. 50). It protects relationships of 'a professional or business nature since it is in the course of their working lives that the majority of people have a significant, if not the greatest, opportunity of developing relationships with the outside world'. (*Niemitz* v. *Germany* (1992) 16 EHRR 97 para. 29). It includes aspects of personal identity, including a person's name or picture (*Von Hannover* v. *Germany* (2005) 40 EHRR 1, para. 50).

There has been much debate about exactly when the right to respect for privacy protects personal information in the public sphere (for example, photographs taken by the media, or CCTV records of public areas). In 1977 the European Court suggested the claim to respect for private life is automatically reduced to the extent that the individual himself brings his private life into contact with public life or into close connection with other protected interests (*Scheuten* v. *Germany* (1977) 3 EHRR 244, paras. 55–8). In *Von Hannover* v. *Germany* [2005] 40 EHRR 1 the European Court recognised that there is a legitimate public interest in publication of information about the lives of politicians (from the perspective of transparency and democratic control), and that there may be a similar legitimate interest in relation to other public figures who exercise public functions. However, in *Von Hannover* the court considered that the innocuous public activities of a known public figure were protected by Article 8(1).

Domestic case law (*Campbell* v. *MGN Limited* [2004] UKHL 22, para. 21) suggests that innocuous daily activities, such as shopping, would not, engage Article 8, since 'the touchstone of private life is whether in respect of the disclosed facts the person in question had a reasonable expectation of privacy'. Accordingly, information about such activities can be shared. *David Murray (by his litigation friends Neil Murray and Joanne Murray)* v. *Big Pictures (UK) Limited* [2008] EWCA Civ 446 makes clear that, in light of *Kay* v. *Lambeth LBC* [2006] UKHL 10, it is the *Campbell* decision that is to be followed, not *Von Hannover*.

Practically, the right to respect for private life must be considered whenever decisions are taken about sharing personal information, particularly, medical data, which is considered fundamental to a person's enjoyment of his/her right to respect for private and family life (*I* v. *Finland* App no. 20511/03, para. 36; *Z* v. *Finland* (1997) 25 EHRR 371, para. 95). Article 8(1) affords a 'right to control the dissemination of information about one's private life' (*Campbell* v. *MGN Ltd* [2004] 2 AC 457 paras. 50–51). Article 8(1) is engaged, when information relating to private and family matters, including issues of personal development, personal identity and family background is requested (*Odievre* v. *France* (2004) 38 EHRR 43)

Practical examples

Article 8(1) is engaged:

- When individuals are obliged to provide personal data for public census purposes (*X* v. *UK* app no. 9702/82 30 DR 239)
- When personal data is disclosed for security vetting purposes (*Hilton* v. *UK* App no. 12015/86 57 DR 108
- When personal data is transferred from one authority to another (*AS* v. *Austria* App no. 15220/89 75 DR 30 – information obtained by police surveillance)
- When personal medical data is shared without consent (*MS* v. *Sweden* (1999) 28 EHRR 313)
- When a telephone servicer provider discloses telephone numbers dialled by an individual to the police (*Malone* v. *UK* (1985) 13 EHRR 448).

Interferences with private life

Interferences, per se, are not unlawful. They must be justified on one of the Article 8(2) grounds, the particular measure taken must be necessary in a democratic society, must be undertaken in accordance with the law and must be a proportionate response to the purpose of interference.

Practical example

The police obtain an individual's itemised calls/billing records from his telecommunications supplier in connection with investigations into a planned robbery. Obtaining the information will be a proportionate response, justified under Article 8(2), provided information is obtained:

- in accordance with statutory provisions authorising disclosure of itemised records and in accordance with the DPA 1998;
- in the interests of prevention or detection of crime; and
- is used only for the investigation and prosecution of crime.

(See *PG and JH* v. *UK* [2001] ECHR 44787/98).

Disclosure of medical records without the patient's consent interferes with private life, and must not only be justified on public interest grounds, but appropriate safeguards must be provided to prevent disclosures which are inconsistent with Article 8. Orders requiring doctors to disclose evidence in criminal proceedings have been considered a proportionate response to preventing crime (*Z* v. *Finland* (1997) 25 EHRR 371).

Orders requiring information to be disclosed, or searched for and seized, can be justified where necessary to protect others' rights. Again, appropriate safeguards must be provided, including regarding use of materials seized (*Chappell* v. *UK* (1989) 12 EHRR 1). The collection and retention of information for national security vetting purposes, and indeed refusals to allow the individual access to that information have been considered justified, under Article 8(2), in the interests of national security (*Leander* v. *Sweden* (1987) 9 EHRR 433). Holding and sharing information for vetting purposes can, therefore, be justified (on national security and public protection grounds) provided safeguards, such as restrictions upon access, are provided.

In many situations, the issue will not be the legality of information sharing, but rather whether information was lawfully obtained. Searches which do not afford procedural safeguards to legal privilege (i.e. information shared with legal advisers for advice purposes) will constitute unjustified interferences (*Niemitz* v. *Germany* (1992) 16 EHRR 97, see also **Chapter 7**).

6.7.2 Right to respect for family life

Family life

Article 8(1) protects family relationships and matters essential to the family relationship, including parental rights to determine their child's upbringing. The concept of family extends to cover many non-conventional family forms, and relationships with a variety of relatives, with the determining factor being whether there are close personal ties (*Marckx* v. *Belgium* (1979) 2 EHRR 330).

Respect for family life requires access to be provided to information about parentage and time spent in public care, where essential to the applicant understanding his childhood and early development (*Gaskin* v. *UK* (1989) 12 EHRR 36). Disclosure of relevant documents to parents in circumstances where substantial interference with family life is proposed is essential to afford requisite protection to the parents' interests as safeguarded by Article 8 (see *McMichael* v. *UK* judgment of 24 February 1995, Series A no. 307-B, para. 92).

Article 8 imposes a positive obligation to provide information regarding environmental hazards to enable families to assess risks posed by living in particular localities (*Guerra* v. *Italy* App no. 14967/89). Note that proactive dissemination of information about hazards (for example exposure to radiation) is not required, simply 'an effective and accessible procedure' which enables those affected to 'seek all relevant and appropriate information'

(*McGinley and Egan* v. *UK* (1998) 27 EHRR 1). There will be no right to access information unless: a positive obligation to disclose exists, the individuals have strong public interest reasons for requiring the information and no contradictory public interest (for example, national security) acts against disclosure.

Justifying interferences with family life

Interferences with family life can be justified.

The fact that records such as social services records, which contain important information about a child's family background, are not routinely disclosed is considered important for ensuring objective, reliable information is retained in such records, and that third parties who have provided or are mentioned in the information are protected. In *Gaskin* v. *UK* (1989) 12 EHRR 36, a system of providing access to records only with the contributor's consent, was considered compatible with Article 8(1) provided disclosure was considered by an independent authority when the contributor was unavailable or unreasonably refused consent to disclosure. It seems DPA 1998, s.7 appropriately balances the private/family life of a requester and private life of third parties.

6.7.3 Right to respect for home

The right to respect for home encompasses a right to access and occupy premises, to enjoy the home without interference and free from pollution. Searches of the home for information may engage private life and respect for the home (*Chapell* v. *UK* (1989) 12 EHRR 1). The right to enjoy a home free from pollution (and to be told when pollution threatens health) may be considered both under the family and home aspects of Article 8 (*Lopez Ostra* v. *Spain* (1994) 20 EHRR 277).

Home is widely defined, covering property used for home and business purposes (*Niemitz* v. *Germany* (1992) 16 EHRR 97). The court has allowed companies to use the right to respect for home to establish rights of respect for registered offices or other business premises (*Societe Colas Est* v. *France* App no. 37971/97).

Where personal information is obtained by virtue of searching homes or offices, it may therefore breach the DPA 1998 and several aspects of Article 8(1), unless justified by reference to Article 8(2), and proportionate. Subsequent sharing will be unlawful.

6.7.4 Right to respect for correspondence

This right, which overlaps to some extent with the notion of privacy, entails a right to share information, both personal and business related, via written and telephone correspondence (*Golder* v. *UK* (1975) 1 EHRR 524). It provides a right to confidentiality of such correspondence (*Niemitz* v. *Germany* 16 EHRR 97, concerning documents held at a lawyer's office).

Privileged correspondence is provided the greatest protection. It should be opened only in exceptional circumstances. Legal professional privilege is recognised as a fundamental right under the Convention, essential to enable individuals to consult lawyers and engage in full and frank discussion with them. Interference with privilege is permissible only where it is abused; for example when information is obtained other than for the purpose of obtaining legal advice and where the contents of correspondence endanger security or the lives of others or are criminal in nature (*Campbell* v. *UK* (1992) 15 EHRR 137).

The individual's desire for privacy in correspondence must frequently be balanced against the public interest in disclosure. Safeguards must, however, be provided to minimise invasions in privacy. (See *Foxley* v. *UK* (2000) 31 EHRR 25 where the European Court considered a bankruptcy trustee to be justified in intercepting and reviewing letters to a bankrupt debtor for the purpose of identifying assets and income available to unsatisfied creditors. However, routine reading and copying of mail intercepted without authorisation, before it was received by the applicant, breached Article 8. It was considered inappropriate for the trustee to read any mail subject to legal privilege.)

6.7.5 Article 8, the other Convention articles and the DPA 1998

The relationship between Articles 8 and 10, increasingly provoking media and public attention, is considered further at **6.8.3**. Other conflicts frequently arise. The child's right to freedom from abuse (Art. 3) may conflict with the parent and child's right to privacy (see *Z* v. *UK*, at **6.5**).

Failure to disclose vital evidence to a parent involved in public child care proceedings potentially breaches Articles 6 and 8 (*McMichael* v. *UK* (1995) 20 EHRR 205).

If personal information is obtained unlawfully it will breach DPA 1998, first principle, and subsequent sharing will not be lawful. More importantly, 'a national measure which is incompatible with Article 8 of the convention . . . also fails to pass the threshold of Article 7(e) of Directive 95/46' (*Osterreichischer Rundfunk and others* [2003] ECR I-4989).

6.8 ARTICLE 10

Article 10(1) affords individuals and organisations a right to freedom of expression, including 'freedom to hold opinions and to receive and impart information and ideas without interference by public authority . . .'

> The right applies not only to information or ideas that are favourably received or regarded as inoffensive or as a matter of indifference, but also to those that offend, shock or disturb the state or any sector of the population. (*Handyside* v. *UK* [1976] ECHR 5493/72, para. 49)

6.8.1 Article 10(1)

The freedom to hold opinions includes a right to express such opinions. This is clearly relevant to information sharing, for example, when a professional shares opinions with colleagues, or where a newspaper editor publishes a public figure's opinions.

The freedom to impart information again encompasses information sharing (for example, affording a father denied contact with his children the right to disseminate his story).

The freedom to receive information imposes negative obligations (public authorities must not restrict the receipt of information which others may wish to impart) and positive obligations (to assist individuals to obtain information imparted by others, where such assistance does not impose an onerous burden (*Appleby* v. *UK* (2003) 37 EHRR 38)). However, the right to receive information is of a limited nature. It does not require the state to provide information. Holding proceedings in private (limiting public access to receive information) does not breach Article 10 (*R (Pelling)* v. *Bow County Court* [2001] 1 UKHRR 165). A failure to disclose a file containing an individual's personal information does not necessarily interfere with their right to receive information (*Leander* v. *Sweden* (1987) 9 EHRR 433). Whilst in *Guerra* v. *Italy* (1998) 26 EHRR 357 the court found a failure to provide information about risks posed by a chemical plant breached Article 8, it did not breach Article 10 (see also *Roche* v. *UK* App no. 32555/96 regarding results of chemical tests on servicemen).

6.8.2 Interferences with Article 10(1)

Article 10 protects information sharing. However, information sharing cannot be unlimited. Exercise of the right involves duties and responsibilities, for example, not to pervert morals (*Handyside*). Accordingly, the right:

> may be subject to such formalities, conditions, restrictions or penalties as are prescribed by law and are necessary in a democratic society, in the interests of national security, territorial integrity or public safety, for the prevention of disorder or crime, for the protection of health or morals, for the protection of the reputation or rights of others, for preventing the disclosure of information received in confidence, or for maintaining the authority and impartiality of the judiciary.
>
> Article 10(2)

Relevant considerations when justifying interferences with Article 10(1) include:

- The type of information to be imparted or received: greater weight is afforded to free expression of political views, than free expression of commercial information. (However, note that in *London Regional Transport* v. *The Mayor of London* [2003] EMLR 4, disclosure of information concerning the London Underground Public Private Partnership was considered appropriate, and in the public interest, notwithstanding the existence of confidentiality agreements.)
- The information giver's identity: weighty reasons are needed to interfere with the rights of those involved in the democratic process (including elected representatives and journalists). However, the special duties and responsibilities imposed upon the armed forces, security services, civil servants and the judiciary justify greater restrictions on their rights to freedom of expression (see *R* v. *Shayler* [2001] 1 AC 247).
- Whether information is already in the public domain: where information is no longer private in nature, and for example, an injunction no longer affords protection to national security or confidentiality, continuing the injunction is futile and therefore cannot be considered 'necessary' (*Plon (Societe)* v. *France* App no. 58148/00; *Observer and Guardian* v. *UK* (1991) 14 EHRR 153 A 216).
- The purpose of the interference: where morals or national security are threatened the UK has a relatively wide discretion.
- The proportionality of the interference to the aim sought: careful consideration must be given to whether the proposed restriction on freedom of expression is such that it may deter others in future from exercising their right to freedom of expression.

Practical example

In *Goodwin* v. *UK* (1996) 22 EHRR 123, a journalist wrote an article concerning a company's confidential plan for raising capital, relying on information from a confidential source. An *ex parte* injunction was made, prohibiting disclosure by national newspapers and relevant journals (recognising the need to protect the company's proprietary and contractual rights). The High Court made an order (upheld by the Court of Appeal and House of Lords) that Goodwin disclose his source, in the interests of justice. (Contempt of Court Act 1980. s.10 prohibits courts from ordering publishers/journalists to disclose their information source unless disclosure is necessary in the interests of justice.) The European Court concluded the injunction achieved the legitimate aim of protecting the company's rights. The order to disclose the source would have a potentially chilling effect on future exercise of Article 10 freedoms, and was not a proportionate interference with the journalist's right to freedom of expression.

Whenever a court application affecting the Article 10 freedoms is considered, those affected must be given the opportunity to comment on the grant of any order and its terms (*X and Y* v. *Persons Unknown* [2007] EMLR 10). HRA 1998, s.12 must be considered in conjunction with Art. 10, explicitly prohibits making without notice orders and other remedies (such as injunctions) which would affect freedom of expression, where the person who will be affected by the order is not in attendance and able to present their views, unless the applicant has taken every reasonable step to notify the respondent, or there are compelling reasons why the defendant should not be notified.

Section 12(3) additionally prohibits the making of interim orders prohibiting publication unless the court is satisfied that at the final hearing the applicant would establish that the order is required. Preventing hasty interim injunctions is particularly important in the context of press publication of public interest issues, given that even a short delay may deprive information of value or interest (*Observer and Guardian* v. *UK* (1991) 14 EHRR 153 A 216 para. 60). However whilst courts should be cautious about making interim restraint orders unless satisfied that the applicant would be more likely than not to succeed in their arguments at trial, where the potential adverse consequences of disclosure are particularly grave, for example, where an interim injunction aims to protect national security, greater flexibility to make interim orders might be merited (*Observer and Guardian* v. *UK* (1991) 14 EHRR 153; *Cream Holdings* v. *Banerjee* [2004] UKHL 44).

6.8.3 Conflicts with other rights

The position becomes complicated when other rights are engaged. HRA 1998, s.12(4) requires any court considering Article 10 rights to have 'particular regard to the importance of the Convention right to freedom of expression'. However, given the section 3 duty to interpret legislation, including the HRA 1998 itself, in line with Convention rights, the courts recognise that priority cannot simply be accorded to Article 10.

Practical examples

In *Green Corns Ltd* v. *Clavery Group* [2005] EWHC 958, information about homes for disturbed children had been publicly available to a limited extent but the information was not widely in the public domain. An injunction was needed to achieve an appropriate balance between rights under Articles 8 and 10.

In *Venables* v. *News Group Newspapers Ltd* [2001] Fam 430, the need to protect the privacy of two boys convicted of murdering another child where a 'real and serious risk' was posed to their Article 2 and 3 rights, justified the indefinite continuation of injunctions to protect information which might reveal their identity.

A conflict most frequently arises between Articles 8 and 10. Neither Article 8 or 10:

> has as such precedence over the other. . . ., where the values under the two articles are in conflict, an intense focus on the comparative importance of the specific rights being claimed in the individual case is necessary. . . . the justifications for

> interfering with or restricting each right must be taken into account. Finally, the proportionality test must be applied to each
>
> *Re S (A Child)* [2005] 1 AC 593 para. 17

Generalisations, for example, that politicians must be expected to have less privacy, are unsustainable – in each case careful consideration must be given to three questions:

- Is this information private?
- Is publication in the publication interest? (If the information is confidential is it also in the public interest to breach confidentiality?)
- Which interest should prevail? (If a matter is of public concern or general interest greater weight may be afforded to Article 10, particularly where interference with the individual's Article 8 right's is not weighty; see *Von Hannover* v. *Germany* (2005) 40 EHRR 1; *HRH Prince of Wales* v. *Associated Newspapers Ltd* [2007] 2 All ER 139; *Mosley* v. *Newsgroup Newspapers Ltd* [2008] EWHC 1777.)

6.9 ENFORCING CONVENTION RIGHTS

When a public authority acts or proposes to act in breach of Convention rights, any victim of that unlawful act may, under HRA 1998, s.7:

(a) bring freestanding proceedings against the public authority in a county or High Court where no other remedy is available, such as an action for breach of confidentiality or judicial review. Where other remedies are available these should be used. The claim should be brought within one year, or if proceedings are brought by way of judicial review, within three months maximum;
(b) rely on the Convention as a defence to proceedings instigated by the public authority;
(c) rely on the Convention when appealing from a decision made by a court or tribunal. For example, where the individual believes that the court failed to act compatibly with Convention rights or to interpret the law in accordance with the Convention and Strasbourg jurisprudence.

A victim may bring a case before the European Court where he has exhausted all domestic remedies or the relevant Convention provision is not a recognised Convention right (see **6.2.1**). The European Court will not substitute its own decision for that of the domestic court. It reviews the domestic decision, and may award damages.

A victim may alternatively waive their rights (provided the right does not protect an important public interest). For example, *Albert and Le Compte* v. *Belgium* (1983) 5 EHRR 533, the right to a public hearing in public was waived.

6.9.1 Victim

A victim includes a living person, non-governmental organisation or group of individuals (Art. 34), who is actually and directly affected by the act complained of or be at risk of being so affected (*Klass* v. *Germany* (1979–80) 2 EHRR 214, para. 33). Non-governmental organisations are not entitled to bring freestanding HRA 1998 proceedings on behalf of the public (*X* v. *Germany* App no. 9234/81), but may bring them on the organisation, or its members' behalf. A victim need not prove specific prejudice or damage (*Eckle* v. *Germany* (1982) 5 EHRR 1 para. 66).

Difficult issues arise where an individual victim believes their Article 8 rights have been breached by police or security service surveillance or intelligence. They must show a 'reasonable likelihood' that they have been the subject of such activities (*Halford* v. *UK* (1997) 24 EHRR 523; *Hilton* v. *UK* App no. 12015/86 57 DR 108).

6.9.2 Remedies

Where a successful claim is brought, domestic courts may award any relief or remedy, or make any order it considers just and appropriate (HRA 1998, s.8).

Civil remedies include injunctions, declarations, the quashing of a decision or damages. The court must be satisfied that taking into account any other remedies granted by that court or any other court, damages are necessary to 'afford just satisfaction' (s.8(2), (3)).

In criminal proceedings the courts may not award damages but may quash an indictment, stay proceedings, allow a submission of no case to answer, exclude evidence or take account of the breach in sentencing. The Court of Appeal (Criminal Division) may quash a conviction where, for example, a trial breached Article 6.

6.10 CONCLUSION

The HRA 1998 and Convention are relevant whenever public authorities, private individuals and companies take decisions whether to share information. Article 8 is particularly relevant to the protection of personal information. Article 10 is important when restrictions upon public dissemination of information are proposed. Public authorities must recognise that Articles 2, 3 and 8 may also oblige information to be shared, particularly for public health and protection reasons.

Given the many justifications for interference with the qualified rights and the need to balance rights against each other, decision makers must carefully consider each information sharing decision afresh giving consideration to the issues outlined in the box below.

Preventing Convention breaches

1. Is one (or more) Convention rights engaged by the proposed action?
2. Is the proposed action discriminatory?
3. Does the action proposed interfere with those rights?
4. Is the right an absolute right? Can interference be justified?
5. If qualified, is the aim of the interference authorised, for example, under article 8(2) or 10(2)?
6. Is interference in accordance with the law?
7. Is the action necessary in a democratic society; does it respond to a pressing social need?
8. How intrusive is the interference; is it proportionate to the aim? Are safeguards provided?
9. If two or more rights are engaged, which interest should prevail?

CHAPTER 7

Disclosure and court proceedings

Claire Bessant

7.1 INTRODUCTION

Anyone involved in proceedings or who may be ordered to share/disclose information (for example, doctors ordered to provide medical records) should understand how the rules governing disclosure in court proceedings apply to them.

Many different types of court proceedings exist, subject to different rules. This chapter therefore focuses on civil proceedings governed by the Civil Procedure Rules 1998, SI 1998/3132 (CPR), and criminal proceedings (excluding provisions which specifically apply to youths, and to terrorist offences). Those public authority professionals involved in proceedings under the Children Act 1989 should also refer to **Chapter 10**.

The disclosure rules (derived from statute, secondary legislation and case law) impose strict obligations upon parties to proceedings to share information with each other and with the court. They can require third parties to share information.

Where information to be disclosed is personal data or is subject to the duty of confidentiality, a court order often provides lawful authority to share that information. It is important nonetheless that those holding information understand when they may legitimately object to disclosure on grounds of privilege or public interest immunity.

7.2 CIVIL PROCEEDINGS

7.2.1 Overview

The CPR govern disclosure of information in proceedings before the county court, High Court and the Civil Division of the Court of Appeal, save insolvency proceedings, non-contentious probate proceedings, Court of Protection proceedings, family and adoption proceedings and election petition and High Court prize court applications (CPR, rule 2.1).

Before proceedings commence
Pre-action protocols require information to be disclosed
Orders for pre-action disclosure (against parties and third parties) may be sought

↓

Claim form detailing the claimant's case issued and served (**Key documents may be appended to the statement of case)**

↓

Defendant acknowledges claim and/or files his defence

↓

Claim allocated to one of three tracks: small claim standard directions, fast track standard directions, multi-track

↓

Parties comply with directions on disclosure, orders for disclosure against third parties are made, parties exchange experts' reports and witness statements. In fast track cases disclosure usually begins within four weeks of allocation. In multi-track cases a longer period may be allowed, depending upon the case's complexity and weight of documentation.

↓

Pre-trial checklists completed, further court directions and possible pre-trial review, followed by the trial and judgment

(In small claims track cases, not considered further, disclosure may either not be ordered at all, or each party may simply be required to provide the other with copy documents upon which they will rely at trial (CPR, rule 27.27)).

Figure 7.1 Information sharing in civil proceedings

In civil proceedings, usually disclosure means:

(a) one party sends a list of documents to the other, informing the other that a document exists or has existed (disclosure);
(b) the other party requests copies of documents they need to view, and inspects or is given a copy of disclosed documents (inspection).

'Document' includes 'anything in which information of any description is recorded' (CPR, rule 31.4). It encompasses electronic documents (CPR PD 31 para. 2A), documents includes: information within photographs, computer hard disks and floppy disks (including deleted items), audio and video tapes, e-mail, hard copy documents, fax transmission logs and other electronic communications, word processed documents and databases, documents stored on servers and back-up systems, deleted electronic documents, and metadata. Copies of documents (anything onto which information recorded in the document has been copied) may also be sought. Although only one copy of a document need ordinarily be disclosed, where a document has been amended, partially obliterated or otherwise marked, it may be disclosed as a separate document (CPR, rule 31.9).

7.2.2 Withholding disclosure

The CPR's overriding objective is that all cases be dealt with justly. The court must ensure parties are placed on an equal footing and that the case is dealt with expeditiously, fairly and proportionately bearing in mind the financial value and importance of the case, complexity of the issues and the parties' financial positions. Whilst dealing with cases justly necessitates provision of key documents, the court must balance the parties' need to access relevant documents against the costs incurred in providing extensive documentation for inspection. It may accordingly dispense with or limit disclosure. Certain documents, which are privileged or subject to public interest immunity (PII), may be withheld from inspection. The very existence of a document subject to PII may not need to be disclosed.

Legal professional privilege

All documents held by a solicitor are not necessarily privileged. A client's identity is not itself privileged information (*Bursill* v. *Tanner* [1885] 16 QBD 1). In fact, legal professional privilege covers two specific situations:

Advice privilege	Litigation privilege
Communications solicitor ← → client	Communications solicitor or client ← → third party
(No proceedings need be contemplated or ongoing)	(Proceedings must be contemplated or current)

ADVICE PRIVILEGE

Confidential letters and other communications between a party and his solicitor (and resulting correspondence with counsel), together with items enclosed or referred to, are privileged from inspection in civil proceedings provided they are written and sent by or to the solicitor in his professional capacity, for the sole or primary purpose of affording the client legal advice and assistance. Advice privilege covers information transmitted by an individual client (or where a company seeks advice, those personnel within the company authorised to retain the solicitor) and recorded by a solicitor, barrister or client in a meeting in which legal advice is provided.

However, advice privilege does not cover non-legal advice such as investment advice (*Three Rivers District Council and Others* v. *Governor and Company of the Bank of England* [2004] UKHL 48). The test is whether advice is sought or given in a 'relevant legal context'. The parties must consider (a) Did the advice relate to the client's legal rights, liabilities, obligations or remedies? (b) Did the way in which communication took place, and its purpose make it reasonable to expect privilege to apply, bearing in mind the policy underlying the privilege (*Three Rivers*, para. 38)?

LITIGATION PRIVILEGE

Litigation privilege applies to documents and communications passing between a third party and a client, or a third party and a solicitor if:

(a) they come into existence once proceedings are contemplated, or have commenced; and
(b) they are made either for the sole or dominant purpose of enabling the client to obtain or the solicitor to give advice in relation to the proceedings, for obtaining evidence for them, or otherwise to aid the client in conducting the proceedings. When a document is produced to identify failings and to address them, and only incidentally to be used in potential future litigation, its dominant purpose is unrelated to proceedings and the document is unlikely to be privileged (*Waugh* v. *British Railways Board* [1979] 2 All ER 1169).

Litigation privilege may include information sought by one individual within an organisation from another, where the information is sought in order to obtain legal advice in relation to current proceedings.

Privilege does not apply where a document comes into being and the purpose of seeking the legal advice is criminal or iniquitous, even if the solicitor is unaware of the illicit purpose. In *Dubai Aluminium Co Ltd* v. *Al Alawi* [1999] 1 WLR 1964 privilege was lost where a search order was obtained using information gathered in breach of the Data Protection Act 1984. The privilege does not extend to doctors, to journalists who receive information from an informant (Contempt of Court Act 1984, s.10 provides some protection to such informants), or to others entrusted with confidences (*Wheeler* v. *Le Marchant* (1881) 17 ChD 675).

Although generally a privileged document is always privileged, privilege may be waived, for example, where a copy of a privileged document (such as a witness statement or expert report obtained for the purpose of proceedings) is served on another party. Where privileged documents are inadvertently produced for inspection or are produced to a party by a non-party, restrictions are placed upon use of that document without court permission, and obviously privileged documents should be returned to the sender immediately (see CPR, rule 31.20; Solicitors' Code of Conduct 2007, rule 4.02).

Privilege against self-incrimination

The privilege against self-incrimination applies to oral and written evidence that a party is compelled to provide (*C plc* v. *P (Attorney General intervening)* [2007] 3 WLR 437). It applies if providing information might materially increase the risk of criminal prosecution or might be relied upon to establish the guilt of a party or their spouse. It does not apply to production of public documents or to documents which incriminate others, and has been removed for certain claims, for example, involving infringement of intellectual property rights (Supreme Court Act 1981, s.72) and certain proceedings to recover stolen property (Theft Act 1968, s.31).

Public interest immunity

A PII claim may be brought by a party, or a third party against whom disclosure is ordered. The courts will withhold disclosure on PII grounds when the public interest in withholding a document overrides the public interest in disclosure. It is well established that PII can attach to certain information types including: confidential information, information held by social services relating to children's welfare and certain types of material obtained in investigations under the Companies Acts. If documents are believed subject to PII a claim for PII should be made in relation to the specific document which it is proposed to withhold from disclosure (rather than for the class of documents, such as all social work records). The person seeking to withhold information must identify the harm which disclosure of this specific document might cause to a particular public interest.

Withholding disclosure of confidential information

Where a third party (for example an NHS Trust) seeks to withhold disclosure upon the basis of a document's confidentiality, the court must decide whether disclosure is necessary for the purpose of fairly disposing of the claim or to save costs and then consider whether, without an order, the applicant would be unable to obtain the document or the information it contains. It must then balance the competing interests of the litigants and the third party and balance any need to keep documents confidential in the public interest, against the public interest in ensuring any trial is conducted with full knowledge of all relevant material. The court may override confidentiality where the interests of justice require it.

To achieve a proportionate balance between the competing interests:

- An order may simply require inspection of identified documents rather than requiring the equivalent of standard disclosure.
- Stringent conditions may be imposed upon the manner and extent of disclosure, (for example, where an action has been brought to enforce obligations of confidence in relation to trade secrets, extensive disclosure may defeat the purpose of proceedings).
- Restricted disclosure or disclosure subject to conditions may be ordered (see *Pharaon* v. *BCCI* [1998] 4 All ER 455 where only those parts of the documents that were relevant to the parties or to the issues in the case were to be disclosed, the rest being redacted).

7.2.3 Disclosure pre-proceedings

Even pre-proceedings, parties may be obliged to share information.

Pre-proceedings protocols

Pre-action protocols encourage the exchange of early and full information about prospective legal claims, to avoid litigation or to enable proceedings to be managed efficiently where litigation cannot be avoided.

Protocols apply to the following claims:

- personal injury;
- clinical negligence;
- construction and engineering disputes;
- defamation;
- professional negligence;
- Judicial Review;
- disease and illness;
- housing disrepair;
- possession claims based on rent arrears.

In other cases the Practice Direction – Protocols, para. 4.1 requires parties to act reasonably in exchanging information and documents relevant to the claim in order to avoid the institution of proceedings. Paragraphs 4.3 and 4.6 suggest that prospective parties should provide sufficient, but concise details of their case, accompanied by copies of essential documents that support their case. Any documents disclosed at this stage may not be used other than for the purposes of resolving the dispute, unless the parties agree (para. 4.8).

Orders for pre-action disclosure

An application may also be made to the High Court or the County Court for an order for pre-action disclosure (Supreme Court Act 1981 (SCA 1981), s.33; County Courts Act 1984 (CCA 1984), s.52), where:

1. Both applicant and respondent would be likely to be parties if proceedings commenced.
2. The respondent would be under a duty by way of standard disclosure to disclose the documents or classes of documents sought.
3. Pre-action disclosure is desirable either to assist in resolving the dispute without proceedings, to reduce costs, or to dispose fairly of the prospective proceedings.

The court should also consider the issues raised by the prospective proceedings, the provisions and application of any relevant protocol, the nature of any documents sought, the applicant's prospects of bringing the proceedings without the disclosure. No order should be made if compliance would be potentially injurious to the public interest (*Black* v. *Sumitomo Corp* [2001] EWCA Civ 1819; SCA 1981, s.35 and CCA 1984, s.54).

An order for pre-action disclosure will specify the documents or classes of documents to be disclosed (usually by standard disclosure) and require the discloser to specify those documents which are no longer in his control or which he claims a right or duty to withhold from inspection. The order may specify a time and place for disclosure and inspection to take place.

7.2.4 Standard disclosure and inspection

Until a court order is made, no party is obliged to disclose any information held, and may be unable to recover their costs if they disclose voluntarily. Normally courts order parties to give standard disclosure and inspection.

Standard disclosure

Standard disclosure (governed by CPR, rule 31 and CPR Practice Direction 31 (PD 31) Disclosure and Inspection) requires a party to disclose only documents which are, or have been, within their control. This means a document that is or was in that party's physical possession, or which they can legally compel a third party to provide to them or to allow them to inspect or copy (rule 31.8). A party need only disclose documents on which he relies or which adversely affect his own or another party's case, or which support another party's case.

Practical example

A claimant brings an action against their employer in relation to a fall at work. The employer undertakes an investigation, and consults their solicitor for advice.

A report prepared by an independent contractor, and paid for by the employer, identifies that the fall may have been caused by a loose fitting carpet, of which the employer should have been aware. The employer has not yet received a copy of the report, but is entitled to a copy. This document may adversely affect the defendant's case yet support the claimant's case. The employer should obtain and disclose the report, giving the claimant opportunity to ask to inspect it or for a copy to be provided.

The advice provided by the employer's solicitor is legally privileged. The correspondence's existence should be disclosed but need not be provided for inspection.

Each party must undertake a reasonable and proportionate search for documents which adversely affect their own or other party's case, or which may support another party's case. In determining whether a search is reasonable, the number of documents, nature and complexity of proceedings, ease and expense of retrieval of documents, significance of any document and the overriding objective are relevant (CPR, rule 31.7; CPR PD 31 para. 2; and para. 2A(4) regarding electronic documents). It may be reasonable to restrict a search to documents coming into existence after a particular date, or to particular categories (in which case any limitation on searches should be stated). There is no need to search for or disclose documents relating to agreed matters.

There is no obligation to speculate about documents that could in future affect the case, however, the duty of disclosure continues until judgment is given. If further documents are identified during proceedings they should be disclosed (CPR, rule 31.11).

An order for standard disclosure requires parties to:

1. Submit a list of identified documents being disclosed (including documents received from or already provided to the other party). 'Without prejudice' documents evidencing settlement negotiations, whilst not admissible in evidence, should generally still be disclosed.
2. Identify documents they claim a right or duty to withhold from inspection on privilege or PII grounds, and documents no longer in their control. Often Part 2 simply details types of documents which the party wishes to withhold from inspection, for example 'confidential correspondence between the defendant and his solicitors', such general descriptions minimise risks of revealing documents' contents (but information must be given about when and why the document was created, and why it is being withheld). If documents are no longer in a party's control, the party should specify what has happened to them.
3. Provide a disclosure statement (made by an individual, or appropriate person on an organisation's behalf) stating the extent of the search made to locate documents and certifying the duty to disclose, including to disclose information detrimental to their case, is understood and has been complied with.

Whilst a privileged document should usually be disclosed even if it is not provided for inspection (*Blunt* v. *Park Lane Hotel Ltd* [1942] 2 KB 253), the existence of documents in which PII is claimed need not be disclosed. A party wishing to prevent disclosure or inspection on PII grounds may apply to court, without notice, for an order to withhold disclosure (CPR, rule 31.19). The court may require the document to be produced for the judge to view it privately to determine its probable evidential value and assist in deciding the application. It may invite any person, whether or not a party, to make representations. Unless the court orders otherwise the order for non-disclosure need not be provided to any other person (rule 31.19(2)), raising questions about compliance with the Convention, Article 6.

Inspection of documents

Once a document's existence is disclosed, whether by standard disclosure or where documents are specifically and directly referred to in a statement of case, a witness statement, a witness summary or an affidavit, the person to whom it is disclosed has a right to inspect it, and may make a written request for inspection or copies of documents (copies being supplied upon payment of reasonable copying costs (CPR, rules 31.14 and 31.15). There is no need to wait for standard disclosure to inspect documents referred to but not served with the statement of case.

The right to inspect is, however, limited where the person who disclosed the document no longer holds it, the discloser has a right or a duty to withhold inspection, or inspection of documents disclosed would be disproportionate (rule 31.3).

If a document disclosed is no longer in the control of the party, the court may, by order for specific disclosure, require that party to obtain a copy. Alternatively the court may order a third party to provide it (see **7.2.5**). Where a party claims a right or duty to withhold inspection of documents, a document or part of a document on the basis of privilege, PII, or proportionality, they do not need to apply to court to withhold inspection. If the inspecting party disagrees that any document or part document should be withheld they may apply for an order for specific inspection. The court may then require the document to be produced to the court and invite any person to make representations (see *Atos Consulting Ltd* v. *Avis plc (No. 2)* [2007] EWHC 323).

Note that subject to CPR, rule 35.10(4), a party may also apply to inspect any document not disclosed but which is mentioned in an expert's report. Inspection should first be requested informally and provided by agreement unless the request is unreasonable. Experts should be made aware that documents to which they refer may be shared. Where numerous documents are referred to and it would be burdensome to copy or collate them, the court will only order inspection where necessary for the disposal of the proceedings, and if the documents cannot be reasonably otherwise obtained (CPR PD 31 para. 7).

7.2.5 Specific disclosure and inspection and search orders

A party who believes inadequate disclosure has been provided may, having first requested further disclosure in writing, apply for an order for specific disclosure (rule 31.12 and CPR PD 31 para. 5). For example, where a document is not mentioned specifically within a statement of case, but its existence may be inferred, an application for specific disclosure or inspection may be appropriate. (In *Rigg* v. *Associated Newspapers Ltd* [2003] EWHC 710 a defence quoted from contemporaneous notes. They were not sufficiently well described to be 'disclosed'. Their specific disclosure was ordered.)

The court will take into account the circumstances of the case and particularly the overriding objective in deciding whether an order is required to ensure compliance with disclosure obligations. Specific disclosure orders may include directions; to disclose specified documents (for example, a document referred to in a disclosed document) or specified classes of documents; or to carry out a wider search for documents.

Search orders under Civil Procedure Act 1997, s.7 (previously Anton Piller orders) may be used to require a respondent to allow specified individuals, supervised by an independent solicitor, onto their premises or vehicles in order to search for, inspect, copy and remove items and documents. Such orders may also require the respondent to deliver documents or to verify information. The claimant must show the respondent's activities pose serious potential or actual risks to the claimant's interests, that incriminating documents or material are held by the respondent and, if the application is without notice, that there is a real possibility the respondent may destroy the material sought before an application on notice can be made. The respondent must be informed of their right to legal advice, to apply to vary or discharge the order, and to take advantage of legal professional privilege or privilege against self-incrimination.

7.2.6 Disclosure by third parties

Various orders may be made to require individuals who are not party to proceedings to disclose information.

Order under CPR, rule 31.17

These orders may be sought by any party to proceedings before the High Court or county court against any third party who appears to the court to be likely to have in his possession, custody or power any documents relevant to issues in those proceedings (SCA 1981, s.34; CCA 1984, s.35).

No order may be made unless:

(a) there is evidence the third party is likely to hold the documents;
(b) the documents sought are likely to support the applicant's case or adversely affect the case of another party; and
(c) disclosure is necessary to dispose fairly of the claim or save costs.

Where numerous documents are sought, the court may order disclosure of all such documents, even if they do not all support the applicant's case/undermine another party's case, both as a matter of practicality, and to ensure documents can be read in context (*Three Rivers District Council* v. *Bank of England (No. 4)* [2002] EWCA Civ 1182).

Witness summons

CPR, rule 34.2 permits the court to issue a witness summons requiring a witness to attend court to give evidence or produce documents specified in the summons (either at the court hearing or on another date). The quantity of material requested must not be oppressive. If, once the witness summons is made, copy documents are delivered to the applicant, they must ensure the documents are shared with other parties and the court.

Witness deposition

If a non-cooperative third party is needed to produce documents and provide evidence, an application may be made for the third party to attend court, before the hearing, both to produce the documents and to give evidence on oath (see CPR, rule 34.8).

Norwich Pharmacal orders

A *Norwich Pharmacal* order (originally derived from *Norwich Pharmacal Co* v. *Customs and Excise Comrs* [1974] AC 133) may be made where a person, albeit innocently, and without themselves having committed a wrongful act, becomes involved in a wrongful act of another. They must provide the only practicable means of obtaining essential information. The person against whom the order is sought is obliged to assist the injured person by providing any information he is able to which discloses the wrongdoer's identity.

Norwich Pharmacal orders are of use where trade secrets have been leaked by an unknown employee and the applicant wishes to prevent further disclosure or to take further action to protect its interests through dismissal of the employee who leaked those secrets. An order may also be made where the applicant suspects contractual confidentiality obligations have been breached by a particular person but needs evidence from the third party to issue a claim form.

Where the applicant is a public authority they may obtain an order only if the disclosure is necessary to enable them to perform their statutory duty (*Broadmoor Special Health Authority* v. *Robinson* [2000] QB 775, *H (A Healthcare Worker)* v. *N (A Healthcare Authority)* [2002] EWCA Civ 195).

Orders concerning banking information

Bankers trusts orders (*Bankers Trust* v. *Shapira* [1980] 1 WLR 1274) require a third party, usually a bank, to disclose information and documents relating to the financial affairs of an individual against whom a tracing claim has been brought, in order to ascertain what has happened to misapplied money.

In non-urgent cases, an order for inspection of bankers books may be made under the Bankers Books Evidence Act 1879.

Practice point

When proceedings are anticipated or as soon as possible once commenced:

1. Consider the issues and identify any relevant documents.
2. Undertake a reasonable, proportionate search for documents. Limitations may need to be imposed in relation to the age, location or type of documents.

3. Identify documents which you may wish to withhold on grounds of legal professional privilege or public interest immunity. If unsure whether documents provided by another person are subject to PII, discuss this with the provider.
4. If information is required from a third party, check whether they will share it voluntarily. If not, the appropriate order may depend upon the extent and nature of the information sought and the third party's objections to disclosure. An order for disclosure against a third party under CPR, rule 31.17 is significantly more onerous than a witness summons, since the order requires the person to whom it is addressed to carry out a reasonable search, may require disclosure by list and may oblige the third party to specify what has happened to documents he no longer holds (*Tajik Aluminium Plant* v. *Hydro Aluminium AS* [2005] EWCA Civ 1218, Moore-Bick at para. 24).

7.2.7 Disclosure of information relating to proceedings

Information disclosed in proceedings need not always be kept confidential. Although applications can be made to prevent further use by the parties, or disclosure to third parties, the possibility of further disclosure should be made clear to third parties before they provide information.

Parties' use of information

Documents may generally be used only to conduct the proceedings in which they are disclosed (CPR, rule 31.22). Misuse may be prevented by injunction. This substantially limits parties' abilities to share documents with others. However, this general rule is subject to exceptions:

- A document read to or by the court or referred to in detail within a public hearing is deemed in the public domain. It may be used for subsequent purposes provided the court has not imposed restrictions on further use. Orders restricting further use may be sought either by a party or a person to whom the document originally belonged, but should only be made where there is a convincing justification for doing so (*Lilly Ocos Ltd* v. *Pfizer Ltd* [2002] EWCA Civ 02, paras. 25–7). The confidentiality of documents may be relevant since permitting further disclosure could discourage use of confidential documents in other cases. In *Bourns Inc* v. *Raychem Corpn* [1999] 3 All ER 154 it was held that confidential documents disclosed for a limited purpose could not be used for another purpose without permission. Any assertion of confidentiality or that publicity will be damaging, should be supported by further specific reasons for requiring restriction of subsequent disclosure.
- Documents may be used again with court permission either for specific purposes (for example, for similar proceedings in a foreign jurisdiction) or with restrictions imposed (for example, requiring documents to be dealt with in private to protect the document owners' interests (*Smithkline Beecham plc* v. *Generics (UK) Ltd* [2003] EWCA Civ 1109).

- Documents may be used for subsequent purposes where the party who disclosed the document and the person to whom the document belongs (if different) agree to that use.

CPR, rule 31.22 does not apply to affidavits sworn under compulsion, documents produced under witness summons and documents produced by virtue of the exercise of statutory powers. Recognising the infringement on privacy resulting from such coercive powers, such documents may not be used by the parties for purposes other than the proceedings in which they were disclosed, nor may they be disclosed to a third party (*Home Office* v. *Harman* [1982] 1 All ER 532, para. 540).

Documents also remain confidential if no trial takes place (*SmithKline Beecham Biologicals SA* v. *Connaught Laboratories Inc* [1999] 4 All ER 498, CA).

Third parties

Generally, civil trials are held in public (CPR rule 39.2(1)). The public can attend, take notes and publish or otherwise use information heard during those proceedings (see *Forbes* v. *Smith* [1998] 1 All ER 973, *Clibbery* v. *Allan* [2002] EWCA Civ 45). This is subject to two exceptions (CPR, rule 39.2(3) and (4)):

1. The court may order proceedings to be heard in private where: publicity would defeat the object of the hearing, reveal matters relating to national security or reveal confidential information and damage that confidentiality; a private hearing is required in order to protect the interests of a child or patient or is in the interests of justice; or an application is being heard without notice and it would be unjust to the respondent to hold a public hearing.
2. The court may prohibit identification of a party or witness.

CPR, rule 5.4 enables courts to keep a publicly accessible register of claims (presently available for some divisions of the High Court, see PD 5 – Court Documents). In addition, third parties may obtain certain documents of court record (judgments and statements of case – but not documents attached to the statement) where all defendants (if more than one) have filed an acknowledgement of service or defence, the case has been listed for hearing, or judgment has been entered, and where no order has been made restricting or preventing disclosure of the statement of case. The court may order disclosure of other documents filed, upon request.

7.3 CRIMINAL PROCEEDINGS

In criminal proceedings, the prosecution (usually represented by the Crown Prosecution Service) brings proceedings against the defendant. The Criminal

Procedure Rules 2005 (Crim PR), with which all parties to criminal proceedings must apply, require that 'criminal cases be dealt with justly' (Rule 1.1). This explicitly obliges respect for the defendant's rights under European Convention, Art.6 and requires proper disclosure to be provided so defendants can defend allegations, and to prevent miscarriages of justice. Primarily, obligations to disclose information are imposed upon the prosecution, although increasingly obligations are also being placed on the defence. Information held by the prosecution may include information obtained by the police from third parties. Third parties should therefore understand the prosecution's disclosure obligations. Third parties may, in any event, be ordered to disclose information.

Disclosure may be withheld on grounds of legal professional privilege or public interest immunity. For a summary of the contents of this section please see Table 7.1 below.

7.3.1 Prosecution disclosure

Broadly, prosecution documents can be divided into two types:

- Used material: evidence the prosecution intends to rely on at trial.
- Unused material: evidence the prosecution is aware of but which does not form part of its case against the defendant.

Whether, and what material is disclosed by the prosecution depends on the type of offence, the defendant's plea, the stage of the proceedings reached and the nature of the material.

Disclosure of used material

A defendant's solicitor must obtain some used material at an early stage in proceedings, to advise his client whether to plead guilty or not guilty, and to advise on the appropriate court.

There is no statutory requirement for the prosecution to disclose advance, or indeed any, information in summary only cases (*R* v. *Stratford Justices*, ex parte *Imbert* [1999] 2 Cr App R 276). The *Attorney-General's Guidelines on Disclosure* (2005) (AG's Guidelines) para. 57, suggest, however, that the prosecution should 'provide to the defence all evidence upon which the crown proposes to rely in a summary trial. Such provision should allow the accused and their legal advisers sufficient time properly to consider the evidence before it is called'.

In either way cases, Crim PR, rule 21.2 requires the prosecutor to notify the defendant of their right to request advance information (including either prosecution witness statements, etc. or a summary of evidence) as soon as practicable after charge or service of summons. The defendant may seek advance information prior to the first magistrates' court hearing. The defendant's solicitor may also request copies or summaries of any tape recorded interviews

Table 7.1 Prosecution and defence disclosure: a summary

Summary only offences (tried before magistrates' court)	Offences triable either way (tried before magistrates' or crown court)	Indictable only offences/ cases to be tried on indictment (tried by crown court)
The investigating officer records and retains information and material gathered or generated during an investigation. The disclosure officer prepares schedules of material which is relevant but unlikely to form part of the prosecution's case (non-sensitive) and material which it is contrary to the public interest to disclose (sensitive).		
Initial prosecution disclosure		
Used material	***Used material***	***Used material***
Disclosed as advance information under AG's guidelines	Disclosure as advance information (Crim PR Part 21). If the defendant is to be committed to the crown court a committal bundle should be provided prior to the committal hearing	Advance information may be provided where fairness requires it. Otherwise provided in a case sent bundle following transfer to the crown court
Unused material	***Unused material***	***Unused material***
To be disclosed as soon as possible but usually within 28 days of entering a not guilty plea to a summary offence or either way offence tried summarily (Magistrates' Courts Protocol para. 3.1)	Depends whether the offence is tried summarily or on indictment	To be disclosed if possible alongside used material or otherwise as soon as reasonably practicable after (a) a not guilty plea is entered to an indictable offence or (b) an either way offence is committed for crown court trial
Defence disclosure		
Optional – within 14 days of disclosure of unused material		Within 14 days of disclosure of unused material a defence statement must be served
The prosecution is under a continuing duty to review unused material.		
Where a defence statement is filed the court has power under CPIA, s.8 to make a disclosure order if the defence can show reasonable cause to believe that there is material falling to be disclosed under the Act.		

conducted at the police station and confirmation of the defendant's previous convictions. A request for advance information may be refused only where disclosure of any particular fact or matter might lead to witness intimidation or interference with the course of justice (rule 21.4) or where PII applies and the prosecutor tells the defendant they are withholding information. The court may adjourn proceedings until satisfied that the defendant's case will not be substantially prejudiced by non-disclosure.

If the magistrates' court accepts jurisdiction to try an either way offence, and the defendant is content to be tried by the magistrates, for disclosure purposes the offence is treated as a summary offence (see above). Where the magistrates' court declines jurisdiction in favour of the crown court or the defendant elects trial by jury a date is fixed for a committal hearing. The prosecution must serve a committal bundle upon the defendant, including further used prosecution material, the draft indictment, typed prosecution witness statements and other evidence, including lists of exhibits. The prosecution need not disclose all used material at this stage, but often does so.

In indictable only cases, Crim PR, rule 21 does not apply. However, the prosecution normally responds to requests for advance information where fairness requires disclosure (for example, to enable the defendant to be properly represented upon a bail application). Used material is otherwise disclosed in a case sent bundle (similar to the committal bundle), within 50 days of the case being sent by the magistrates to the crown court if the defendant is in custody, or otherwise within 70 days, unless an extension is granted (Crime and Disorder Act 1998 (Service of Prosecution Evidence) Regulations 2005, SI 2005/902).

Disclosure of unused material

Where a defendant pleads not guilty to an offence, unused material must be disclosed in accordance with the Criminal Procedure and Investigations Act 1996 (the CPIA 1996). There may also need to be some disclosure, in the interests of justice, of information relevant to sentence, where an accused pleads guilty (see AG's guidelines, para. 58.)

THE CPIA CODE

The Code of Practice, Home Office, (2005), made under CPIA 1996, s.23 requires certain information to be recorded and retained by the police in relation to a criminal investigation (para. 5). Paragraph 6 requires two schedules to be prepared, listing:

(a) material relevant to the investigation but which the police consider unlikely to form part of the prosecution's case (the schedule of non-sensitive material);
(b) material which it would not be in the public interest to disclose (the sensitive schedule).

The schedules are provided to the prosecution to help them decide whether to inspect the material.

DISCLOSURE OF UNUSED MATERIAL

Unused material should be provided to the defence as soon as reasonably practicable after a defendant indicates an intention to plead not guilty, or where a defendant pleads not guilty to an either way or indictable offence, as soon as possible after committal or transfer to the crown court.

Specifically the prosecution must provide material in their possession or which they have inspected and not previously disclosed to the defendant, which might objectively be considered to undermine the prosecution case or assist the defendant's case (CPIA 1996, s.3). Examples include material casting doubt on the accuracy or reliability of the prosecution evidence, material pointing to another person being involved in committing the offence, material supporting the defence, material relating to the credibility of a prosecution witness or relevant to admissibility of prosecution evidence (the AG's Guidelines paras. 10–14). A copy of the non-sensitive schedule should also be provided (CPIA 1996, s.4). If no material contrary to the prosecution case or helpful to the defence case exists the prosecution must state this in writing.

The prosecution must continue to review the need to disclose unused material until acquittal or conviction, particularly if the defendant files a defence statement. After the defence statement is filed further disclosure must be provided or the prosecution must state they believe no further disclosure is needed (CPIA 1996, s.7A and see **7.3.3**). The prosecution may also need to review disclosure post conviction, where information comes to light which might cast doubt upon the safety of the conviction (AG's guidelines, paras 59–60).

Defence applications for prosecution disclosure

The defence may only apply for further prosecution disclosure if they have filed a defence statement and, if they reasonably believe the prosecution hold further material which might assist the defence. The prosecution must only provide information they hold or have inspected, and material retained by the police which the prosecution would be given a copy of or be allowed to inspect if they so requested (CPIA 1996, s.8).

7.3.2 Defence disclosure

In a case that has been committed or sent for trial to the crown court, once the defendant has received disclosure of the prosecution's unused material, he must, within 14 days, submit a written defence statement to the court and to the prosecution (and may need to serve the statement on any co-accused (CPIA 1996, s.5). The defence statement should include information about:

- the accused's defence, including particular defences which will be relied on;
- the facts on which he takes issue with the prosecution, and why he takes issue;
- particulars of factual matters on which he intends to rely in his defence;
- any point of law he wishes to take (including points as to admissibility of evidence or any abuse of process) and any authority which will be relied on;
- details of any alibi (CPIA 1996, s.6A).

An updated defence statement must also be filed prior to the start of the trial. If no changes need making to the defence statement, a witness statement confirming this may instead be filed (s.6B).

Where a defendant fails to file a defence statement, sets out inconsistent defences, or puts forward a different defence at trial, the court or jury may draw appropriate inferences when deciding the defendant's guilt (CPIA 1996, s.11). Inferences can also be drawn if the disclosure is late, if D raises facts which were not disclosed under section 6A or relies on an alibi that was not disclosed. Although an inference alone cannot prove guilt, the prosecution can use the defence statement to prove inconsistencies in a defence or for the purposes of further enquiries. The AG's Guidelines suggest such statements also offer positive benefits to the defence, provoking the prosecution to reconsider any remaining unused material and to provide further disclosure, or to consider the appropriateness of discontinuing the case (para. 15).

Where a defendant pleads not guilty to an offence tried by the magistrates, they are not obliged to provide a defence statement (CPIA 1996, s.6), and defence statements are not routinely provided in summary cases where there is often little gained by it.

7.3.3 Third-party information

When the police, complying with their duties to pursue all reasonable lines of inquiry, become aware that a third party, for example, a local authority or a hospital, have material or information which might be relevant to the prosecution case, the police must take appropriate steps to obtain that material, retain it and make it available to the prosecution to disclose (disclosure is required if the material is used or unused material). Material held by third parties is not prosecution material if it has not been inspected, recorded and retained during the course of the relevant criminal investigation.

Where the police and prosecution need to inspect third party material to determine its relevance, such third parties must consider whether any statutory provision prevents disclosure, and identify statutory provisions which authorise information sharing. A DPA 1998, s.29 exemption may apply where personal data is shared for investigation and prosecution purposes, but suitable Schedule 2 (and possibly Sched. 3) conditions must be identified.

Where information is held by a third party, the prosecution should establish whether that third party wishes to withhold disclosure on public interest grounds, and whether an application for PII must be made. CPIA 1996, s.16 enables third parties to be heard in relation to a PII claim.

If the third party refuses to allow inspection but it is reasonable to seek production of the information, or where the third party requires the prosecution to obtain an order for disclosure (to ensure confidential information is lawfully disclosed) the prosecution may need to obtain a witness summons. The defendant may also seek a witness summons where the third party refuses voluntary disclosure and the prosecution decides they do not need to seek a summons. A witness summons may be issued by the magistrates or the crown court where a person within the jurisdiction can provide material evidence and it is in the interests of justice to issue the summons (Magistrates Court Act 1980, s.97; Criminal Procedure (Attendance of Witnesses Act) 1965, s.2). Material evidence means evidence immediately admissible in evidence in the proceedings (not merely to be used for purposes of cross-examination). The applicant must show a real possibility that the third party has the information. A witness summons cannot therefore be used simply to find out if someone has information. There is no provision for the parties to examine documents before they are produced and accordingly a witness summons to produce a document may not in reality elicit the required information (see *R* v. *Alibhai and others* [2004] EWCA Crim 681).

In relation to banking material either party may apply to the magistrates' or crown court for an order to inspect or take copies under the Bankers Books Evidence Act 1879.

Where information is sought in relation to other proceedings, rather than from a particular authority (for example, where information disclosed in proceedings under the Children Act 1989 reveals that a parent has assaulted their child), it is suggested that a party to those proceedings, such as the local authority (who may not disclose information to the police or prosecution without court permission), should seek an order authorising disclosure, detailing what may be disclosed, to whom and for what purposes (*Disclosure: A Protocol For the Control And Management Of Unused Material In The Crown Court* (2006) paras. 52–62; Crim PR Part 28).

7.3.4 Withholding information

Documents protected by advice or litigation privilege (defined at **7.2.2**) are privileged from disclosure in criminal proceedings. Where privileged material is inadvertently disclosed the court may restrain use of the material, where required in the interests of justice (*R* v. *G and B* [2004] 2 Cr App R 37).

The privilege against self-incrimination may be asserted in criminal proceedings, where a party is compelled to provide evidence. Where it is asserted, the court must be satisfied there are reasonable grounds for apprehending a real and appreciable danger to the witness, taking account of the circumstances of the case and the nature of the evidence the witness is called to give (*R (CPS)* v. *Bolton Magistrates Court* [2004] 1 Cr App R 33). If the court is so satisfied (and latitude is given to the witness in judging this) it must uphold the privilege, even if the witness themselves does not appreciate the risk of incrimination, or is refusing to answer in bad faith.

The disclosure of information covered by the Sexual Offences (Protected Material) Act 1997 (statements, photographs or medical reports relating to victims of sexual offending) is carefully regulated. Where such information would ordinarily be provided to a defendant it should instead be provided to the defendant's legal representative who must provide undertakings with regard to how the information may be used, for example, to only allow the defendant to view the material under supervision.

PII is the primary reason for withholding prosecution material.

The prosecution may apply, on public interest immunity grounds, to withhold information they must otherwise disclose to the defence (CPIA 1996, ss.3(6), 7(8), 8(5)), for example, to protect confidential information (see *R (On the application of B)* v. *Crown Court at Stafford* [2007] 1 WLR 1524, in which PII attached to the victim's psychiatric records).

> Circumstances may arise in which material held by the prosecution and tending to undermine the prosecution or assist the defence cannot be disclosed to the defence, fully or even at all, without the risk of serious prejudice to an important public interest. The public interest most regularly engaged is that in the effective investigation and prosecution of serious crime, which may involve resort to informers and under-cover agents, or the use of scientific or operational techniques (such as surveillance) which cannot be disclosed without exposing individuals to the risk of personal injury or jeopardizing the success of future operations.
>
> *R* v. *H* [2004] 2 AC 134, para. 18

(Restrictions are also imposed upon disclosure of unused material relating to the interception of communications (ss.3(7), 6(9), 8(6)).

Before applying to the court to withhold material which should otherwise be disclosed, on the basis of a:

> real risk of serious prejudice to an important public interest, prosecutors should aim to disclose as much of the material as they properly can (for example, by giving the defence redacted or edited copies or summaries). . . . It is only in truly borderline cases that the prosecution should seek a judicial ruling on the disclosability of material in its possession.
>
> AG's guidelines para. 20

If no PII application is brought by the prosecution, or it is the prosecution who seek information, a third party who objects to disclosure may make a PII claim themselves in relation to material they hold. In any event, where a third party demonstrates they have an interest in material allegedly subject to PII, the court must not make an order until that third party has been heard (s.16).

The European Court has confirmed that disclosure may be withheld from the defence, but any restriction to a defendant's rights should be proportionate to the protection of public interests, and protected by procedural safeguards (*Rowe and Davis* v. *UK* (2002) 30 EHRR 1). Ordinarily, the defence should be informed of any PII application and of the type of material being withheld. The defence should be permitted to make representations in favour of disclosure. If an application is made without notice the judge should, having considered the document, conclude whether to inform the defence and afford them opportunity to make representations. There are concerns that ex parte PII hearings may not satisfy Article 6 (*Edwards and Lewis* v. *UK* [2003] All ER (D) 368).

Where public interest immunity is argued:

> . . . a judge is balancing on the one hand the desirability of preserving the public interest in the absence of disclosure against, on the other hand, the interests of justice. Where the interests of justice arise in a criminal case touching and concerning liberty or conceivably on occasion life, the weight to be attached to the interests of justice is plainly very great indeed
>
> *R* v. *Ward* [1993] 1 WLR 619

If 'the disputed material may prove the accused's innocence or avoid a miscarriage of justice, then the balance comes down resoundingly in favour of disclosing it' (*R* v. *Keane* [1994] 1 WLR 746, per Lord Taylor CJ).

Should information be withheld?

1. What is the material which the prosecution seek to withhold?
2. Might the material weaken the prosecution case or strengthen that of the defence? If No, disclosure need not be ordered. If Yes, full disclosure should be ordered (subject to (3), (4) and (5)).
3. Is there a real risk of serious prejudice to an important public interest if full disclosure of the material is ordered? If No, full disclosure should be ordered.
4. If the answer to (2) and (3) is Yes, can the defendant's interest be protected without disclosure or disclosure be ordered to an extent or in a way which will give adequate protection to the public interest in question and also afford adequate protection to the interests of the defence (for example, by providing summaries, extracts of evidence, or anonymised documents)? In appropriate cases the appointment of special counsel may be a necessary step to ensure that the contentions of the prosecution are tested and the interests of the defendant protected.
5. Do the measures proposed in answer to (4) represent the minimum derogation necessary to protect the public interest in question? If No, the court should order such

greater disclosure as will represent the minimum derogation from the golden rule of full disclosure.

6. If limited disclosure is ordered pursuant to (4) or (5), may the effect be to render the trial process, viewed as a whole, unfair to the defendant? If Yes, then fuller disclosure should be ordered even if it may lead the prosecution to discontinue the proceedings so as to avoid having to make disclosure.

It is important that the answer to (6) should not be treated as a final, once-and-for-all, answer but as a provisional answer which the court must keep under review.

(See *R* v. *H* [2004] 2 AC 134, para. 36)

7.3.5 Disclosure of information relating to criminal proceedings

Criminal proceedings usually take place in open court. Information provided in open court may be reported, shared, etc. unless the court imposes specific restrictions. However, whilst material gathered during the course of a criminal investigation and disclosed by the prosecution under the CPIA 1996 may be used for the purpose of the current proceedings, e.g. disclosed to an expert witness, barrister, client, etc. it may not otherwise be used or disclosed by the defence, (CPIA 1996, s.17(1)), save:

(a) for the purpose of further criminal proceedings (for example an appeal);
(b) to the extent that it has been communicated to or displayed to the public in open court (save where the proceedings are for contempt);
(c) where it is used in accordance with a court order, sought under Crim PR, rule 26, authorising such further use. If a third party with an interest in the document, or the prosecution applies to be heard, no order may be made before hearing them.

It is a contempt of court to disclose information in breach of section 17. Sections 17 and 18 effectively prevent the defendant from disclosing to friends and family disclosed information about, for example, a witness.

The common law, which applies to all disclosure not made under the CPR 1996, achieves the same result by the creation of an implied undertaking not to use the material for any purposes other than the proper conduct of the particular case (see *Taylor* v. *Director of the Serious Fraud Office* [1999] 2 AC 177).

If information is required for related proceedings before the family courts, for example, consent to disclosure should be sought from the prosecution (and possibly the court).

7.4 COURT DISCLOSURE AND THE KEY LEGAL REGIMES

The courts' approach to determining applications for disclosure and claims for PII reflects their obligations to comply with the Convention. Article 6 plays a key role in ensuring parties receive a fair trial. However, as we have also seen, this may need to be balanced against the rights of witnesses, victims, etc., afforded rights by Articles 8 (privacy), 2 (right to life) and 3 (freedom from torture), etc.

We have also identified numerous situations in which confidentiality impacts upon disclosure obligations (whether information is held by a party or sought from a third party), the law recognises important public interests in maintaining obligations of confidence, but also that confidentiality obligations must be balanced against the public interest in disclosure.

Practical examples

In *South Tyneside Metropolitan Borough Council* v. *Wickes Building Supplies* [2004] EWHC 2428 no order for disclosure of confidential information was made since disclosure would have had the effect of opening up commercially sensitive information to a rival.

In *Frankson* v. *Home Office* [2003] EWCA Civ 655 where prison officers had made statements to the police in confidence in relation to complaints of criminal assault on prisoners, the court held that the balance of two competing public interests came down in favour of disclosure but laid down stringent conditions as to the manner and extent of disclosure.

It is primarily when information is sought from a third party that careful consideration must be given to DPA 1998 compliance. Often the section 35 exemption from the non-disclosure provisions can be used: where disclosure is necessary for the purpose of, or in connection with, any legal proceedings (including prospective legal proceedings) or for the purpose of obtaining legal advice, for otherwise establishing, exercising or defending legal rights. If there is doubt about DPA 1998 compliance, it may be prudent to raise the issue with the court. Section 35 clearly applies where a court orders disclosure. Schedule 2, paragraphs 3 and 5; Schedule 3 paragraphs 6 and 7 can be used to justify sharing if an order is made.

Practical example

In *Totalise plc* v. *Motley Fool Ltd and another* [2001] All ER (D) 213, Owen J made clear that where defendants operated websites but exercised no legal or editorial control over the content of postings, a Norwich Pharmacal order could be made requiring the defendants to disclose the identity of an individual (Z) who had posted defamatory allegations about Totalise. The court concluded that DPA 1998, s.35 clearly preserved and did not restrict the right of the claimant to obtain disclosure of a tortfeasor's identity. It was clear that Z had defamed Totalise, as part of a concerted campaign. The potential audience was vast with no geographical limit and Totalise was at risk of serious damage. Z was hiding behind anonymity and Totalise had no other practical means of establishing his identity. The balance weighed clearly in favour of granting the relief sought. If it were otherwise, it would be possible for individuals to defame on websites with impunity.

DPA 1998, s. 7 may also be used where a party wishes to obtain their own personal data for the purpose of court proceedings in which they are involved (for example to obtain medical records for personal injury proceedings). However, in criminal proceedings, section 29 may prevent disclosure, if disclosure would be likely to prejudice the prosecution of crime (it may be difficult to demonstrate prejudice where information sought is material which would later be disclosed in any event; see also **Chapter 12**).

FOIA 2000 and the EIR 2004 provide another means by which litigants may obtain information for the purpose of proceedings in which they are involved, supplementing the disclosure rules relating to disclosure by parties, and by third parties. Accordingly it may not, in fact, be necessary to obtain a witness summons or order for disclosure if the third party from whom information is sought is a public authority. The advantages of obtaining information under FOIA 2000 or the EIR 2004 are, of course, that ordinarily no restriction is imposed upon further use of the information once obtained. It is deemed within the public domain and may be shared with anyone.

Having said this, of course, there may be a number of exemptions from disclosure which, in practice, subject to the public interest test, will limit use of FOIA 2000 and the EIR 2004 where the information is accessible by other means, is personal data, is confidential information, relates to commercial interests or intellectual property rights, or relates to criminal investigations (see EIR 2004, reg. 12(3) and (5); FOIA 2000, ss.21, 30, 31, 40, 41 and 43). Many of the exemptions listed above will also prevent third parties accessing information relating to proceedings.

7.5 CONCLUSION

The courts have extensive powers to require parties to civil and criminal proceedings to share information with other parties, even where information was obtained by that party from another person (and that third party does not wish that information to be disclosed). The courts also have extensive powers to require third parties to share material/relevant information, again against their wishes.

If an individual or organisation wishes to withhold disclosure, they must understand when and how privilege and public interest immunity may be claimed. Of some comfort to those obliged to disclose information contrary to their wishes must be the clear restrictions upon further disclosure of information acquired to conduct court proceedings.

To fully understand when parties may be obliged to share information, or when they can obtain information, the DPA 1998, HRA 1998, FOIA 2000 and EIR 2004 should be read in conjunction with the rules on disclosure.

PART II

Application of the law

CHAPTER 8

Healthcare

Helen Kingston

8.1 INTRODUCTION

This chapter considers the legal provisions relevant both to practitioners working within healthcare settings and to practitioners seeking healthcare information.

In the healthcare context, perhaps more than any other, legal, ethical, moral and professional obligations of confidence have long played a key role in determining whether information is shared. The Hippocratic Oath states clearly:

> All that may come to my knowledge in the exercise of my profession or in daily commerce with men which ought not to be spread abroad, I will keep secret and will never reveal.

Whilst in reality health information is no longer kept secret, the British Medical Association (Confidentiality and Disclosure of Health Information, 1999) recognises a 'moral duty of confidentiality' is 'an essential requirement for the preservation of trust between patients and health professionals'. The General Medical Council confirms: 'Doctors hold information about patients which is private and sensitive. This information must not be given to others unless the patient consents or you can justify the disclosure.' (GMC 2004 *Confidentiality: Protecting and Providing Information* (the GMC Guidance)).

The Department of Health's key guidance in this area also emphasises the obligation stating all 'parts of the NHS need to establish working practices that effectively deliver the patient confidentiality that is required by law, ethics and policy', The Department of Health 2003 (*Confidentiality, NHS Code of Practice* (the NHS Code) p. 3).

Although clear professional and legal obligations (both in domestic and European Convention case law) exist to maintain and protect the confidentiality of the medical record, the precise nature of the obligation and questions about disclosure without consent in the public interest, can cause difficulties in practice. This becomes particularly apparent when dealing with certain groups, such as children or adults who lack capacity, and the deceased (see **8.6**).

Since the information obtained by health professionals will usually be sensitive personal data under the DPA 1998 this already complex picture becomes yet more involved. To assist practitioners throughout this chapter cross-references are used to illustrate when and how lawful sharing under the duty of confidentiality, for example, also ensures compliance with the Convention and the DPA 1998. Whilst relatively few cases offer specific guidance on sharing health information, fortunately, practical advice should also be available in the healthcare context from several sources, including the Caldicott Guardian (previously considered at **5.5**).

8.2 THE DUTY OF CONFIDENTIALITY

Having identified in Chapter 5 that a duty of confidence arises only in relation to information of a confidential nature, which has been disclosed in circumstances where it is reasonable to impose a duty, we now consider when the duty arises in the healthcare context.

8.2.1 Confidential health information

This chapter focuses on healthcare information, particularly medical records. Some of the information contained in such records may not legally be confidential information (because it is trivia or is already in the public domain). This very issue was considered in *Stevens* v. *Plymouth City Council* [2002] EWCA Civ 388, para. 33 in the context of care provided by the local authority to an adult, subject to guardianship under the Mental Health Act 1983. The patient's mother sought access to local authority records about her son. The court observed that:

> some of the information will indeed be confidential to C: the most obvious examples are the medical reports and recommendations but social workers and other professionals also owe him a duty to respect his confidences. Some of the information may be confidential to other people: opinions shared at professional's meetings could fall within this category. But some of it may not be confidential at all: straightforward descriptions of everyday life are not normally thought confidential.

The court was, however, 'content to assume that most if not all of the information sought is covered by a common law obligation of confidence'.

Practical example

Dan, who suffers from schizophrenia, has been receiving inpatient treatment for mental disorder, for nine months. During this time records have been kept relating to his care, including medical records recording his diagnosis, details of his treatment, medication and nursing notes relating to his presentation on the ward and nursing interventions. The records contain details of his diet and daily activities on the ward, and include references to visits by friends, family and fellow inpatients. The records also contain copies of correspondence with Dan's GP and social services, including the social worker involved in Dan's care.

Whilst some records contain information which is clearly confidential (e.g. details of his diagnosis and medical treatment), others contain descriptions of everyday life which might not normally be thought confidential. In practical terms it is safest to start by assuming that all information within health records is confidential.

8.2.2 When the duty arises

Under common law a duty of confidentiality arises in relation to confidential medical information as a result of the nature of the relationship between health professional and the patient. The range of individuals who may be subject to such a duty includes doctors, nurses, nursing assistants, secretaries, ward clerks, receptionists, porters and radiographers, etc. Contractual duties of confidence may also be imposed on healthcare professionals through their employment contracts.

8.2.3 Lawful sharing

The fact that information is subject to the duty does not prevent it from ever being disclosed. Indeed such information will frequently be shared between health professionals and may be shared with third parties, such as solicitors, insurance companies offering critical illness, travel and life insurance, pension fund providers, occupational health departments, employers, social services and the police.

Legal authority to share confidential information is provided when:

- the patient (or someone empowered to act on the patient's behalf) consents;
- disclosure is in the public interest;
- disclosure is required by court order or statutory provision.

Consent

Where the patient expressly or impliedly consents to information being disclosed then it may be disclosed (assuming no statutory provision prohibits its disclosure). The requirements for valid consent, and distinctions between express and implied consent are considered in the **Introduction**.

Frequently where health information is disclosed within the healthcare context, this is done on the basis of implied consent. The NHS Code paragraphs 14–16 notes that where patients:

> . . .have been informed of:
>
> (a) the use of their information associated with their healthcare; and
> (b) the choices that they have and the implications of choosing to limit how information may be used or shared;

then explicit consent is not usually required for information disclosures needed to provide that healthcare.

Generally information is provided to patients by means of NHS leaflets and booklets (see NHS Code, Annex B at p. 29). However, since consent is only validly provided if the patient understands how their information will be shared, careful consideration must always be given to whether individual patients are able to read these leaflets, or whether information needs to be provided in another form.

The same reliance upon implied consent is not appropriate for non-healthcare disclosures (para. 16). Where information is sought by a third party, such as a solicitor (for example, in order to represent a client in relation to a complaint or claim arising out of the provision of health care), express consent should be obtained.

Practical example

Dan's health information is held in several different places. His general medical records are held by his GP, his mental health, nursing, medical and statutory (under the Mental Health Act 1983) records are held by the hospital where he is an inpatient. On a daily basis his records are accessed by administrative staff, as well as the nursing and medical staff who provide his care. Dan's GP also needs to be kept informed of Dan's condition and is involved from time to time in reviews of Dan's care. Dan's social worker is also involved with the care reviews.

It is likely that the sharing of information described above is covered by implied consent, in particular in relation to the sharing of information within the hospital. It is important, however, that Dan is informed about how his information may be shared, both within and outside the healthcare setting (to also comply with the DPA 1998 first principle). Care needs to be taken to ensure that too much or inappropriate reliance is not placed on Dan's implied consent. Whenever in doubt whether disclosure is covered by implied consent, express consent should be obtained and recorded.

If Dan refuses to consent to his GP being kept informed, or information being shared with his social worker then information sharing will need to be justified on other grounds.

Whilst it should be presumed that Dan, as any other adult, has capacity to consent to sharing information (Mental Capacity Act 2005, s.1), in certain circumstances patients may not be able to consent due to age, lack of capacity or otherwise. Consideration should always be given to such issues (see the **Introduction** and **8.6**). Even if unlikely to be forthcoming, consent should, other than in exceptional circumstances, be sought in advance. The patient should be informed (see GMC guidance, para. 27) and given an opportunity to raise objections and seek advice where necessary. For obvious reasons, if there is a challenge to disclosure it is preferable for that to be dealt with prior to, rather than after, disclosure. In particularly difficult cases guidance from the court may be sought. In emergency circumstances, however, this may not be possible.

Where consent is provided information should only be shared on a 'need to know' basis, and anonymised where possible. Appropriate systems to protect against unnecessary disclosure will be crucial in ensuring information is only shared within the terms of any consent, whether implied or explicit. (The DPA 1998, third and seventh principles also require no more information than necessary to be shared, and to ensure appropriate security arrangements are in place to prevent inappropriate sharing).

Further guidance on consent in the medical context can be obtained from the DoH website (see A–Z policy guidance under consent). Guidance is also given in the NHS Code at pages 30–3.

Public interest disclosure

For disclosure of confidential information to be justified in the public interest it is necessary that:

- there is a public interest in disclosure; and
- this public interest in disclosure outweighs the public interest in maintaining the confidentiality of the information.

Essentially, what is required is a balancing exercise; balancing the importance of the information being kept confidential with the importance of sharing the information.

***W* v. *Egdell* [1990] 1 All ER 835**

W was detained in a high secure hospital receiving treatment for mental disorder following an incident (some years previously) where W had killed and seriously injured a number of people. An independent consultant psychiatrist examined W at the request of W's solicitors in order to provide a report to be used in connection with an application to a Mental Health Tribunal. The report identified several concerns concerning W's mental health and appropriateness of discharge from hospital. Dr Egdell considered it was necessary for his report to be shared with the Secretary of State and the hospital with responsibility for W's treatment. W refused to consent to such disclosure. The report's disclosure was challenged by W as unlawful and a breach of confidentiality. The court ultimately held that on balancing the two competing public interests (the public and private interest in W's confidentiality being maintained versus the public interest in the disclosure of the report), the balance came down firmly in favour of disclosure.

Although *Egdell* provides an example of when and how information may be disclosed in the public interest, determining in any given scenario where the balance falls may be very challenging. Ultimately it will be a matter for the courts to decide.

From a practical point of view, it is important to be able to demonstrate how any decision was made, where disclosure is being justified 'in the public interest'. Records should demonstrate factors considered, the balancing exercise (including factors both 'for and against' the decision ultimately taken) and reasons for conclusions reached. In difficult cases it may well be prudent to seek advice in advance, for example, from Trust solicitors, the Caldicott Guardian, insurers or professional bodies (although in seeking advice careful thought will need to be given to the information that needs to be shared and particularly where professional bodies are consulted, whether any patient identifying information needs to be disclosed).

In all cases it is important to be clear why and with whom information needs to be shared. The identity of the individual to whom information is disclosed can be crucial. It may be justifiable to disclose the information to another professional, for example social services or the police who will also be subject to obligations of confidentiality, but not to a family member. Once information has been disclosed, any control over it is effectively lost.

It is equally important to consider the amount of information disclosed. Whilst this should be the minimum necessary to achieve the purpose of sharing (this proportionality is also key to compliance with Article 8 of the Convention), sufficient information needs to be disclosed to enable appropriate actions and decisions to be taken by the recipient.

Practical example

Dan is now ready for discharge from hospital. A care plan is to be drawn up to cover his discharge and care in the community. A meeting of the professionals who may be involved in his community care is arranged. This includes Dan's consultant and representative of the nursing team caring for Dan in hospital, Dan's GP, Dan's social worker and a community psychiatric nurse who will supervise Dan in the community. A representative of a local housing association which has agreed to accommodate Dan is present. In addition a police officer attends, since there is a small possibility that, should Dan's condition deteriorate, he could pose a risk to himself or others.

Certain disclosures at the meeting, about Dan and his medical condition, may be covered by implied consent. However it is unlikely this would cover disclosures to the police or housing. Express consent should, therefore, be sought from Dan. If Dan cannot or will not consent, it may be justified to disclose information to the police and housing in the public interest. This will require Dan's refusal, the importance of maintaining confidentiality and the impact on the therapeutic relationship with Dan to be balanced against the need for the information to be shared in the wider public interest. Relevant factors will include level of risk, likelihood of the risk occurring and why it is necessary for information to be shared. If the information cannot be shared, it may not be appropriate for Dan to be discharged.

Ultimately it should be borne in mind that any decision to disclose without consent is a serious decision which the professional may be called upon to justify, for example to a court or their professional body.

8.2.4 Court order

The civil courts have extensive powers to order disclosure of documents by parties and sometimes non-parties, for example when a civil claim is brought for clinical negligence or a local authority applies for a care order. The criminal courts may also order disclosure of the medical records of the defendant, victim and even witnesses (see **Chapter 7**). The Court of Protection may order disclosure under the Mental Capacity Act 2005.

The NHS Code states that where courts and tribunals order disclosure (p. 28):

> This does not require the consent of the patient whose records are to be disclosed but he/she should be informed, preferably prior to disclosure. Disclosures must be strictly in accordance with the terms of a court order and to the bodies specified in the order. Where staff are concerned that a court order requires disclosure of sensitive information that is not germane to the case in question, they may raise ethical concerns with the judge or presiding officer. If however the order is not amended it must be complied with.

Where a court orders disclosure, this provides lawful authority to share confidential information (it will also satisfy Sched. 2 para. 3, Sched. 3 para. 6, and under DPA 1998, s.35 exempts the data controller from complying with the non-disclosure provisions, see **8.4**).

Information should be shared in accordance with the order (which will, for example, detail time limits for disclosure). However, as the NHS code recognises, steps should still be taken before providing disclosure, to clarify exactly what the order covers, to whom disclosure is required, and why the information is sought. This enables proper consideration to be given to the extent of disclosure required (as required to comply with the Article 8 requirement of proportionality and the DPA 1998 third principle).

Whilst the NHS code states that consent is not required, this should be read in the light of the decision in *TB* v. *Stafford Combined Court & Others* [2006] EWHC 1645 Admin. The High Court was asked to consider an order made by the crown court for disclosure of psychiatric records of a 14-year-old girl, who had previously attempted suicide and was said to be vulnerable, in the context of the prosecution of a man accused of sexual offences against her. The High Court in judicially reviewing the decision to order disclosure, criticised the failure to notify the girl of the application, or to provide her with an opportunity to object to disclosure. Criminal Procedure Rules 2005, rule 28 has subsequently been amended to ensure that where confidential documents are sought from an NHS Trust, for example, the patient should be notified to enable them to make appropriate representations.

In addition to ordering disclosure, the court may be asked (and with the complexities of balancing conflicting rights, increasingly so) to determine whether a particular disclosure is lawful or should be prevented. The court's assistance may be particularly helpful in relation to adults who lack capacity, and may be sought, even where the incapable person agrees to disclosure, when concerns that disclosure is not in their best interests arise (see *E* v. *Channel Four, News International Limited and St Helen's Borough Council* [2005] EWHC 1144).

It may also be necessary to ask the court to reconsider a court order for disclosure on the basis that information is protected by public interest immunity (see **Chapter 7**).

Practical example

Julie is a severely learning disabled adult, cared for in a residential unit by the Local Authority and NHS Trust. She lacks capacity for many decisions, including to consent to disclosure of information about her. An allegation has been made by Julie and her carers that Julie has been assaulted by a male relative. The police have been involved and have investigated the allegations. They have now approached the staff of the residential unit asking for copies of all Julie's records including her medical records and social services file. They request to see everything so that the investigation can be completed and a decision taken whether to prosecute.

Care must be taken not to confuse this request with a court order requiring disclosure. Where such a request is made authority will be needed for any disclosure in the usual way (consent or disclosure in the overriding public interest) (see commentary in GMC 2004 *Confidentiality: Protecting and Providing Information*, para. 20.)

Although the police obtain Julie's consent (and that of her mother) staff are concerned that Julie does not understand what she has consented to. It is decided, however, that it is in Julie's best interests for some of her medical records relating to her mental state, which could be relevant to the trial, to be disclosed.

Some months later the police approach the unit again. The case is proceeding to trial and the defence are insisting they need to see all Julie's records. Again, due to concerns about the nature of the material and its relevance, the request is refused. The police return with a court order requiring disclosure and the attendance of the Unit Manager at court with the records. Julie's consultant psychiatrist is concerned that full disclosure of the records, which may come into the public domain during the trial, could be seriously detrimental to Julie's health. The unit request a PII hearing at which the records a summary and explanation of the unit's concerns are presented to the judge. The judge balances the competing interests and orders additional disclosure of some records, but does not order disclosure of the sensitive material that the unit was particularly concerned about.

8.2.5 Statutory provisions

In **Chapter 4** we identified several situations in which health professionals may be obliged to share information (for example, when a medical practitioner terminates a pregnancy, to prevent the spread of serious diseases and in order to prevent fraud against the NHS). National Health Service Act 2006, ss.251 and 252 (previously Health and Social Care Act 2001, ss.60 and 61) additionally empower the Secretary of State for Health to make further regulations enabling certain information to be disclosed without consent.

As with court orders, it is important to be clear exactly what information is covered by any statutory provision, before information is shared. It is important to clarify whether provisions require information to be disclosed or are simply gateway provisions which provide power, but not a duty, to disclose. (Similar considerations apply under the DPA 1998, where the section 35 exemption from the non-disclosure provisions applies when a statute obliges disclosure to be made. A statutory power to disclose does not enable a data controller to rely on section 35.)

8.2.6 Disclosures to family

Listening to information (for example, where a family member has information) should not generally involve any breach of confidentiality (though the family member should be informed that the patient may well have a right to access any information held about them as a result). Care needs to be taken, however, that information is not inappropriately disclosed in seeking information in such circumstances. The impact on the therapeutic relationship with a patient must be considered, particularly where a patient does not want family to be approached.

8.3 HUMAN RIGHTS

Health professionals employed within the NHS must, as public authority employees, ensure that they act in accordance with the Convention (HRA 1998, s.6 see **Chapter 6**). In the health context, particular care needs to be taken not to breach Article 8 of the Convention, which affords a right to respect for private and family life.

> The protection of personal data, in particular medical data, is of fundamental importance to a person's enjoyment of his or her right to respect for private and family life as guaranteed by Article 8 of the Convention. Respecting the confidentiality of health data is a vital principle in the legal systems of all the Contracting Parties to the Convention. It is crucial not only to respect the sense of privacy of a patient but also to preserve his or her confidence in the medical profession and in the health services in general.
>
> *I* v. *Finland* App no. 20511/-3, para. 38

Domestic law must afford appropriate safeguards to prevent such communication or disclosure of personal health data as may be inconsistent with the guarantees in Article 8 of the Convention (*Z* v. *Finland* (1997) 25 EHRR 371, paras. 95–6).

The NHS Code suggests that 'current understanding is that compliance with the Data Protection Act 1998 and the common law of confidentiality should satisfy Human Rights requirements' (para. 34). Whilst compliance with the DPA 1998 principles will certainly assist in demonstrating safeguards have been provided, there are undoubted differences between the three different legal regimes, and it is important to be clear exactly what needs to be demonstrated to ensure that information sharing is lawful for Convention purposes.

As *MS* v. *Sweden* [1997] ECHR 20837/92 confirms, disclosure of a person's medical records to another public authority (in this case disclosure by a clinic to the Social Insurance Office for purposes of investigating fraud), may constitute interference with Article 8.

Article 8 is, however, not an absolute right. Disclosure even against the person's wishes may be justified, provided the disclosure is made lawfully, is necessary in a democratic society to achieve certain aims (including assuring the country's economic well-being, public safety, prevention of disorder or crime, protection of health or morals, and the protection of the rights and freedoms of others), and is a proportionate response to those aims. In *MS* v. *Sweden* the European Court considered that disclosure to the social insurance office was lawful, served the legitimate aim of protecting the economic well-being of the country, and since the disclosure was relevant to a benefits claim the applicant herself had made, was not disproportionate to the aim pursued.

To determine whether interference breaches Article 8, a similar balancing act to that undertaken under the duty of confidentiality must be carried out.

> The interests in protecting the confidentiality of such information will . . . weigh heavily in the balance in determining whether the interference was proportionate to the legitimate aim pursued. Such interference cannot be compatible with Article 8 of the Convention (art. 8) unless it is justified by an overriding requirement in the public interest. . . . any State measures compelling communication or disclosure of . . . information [in this case confidential information relating to HIV infection] without the consent of the patient call for the most careful scrutiny . . . as do the safeguards designed to secure an effective protection . . . At the same time, the Court accepts that the interests of a patient and the community as a whole in protecting the confidentiality of medical data may be outweighed by the interest in investigation and prosecution of crime and in the publicity of court proceedings
>
> *Z* v. *Finland*, paras. 95–7

Practical example

John attends A&E with head injuries consistent with being in a fight. He is treated and admitted to a ward for observations. The next day the police attend A&E asking for information. John is said to have been involved in a serious incident where a fight broke out in a nearby pub and a young man has been killed. The police ask for disclosure of the medical records and a report from the A&E doctor on John's condition and injuries.

John refuses to consent to disclosure. He argues that if information is shared with the police he will sue for breach of his human rights.

Whilst disclosure of John's medical records will constitute interference with his article 8 rights, the information can be disclosed.

In accordance with the law

The information can be disclosed under common law in the public interest, see also Crime and Disorder Act, s.115. Disclosure will not breach the Data Protection principles (see **8.4**).

Pursues a legitimate Article 8(2) aim

Information can be disclosed for prevention of crime.

Proportionate

Disclosure is a proportionate response bearing in mind the severity of the allegations and nature of the information requested.

In certain circumstances a further balancing exercise may need to be carried out, to balance competing rights within Article 8 itself, for example in relation to a parent and their child, or to balance Article 8 against other articles. In *Andersson* v. *Sweden* Application no. 20022/92, where a mother's medical records which disclosed information relating to her mental health problems were shared with social services, the European Court recognised that whilst the referral did interfere with the right to respect for private life, it also pursued the legitimate aim of protecting health or morals and the rights and freedoms of others and was necessary in a democratic society.

Undoubtedly, therefore, whilst the focus for health professionals may be Article 8, the positive obligations imposed upon public authorities (to prevent inhuman and degrading treatment (Article 3) and to act to preserve life (Article 2 and *Osman* v. *United Kingdom* (1990) 1 FLR 193) cannot be ignored (see **Chapter 6** for further consideration of conflicts between the articles). Whilst we have hitherto, therefore, considered how we can ensure that it is legally possible to share, we must also recognise that there may be situations when there may be a duty to a third party, for example, to warn them of possible risk/harm posed by a patient, which requires the disclosure of confidential information about that patient. This involves difficult legal considerations and expert advice may be necessary to assist with what is essentially a balance of competing public interests and potential legal (and other) risks involved in disclosure or non disclosure.

8.4 DATA PROTECTION ACT 1998

8.4.1 When the DPA 1998 applies in the healthcare context

Having considered the obligations imposed by the DPA 1998 in some detail in **Chapter 2**, we now consider their specific application in the healthcare context.

Application of key DPA 1998 provisions to health information

Data

This includes information which is:

(a) stored on or accessed via a computer in, for example, a GP's surgery or an electronic patient database or is recorded with the intention of being so stored;
(b) information which is not held electronically but is organised in a filing system by, for example, patient name; or
(c) in a health record.

Health record

A health record is a record which consists of information relating to the physical or mental health or condition of an individual and has been made by or on behalf of a health professional in connection with the care of that individual.

Personal data

This means data which identifies the patient, or data which when read with other information held by the data controller will identify the patient. If information has been completely anonymised then it will not be caught by the DPA 1998. However, in practice it may be difficult to completely anonymise such data. For example, the fact that individual identifying details have been removed from a particular report does not prevent it from being personal data, where the data controller still holds the original information.

Of course, the DPA 1998 does not apply to the deceased patient (although it seems the duty of confidentiality and Article 8 will do so).

Sensitive personal data

Personal data which relates to the physical or mental health or condition or the sexual life of an individual (for example information disclosed by a minor in order to obtain contraceptive advice) will always be sensitive data.

Health professional

This is defined in section 69, and includes for example, doctors, dentists, nurses.

Data subject

If a patient's personal data is held by a data controller then the patient will be a data subject.

Generally, any sharing of patient information (as well as the collection, recording, etc. of such information for such purposes) will be processing of personal data for the purposes of the DPA 1998. Consequently it must be carried out in accordance with the DPA 1998 principles, unless an exemption from part or all of any principle applies.

8.4.2 The First Data Protection Principle

The first principle is particularly important in the healthcare context. As noted in **Chapter 2**, the first principle requires information sharing to be:

- lawful;
- fair;
- undertaken in accordance with one of the Schedule 2 conditions, and where it concerns sensitive personal data (healthcare data will mainly consist of sensitive personal data) in accordance with one of the Schedule 3 conditions.

Lawful

The NHS Code confirms the first principle imposes a requirement which includes meeting common law confidentiality obligations (Annex B, p. 36, para. 39). It also requires compliance with article 8 provisions and adherence to any obligations to disclose or not to disclose which are imposed by statute.

Fair

Fairness requires patients to be properly and appropriately informed about how their information will be dealt with and how it may be shared. Consideration should be given to whether the patient would be surprised as to the use their information is put to; 'if so then they are not being effectively informed' (NHS Code para. 23).

Patients should be told:

- Who the data controller is, for example, identifying the particular GP practice or NHS Trust.
- The purposes of any processing. Here a balance needs to be struck between providing more information than the parent can practically read, and providing too little. Generally, saying data will be used for healthcare purposes is unlikely to be sufficient.
- Any further information which is necessary having regard to the specific circumstances, for example: what will be recorded; any specific non-routine disclosures; where disclosure is optional. (see Sched. 1 Part 2).

Essentially, information needs to sufficiently inform a patient so they are able to (a) validly consent to any disclosure, (b) exercise any rights they may have and (c) assess any risks involved in providing the information (ICO 2002 Use And Disclosure of Health Data, Guidance on the Application of the Data Protection Act, (the DPA 1998 guidance), p. 7).

Information should be provided at the outset, with the patient being given reminders from time to time, particularly regarding any unusual disclosures. Where data may be used for additional purposes (for example disclosure to social services) patients should be informed (see DPA 1998 Guidance, p. 8). However, in those instances where patient data is shared for statistical purposes, for example, and the number of patients affected is so great that it is disproportionate to notify every patient about such processing, an exemption-from providing such information applies (but general information in this regard could in any event be dealt with in a standard notice provided to all patients upon first contact).

There are clear overlaps between the fair processing requirements, and the steps that need to be taken to ensure that valid consent to sharing confidential information is provided (considered above).

Relevant Schedules 2 and 3 conditions

The following conditions are of particular relevance in the healthcare context:

SCHEDULE 2

Processing:

- with the data subject's consent (condition 1);
- to comply with a legal obligation (condition 3);
- necessary to protect the data subject's vital interests (condition 4);
- necessary for the exercise of statutory functions; or the exercise of other public functions in the public interest (condition 5);
- necessary for the purpose of legitimate interests pursued by the data controller or a third party to whom the data are disclosed, except where the processing is prejudicial to the rights and freedoms or legitimate interests of the data subject (condition 6).

SCHEDULE 3

Processing:

- with the data subject's explicit consent (condition 1);
- necessary to protect the vital interests of the data subject or another person; where consent cannot be given by or on behalf of the data subject or the data controller cannot reasonably be expected to obtain the data subject's consent; or where necessary in order to protect the vital interests of another person, where consent by or on behalf of the data subject has been unreasonably withheld (condition 3);
- necessary for the purpose of, or in connection with legal proceedings, rights or advice (condition 6);
- necessary for medical purposes, and undertaken by a health professional or a person owing a duty of confidentiality equivalent to that of a health professional (condition 8). 'Medical purposes' is defined in Schedule 3, s.8(2) to include 'the purposes of preventative medicine, medical diagnosis, medical research, the provision of care and treatment and the management of healthcare services';
- necessary for the provision of confidential advice, counselling or support (2000 order, condition 4);
- of medical data or data relating to ethnic origin for monitoring purposes (Data Protection (Processing of Sensitive Personal Data) Order 2000, SI 2000/417, condition 9).

Since only one of the conditions in each Schedule needs to be met this means that consent (although it is one of the possible conditions in both Scheds. 2 and 3) is not always necessary. It may not indeed be possible in DPA 1998 terms. Although the NHS guidance suggests that implied consent is sufficient (at least under the duty of confidentiality) to enable sharing for healthcare purposes, such implied consent would not satisfy Schedule 3, para. 1 (which requires explicit consent). The reality is, however, that it is not possible to obtain explicit consent for every healthcare disclosure, and lawful sharing for healthcare purposes is still possible and justified under Schedule 2, para. 1 (which does enable sharing with implied consent) and Schedule 3, para. 8 (sharing for medical purposes).

The conditions also provide adequate power for information sharing with non-healthcare professionals for many of the purposes already considered in the context of confidentiality or the HRA 1998 (to prevent crime, to protect an individual from serious harm or death, and to ensure effective administration of justice/that Article 6 rights to a fair trial are respected).

8.4.3 The remaining DPA 1998 principles

The other seven DPA 1998 principles, in addition to the first principle will, of course, also have to be considered in the context of information sharing. The NHS Code (para. 32), considers other key principles in the health context to be the second principle and the seventh principle. We also consider the third and fourth principles.

Second principle

Careful consideration must be given when a patient's data is first collected to any possibility that information will subsequently be disclosed to other public authorities (police, social services, the Audit Commission, etc.), both to comply with the first and second principles. The second principle is clear that subsequent use of data must be for purposes which are not incompatible with the original purposes of processing. This issue can largely be resolved through carefully considered fair processing information.

Third principle

We considered this principle briefly in the context of court orders for disclosure (see **8.2.4**). Whenever information is shared, whatever the legal basis for sharing, no more information than is necessary and relevant should be shared. This again ties in with the need for proportionality under Article 8.

Fourth principle

Considered at **2.5.4**, this principle requires information to be accurate and up to date. Compliance with this principle is essential in order to ensure that patients are treated appropriately, taking account of all health conditions diagnosed. It is crucial that a patient's contact details remain up to date, to ensure that information is not inadvertently disclosed to third parties (for example where routine reminder letters are sent).

Seventh principle

This principle requires data controllers to protect data from accidental or unlawful processing. *Z* v. *Finland* considered above, of course, requires effective measures to be put in place by state authorities, i.e. the NHS to ensure that confidential information is not disclosed in contravention of Article 8. Having sufficient organisational and technical measures to ensure information is only disclosed to those who need to have access is key to complying with Article 8, the duty of confidentiality and the DPA 1998.

8.4.4 Exemptions

The exemptions in conjunction with the appropriate Schedule 2 and 3 conditions also enable lawful sharing of health information, particularly with other public authorities.

Of particular relevance are sections 29(3) and 35. Both afford data controllers exemption from the non-disclosure provisions (the first data protection principle except for the requirement to comply with a condition in Schedule 2 or 3, the second, third, fourth and fifth data protection principles, sections 10 and 14(1) to (3)) in certain circumstances.

Practical example

When John was admitted to A&E he was told that his information would be shared for medical purposes. The police state that DPA 1998, s.29(3) enables them to obtain John's medical records and a report on John's condition notwithstanding John's objections to disclosure.

Section 29(3) does not oblige the A&E department to provide information. However, it enables information to be shared, provided:

(a) conditions under Schedule 2 and Schedule 3 are satisfied, for example, Schedule 2, para. 6 (legitimate interests) and Data Protection (Processing of Sensitive Personal Data) Order 2000 SI 2000/417 Schedule, para. 10 (processing to enable police constables to exercise their functions);
(b) disclosure is to prevent or detect crime or apprehend or detect offenders and applying the non-disclosure provisions would prejudice the prevention/detection of crime, etc.;
(c) disclosure will not breach the duty of confidentiality or obligations under the HRA 1998.

If the A&E department did not consider disclosure could be undertaken without breaching confidentiality it might be suggested to the police that a court order for disclosure be obtained (ensuring compliance with the duty of confidence and affording an alternative exemption under section 35 and Sched. 2, para. 3 and Sched. 3, para. 6).

8.5 PATIENT REQUESTS FOR INFORMATION

Whilst the focus for many will be sharing information with other professionals, health information may also be obtained by the patient (or others on their behalf).

8.5.1 DPA 1998, s.7

Section 7 entitles the patient to be told what personal data about them is held by the data controller. The data controller must also tell the patient why and with whom the Trust has shared or may share information, and where information has come from.

The patient is entitled to access to, or copies of information the data controller holds. The patient should within 40 days of submitting a written request and the necessary fee (currently £50), or if further information is required in order to comply with any request, 40 days from when this information is provided, be provided with a copy in permanent form of their records. However, where health professionals receive numerous repeat requests for access, any identical or similar request need not be complied with unless a reasonable interval has elapsed since previous data was supplied (s.8(3)). Copy information must also only be provided if it is not disproportionate to do so, the alternative being for the patient to be invited to view the records instead.

In addition to receiving copies, the patient is entitled to an explanation of records which would otherwise be unintelligible (for example where a code is needed to interpret records stored in a particular way). It is unclear whether explanations of medical information must be provided. In reality, where access is requested in the context of legal proceedings, the patient will be advised by an appropriate medical expert in any event.

8.5.2 Requests by solicitors, etc.

DPA 1998, s.7 confers a right of access to records to the patient (the data subject). It does not confer rights of access to anyone other than the patient (a solicitor has no legal right to access information on their client's behalf). Those individuals who may be required to deal with requests should understand how they can clarify whether the request is indeed made by a patient or on their behalf (thus ensuring the duty of confidentiality, HRA 1998 and the seventh principle are not breached). Obtaining a signed consent form ensures authority is provided for section 7 purposes and additionally ensures that confidential information is disclosed with consent.

8.5.3 Information that cannot be accessed under section 7

It is important to note there are limitations on the section 7 right of access.

Where the information sought is general information, for example about the data controller's policies/systems, access should be provided under FOIA 2000 or the EIR 2004.

There are also some important limitations on exactly what information held in the patient's records the patient can access. In particular, the patient cannot access certain information about other people, or information which if disclosed, might cause harm.

Third-party information

It is not uncommon for patient records to contain information about, or received from, a third party. Generally the patient is not entitled access to such information if it is information from which the third party can be identified (whether from the information alone or when taken together with other information the data controller believes the patient has or may obtain (s.8(7)). This does not apply, however, where the third party identified is a health professional who has provided the information in a professional capacity (s.7(4)). Health professionals must be made aware that the patient may request and read comments made in their records.

Where the third party is not a health professional, the data controller does not have to comply with the request if it cannot do so without identifying the third party, unless the third party consents to the disclosure, or the data controller deems it reasonable in the circumstances to disclose without consent (s.7(4)(b)). This necessarily involves very careful consideration and balancing of factors including any duty of confidentiality owed to the third party, whether the third party can consent and whether they have refused to do so (s.7(6)). The data controller must be prepared to justify any decision, whether to withhold or provide disclosure.

It may, however, be possible to comply with most of the patient's request by simply removing reference to the third party. Care must be taken here to ensure all necessary information is removed. It may still be possible for the patient to be able to identify a third party even though their name is removed.

Data Protection (Subject Access Modification) (Health) Order 2000 SI 2000/413

This order provides the other important qualification to patients' access rights. It applies to personal data consisting of information as to the physical or mental health or condition of the data subject (thus medical records). This order provides an exemption to access where a health professional considers disclosure would be likely to cause serious harm to the physical or mental health of the data subject or any other person. If the data controller is not a health professional (e.g. a Trust) then the appropriate health professional, usually the health professional in charge of the patient's care (the order refers to the health professional who is currently or was most recently responsible for the clinical care or if more than one such professional, the one who is the most suitable), must be consulted. If there is no such professional, any professional with necessary experience and qualifications can carry out the task. The order requires the data controller to determine whether the exemption applies before any disclosure is made (unless the application of such an exemption has been considered by a health professional in the last six months, and the position confirmed in writing).

Article 4 of the Order also exempts the data controller from its obligation to satisfy the fair processing requirement of the first principle, and from its obligation to comply with section 7, where certain documents have been prepared for certain court proceedings concerning children (this aligns the DPA 1998 with the court rules that enable the court to withhold such documents).

Practical example

Jason has a history of schizophrenia and has spent lengthy periods in hospital. His nursing and medical records are substantial, recording details of his treatment and care whilst in hospital. They include references to other patients on the ward and Jason's interaction with them. They also detail an incident that occurred on the ward, including the response and involvement of a nurse on the ward.

Jason is bringing a claim against the NHS Trust responsible for the hospital and has signed a consent form authorising his solicitor to access his records.

Before access is given, the consultant psychiatrist in charge of Jason's care reviews the records to consider whether any exemptions to disclosure apply. He concludes that the third-party information relating to other patients should be redacted from the copy records sent to Jason's solicitor. The details relating to the nurse need not be redacted.

8.6 SPECIAL GROUPS

Having considered generally when information may be shared, when it may not be shared and when it must be shared, we now turn to the additional considerations relevant to three groups: children, those who lack capacity and the deceased.

8.6.1 Children

The starting point should be that a child (generally anyone under 18), is entitled to the same duties and rights as an adult (under the common law, DPA 1998 and HRA 1998). In reality, however, some children are insufficiently mature to exercise their rights. (A child's ability to request information under DPA 1998, s.7 and the parent's role where the child is incapable of making such a request is considered in **Chapter 10**.)

If a child is incapable of providing consent to disclosure, or refuses to do so, there are alternative means by which legal authority to share information (for healthcare or for other purposes) may be provided.

- Where 'a competent young person or child refuses treatment for a life threatening condition, a doctor's duty of care would require confidentiality to be breached to the extent of informing those with parental responsibility for the child who might then be able to provide the necessary consent to the treatment' (NHS Code, para. 9).
- Where the child is not competent or is incapable of consenting to disclosure, although there is no direct case law or statutory guidance on this point, it seems that someone with parental responsibility can consent to disclosure on their behalf, for example to enable treatment which the adult has consented to being carried out. (We considered in our introductory chapter how the child's ability to consent to treatment is determined, and the ability of a parent to consent on the child's behalf.)
- Confidential information can be shared by one health professional with another, if the disclosure is made to provide appropriate care for the child, and provided it is demonstrably in the overriding interest to share that information to protect the child's health. The minimum amount of information should be disclosed only to those health professionals who need to see it. Justifications for such disclosure can also be found in the DPA 1998, Sched. 2 para. 4 (vital interests), para. 5 (to exercise statutory or public functions) and para. 6 (legitimate interests), and under Schedule 3 para. 3 (vital interests), para. 7 (to exercise statutory functions) and para. 8 (medical purposes). Such disclosure would not breach Article 8 of the Convention where information sharing was a proportionate response to the need to protect the child's health.
- Where neither the child or parent will consent to disclosure to another organisation (for example to social services), again, health information may lawfully be shared provided the action has been taken in the overriding public interest, can be justified under the HRA 1998 as a proportionate response to the reason for sharing and where the DPA 1998 principles are satisfied (unless an exemption applies).
- The court may also be asked to consent to or confirm the legality of disclosure, in the child's best interests.

One of the biggest problems in practice is likely to be raised when a parent seeks information about her child's healthcare. Although a parent can act upon her child's behalf, she does not have a right in her own regard to access her child's health information. Sharing information because the parent has requested information, or indeed in order to simply inform the parent is unlikely to be justifiable under Article 8, the DPA 1998 or the duty of confidentiality, particularly where the child is themselves competent to consent to treatment (see *On the application of Axon* v. *Secretary of State for Health* [2006] All ER (D) 148).

8.6.2 Incapable adults

We have already seen that whilst it is common practice for patients to be asked to consent to information sharing, it is not always necessary to obtain patient consent. When a patient lacks capacity to consent, but information still needs to be shared, whether amongst health professionals and other carers or with other agencies (such as social care), alternative avenues for justifying disclosure must be found, unless the patient provided consent while they still had capacity. As for the incapable/incompetent child, it may be perfectly possible to justify disclosure of confidential information in the public interest (to protect the patient's health), and, as for children, it should not be too difficult to justify disclosure either under the DPA 1998 or the HRA 1998, for healthcare purposes. Consent to disclosure can also, post implementation of the Mental Capacity Act 2005 (MCA 2005), now be obtained from another person.

The MCA introduces processes for proxy decision making, namely Lasting Powers of Attorney (LPAs), together with granting very wide jurisdiction to the new Court of Protection (including the power to appoint Deputies to make certain decisions). Such proxy decision makers will be entitled to make a section7 request for access to relevant information where necessary to enable them to exercise their decision-making powers, and subject to the Data Protection (Subject Access Modification) (Health) Order 2000, which also applies to an incapable adult.

Disclosure is also impliedly permitted to enable care and treatment to be provided in the patient's best interests. The assessment of best interests (s.4), which requires consideration of the patient's own wishes, and consultation with relevant carers and family, clearly suggests that information will be shared (although no more than is necessary and would be expected by the patient).

Although MCA 2005 does not expressly consider confidentiality or information sharing, guidance can be found in pre-MCA 2005 guidance (the NHS Code, Annex B, paras. 11–15). This suggests that 'information should only be disclosed in the patient's best interests, and then only as much information as is needed to support their care' (para. 13). Similar guidance is given by the GMC (the GMC Guidance, paras. 38–9), which provides for disclosure (even against the patient's wishes) in the patient's best interests where the health professional is 'convinced that [such disclosure] is essential in the patient's best interests'. In the case of *E* v. *Channel Four, News International Limited and St Helen's Borough Council* [2005] EWHC 1144 (Fam)) (again pre-MCA 2005), the court considered the assessment of best interests in the context of disclosure, and noted that this involves 'taking into account not just medical but a wide range of ethical, social, moral, emotional and welfare considerations' (see para. 62). The court concluded that when an individual lacks capacity to make a decision for themselves, the court can decide what is in the person's best interests under the court's inherent jurisdiction (or now post-MCA 2005 under the jurisdiction of the new Court of Protection, see Chapter 16 of the MCA 2005 Code).

Interestingly, the draft revised GMC guidance on confidentiality (*Confidentiality: A draft for consultation*, GMC, 2008, para. 58) suggests it is 'reasonable to assume that patients would want those closest to them to be kept informed of their general condition and prognosis'. However, this comment must surely be approached with some care. Any disclosure to a family member must be carefully considered, to ensure that full account is taken of the relationships between family members and the patient.

8.6.3 The deceased

There has been much legal debate as to the existence or nature of any duty of confidentiality post death. *Bluck* v. *The Information Commissioner and Epsom and St Helier University NHS Trust* EA/2006/0090 and *Lewis* v. *The Secretary of State for Health* [2008] EWHC 2196 both suggest that the duty continues after death. The GMC guidance clearly indicates a continuing obligation to maintain confidentiality of personal information after death (see GMC 2004 *Confidentiality: Protecting and Providing Information*, para. 30). For practical purposes it should be assumed that health information should be kept confidential after the patient dies, and not disclosed without lawful authority.

It is suggested by the GMC that:

> The extent to which confidential information may be disclosed after a patient's death will depend on the circumstances. If the patient had asked for any information to remain confidential his or her views should be respected. Where you are unaware of any directions from the patient, you should consider requests for information taking into account:
>
> – whether the disclosure of information may cause distress to, or be of benefit to, the patient's partner or family;
> – whether disclosure of information about the patient will in effect disclose information about the patient's family or other people;
> – whether the information is already public knowledge or can be anonymised;
> – the purpose of the disclosure.

Plon (Societe) v. *France* App no. 58148/00 also recognises that whilst Article 8 can be used to protect medical confidentiality after death, the circumstances in which that protection is sought must be taken into account. As time elapses the public interest in disclosure may prevail over the requirement to protect an individual's medical confidentiality.

The GMC guidance is currently under revision. The draft guidance, GMC 2008 *Confidentiality: a draft for consultation*, paras. 63–4, specifies certain circumstances when information may be disclosed: to a coroner (or similar officer), on death certificates, to a parent who requests information about the circumstances and causes of a child's death, to a partner, close relative or friend who requests information about the circumstances of an adult's death, where there is no reason to believe the deceased would have objected and to National Confidential Inquiries, for clinical/audit purposes, education, research, public health surveillance (such information should be anonymised or coded if possible).

In addition, although the DPA 1998 does not apply to the deceased, the deceased's personal representatives and any person who may have a claim arising out of the patient's death may lawfully obtain medical information relating to the deceased under the Access to Health Records Act 1990.

This Act affords access to a health record. A record that:

> consists of information relating to the physical or mental health of an individual who can be identified from that information and, or from that and other information in the possession of the holder of the record; and has been made by or on behalf of a health professional in connection with the care of that individual.

Under sections 4 and 5, disclosure may be limited where:

- disclosure would identify a third party (unless that third party consents to the disclosure, or is a health professional who has been involved in the patient's care);
- disclosure would be 'likely to cause serious harm to the physical/mental health of another (s.5(1), (2));
- the patient objected to access being given or to any information;
- the discloser believes disclosure would reveal information that was provided by the patient in the expectation that it would not be disclosed to the applicant;
- disclosure would reveal information obtained as a result of any examination/investigation to which the patient consented on the basis it would not be so disclosed.

Where information is provided to enable a claim to be brought, relevant information only need be disclosed (s.5(4)).

8.7 CONCLUSION

The emphasis for many health professionals when considering whether to share information will undoubtedly be their legal, ethical and professional duties to maintain patient confidentiality. The need to protect such confidentiality is clearly reflected in the case law emanating from the European Court. However, it is clear that neither the duty of confidentiality or Article 8 are breached by information sharing which is undertaken in the overriding public interest, and is proportionate to the aim pursued. In both instances a careful balancing act between the public interest in maintaining confidentiality and the public interest pursued by disclosure is required (it is this balance that in practice is undoubtedly difficult to achieve, and in many instances guidance from legal advisers, a Caldicott Guardian or the court may be needed).

The DPA 1998 is also clearly relevant within the healthcare context, with most of the data to be shared being sensitive personal data for DPA 1998 purposes. The first principle clearly requires any information to be shared in accordance with the duty of confidentiality and HRA 1998. The three regimes together provide a framework for ensuring that patients are appropriately informed about the use of their information. All recognise the importance (if not the need) for patient consent to disclosure to be considered. Again it is clear that it is possible to share information obtained in the healthcare context, without consent, for a wide range of health and non-health purposes, with wide-ranging justifications for disclosure provided under DPA 1998, Scheds. 2 and 3, and several exemptions (particularly disclosures for the purpose of crime prevention and where required by law) afforded to enable lawful information sharing.

CHAPTER 9

Employment context

Liane Atkin and Elisabeth Griffiths

9.1 INTRODUCTION

Employers process vast amounts of employee information. They often need to share information; with employment agencies, pension scheme providers, occupational health providers, accountants, marketing companies and HR consultants. They may be obliged to share information by statute (for example to vet prospective employees). In addition, where employers have associated offices, or are involved in mergers or takeovers, employee data is inevitably shared.

The DPA 1998 and the duty of confidentiality play an important role in regulating information sharing. We explore the application of both regimes in detail; from recruitment, throughout the employment relationship and post-termination of employment.

9.2 THE DUTY OF CONFIDENTIALITY

The duty of confidentiality is relevant when an employee wishes to use information shared by their employer, and when an employer considers whether to disclose employee information to third parties.

The courts recognise that an employment relationship is of a special nature, with employee and employer enjoying a relationship of trust, confidence and faith. It is important that an employer and employee can rely on the other's integrity (for example, an employee should be able to discuss health problems to assist the employer to arrange cover without worrying widespread disclosures will be made to colleagues).

The employment contract may incorporate terms specifically requiring confidentiality, and there is extensive statutory regulation protecting sensitive and confidential information. If an employee proposes to, or breaches the common law duty of confidentiality by inappropriately sharing information, their employer may take court action to prevent or remedy this. Such conduct may, in any event, breach the employment contract.

However, confidential information may be shared in certain circumstances: where consent is provided, where disclosures are made to comply with a court order or statutory obligation and where disclosure is in the overriding public interest (see also **Chapter 5**). Information that is trivial or well-known can be disclosed by employer or employee during or after employment.

9.2.1 Employee use of employer's information

Employees may use information provided by their employer only in limited circumstances, as illustrated below.

Faccenda Chicken v. *Fowler [1986] IRLR 69*

Fowler was employed to set up and operate a fleet of refrigerated vans. When he resigned he set up a rival refrigerated van operation, utilising sales information (customer names, requirements, etc.).

The Court of Appeal considered that, where parties are, or have been, linked by an employment contract, the employee's obligations should be determined by that contract. In the absence of any express term, the employee's obligations in respect of use and disclosure of information are subject to implied terms. Fowler's employment contract contained no express confidentiality clause, nor any express post-termination restraint. The employer sought to establish breach of the implied term of confidentiality.

The Court of Appeal drew distinctions between the duty during employment and the duty after employment.

While the employee remains in the employer's employment he is subject to implied duties of good faith or fidelity (confidentiality). The extent of the duty will vary according to the nature of the contract. The duty will ordinarily be broken if an employee, during his employment, makes or copies his employer's customer list for use after his employment ends.

Faccenda Chicken sought to restrain Fowler's actions after his employment ended. The Court of Appeal concluded that after the termination of employment, the obligations imposed on the employee are narrower. If information is implicitly or explicitly confidential but becomes part of the employee's skill and knowledge (for example, through the continued use of methods and processes, or customer information), it cannot be disclosed during the employment term. However, such information can be used after employment ends (even when used in competition with the previous employer). Employers can use contractual clauses to prevent using such information post-termination to a limited extent.

In order to determine whether an implied duty applies the Court of Appeal concluded that all circumstances must be considered. Where confidential material is habitually handled a higher obligation of confidentiality may be imposed, since the employee can be expected to realise its sensitive nature.

The Court of Appeal clarified that information will always be protected if it is a trade secret or material which, while not properly to be described as a trade secret, is in all the circumstances of such a highly confidential nature as to require the same protection (for example secret processes of manufacture, chemical formulae and designs or special methods of construction). Since it may be unclear whether something is tantamount to a trade secret, employers should include a specifically drafted confidentiality clause to support this common law duty and include a list of all confidential information they wish to protect which they believe amounts to a trade secret.

9.2.2 Whistleblowing

Both statute and common law now allow an employee to divulge confidential information (whistleblow) in the public interest.

Initial Services Ltd v. *Putterill* [1967] 3 All ER 145 confirmed that an employee could be justified in making public disclosures about their employer's malpractices, in the public interest, for example, in cases of crime or fraud. *Lion Laboratories Ltd* v. *Evans* [1984] 2 All ER 417 subsequently confirmed that the public interest in being informed of matters of real public concern (namely that a breathalyser gave inaccurate readings and might therefore result in wrongful convictions) can outweigh the public interest in preserving organisations' rights to maintain the secrecy of confidential information.

Part IVA Employment Rights Act 1996 (as amended by the Public Information Disclosure Act 1998) now protects, and makes it automatically unfair to dismiss, employees who make certain disclosures, even if disclosure breaches contractual duties of confidence (s.43J).

Disclosures will be protected unless they constitute a criminal offence (for example certain disclosures which breach the Official Secrets Acts). They must be made in good faith to specified individuals (including the employer, a legal adviser, the government and certain public bodies). The employee must reasonably believe disclosure will show that:

(a) a criminal offence has been, is being or is likely to be committed;
(b) a person has failed, is failing or is likely to fail to comply with their legal obligations;
(c) a miscarriage of justice has occurred, is occurring or is likely to occur;
(d) the health or safety of any individual has been, is being or is likely to be endangered;
(e) the environment has been, is being or is likely to be damaged; or
(f) information relating to any of the above matters has been, or is likely to be deliberately concealed.

9.3 THE DPA 1998 AND ITS CODES OF PRACTICE

The DPA 1998 is particularly significant in the employment context. This chapter focuses upon its application to common employment situations (although further consideration is also given to confidentiality and the HRA 1998).

9.3.1 How the DPA 1998 applies in the employment context

In most situations, employers processing employee information are data controllers processing personal data. They must comply with the DPA 1998.

Processing?

Processing is defined broadly to include obtaining, recording, sharing and merely holding data (see **2.2**). Numerous employment functions (for example, recruitment and selection, disciplinary and grievance procedures) potentially involve data processing.

Personal/sensitive personal data?

Data includes information which is processed or intended to be processed by equipment operating automatically (see **2.3**). In the employment context data could include application details, records of sickness absence or staff contact details stored on a computer database.

In addition, data includes manual information stored as part of a relevant filing system (see **2.3.2**); where information is structured either by reference to individuals (e.g. by names) or by reference to criteria related to individuals (e.g. job titles) in such a way that specific information related to an individual is readily accessible.

Practical example

In the context of recruitment and selection of employees, a filing cabinet which contains files for each job applicant sorted into alphabetical order and then sub-divided into sections for CV, covering letter, interview notes, references and decision would be a relevant filing system since it would be easy to locate any particular document for any particular applicant. By contrast a filing cabinet storing application documents in chronological order without division is unlikely to be a relevant filing system.

In the employment context, data might also include employee health records.

Whilst unstructured manual data held by a public authority is also data, such data is exempt from numerous parts of the DPA 1998 where the data relates to appointments, removals, pay, discipline, superannuation or personnel matters in relation to those serving in the armed forces or employed by any public authority or the crown (DPA 1998, s.33A, see **2.8.8**).

Personal data is data relating to a living individual who can be identified from (a) those data or (b) those data and other information in the possession of the Data Controller. (It would cover a database of anonymised test results linked by reference codes to a database of employee names, thus enabling an employer to identify individual scores, see **2.4**.)

Data held by an employer and relating to identifiable employees will be sensitive personal data if it relates to the employee's racial or ethnic origin (particularly relevant to equality monitoring), political opinions, religious or other similar beliefs, trade union membership, physical or mental health, sexual life, commission or alleged commission of any offence or any proceedings or sentence relating to any offence.

Best practice

Although consideration should always be given to the definition of personal data and whether particular employee information is caught by the definition, it is in the interests of employer/employee relations for an employer to comply with the DPA 1998 whenever dealing with employee information.

9.3.2 The DPA 1998 Code

The ICO 2005 *Employment Practices Data Protection Code* (the Code), published by the ICO under DPA 1998, s.51, aims to assist employers to comply with the DPA 1998. It is accompanied by guidance (the supplementary guidance), which contains more detail and in-depth examples of certain issues raised in the Code. It is not unlawful for an employer not to follow the Code, provided the employer complies with the DPA 1998. However, the ICO will take compliance with the Code into account when deciding whether to take enforcement action.

The Code offers practical advice on the steps employers should take in various situations, specifically considering:

- Part 1: Recruitment and selection; including how to comply with the DPA 1998 when advertising vacancies, receiving applications, interviewing and verifying a prospective employee's information.
- Part 2: Employment records; this covers the collection, retention and use of employment records from appointment through to destruction.
- Part 3: Monitoring at work.
- Part 4: Medical records; the operation of occupational health schemes, medical examination and testing of workers, drug and alcohol testing and genetic testing in the workplace.

9.4 SHARING INFORMATION WITH RECRUITMENT/EMPLOYMENT AGENCIES

Employers often use agencies to recruit employees. This necessarily involves information sharing between the employee, agency and employer. The Data

Protection principles (detailed at **2.5**) are key to lawful sharing. The first three principles are of particular relevance to recruitment and are considered in this section. These and the other principles are also explored, where appropriate, in subsequent sections.

9.4.1 The first principle

Since the first principle requires personal data to be processed fairly, the employer should, as far as practicable, ensure the prospective employee is informed of the fair collection information when personal data is obtained (para. 2(3) Part II Sched. 1). Advertisements should, therefore, include:

(a) the employer's identity (not simply an address without further details);
(b) the purposes for which data is to be processed if this is not obvious from the advertisement (if for example the advertisement is advertising one specific job the purpose should be clear but if it is inviting speculative applications it may not be);
(c) other relevant information.

Similarly, application forms should contain this information, to ensure that applicants know who they are sending their information to and what it will be used for.

Data sharing and fair processing

If an employer uses a recruitment agency the Code, paragraph 1.1.2 suggests that the agency should identify itself in the advertisement. If the employer does not wish to identify itself, only anonymised information should be sent to the employer (until it reveals its identity). In addition, the purposes of obtaining information sought by the recruitment agency for a particular vacancy must be made clear. Any additional purposes (e.g. using the information for other vacancies which may arise) must be specified in the advertisement.

The same issues will be relevant to shortlisting and interview, and, indeed, throughout the recruitment process.

*Schedule 2 (see also **2.6**)*

In the recruitment context, consent (condition 1) is likely to be the most relevant justification for processing. By submitting an application form or CV, applicants impliedly consent to their data being processed by the recruitment agency and the employer for the purposes of recruiting into the vacancy applied for.

Condition 6 may also be relevant, since it is likely that a recruitment agency and an employer would have a legitimate interest in processing information obtained from a job applicant for the purpose of filling a vacancy although whether it would be necessary as required by condition 6 is another matter.

Processing would be unlikely to prejudice a job applicant who applied for the job.

Schedule 3

There is no legitimate interests justification under Schedule 3. An employer can, however, rely upon conditions 1 and 2:

- The data subject has given explicit consent to the processing (para. 1). Note the difference from Schedule 2, where implied consent suffices.
- The processing is necessary for the purposes of exercising or performing any right or obligation which is conferred or imposed by law on the employer in connection with employment (para. 2). There are many rights and obligations imposed on employers concerning health and safety, equal opportunities monitoring, maternity and sick pay records.

Obtaining sensitive personal data

Employers and recruitment agencies should ensure they do not request any data at the recruitment stage which is not relevant to the job or necessary at the recruitment stage.

The supplementary guidance gives the example of a driving company requesting information about driving convictions (which constitute sensitive personal data) from all of its drivers. The supplementary guidance points out that information regarding convictions is only necessary if relevant to the job sought (a receptionist in the driving company need not be asked about driving convictions). The question on the application form should be appropriately phrased to prevent unnecessary information being obtained, for example asking 'have you had any driving convictions in the last five years' avoids the applicant mistakenly believing they need to reveal spent or other convictions. The form should then require the applicant to explicitly confirm their consent to the information in the form being processed, to enable the employer to process the sensitive and other personal data. (For more information on obtaining specific details of criminal convictions see **9.5.2**.)

9.4.2 The second principle

Since this principle requires consideration to be given to the notified purpose of processing, it ties in with the first data protection principle. It is further reason for employers and recruitment agencies to ensure advertisements and application forms state clearly the purpose of obtaining job applicants' personal data.

Best practice

If personal information may be used for other future purposes (for example, sharing personal data with similar or associated employers to assist in filling their vacancies) this must be made clear when information is obtained to avoid breaching the second principle. Similarly, if a recruitment agency intends to use information to fulfil other vacancies, or to market services to the applicant, this must be stated on the advertisement/application form.

9.4.3 The third principle

This principle requires personal data to be adequate, relevant and not excessive having regard to the purpose of processing. Whilst it may be tempting for employers and recruitment agencies to ask questions not directly relevant to the advertised job, or to use a lengthy pre-printed application form for all applicants irrespective of job type, this could breach the third data protection principle.

Best practice

Employers should think carefully what information they actually need to decide whether to interview a prospective applicant. They should only request information specifically relevant to the job. More information can be obtained if necessary, once the applicant is offered the job.

9.5 VERIFICATION AND VETTING

The Code distinguishes between verification and vetting:

- Verification means checking information supplied by the job applicant and taking up references.
- Vetting 'covers the employer actively making its own enquiries from third parties about an applicant's background and circumstances' (The Code, Part 1, p. 14).

Most employers are likely to verify information to a greater or lesser extent whereas vetting will only be justified in certain areas of particular sensitivity or risk (for example, protection of children or government defence). Both may require the applicant's personal data to be shared.

9.5.1 Verification

The first and second data protection principles are both relevant to verification. The act of requesting and obtaining verification of information from third parties (e.g. former employers or educational establishments) will be processing. Accordingly, the application form (or other documents) must state what information will be checked and how in order to ensure data is fairly obtained for that further purpose and is processed is accordance with the original purpose.

9.5.2 Criminal convictions

If an employer requires details of a job applicant's criminal convictions these should be sought from the Criminal Records Bureau (CRB) in compliance with the Code of Practice and CRB (undated) *Explanatory Guide for Registered Persons and Recipients of Disclosure Information*. In any event, information should only be sought where necessary for the job applied for (for example, work with children) and, to avoid breach of the third data protection principle, only when the applicant has been provisionally selected for the job (the information sought should only be that which is necessary for appointment to the job).

9.5.3 Criminal offences

Under DPA 1998, s.55 it is a criminal offence for a person to knowingly or recklessly obtain, disclose or procure disclosure of personal data without the data controller's consent. If a prospective employer misleads a previous or current employer into believing the applicant has consented to information being checked, this could breach section 55 (the third-party data controller has not given informed consent to disclosure). It is important for employers to ensure appropriate consents are obtained from job applicants and that these are clearly communicated to the third parties involved.

Best practice

If an employer wishes to check information with a third party it should obtain a signed approval from the job applicant authorising the third party to release the information without breaching the DPA 1998.

9.5.4 Ensuring accuracy of data

The fourth data protection principle requires personal data to be factually accurate and, where necessary, kept up to date. Employers should not simply assume information they obtain from third parties about job applicants is correct. They must take reasonable steps to ensure accuracy, and where an employee identifies an inaccuracy, the employer must record any conflict in information on the records (see DPA 1998, paragraph 7, Part II, Sched. 1).

Best practice

Employers should take reasonable steps to ensure information obtained from third parties is accurate by asking the job applicant about discrepancies, enabling the applicant to explain why contradictions may have arisen. If the job applicant believes the information provided by the third party is inaccurate, the employer should record this within the personal data.

9.5.5 References

An employer may wish to obtain a reference from the job applicant's previous employer or education provider and would usually ask the applicant to provide contact details for their referees. By providing these contact details, the applicant impliedly consents to the referee being contacted. The requirements of the first data protection principle should therefore be met (the same will be true where character and financial references are sought). Under, DPA 1998, Sched. 7, para. 1 confidential references given by a third-party data controller for the purposes of education, training, employment, appointment to any office or provision of any service will be exempt from the right of subject access in so far as the third-party data controller is concerned. The job applicant would not be entitled to receive a copy of the reference under DPA 1998, s.7 if he put his request to his old employer. However, this exemption does not extend to the new employer so, if the job applicant put in a request for the reference to his new employer, the new employer would need to consider whether the reference was personal data (taking account of whether the information was received and is stored electronically or, if the reference was received as a hard copy whether it is filed in a relevant filing system) and whether it could comply with the subject access request (or whether another exemption applies).

Best practice

Employers giving references should be aware that the reference can be seen by an individual who submits a subject access request to their new employer. This is particularly relevant in light of *Spring* v. *Guardian Assurance plc* [1995] 2 AC 296 in which the House of Lords held that an employer must take reasonable care when writing a reference to ensure the reference is accurate and not misleading. *Bartholomew* v. *London Borough of Hackney* [1999] IRLR 246 subsequently confirms that, whilst there is no obligation to provide a reference, if one is provided it must be fair and balanced.

9.5.6 Vetting

Many issues highlighted above are equally relevant to vetting. Since vetting is more intrusive than verification, employers should be even more careful to ensure checks are proportionate to the risks faced by the employer in employing the applicant. Such risks might relate to the employer's security, to employing unsuitable people to work with children or to the theft of highly confidential commercial information.

In order to comply with the first data protection principle, information on any vetting that may take place must again be made clear early in the recruitment process (e.g. on the application form). In order to comply with the third data protection principle, employers should only seek information relevant to the job applied for and should not attempt to use vetting as general 'intelligence gathering' (The Code, Part 1, p. 22).

Best practice

Vetting should only be carried out when applicants have been selected for the job. Vetting all shortlisted applicants could be excessive. In order to comply with the fourth data protection principle, the reliability of the information source should be assessed. The job applicant should be offered the opportunity to make representations, particularly if the information dissuades the employer from appointing them.

9.5.7 Information about employee family members/associates

The supplementary guidance suggests that in exceptional cases, for example, upon recruitment of police or prison officers, it may be necessary for an employer to obtain information about the family (or close associates) of the job applicant. If the employer does obtains personal data about such third parties, then collection of the information must comply with the first data protection principle. Thus third parties must be informed of the employer's identity (as the data controller), the fact that information has been obtained and the purposes of the processing, unless providing such information would involve a disproportionate effort or the recording or disclosure of the data is necessary for the employer to comply with statutory obligations.

Practical example

The supplementary guidance suggests that it could be disproportionate effort to provide the fair processing information to the third party if the employer does not hold contact details for the third party and will only be retaining the information for a very short period. Finding and providing information to the third party would be disproportionate to the short time period the data is retained.

9.6 MANAGING EMPLOYEE DATA

Employers often keep general records of employees' personal details, including contact details and next of kin. Further details, for example, of work absences, equal opportunities monitoring and pensions may be stored, either in an employee's general personnel file or separately. If the information constitutes personal data, employers must ensure compliance with the DPA 1998 and, if sharing information with external HR consultants or otherwise outsourcing personnel functions, they must ensure these external organisations comply with the DPA 1998.

9.6.1 Pension schemes

In most situations where employers offer pensions or insurance to employees, these schemes are controlled by a separate pension provider or insurance company. Employers must ensure they do not process employee information obtained for the purposes of such pension/insurance provision for unrelated, general employment purposes. This will breach the first and second data protection principles.

9.6.2 Security

Employers must ensure they have appropriate security systems to protect employees' personal data both when they share data and when it is held by another body on their behalf. The seventh data protection principle (see **2.5.7**) requires technical (passwords, computer encryption) and organisational measures (ensuring areas where personal data is stored are locked, that staff who can access personal data are reliable, and that only authorised staff can access the data) to be put in place to protect personal data. Security should be regularly monitored and reviewed.

The Code suggests employers should obtain the Code of Practice for Information Security Management BS 7799:1995 which provides guidance on addressing security risks. (See also ISO/IEC 27001:2005 – Information technology – Security techniques – Information security management systems – Requirements.) The Code and supplementary guidance also provide practical guidance on ensuring compliance with the seventh data protection principle and maintaining an appropriate level of security for employee data.

Security will be especially relevant for employers who share employee information with other organisations (for example by outsourcing payroll). Employers must ensure such data processors provide adequate security, must regularly review the situation to verify compliance and must enter into a written contract which requires the data processor to (a) only act when it receives instructions from the data controller and (b) to comply with equivalent obligations to those imposed by the seventh principle (DPA 1998, Sched. 1, Part II, paras. 11 and 12).

Best practice

Under DPA 1998, s.4(3) only data controllers are obliged to comply with the DPA 1998, therefore, in the event of sharing data with a data processor, the employer must protect itself by contractually obliging the data processor to comply with the DPA 1998.

In addition to satisfying the DPA 1998, the contract should contain confidentiality provisions and include:

- a requirement that the data processor complies with obligations equivalent to the eight data protection principles;
- a requirement that the data controller be entitled to review and monitor the data processor's activities (affording rights of access to premises/documents, rights of inspection, etc. to enable the data controller to do this);
- a prohibition on subcontracting (or require subcontracting on the same terms as the head contract).

9.7 SUBJECT ACCESS AND THIRD-PARTY ACCESS

9.7.1 Employee access to information about themselves

Under DPA 1998, s.7, all employees are entitled to be informed whether the employer or someone on its behalf is processing their personal data and if so to be given a description of:

(a) the personal data;
(b) the purpose or purposes of the processing;
(c) who the data are or may be disclosed to.

Disclosure of an employee's personal data may reveal third-party data. This might include information which identifies that another employee has provided information (for example within a letter of grievance relating to the employee requesting information). It might include information from which a third party could be identified when considered together with other information which the data controller reasonably believes is or is likely to be in the possession of the data subject (for example when the third party is only identified by job title but the employee only works with one particular individual with that job title).

An employer may disclose third-party information if the third party consents to disclosure or it is otherwise reasonable in the circumstances to disclose. If the third party consents to disclosure, an employer should ensure this is confirmed in writing. If there is no consent, the employer must consider whether it is reasonable to disclose, taking account of any duty of confidentiality owed to the third party, any steps taken by the employer to obtain consent, any express refusal of consent and the capability of the third party in giving consent.

Practical example

If the third party is an existing employee who has raised a complaint against the data subject, there may be a high duty of confidentiality to that employee such that an express refusal of consent to disclosure would make it unreasonable to disclose information identifying the employee. However, if the third party is a manager who conducted an investigation, it may be reasonable for them to be identified, in view of their position of responsibility and the fact they should only have recorded relevant information. Even where an employer is unable to disclose information identifying a third party, the employer must still communicate as much information as possible without disclosing the identity of the third party (so, for example, by deleting names or other identifying information).

9.7.2 Disclosure requests from third parties

Third parties may ask employers to disclose employee personal data for reference purposes (considered at **9.5.5**) or to comply with legal obligations. In an employment context, for example, the employer would be legally obliged to comply with requests for payroll information from the Inland Revenue or requests about salary details from the Child Support Agency or the Benefits Agency. Where disclosure is required by any enactment, rule of law or a court order, personal data are exempt from the non disclosure provisions (see DPA 1998, s.35 and **2.8**).

Employers should ensure staff are trained to respond to requests, understand the legal obligations to which they are subject and always check the identity of the requester before disclosing any information. If personal data is disclosed to someone other than the data subject in breach of the DPA 1998 this could result in the person who released the information being personally criminally liable (DPA 1998, s.61). The data subject may also be able to claim compensation against the employer if they have suffered damage or damage and distress (DPA 1998, s.13 and see **5.8.2** regarding breach of confidentiality).

Where requests are made, but no legal obligation to disclose personal data applies, the supplementary guidance suggests that the following exemptions may be relevant to determining the legality of disclosure:

- Section 29: this would be relevant in the context of criminal or tax investigations. However, even if the exemption applies, employers should carefully consider whether to disclose balancing (a) the public interest in disclosure against (b) the duty of confidentiality owed to the worker. There must be a substantial chance that investigations would be significantly damaged by any failure to disclose.
- DPA 1998, s.37 and Sched. 7, para. 10, disclosure required for legal proceedings, prospective legal proceedings or obtaining legal advice; for example where an employer seeks to defend employment tribunal proceedings, and needs to disclose personal data regarding the complaining employee to its legal advisers.

9.7.3 Publication of staff details

The Code contains specific guidance on disclosures by way of publication (for example of staff details in a client newsletter). If there is no legal obligation to publish information, employers should ensure one of the Schedule 2 fair processing conditions is met, for example, by obtaining employee consent to publication (Sched. 2, para. 1) in which case the worker should be fully informed of the extent of any publication and how the information will be published). Alternatively, the employee may have a legitimate expectation that the information will be published (Sched. 2, para. 6), although whether it will be necessary as required by paragraph 6 is more difficult to show.

Best practice

When considering the legitimate interests condition, first, it must be necessary for the data controller to pursue the particular legitimate interest, so in this case it would need to be shown it was necessary for the benefit of publishing information about its employees, for example on a company website. Second, the processing must not be unwarranted by prejudicing the rights, freedoms or legitimate interests of the data subject. It is therefore necessary to weigh up the employer's legitimate interests against the reasonable expectations of an employee that their privacy will be respected (bearing in mind that the data subject's interests will generally override the data controller's interests, particularly where disclosure is prejudicial).

9.8 MERGERS, ACQUISITION OR BUSINESS REORGANISATION

In the event of a merger, acquisition or business reorganisation involving transfer of employee data from one legal entity to another, an employer will usually need to provide the prospective partner or purchaser with some employee information during pre-transfer negotiations.

9.8.1 Use of anonymous information

Employers should, wherever possible, use anonymous information about employees (details of employee numbers, job titles, salaries, etc. with no names); if the information is not personal data there is no risk of breaching the DPA 1998.

However, at some stage before the deal is finalised, non-anonymised information must usually be disclosed (particularly if the Transfer of Undertakings (Protection of Employment) Regulations 2006 (TUPE) applies, see **9.8.3**). One of the Schedule 2 fair processing conditions will need to be met and, if sensitive personal data such as sickness records are being disclosed, one of the sensitive data conditions in Schedule 3 also satisfied. The legitimate interests condition, Schedule 2, para. 6 is likely to be relevant; where it is demonstrably in the company's legitimate interests to release employee personal data during the acquisition process and where employees would expect this to be done at some stage (provided safeguards are in place).

Practical example

To rely on the legitimate interests condition, employers should ensure they obtain assurances from any third-party purchaser that they will keep the information confidential, will only use it for the purposes of evaluating the business and that the information will be securely destroyed or returned after use if the transaction does not proceed. All information should be accessed via a secure data room into which only those who agree to the confidentiality provisions may enter. Where possible, employers should ensure employees are aware of disclosures and the proposed transfer of their records to the partner/purchaser, to ensure compliance with the first data protection principle. The employer will require explicit consent if sensitive personal data is involved (unless one of the other Schedule 3 conditions applies, see **Chapter 2**). It may be sensible to seek consent, in any event.

9.8.2 Corporate finance exemption

The supplementary guidance recognises that informing employees of a proposed transfer/disclosure may not always be commercially viable for reasons of confidentiality or restrictions on insider trading (for example when providing an explanation to workers could affect a company's share price). However, an exemption from the fair collection requirements of the first data protection principle applies where:

(a) personal data is processed for the purposes of a corporate finance service (meaning underwriting in respect of issues on any instrument or, advice to undertakings on capital structure, industrial strategy, mergers or purchase of undertakings, Sched. 7, para. 6 (3));
(b) where the data controller reasonably believes application of these provisions could or where application could indeed affect the price of any instrument listed in Investment Services Regulations 1995, SI 1995/3275, Sched. 1 including shares already in existence or to be created (Sched. 7, para. 6(1)(a)).

An exemption may alternatively apply if exemption is required for the purpose of safeguarding an important economic or financial interest of the UK (Sched. 7, para. 6(1)(b)). The Data Protection (Corporate Finance Exemption) Order 2000 SI 2000/184 offers guidance to determine whether this exemption applies. To be taken into account are: either the inevitable prejudicial effect on the orderly functioning of the economic markets, or the efficient allocation of capital which would result from supplying information about the decision of any person to deal, not to deal, subscribe for or issue any instrument or the decision of any person to act or not to act in any way likely to have an effect on any business activity. This is only likely to apply to very large organisations.

If sensitive personal data is transferred the employer must ensure one of the sensitive personal data conditions is met. If the employer is under a legal obligation to disclose, Schedule 3 condition 2 will be satisfied, otherwise, the employer may need to obtain specific consent from its workers (Sched. 3, condition 1).

9.8.3 TUPE guidance

TUPE covers the transfer of any business (as opposed to shares only) and can also include a change of service provider (so, for example, a change from using one company to service a cleaning contract to another). TUPE will cover most mergers and acquisitions. TUPE requires specific employee information (including name, age, details of pay, disciplinary and grievance records, etc.) to be given to the new employer at least two weeks before the transfer takes place. Employers are unable to keep the required information anonymous after that time. The DPA 1998 permits such disclosure since it is required by law, however, the data protection principles must still be satisfied. In June 2008 the ICO issued new guidance to organisations on the transfer of employee information under TUPE, which should be considered alongside the more general Code guidance where TUPE applies.

Recommended good practice

- Think about data protection early in the TUPE process.
- Agree what information you should transfer, and how, well before a transfer takes place.
- Make sure those responsible for negotiating the transfer of staff are aware of their responsibilities to comply with data protection principles, for example, to keep personal information up to date and secure.
- Make sure you transfer enough information to meet your TUPE obligations and to allow the new employer to run the business and manage the staff. However, both parties should ensure excessive and irrelevant information is not transferred.
- Make sure any information handed over is used only for the purposes of TUPE until the staff transfer is completed.
- Tell employees their information will be passed to the new employer. This may not always be possible if, for example, insider trading restrictions apply.
- Consider whether personal information could be anonymised before providing any information not required by TUPE.
- Make sure once the transfer of staff has been completed, that employment records are accurate, relevant and up to date and any unnecessary information is destroyed securely.

ICO 2008 *Data Protection Good Practice Note, Disclosure of employee information under TUPE*

9.9 DATA TRANSFER ABROAD

Transfers of personal data outside of the EEA may arise where an international company uses a shared computer network or has a central HR department outside of the EEA, in which case the eighth data protection principle must be considered. The aim of the eighth principle is to ensure personal data cannot be transferred outside of the area where it is protected by the European Data Protection Directive without adequate protection being in place.

As discussed at **2.5.8**, information may be shared outside the EEA provided:

- The destination country provides adequate protection (i.e. the European Commission has either specified that the country provides adequate protection, or the employer assesses the country provides adequate protection (taking account of DPA 1998, Sched. 1, Part II, para. 13 and the ICO's guidance *The Eighth Data Protection Principle and International Data Transfers*, ICO, (2008)).

- The information is transferred to a company in the United States, which has signed up to a Safe Harbor Scheme.
- One of the exemptions in DPA 1998, Sched. 4 applies (for example where the employees have given consent to the transfer (although this may be difficult to rely upon due to the inequality of bargaining power of employers as against employees); if the transfer is made in connection with current or prospective legal proceedings, is necessary for the purpose of obtaining legal advice, or is otherwise necessary for the purposes of establishing, exercising or defending legal rights (for example, if the employer has an HR department outside of the EEA and wishes to send information regarding a potential unfair dismissal claim to that HR department with a view to preparing a defence); or where the transfer is authorised by or made on terms which are of a kind approved by the ICO as ensuring adequate safeguards for the rights and freedoms of data subjects.
- The recipient is subject to binding corporate rules which have been approved by the ICO under Schedule 4, para. 9. Binding corporate rules are effectively codes of conduct which substantially conform to the Data Protection Directive and DPA 1998 and are binding or legally enforceable. They must operate across a corporate group (a company or group of companies) for the purposes of international data transfers. They might be used in an employment context by a multinational company to ensure consistent protection for international data transfers by all its offices worldwide.

Practical example

When assessing the level of protection offered by a non-EEA country the ICO distinguishes between issues of general adequacy (such as the nature and extent of risks to the data subject's rights from the transfer and subsequent processing) and legal adequacy (the protection offered by domestic and international obligations applicable to the third country). Where the general criteria are assessed as low risk, the ICO suggests exhaustive consideration of the legal issues may not be required.

If a company intends to transfer a list of its employee's business e-mail addresses to its office in a third country this may be considered low risk; the data relates to business rather than home e-mail addresses and the purposes of the transfer are for internal company communication use (rather than marketing or advertising). Even where the general criteria is assessed as low risk, the employer must still assess the legal criteria to some extent, for example, to establish whether there would be a significant risk of harm due to instability in the third country.

9.10 MONITORING AT WORK

9.10.1 Equal opportunities monitoring

The monitoring of sensitive data about a worker's health or disability may be necessary under the Disability Discrimination Act 1995 in particular to satisfy the employer's duty to make reasonable adjustments and ensure equality of opportunity. It may also be necessary to share this information with external advisers to ensure the employer is doing everything possible to comply with equality legislation. Processing such sensitive personal data is justified when an employer complies with a legal obligation in connection with employment (Sched. 2, para. 3, Sched. 3, para. 2).

Information about an individual's racial or ethnic origin, religion or belief, sexual orientation and disability may also be processed under various anti-discrimination provisions because of the duty placed on an employer not to discriminate against job applicants or employees on grounds of race and gender (see Race Relations Act 1976 and Equality Act 2006).

9.10.2 Monitoring performance, etc.

Part 3 of the Code defines monitoring as:

> activities that set out to collect information about workers by keeping them under some form of observation, normally with a view to checking their performance or conduct.

This might include use of: CCTV, audio bugging, mobile phone tracking, monitoring e-mail, internet and keyboard use, drug and alcohol testing and biometric tests. An employer may not, however, intercept an electronic communication (telephone, fax, e-mail, etc.) on its system or anyone else's, without lawful authority (Regulation of Investigatory Powers Act 2000, s.1, and see Telecommunications (Lawful Business Practice) (Interception of Communications) Regulations 2000, SI 2000/2699). This can be established where there is consent and monitoring is for business related communications and to decide if the communication is business related. These provisions will have most impact in the workplace on unopened incoming e-mails (once they are open it is unlikely to be classed as an interception) and the interception of a worker looking at an internet site whilst they are in the process of looking at it (if it is an historical account of sites actually visited by an employee, again, it is unlikely to be covered).

Monitoring at work raises issues under the right to respect for private life (Article 8 of the European Convention) and under the DPA 1998 (although only if a record is kept of the specific monitoring activity). However a certain degree of monitoring may be necessary to protect the employer's business interests and the interests of clients or other employees (for example, it may be necessary to monitor an employee's efficiency and productivity, to act to avoid a potential harassment claim, to ensure effective security measures are in place, to record information as part of employee training, to prevent theft, to control trade secrets or to prevent soliciting employees/customers).

The aim of any reasonable employer is to strike a balance between the needs of the organisation and the rights of the employee in contract, especially in relation to the duty to protect the mutual trust and confidence between the employer and the employee, and the individual's right to respect for privacy (see Part 3 of the Code, and the Supplementary Guidance). Employers should, before undertaking any monitoring, therefore:

(a) undertake an impact assessment (assessing the impact on privacy) to determine whether to undertake, and how to undertake monitoring;
(b) provide clear policies on, for example, monitoring electronic communications, informing employees how such information will be processed, as required by the first data protection principle (the Code, Part 3).

Workplace monitoring may, depending on the type of monitoring and why monitoring was thought necessary, result in information being shared across departments, for example, for the purpose of disciplinary or grievance appeal panels. Since information about an employee gathered during monitoring may have an adverse impact on the employee, it should always be presented to the employee for comment before the employer decides whether or not to take matters further, for example by instigating disciplinary action or sharing information with others in or outside the workplace (i.e. external HR consultants).

Practical example

An HR manager decides to record a telephone conversation between an employee and a client. The employee's manager has reasonable grounds to believe the employee intends to divulge trade secrets to the client. If the HR manager listens to the conversation but does not record that fact or does not record any personal information the DPA 1998 will not apply (although the right to respect for privacy requires consideration). If the HR manager makes a record of the call, including, e.g. the employee's name and what was said in the phone call, depending upon whether the record constitutes personal data, the DPA 1998 may apply. If the employee was not provided with the fair collection information when information was obtained it should be provided to him when the monitoring information is shared with the manager, and the employee should also be afforded an opportunity to comment upon the monitoring information. If information is not shared with the employee's consent, sharing may instead be justified under the legitimate interests condition (Sched. 2, para. 6).

Third parties may also be involved in monitoring employees in the workplace, particularly where covert monitoring or private investigators are used (in which case information about the employee shared by and with the employer, must be shared in accordance with the DPA 1998). The Code defines covert monitoring as 'monitoring carried out in a manner calculated to ensure those subject to it are unaware that is it taking place'. Covert monitoring is very difficult to justify legally unless the exemption in DPA 1998, s.29 applies (where necessary to prevent or detect, apprehend or prosecute crime). Therefore, if an employer suspects that the employee is involved in some kind of illegal activity, such as theft in the workplace then covert monitoring may be justified. The Code suggests that there should always be a limit to the number of people involved in the monitoring and there should be a very clear set of rules restricting access to and disclosure of any personal information obtained (for example, to the police). Anything collected about the employee that is nothing to do with the suspected wrongdoing should be completely disregarded by the employer (see Part 3 of the Code).

Best practice

- Monitoring must be undertaken only for specific identified purposes.
- Organisations should adopt a monitoring policy explaining the purposes and extent of any monitoring and the means employed to carry out the monitoring activity. Such a policy should inform employees how information will be used, who will have access to the data and any other relevant information (to be fair, as required by the first principle). The contract of employment might refer to the policy with express consent to monitoring provided when employees sign the contract; alternatively employees might sign a separate acknowledgement as to the contents of the policy and their agreement to monitoring and recording.
- When monitoring is undertaken consideration should also be given to reminding employees about the policy, for example by an all-staff e-mail or newsletter or on a staff notice board.
- If the employee's consent has not been obtained, employee personal data can only be processed if an alternative Schedule 2 (and possibly a Schedule 3) condition is satisfied.
- An employer must always use the least intrusive method to establish facts sought. Spot checks might be used instead of continuous monitoring, or monitoring might be restricted to employees who work in jobs that pose a high risk to the employer.
- A policy allowing an employer to read all employee e-mails to monitor employee use of e-mail at work is likely to be excessive and therefore contrary to the third data protection principle.
- Organisational and technical measures must adequately protect against unauthorised and unlawful processing. Monitoring data should be provided only to those who need to know, for example senior management. Employers should set audit trails to identify which employees have had access to the data. Any data removed, for example on laptops, should be subject to rigorous access controls.

9.11 SHARING HEALTH INFORMATION

Part 4 of the Code recommends employers should conduct an impact assessment to decide whether or not it is justified to process health information. In doing so the employer can establish whether there are benefits to the employee from processing health information and whether those benefits justify the inevitable intrusion into an employee's private life and the adverse impact the intrusion might have.

In reality, employers often need to collect, use and share information about a worker's health during and sometimes even before the employment contract begins (for example, for equal opportunities monitoring purposes). Health information may be gathered through examination or questionnaire (the least intrusive method appropriate should be used).

Employers may need to share health-related information in order to properly manage their organisations, and manage sickness absences, for example, if a line manager needs to arrange sickness cover, if a doctor's report is required, or if external occupational health consultants are used. It may need to be shared if an employee is involved in an accident at work (if the employee is unconscious and in a critical condition information sharing would be justified in the employee's vital interests (Sched. 2, para. 4, Sched. 3, para. 3)). The DPA 1998 does not prevent employers from collecting or sharing employees' health information, however, such processing must be justified, and must comply with the data protection principles. Employers should also remember they owe a duty of confidentiality to the employee in respect of health information.

The first data protection principle will apply when an employer obtains information about an employee's health. An employer should identify a clear purpose for collecting health information and ensure only information necessary to meet the purpose is collected. The use of pre-employment questionnaires, for example, should be used with caution where the questions asked are not relevant to the particular job or for the purpose designated (third principle). The employee must be informed of the purposes for which information will be held and shared, and with whom it may be shared. The information should not be shared for any other purpose (second principle). Any sharing must be in compliance with the employer's obligations of confidence (and disclosures should only be made in the public interest, to meet a legal obligation or with the employee's consent). A Schedule 2 and a Schedule 3 condition must each be satisfied.

Practical example

An employer must not use health information that was gathered for the purpose of health insurance to decide how to manage an employee's sickness absence without informing the employee that this information will be used for that further purpose.

Information should be held only for as long as is necessary for the purpose (fifth principle) and should only be shared with those who need to know, for example, senior management (third principle). Health data should ordinarily be shared with the employee's work colleagues only where explicit consent is provided (to satisfy Sched. 2, para. 1 and Sched. 3 para. 1). Where the employee has not been informed that his or her health information will be shared with colleagues, sharing may breach the first principle (being unlawful if in breach of confidence or contrary to the employee's legitimate expectations) and the third principle (if it is not relevant and is excessive given the purpose of processing).

Since an employee will have high expectations of privacy in relation to health information the employer must ensure the organisation has a clear policy on access to such information, to avoid inappropriate information sharing (seventh principle).

9.11.1 Employees and job applicants who have a disability

The Disability Discrimination Act 1995 (DDA 1995) applies to all employers and all workers who have a disability. There are two key duties within the DDA 1995: a duty not to discriminate against employees and job applicants who have a disability and a duty to make reasonable adjustments in working arrangements, working practices and premises to accommodate their needs.

In order to fulfil their obligations towards disabled employees or job applicants, employers must collect, retain and possibly share data about: the individual's condition, its effects on his or her ability to carry out normal day to day activities in the workplace, and any effect the disability may have on the individual's ability to perform his or her job. Employers should talk to the employee who has a disability to ascertain the support he is going to need. If information needs sharing, for example, with occupational health, the employee should be told exactly what use will be made of the information, with whom it will be shared, and for what reasons (the first data protection principle). It should not be shared for any other purposes (the second principle). Whilst usual for the employee's consent to be obtained, sharing may, in any event, be justified under Schedule 2, para. 3 and Schedule 3, para. 2 (compliance with legal obligations, which might include health and safety obligations); and Schedule 3, para. 9 and the Data Protection (Processing of Sensitive Data) Order 2000, SI 2000/417 which additionally authorises processing of health information for equality monitoring purposes.

9.11.2 Medical reports

A GP may not voluntarily disclose health information to an employer. If an employer wants a report from a doctor, for example, in connection with a sickness absence, the employer must comply with the Access to Medical Reports Act 1998 as well as the DPA 1998. Employers must not apply to a GP for a medical report without first obtaining the employee's consent. The employee has the right to see the report before it is sent to the employer, request that the report be amended, and refuse consent for it to be shared with the employer. If consent is refused, an employer may decide they have enough information to dismiss an employee who has been absent from work on the grounds of capability, without seeing the medical report. A tribunal may decide that this is fair if consent is withheld. Even if the report contains information that may have prevented the dismissal, the employer is not reasonably expected to know this if he is not allowed to see the report.

Where an employer needs a medical report or medical records for the purpose of employment tribunal proceedings, the tribunal may order disclosure (this provides an exemption from the non-disclosure provisions, with processing justified under Schedule 2, para. 5 or 6, and Sched. 3, para. 6). Since only certain medical records may be relevant, employers should be specific in their requests to avoid breach of the third principle.

9.11.3 Sharing the results of medical examinations and drug and alcohol testing

To ensure the maintenance of health and safety in the workplace and to provide a safe working environment, employers will sometimes require employees to undergo medical testing. The right to test should be contained in a written clause in the employee's contract of employment. Employees should be made fully aware what testing will be carried out, and why, to ensure the validity of any consent given by an employee (this consent should cover both the actual testing itself and the recording and sharing of the information). Testing should be clearly justified (for example, to identify a specific impairment in relation to a particular job). Employees must also be appraised of the consequences of not consenting to the medical testing and the consequences of testing positive or negative especially in relation to drug testing. In order to comply with the first principle, employees should be told how the test results will be stored and used and who will have access to them. It may be particularly important for an employee to know to whom positive drug test results will be disclosed. To comply with the DPA 1998 (third principle) and the HRA 1998, any drug test and any subsequent sharing of the results should only be undertaken where necessary and relevant to the employment, for example, where relevant to competence to perform a specific job.

Practical example

Where an employee has been absent on ill-health grounds, and a medical examination is undertaken, only relevant information should be shared with managers (for example, managers would need to know a prognosis as to when the individual might be able to return to work). However, sometimes a manager may need to know details about an illness or disability so they can decide how to manage the employee appropriately and with compassion. A manager may need to consider making reasonable adjustments to the workplace or to the duties carried out by the employee to enable them to return to work. The individual should be told what information will be shared with their manager, and who it may subsequently be shared with. Explicit consent to sharing should be sought, where possible, and any objections to sharing that the individual may have should be recorded and taken into account.

9.12 CONCLUSION

The employment relationship is a complex one. This complexity can be exacerbated when employers need to share information with others. Data protection laws, the HRA 1998 and the duty of confidentiality provide some protection to employees in the way employers handle and process that information. It is important not only that employers have regard to the DPA 1998 principles, and the guidance contained within the ICO Code and supplementary guidance, when sharing information but that they also ensure that where information is legitimately shared, the third party whom it is being shared with complies with the same principles and guidance.

CHAPTER 10

Safeguarding and promoting the welfare of children

Claire Bessant

10.1 INTRODUCTION

In 2003 the government proposed that all children be protected from risk 'within a framework of universal services which support every child to develop their full potential and which aim to prevent negative outcomes' (HM Government 2003 *Every Child Matters*, CM 5860 (the Green Paper) Executive Summary, para. 5). Information sharing is crucial to achieving this aim. This chapter explores the statutory powers afforded to professionals to share information for this purpose. It explains when the DPA 1998, the HRA 1998 and the duty of confidentiality apply, and considers how information can nonetheless be lawfully shared.

Recognising that when action is taken to safeguard children's welfare court proceedings may need to be instituted, we consider the court rules which either oblige information sharing or impose confidentiality in the child's interest. We also consider how children may obtain information about themselves.

10.2 THE DATA PROTECTION ACT 1998

When information is shared about children and their families the DPA 1998 will often be engaged, as we see throughout this chapter.

The DPA 1998 applies to: information held in the ContactPoint database (see **10.5**), CCTV recordings of children writing graffiti, information held on paper and structured by reference to children's names or organised by reference to specific criteria (i.e. paper registers for children organised by form group), children's medical and social, services records, information recorded by maintained and special schools, and information which is not automatically processed or held in a structured way, but which is held by local authorities, health, the police, etc. (The DPA 1998 does not apply to anonymised information, provided no child could be identified from that information and other information available to the data controller.)

Processing occurs whenever a child's personal data is obtained (whether from the child, their parent or another professional) and when it is shared with other professionals.

In many instances information shared will not only be personal data, but will be sensitive personal data, for example, information about a child's physical or mental health, their sexual life, the commission or alleged commission of a criminal offence or the proceedings or sentence relating to that offence, the child's racial and ethnic origin and information about their religious beliefs.

Practice point

When a child is looked after by a local authority, the authority must consider the child's religion and race (Children Act 1989, s.22(5)). When such information is obtained, recorded or shared, the data protection principles must be satisfied, as must conditions under DPA 1998, Scheds. 2 and 3.

All data controllers are obliged to comply with the data protection principles. The term data controller encompasses schools, local authorities, police forces and hospitals. Employees or agents of a data controller (for example, a social worker employed by a local authority) are treated as part of the data controller (ICO (undated) *Data Protection Act 1998: Legal Guidance*, para. 2.8).

Joint data controllers

Increasingly, health and social care professionals are co-located, co-funded and work closely together, although they are employed by different authorities. If social workers and health professionals work together on an assessment of a child's needs, and there is only one file for the child, including data from both a local authority and a Trust, they are probably joint data controllers. To ensure clarity, a data sharing protocol should be drawn up. If both organisations are data controllers technically a DPA 1998, s.7 subject access request could be made to either. Any protocol should clarify how subject access is handled.

10.3 THE DUTY OF CONFIDENTIALITY

A duty of confidence arises when information having the necessary quality of confidence, for example, information about a child's sexual behaviour, is disclosed or obtained in circumstances which impose an obligation of confidence. This includes where information is disclosed to a teacher, social worker or doctor (or is received by a professional from another professional in the knowledge that the duty arises). Whilst the DPA 1998 does not apply to information once a child dies, the duty of confidentiality continues (*Lewis* v. *The Secretary of State for Health* [2008] EWHC 2196; *Bluck* v. *Information Commissioner* EA/2006/0090). This is important to appreciate where information about a deceased child is discussed in the context of serious case reviews established to learn lessons from the death.

However, confidentiality does not prevent all information sharing. A professional can disclose confidential information if the confider (the child, or their parent) consents, a court order or other legal obligation requires disclosure or the public interest in disclosure overrides the public interest in maintaining confidentiality. Confidential information can be shared for the purpose for which it was brought into existence (for example if a social worker asks a doctor, outside court proceedings, to assess a child's mental health so the social worker can provide appropriate support, that assessment could be shared. If the child agrees to the assessment, arguably consent to sharing is, in any event, implied).

The meaning of public interest often raises problems in practice. Whilst rarely disputed that the public interest in disclosure outweighs the public interest in maintaining confidentiality where a child risks serious physical or mental injury or death, the position is less clear in other situations. Issues such as the nature of the information (its sensitivity) and the confider's specific expectations when it was disclosed are relevant.

Guidance on disclosure should be available, within health and social care at least, from the Caldicott Guardian, who has responsibility for ensuring confidentiality and advising when information sharing is appropriate. Ultimately, if one professional believes disclosure is necessary, but another believes information should be kept confidential, a court application to disclose or to withhold disclosure may be needed. An order will require specified information to be disclosed (care should be taken to ensure any order specifies precisely what is needed. Disclosure of an entire file, without appropriate consideration of the relevance and content of all documents, raises issues of proportionality under the HRA 1998 and may breach the DPA 1998 third principle).

10.4 THE HUMAN RIGHTS ACT 1998 AND THE EUROPEAN CONVENTION

Many agencies who share information about children are public authorities for the purposes of the HRA 1998; local authority social services, NHS Trusts and primary care trusts, the police, etc.

Before sharing information, to ensure compliance with the Convention (as required by HRA 1998, s.6), relevant Convention rights must be identified:

- Article 2 imposes positive obligations to protect life.
- Article 3 requires authorities to take all reasonable steps to prevent real and immediate risks of ill-treatment, i.e. parental abuse or neglect of which they are or should be aware (*Z* v. *United Kingdom* App no. 29392/95 Commission rep 10.9.99 and (2002) 34 EHRR 3). Articles 2 and 3 together impose positive obligations on local authorities, health authorities, the police, etc. to investigate, or to cooperate with investigations into allegations of abuse and neglect, including by sharing information.

- The Article 6 right to a fair trial affords parents extensive rights to information both within public Children Act 1989 proceedings, and when a local authority determines how it should be protecting children.
- Article 8 affords children and their parents' rights to respect for their family and private life:
  - The right to respect for family life affords parents' decision-making powers, particularly regarding children's medical treatment (*Glass* v. *United Kingdom* App no. 61827/00). Exercise of such rights implies some information sharing to enable parents to provide informed consent, at least until the child is sufficiently mature to determine their own best interests, at which point the child's right to confidentiality/privacy prevails (see *R. (on the application of Axon)* v. *Secretary of State for Health* [2006] All ER (D) 148)). The right to family life affords children rights to access information about their family background (*Gaskin* v. *UK* [1989] Series A no. 160, 12 EHRR 36). It also encompasses a right for parents to be involved in child protection investigations, to be provided with information and to be able to provide information relevant to decisions to place a child in protective care (*W* v. *UK* (1987) 10 EHRR 29, paras. 62–4). In such cases objective, careful consideration must be given to the precise information disclosed to parents, taking account of others' interests (*TP and KM* v. *UK* App no. 28945/95).
  - The right to respect for privacy is engaged when professionals undertake assessments, when a professional shares information about a child or their parents, and when a court orders disclosure of medical records. Where information is shared contrary to a parent's express wishes the right to respect for private life will be breached, unless disclosure is justified on one of the Article 8(2) grounds as necessary in a democratic society, and the action taken is proportionate to the aim. Interference with the Article 8 right, may, therefore, be justified, to protect health or morals or the rights and freedoms of others, for example, if disclosure is made to social services in order to prevent potential harm to a child from a mother suffering from mental health problems (*Andersson* v. *Sweden* App no. 20022/92). In *Andersson* the court expressly approved the fact that the applicant had been informed of the disclosure and that information was not made public but remained protected by the same confidentiality as that applicable to psychiatric records. The court also recognised that to assess the need for intervention, social services needed information not only about the applicant's son but also about the applicant.

Conflicts may arise between parents'/children's rights under Article 8 and the child's rights to protection. In such instances the courts must balance the respective rights against each other, recognising that whilst Article 8 is qualified, Articles 2 and 3 impose absolute obligations, and that:

> . . . the seriousness of child abuse . . . demands that [health] professionals, acting in good faith in what they believe are the best interests of the child, should not be subject to potentially conflicting duties when deciding whether a child may have been abused, or when deciding whether their doubts should be communicated to others, or when deciding what further investigatory or protective steps should be taken. . . . 'the interests of the child are that the [doctor] should report any suspicions he may have and that he should carry out further investigation in consultation with other child care professionals. . . . 'the well-being of innumerable children up and down the land depends crucially upon doctors and social workers concerned with their safety being subject by law to but a single duty: that of safeguarding the child's own welfare.
>
> *JD* v. *East Berkshire Community Health NHS Trust; MAK* v. *Dewsbury Healthcare NHS Trust; RK* v. *Oldham NHS Trust* [2005] 2 FLR 284

See **Table 10.1** for a summary of the situation relating to Article 8.

Table 10.1 Article 8 and information sharing

Question	Action
Are my actions lawful? Which legal provision empowers me to take this action?	Where issues are raised in relation to impairment of a child's health or development, or child abuse, the Children Act 1989 may provide statutory authority to share information. (**10.5** details other statutory information sharing powers.)
Do I have a legitimate aim for interference, which corresponds to a pressing social need?	Article 8 authorises interference '. . . for the prevention of disorder or crime, for the protection of health or morals, or for the protection of the rights and freedoms of others'.
	Interference (including through inter-agency information sharing) can be justified to protect a child's life (in accordance with Article 2) or to prevent abuse and torture.
Is the interference necessary?	Will this action achieve the intended aim?
Are my actions proportionate?	Interference should be kept to the minimum possible. Ideally obtain the child's and the parents' consent. If consent cannot be obtained, inform the child/parents what actions will be taken unless it is inappropriate to do so (i.e. it will heighten risk of harm, breach a duty of confidentiality, or prejudice criminal investigations).
Am I discriminating?	There should be no discrimination on the grounds of sex, race, colour, language, religion, national or social origin, national minority, birth or other status (Article 14).

10.5 SAFEGUARDING AND PROMOTING CHILDREN'S WELFARE

Safeguarding and promoting children's welfare means:

> the process of protecting children from abuse or neglect, preventing impairment of their health and development, and ensuring they are growing up in circumstances

> consistent with the provision of safe and effective care that enables children to have optimum life chances and enter adulthood successfully.
>
> *Working Together to Safeguard Children*, HM Govt, 2006 (Working Together) Glossary

Safeguarding and promoting is to be distinguished from child protection, which focuses on protecting individual children identified as either suffering, or at risk of suffering, significant harm as a result of abuse or neglect (Working Together, Glossary).

Safeguarding and promoting welfare is directed towards ensuring all children meet five outcomes: being healthy, staying safe, enjoying and achieving, making a positive contribution, achieving economic well-being. It depends upon the information being shared, and extensive statutory powers are afforded for this purpose.

Whilst this section focuses upon the Children Act 1989 (CA 1989) frameworks for promoting welfare and protecting children (and supporting legislation), the CA 1989 focuses primarily upon outcomes 1 and 2. To understand how outcomes 3 (which expects that school age children attend and enjoy school), 4 (which assumes children will engage in law abiding and positive behaviour) and 5 (which aspires for children to engage in further education, employment and training when they leave school) are satisfied, we must consider aspects of other legislation which enable information sharing. We must also understand the fundamental aspects of the Government's Every Child Matters (ECM) programme.

10.5.1 Every Child Matters

The ECM programme establishes new governance structures. Local authority children's services authorities/departments (children's services) must establish and lead cooperative arrangements with other key local authority services such as housing, transport, planning and leisure, and public, private, voluntary and community partner organisations. All those under the duty to cooperate in Children Act 2004, s.10 must work with other stakeholders, sharing information, to assess local needs to formulate a Children and Young People's Plan (CYPP) reflecting national and local priorities for improving outcomes. Children Act 2004, s.17 provides the statutory basis for CYPPs. The detailed requirements in relation to such plans, including consultation and publication, are found in The Children and Young People Plan (England) Regulations 2005, as amended. These Regulations provide statutory power for extensive information sharing.

Several new processes and roles have also been developed to facilitate inter-agency working:

- a common assessment framework (CAF) designed to reduce duplication and improve referrals. The CAF assesses the full range of children's needs, not just needs that individual services (health, education, social care) are

most interested in. It can be undertaken whenever a practitioner has concerns that a child will not progress towards the five outcomes, save when the issue is risk of significant harm. Providing a structure for recording information with the family's consent, it can be used to support requests for help from other services, who will also use and understand such an assessment;
- a lead professional to coordinate services provided by several agencies and to keep the family and other agencies informed;
- the ContactPoint database (see further below); and
- Children's Trusts, embodying the local partnership between children's services and other providers (or potential providers) of services for children. They are involved in planning how front line services should work together to improve outcomes, notwithstanding different professional and agency agendas.

Information sharing is key to the effectiveness of the initiatives outlined above and the ECM programme generally (see **www.everychildmatters.gov.uk**).

10.5.2 The Children Act 1989

Three key principles underpin CA 1989:

1. Children are generally best looked after within the family.
2. Partnership between parents and local authorities will best ensure that children's needs are met. Recourse to court is a matter of last resort (reflecting the Article 8 requirement of minimum intervention in family life). Where parents are having difficulties caring for their child, they should be encouraged to seek assistance from and to work with children's services to determine what assistance is required. Consent to disclosure of information should ideally be obtained from parents, both when information is to be shared within the local authority, and when it is shared by a local authority with another agency.
3. Effective public service cooperation ensures appropriate responses to the needs of children and families.

> Safeguarding and promoting the welfare of children – and in particular protecting them from significant harm – depends on effective joint working between agencies and professionals that have different roles and expertise. Individual children, especially some of the most vulnerable children and those at greatest risk of social exclusion, will need coordinated help from health, education, children's social care, and quite possibly the voluntary sector and other agencies, including youth justice services.
>
> (*Working Together to Safeguard Children, HM Government,* (2006) (Working Together) para. 1.14).

CA 1989 thus emphasises the importance of early intervention. It implicitly acknowledges the importance of information sharing. It acknowledges, however, that there are situations when children's services, in conjunction with other agencies need to take strong action to protect children from harm. We consider first the legislative framework for early intervention and then the provisions on child protection.

Early intervention

CA 1989, s.17 obliges local authorities to safeguard and promote the welfare of 'children in need', and so far as is possible, to promote the upbringing of children within their families, through the provision of a range of services. Before providing services the local authority should, so far as is reasonably practicable, ascertain the child's wishes, and give them due consideration (s.17(4A)).

A child in need is a child who:

(a) is unlikely to achieve or maintain, or to have the opportunity of achieving or maintaining, a reasonable standard of health or development without the provision for him of services by a local authority under this Part; or
(b) whose health or development is likely to be significantly impaired, or further impaired, without the provision for him of such services; or
(c) who is disabled (CA 1989, s.17(10)).

To determine whether a child is in need an in-depth assessment by children's services must be undertaken, analysing the child's developmental needs, the parents' capacity to meet these needs, and wider family and environmental factors which influence whether a child's needs are met. Such an assessment requires information to be obtained from parents and carers, the child and professionals involved with the family. Consent to information sharing should be obtained and recorded wherever possible. If a parent indicates that they do not wish a particular professional to be consulted, their views should be considered, but are not determinative.

Even if consent is not provided, information can be obtained from other professionals, provided:

(a) a legal power to share information exists (see immediately below);
(b) information is shared in compliance with the DPA 1998;
(c) information subject to a duty of confidentiality is only shared in the overriding public interest, or where permitted by court order;
(d) no more information is shared than absolutely necessary to achieve the Article 8(2) aims;
(e) there is no statutory or court prohibition on information sharing.

POWERS TO SHARE INFORMATION

- CA 1989, s.17 provides implied power for children's services, to share information with other professionals who can assist in assessing whether a child is in need and, to share information with agencies which provide certain services for children in need.

- CA 1989, s.27 permits children's services to seek assistance from health, education and housing where these agencies/departments may assist the local authority in meeting its section 17 obligations. Such authorities should comply with any request unless it prejudices the discharge of their own statutory or other duties and obligations (s.27(2)). If a child in need's family requires improved housing, section 27 enables children's services to share information with housing for those purposes.
- CA 1989, Sched. 2, para. 4(2) requires any local authority who believes that a child lives or will be living in another local authority area to inform that authority if they believe that the child is likely to suffer harm (specifying the type of harm and, if possible, where the child lives or will live).
- CA 1989, Sched. 2, para. 7 requires every local authority to take reasonable steps to reduce the need for care proceedings, and to reduce youth offending.
- Children Act 2004 (CA 2004), s.10 requires certain partners (including police authorities and chief police officers, local probation boards, probation service providers, youth offending teams, Strategic Health Authorities and primary care trusts, Connexions and the Learning and Skills Council) to make arrangements to cooperate with children's services authorities, with a view to improving children's well-being. Information sharing powers are clearly implied.
- CA 2004, s.11 imposes a requirement, to consider the need to promote and safeguard the welfare of children when undertaking statutory functions, upon children's services authorities and district councils which do not exercise children's services functions, strategic health authorities, primary care trusts, NHS Trusts and NHS foundation trusts, certain designated Special Health Authorities, police authorities and chief police officers, the British Transport Police Authority, local probation boards, youth offending teams, governors of prison or secure training centres and Connexions. Section 11 implies power to share information where information sharing is necessary to safeguard and promote children's welfare (as a group and individually). It arguably implies that information will not be shared if it may harm a child's welfare.
- Education Act 2002, s.175 (in relation to Local Education Authorities, the governing bodies of maintained schools, and the governing bodies of Further Education institutions) and Education Act 2002, s.157 and the Education (Independent Schools Standards) (England) Regulations 2003 SI 2003/1910 in relation to independent schools impose duties which mirror CA 2004, s.11.
- CA 2004, s.12 and the Children Act 2004 Information Database (England) Regulations 2007 SI 2007/2182 provide authority for operation of the children's database, ContactPoint. For every child, this will provide the name; address; gender; date of birth; identifying number; name and contact of details of those with PR or caring for him; school; GP; health visitor, midwife or school nurse (as appropriate); any person providing other services; information in relation to any common assessment undertaken; information about

any lead professional and the relevant local authority's name. Case notes and histories will not be included. The Regulations specify who may access the database and which bodies will provide information to be included within it, and clarify that certain disclosures made in compliance with the Regulations will not breach the duty of confidentiality (reg. 13). Note that specialist or targeted services for sexual health, mental health or substance abuse may only provide information where the child consents and the service provider considers there is reasonable cause to suspect the child or participating young person is suffering, or is likely to suffer, significant harm (reg. 11(3)).

- Local Government Act 2000, s.2(1) affords every local authority power to do anything they consider likely to achieve certain aims, including promotion or improvement of social well-being in their area. Local authorities may enter into arrangements with, cooperate with or exercise other bodies' functions (s.2(4)). Although section 3 prohibits a local authority from doing anything they are prevented from doing by another statute (i.e. the DPA 1998 or HRA 1998), section 2 provides extensive implied information sharing powers.
- Housing Act 1996, s.213A requires housing authorities when dealing with applications by homeless persons who appear to be ineligible for homelessness assistance or to be intentionally homeless, if a dependent child lives with them, to invite them to consent to disclosure of essential case facts to children's services (and if consent is provided, they should inform children's services whether they have decided to provide housing).

Although important to establish which powers enable information to be shared, information can still only be shared if sharing does not breach the DPA 1998, HRA 1998 or the duty of confidence. Where confidential, sensitive personal data is involved, it is not always clear that information may lawfully be shared where concerns do not suggest risk of significant harm.

Practical example

Helen, aged 14, discloses to her teacher, in confidence that she is feeling ill and falling behind at school because she has been caring for younger siblings since her mother is unwell. Although the teacher discusses the benefits of sharing information with social services, Helen refuses to consent to disclosure.

Education Act 2002, s.175 (akin to CA 2004, s.11) is likely to provide lawful power to share information.

In the absence of consent, careful consideration must be given to whether information can be shared, under the DPA 1998, HRA 1998 and the duty of confidentiality.

Helen should be told if the information will be shared, with whom and why. No more information should be shared than is necessary. Recognising that Helen's and her mother's personal data (including information about their health) need to be shared, a condition under Schedules 2 and 3 should be satisfied. The legitimate interests under Schedule 2 might be used. No Schedule 3 condition is obviously appropriate. Could processing to exercise statutory functions be argued (para. 7)? It does not appear to be a matter of vital interests (which are narrowly construed, see **2.6.2**).

The duty of confidentiality also poses difficulties. No court order is likely to be sought. Is it in the overriding public interest to disclose information in order to improve outcomes for Helen and her siblings? What is the level of risk posed? Could Helen be harmed by undertaking responsibilities inappropriate to her age? Is harm to education sufficient? Since life and limb are not at stake many professionals (for example those bound to follow *Confidentiality: Protecting and Providing Information* General Medical Council (GMC) April 2004) might consider disclosure unwarranted.

Sharing information without consent clearly constitutes interference with the child's private life. Might disclosure be justified on grounds of health (the mother's or children's)?

Protection from significant harm

Significant harm, usually associated with the concept of child abuse, whether physical abuse, sexual abuse, neglect or emotional abuse, is the criteria by which children's services and courts measure whether child protection procedures need to be invoked and court orders made to safeguard and promote a child's welfare.

Significant harm

Harm means ill-treatment (including sexual and physical abuse and non physical ill-treatment), or the impairment of physical or mental health or physical, intellectual, emotional, social or behavioural development including, for example, impairment suffered from seeing or hearing the ill-treatment of another.

Where the question of whether harm suffered is significant turns on the child's health or development, health or development should be compared with that to reasonably be expected of a similar child (CA 1989, s.31(9), (10))

INVESTIGATING ALLEGATIONS OF SIGNIFICANT HARM

There is no specific statutory duty which requires any person or body to inform a local authority that a child is, or is at risk of, being harmed, although Article 2 and 3 require public authorities to act to prevent child abuse and to preserve life. Where a referral is provided by another professional, the statutory power to share such information will often be CA 2004, s.11 (or for education professionals Education Act 2002, ss.157 and 175).

Children's services have statutory duties to investigate child protection concerns. CA 1989, s.47 applies when a child is subject to an emergency protection order, is in police protection, has breached a curfew order or is subject to a referral which suggests there is reasonable cause to suspect he is suffering or likely to suffer significant harm. It requires children's services to carry out enquiries to decide what action to take to safeguard or promote a child's welfare. (The investigative process is detailed in Working Together, Chapter 5.)

During the course of investigations extensive information will need to be shared amongst professionals; CA 2004, ss.10, 11 and 12 remain relevant.

CA 1989, s.47 itself implies information sharing powers. Section 47(5) obliges children's services to consult with education departments/authorities where education issues need investigation. Section 47(9)–(11) enable children's services authority to seek assistance from another local authority, a local education authority, a local housing authority, and certain health providers, such bodies being required to assist with enquiries unless unreasonable in the circumstances to do so.

It is often easier to justify information sharing when significant harm is alleged, but again careful attention must be paid to satisfying the requirements of DPA 1998, HRA 1998 and duty of confidence.

Practice point

A child discloses to a doctor that he is being physically abused. The doctor wishes to disclose this information to a social worker.

1. The child should be asked for their consent and in any event should be told what information will be shared and with whom (for sharing to be fair).
2. To be lawful, compliance with the Convention and duty of confidence is required:
   (a) Confidential information may be disclosed with consent or if necessary to protect the child from imminent or serious physical harm.
   (b) Article 8 will be engaged but disclosure may still be justified if necessary and proportionate action to protect the children health.
3. Schedule 2 conditions (consent, legitimate interests) and Schedule 3 conditions (consent, exercise of statutory functions) may be satisfied. Unless Schedule 2 and 3 conditions are satisfied information should not be shared.
4. The minimum information necessary should be shared and in a secure manner.

EMERGENCY PROTECTION

Where investigations identify a grave and immediate risk of significant harm to a child, or imminent threat to their life, two remedies are available: police protection or an emergency protection order. In both instances the CA 1989 may require information to be shared.

A child may be taken into police protection under CA 1989, s.46 (without court order) if a police constable believes the child would be likely to suffer significant harm unless they are removed to and kept in suitable accommodation or reasonable steps are taken to ensure the child is not removed from hospital or another place. Once a child becomes subject to police protection, the police must share information with:

(a) children's services in whose area the child was found, detailing steps taken or proposed and reasons for taking them;

(b) children's services where the child ordinarily resides, where the child is being accommodated;
(c) the child (if capable of understanding), advising them of steps taken and proposed and reasons for taking them and seeking information about the child's wishes;
(d) the child's parents, those with parental responsibility, or who were caring for them, detailing steps taken or proposed and reasons for taking them.

An emergency protection order may be sought by children's services, the NSPCC or any other individual (including the police), where there is reasonable cause to believe the child is likely to suffer significant harm if he is not removed to accommodation provided by or on behalf of the applicant; or he does not remain in the place in which he is being accommodated (s.44(1)(a)). When making the order the court can order someone who has information about the child's whereabouts to disclose that information to the court and the applicant (s.48). If an order is sought by the police or another individual it may subsequently be transferred to children's services. The Emergency Protection Order (Transfer of Responsibilities) Regulations 1991, SI 1991/1414, reg. 3 requires children's services to consult with the applicant to determine whether the order should be transferred to them. A wide range of information must be considered and obtained from the applicant (if not already within children's services knowledge), including the child's wishes and feelings, their needs, age, sex and family background.

LONGER TERM PROTECTION

Care, supervision and adoption orders (under Adoption and Children Act 2002) may be obtained to protect children suffering or at risk of significant harm, long term. A care order (CA 1989, s.33) requires the local authority to receive the child into its care, provide accommodation and maintain the child, and grants the local authority parental responsibility. Although the local authority may veto parental decisions where necessary to safeguard and promote the child's welfare, the local authority should exercise parental responsibility in partnership with the child's parents. Information must therefore be shared by the local authority with the parents.

A supervision order (CA 1989, s.35) places the child under the supervision of a local authority officer, who must advise, assist and befriend the child and take steps to give effect to the order. Information may need to be shared with and by the local authority to monitor whether the child or parent is complying with the terms of an order.

Under an adoption order the adoptive parents become the child's legal parents. Whilst ongoing contact between the child and their biological family may be ordered, where the adopted child is very young, adoption may result in a clean break between the child and their old family. Adoption therefore raises several difficult information sharing issues: how and to what extent should the facts of the adoption be kept private? What information should be shared with biological parents about adoptive parents? What information should be shared with the child about biological parents? (see further **10.7**).

The ability of the court to determine the order necessary depends upon evidence of current or future harm, and the likely cause. Whilst children's services play a key role in investigating the child's circumstances and collating evidence, the input of other agencies is necessary for the court to understand the whole picture.

If an individual or agency is unsure which legal power enables them to share information lawfully for the purposes of proceedings, or is unclear whether information sharing is justified under DPA 1998, Scheds. 2 and 3 or the duty of confidentiality, consideration should be given to obtaining a court order. (Where an expert opinion is needed to clarify how injuries have been sustained, a court order will be made authorising disclosure of court documents to the expert. The order requiring the report to be filed enables information to be shared in accordance with the DPA 1998 and duty of confidentiality.) Disclosure in care proceedings is more fully considered at **10.6**.

10.5.3 Other information sharing powers

The fact that a child is not attending school may be an educational issue but the ability to lawfully share that information is important where non-attendance flags up health or child protection concerns. Where a child has special educational needs support may be required from numerous agencies. While the youth justice system focuses on key elements of the 'making a positive contribution' outcome (encouraging young people to choose to engage in law-abiding behaviour and ensuring children and young people are safe from crime, exploitation, bullying, discrimination and violence), it also makes a vital contribution to all five outcomes, for example, where criminal offending is part of a larger problem (see *Every Child Matters: Change for Children in the Criminal Justice System*, DfES, 2004 p. 1). For these reasons, it is of benefit to all professionals involved with children to understand the wide range of statutory powers which permit information sharing, even where provisions seem relevant only to other professionals (see **Table 10.2**, pp. 266–7).

10.6 CHILDREN AND THE COURTS

10.6.1 CA 1989 proceedings

Care and supervision proceedings may need to be brought to protect a child from significant harm. In such proceedings, all parties (local authority applicant, parent respondents and children's guardian) and their legal advisers owe

Table 10.2 Further statutory information powers

Powers to prevent youth offending	Powers to identify whether children are attending school and provide education support
The Crime and Disorder Act 1998 focuses on preventing offending (as opposed to punishment). Its provisions are underpinned by the need for certain partners (including local authorities and the police) to work together (and to share information) in order to: • formulate strategies to reduce crime and disorder and to combat drug misuse (ss.5 and 6); • implement curfew schemes applying to children aged under 10 (s.14); • ensure appropriate youth justice services are available (s.38); • establish youth offending teams for that area (s.39). Further provisions provide implied and explicit powers to share information: • Section 17 requires local authorities, fire and police authorities to consider how to reduce crime and disorder. • Section 37 imposes obligations on all those who carry out functions in relation to the youth justice system to have regard to the aim of preventing youth offending. • Section 66 requires the police to share information about child offenders with youth offending teams within one working day of giving a reprimand or final warning. • Section 115 provides explicit power for the police, local authorities, probation and various health authorities to disclose information where 'necessary or expedient for the purposes of any provision' of the Act.	Education Act 1996, s.436A requires local education authorities to make arrangements to establish which children of compulsory school age are not registered schools pupils and are not otherwise receiving suitable education. DCSF, 2009, Revised statutory guidance for local authorities in England to identify children not receiving a suitable education suggests a long list of partners with whom arrangements should be made (and information impliedly shared) including from within health, education, youth justice and government agencies such as HM Revenue and Customs, UK Border Agency, voluntary and community organisations. Education (Pupil Registration) (England) Regulations 2006 SI 2006/1751 apply where children are registered at school but are not regularly attending. Certain school proprietors must maintain admissions and attendance registers for pupils registered at the school, and make these registers available to OFSTED and the local education authority. Information must regularly be passed to local education authorities about pupils who fail to attend school regularly or who absent without authorisation for more than 10 days continuously. Education (Special Education needs) (Consolidation) Regulations 2001 SI 2001/3455 enables information to be shared about children with special educational needs: • Before the child is assessed information may be shared with parents, social services, the primary care trust, the child's head teacher or early education provider. • After special educational needs are assessed, information may be shared with relevant head teachers, primary care trusts and Connexions. No further disclosure of statements is permitted without the child's or their parent's consent (if the child lacks capacity) save in prescribed circumstances (for example within court proceedings, or where in the child's interests)

Education (Information about Individual Pupils) (England) Regulations 2006 SI 2006/2601 requires maintained schools to provide the relevant local education authority, upon request, with a range of personal information about their pupils, excluded pupils and former pupils (including name, address, date of birth, gender, ethnic origin, type of special educational needs, if any, whether the school is aware that the child is 'looked after' by the local authority).

Local authorities must also share information with the Secretary of State about pupils attending or previously attending pupil referral units (reg. 3A), about pupils over compulsory school age attending maintained schools, and about pupils at non-maintained special schools, city technology colleges, city colleges for the technology of the arts and academies.

To enable local education authorities to arrange, through Connexions, to support young people and those with learning difficulties in education and training, certain schools and colleges, pupil referral units, further education colleges and institutions receiving funding from the Learning and Skills Council must provide personal information about pupils and their parents, upon request (Education and Skills Act 2008, s.72), unless a child aged 16 or above, or the parent of a younger child object to information being shared. Social security information may also be provided to local education authorities or Connexions (s.76). Section 77 enables information about young people receiving services to be provided to Connexions by a local authority, the Learning and Skills Council, a Primary Care Trust, a Strategic Health Authority, a chief officer of police, a provider of probation services, a local probation board, and a youth offending team.

a duty to provide full and frank disclosure, to enable the court to determine what order is in the child's welfare (*Practice Note (Case Management)* [1995] 1 FLR 456). However, the rights under Articles 6 and 8 of the child and others (victims, parties and witnesses) may override this duty of disclosure (*Re B (Disclosure to other parties)* [2001] 2 FLR 1017).

Disclosure obligations

The Public Law Outline (PLO), which applies to care proceedings brought after 1 April 2008, specifies certain information that children's services must file, including documents on their files (assessments and reports, including joint or inter-agency materials, records of discussions with the family, key meeting minutes, child in need plans, looked after child plans, and child protection plans, a social work chronology and letters before proceedings), and documents prepared for the proceedings (a schedule of proposed findings, the initial social work statement, the care plan, allocation record and timetable for the child).

Many documents held on children's services files include information provided verbally or in writing by other professionals or agencies. Children's services must ensure that when information is provided by third parties they explain the disclosure obligations under the PLO. Where the discloser might wish to withhold information from disclosure this should be recorded and consideration given to the need for a public interest immunity (PII) hearing.

A wide range of further information may also be needed to determine the issues: the children's guardian's report, children's and parents' medical records; police interview records, etc.

- A children's guardian is appointed in care and supervision proceedings to safeguard the child's interests (CA 1989, s.41). The guardian has a right to access local authority records (CA 1989, s.42). The guardian must bring to the court's attention and, unless the court directs, to the attention of other parties, all records and documents they believe may assist in determining the proceedings (FPR 1991, rule 4.11A(9)). If they identify that children's services has failed to disclose relevant material they should bring this to their attention to enable them to remedy their default. Since the guardian is unable to disclose children's services documents covered by PII, if necessary they should apply to the court for disclosure (*Re C (Expert Evidence: Disclosure: Practice)* [1995] 1 FLR 204).
- Where an adult's medical history or records are relevant, the person concerned (whether a party or not) should be asked to produce and disclose the documents voluntarily. If consent is withheld, a party may be ordered to disclose, where necessary to fairly dispose of the proceedings (FPR 1991, rule 1.3(1), RSC Ord 24 and CCR Ord 14). A non-party may be required to produce records to the court by way of a subpoena or witness summons, where it is in the public interest to do so (to provide

justice to the parties, and to safeguard the child's welfare). Compliance with such an order will not breach the duty of confidentiality, and exempts a data controller from compliance with the non-disclosure rules (DPA 1998, s.35).

- Whilst a child may not wish details of confidential interviews which allege sexual abuse to be disclosed to her parents, a child has no more right to withhold information than any other party or witness. In determining whether disclosure is to be provided the court must decide the matter in the child's best interests, taking account of the need to do justice to the parents (*B* v. *B (Child Abuse: Evidence)* [1991] 2 FLR 487).
- Ideally police records will be produced for use in proceedings, by agreement (*Re M and K* (child abuse: video evidence) [1995] 2 FLR 571). In *Re A and B (Minors)(No. 2)* [1995] 1 FLR 351 the court considered that whilst it would invite cooperation, the court should not hesitate to use its powers to compel police disclosure where necessary for the proper determination of the proceedings, and to address police concerns about use of the material (recognising the police may require a court order to release material obtained in the course of its investigation but not used for a prosecution and will require the parties to undertake to respect the confidentiality of the material).

Withholding disclosure from parties

In civil and criminal proceedings information may be withheld from another party on the basis of privilege and PII (see **Chapter 7**). PII may be claimed, but the rules regarding privilege apply very differently to children proceedings.

PUBLIC INTEREST IMMUNITY

PII may attach to many documents relevant to children proceedings: social work records, confidential medical records, information about police investigations, etc. (see **7.3.4** regarding immunity for social work records sought for use in criminal proceedings). If a claim for PII is made, the court must exercise its discretion and weigh up whether the public interest in protecting identified social work records outweighs the public interest in affording the parties a right to legal redress (*Re R (Care: Disclosure: Nature of Proceedings)* [2002] 2 FLR 755).

The courts have made clear (*Re C (Disclosure)* [1996] 1 FLR 797; Re B [2001] 2 FLR 1017, para. 64) that whilst a limited qualification of a party's right to see documents may be acceptable if reasonably directed towards a clear and proper objective (protection of witnesses, etc.) the case for non-disclosure must be compelling, the court must be rigorous in its examination of the risk and gravity of the feared harm posed by disclosure, procedures adopted must ensure all parties receive a fair trial.

Practical example

Re W (Care Proceedings: Disclosure) [2003] EWHC 1624
A local authority received confidential information from police about a man living with a mother and her five children who were subject to interim care orders. Social workers were told not to disclose information to the mother to avoid prejudicing the police operation or putting the informant's life at risk. The court granted the local authority permission to disclose information to the mother and all documentation to her solicitors. (Where the police or Crown Prosecution Service have provided information on the basis that it would not be disclosed, it should not be disclosed without court permission.) Confirming that non-disclosure was an exception rather than the rule, the court considered it essential the mother be informed of the substance of allegations against her (with her solicitors being provided with information relating to the applications and the wider picture to ensure fair process).

LEGAL PRIVILEGE

Since public law CA 1989 proceedings are essentially investigative and non-adversarial, litigation privilege does not apply (*Re L (A Minor)(Police Investigation: Privilege)* [1997] AC 16). A report by a third party prepared on the instructions of a party to proceedings should be disclosed to other parties (see also *S County Council* v. *B* [2000] 2 FLR 161). In *Essex County Council* v. *R* [1994] Fam 167 p. 168 Thorpe J also suggested that the case law should go further:

> to make it plain that the legal representatives in possession of such material relevant to determination but contrary to the interests of their client, not only are unable to resist disclosure by reliance on legal professional privilege, but have a positive duty to disclose to the other parties and to the court.

PRIVILEGE AGAINST SELF-INCRIMINATION

In public law proceedings, section 98(1), again recognising the importance of the court being able to undertake its investigative function, states no person is excused from giving evidence or answering any question on the basis that it would incriminate them or their spouse. Whilst section 98(2) confirms any admission or statement is inadmissible against that person or their spouse for an offence in criminal proceedings, and cannot be used as evidence unless the incriminated person puts forward a contrary defence, if the prosecution become aware that a parent has admitted to harming their child, even if the statement itself cannot be used as evidence, there is nothing to prevent the police from seeking an order to obtain a copy statement, using such admissions as a basis for further investigations.

Confidentiality of proceedings

The ability to disseminate information regarding children proceedings is relatively restricted. Cases may be heard in private in the Family Proceedings

Court to protect the child's interests. Cases are usually heard in chambers in the county and High Courts (see FPR 1991, rule 4.16(7), FP(CA1989)R 1991, rule 16(7)). (Note from 27 April 2009 accredited media will be able to attend children hearings, even where heard in private, unless the court orders restrictions in the interests of the child, a party, a witness or connected individuals, or to ensure the effective administration of justice and orderly conduct of proceedings (FPR 1991, rule 10.28)).

Information from CA 1989 proceedings may be disclosed to specified individuals in accordance with FPR Part XI (parties to proceedings and their legal representatives, a CAFCASS officer, or welfare officer, the Legal Services Commission, an expert whose instruction by a party has been authorised by the court, or a professional acting in furtherance of the protection of children, a relevant independent reviewing officer). Information may also be disclosed to certain other individuals and professionals, but only for prescribed purposes. For example, rule 11.4 enables limited disclosure to be made by a party, to a police officer for the purpose of a criminal investigation or to a health care professional or a person or body providing counselling services for children or families to enable a party or their child to obtain health care or counselling. (Note disclosure may be made to a police officer both as a professional acting in furtherance of the protection of children and for criminal investigations; in the former case disclosure encompasses any information relating to proceedings.) FPR 1991, rule 11.2(2) prohibits communication of information about CA 1989 proceedings to the public at large.

Summaries or texts of orders and information which protects the anonymity of those involved in the case may be disclosed, unless the court prohibits such disclosure.

Numerous provisions otherwise prevent publication:

- Administration of Justice Act 1960, s.12 makes it a contempt of court to disseminate information about CA 1989 proceedings even after proceedings conclude, unless authorized by the court or FPR 1991, rule 10.20A.
- CA 1989, s.97(2) makes it a criminal offence to disseminate material intended or likely to identify that any child is currently involved in CA 1989 proceedings or identifying an address or school as the address or school of a child involved in such proceedings.
- Children and Young Persons Act 1933, s.39(1) empowers the court to prohibit newspaper reports of proceedings which reveal certain information about children involved in proceedings.
- The High Court may grant an injunction to protect Convention rights, i.e. Article 8 (*Clayton* v. *Clayton* [2007] 1 FLR 11; *Re S (A Child) (Identification: Restrictions on Publication)* [2004] UKHL 47).
- Where a court chooses to sit in public but to withhold information such as parties' names, the court may impose reporting restrictions under Contempt of Court Act 1981, s.11.

Applications for court permission to disclose may be brought be a party to proceedings or a third party (such as the police), ordinarily with notice given to the other parties, and the children's guardian. Before granting permission to disclose the court must undertake a balancing exercise weighing the importance of confidentiality in children cases and the resulting frankness and cooperation of parties, experts and other professionals giving evidence against factors such as the public interest in seeing that justice is served, and where disclosure is sought for criminal prosecution purposes: the public interest in the prosecution of serious crime; the gravity of the offence; relevance of evidence to be disclosed; the importance of inter-agency cooperation; fairness concerning incriminating questions and the defendant's right to fair trial, and the extent of previous disclosure (*Re X (Children)* [2008] 1 FLR 589). The child's welfare is important, but not paramount. Even if disclosure is ordered, requirements to keep documents confidential and restrictions upon use may be imposed.

10.6.2 Adoption proceedings

Where adoption is proposed as a means to secure permanence for children, much information will be shared with and by the local authority before adoption proceedings commence (see Adoption Agencies Regulations 2005 SI 2005/389 (AAR 2005)). Information will be obtained from the birth family, including health information and detailed life story information, to be provided to the adoptive family to be shared with the child when they are older (AAR 2005, reg. 35 and Sched. 5). Information obtained from prospective adopters is shared with the adoption panel deciding whether the adopters are suitable to adopt and if they should be matched with a particular child. Adoption panels will (and prospective adopters may, with court permission) be provided with significant details of care proceedings and court documents such as expert or medical reports concerning the child. Information must also be shared with health and education providers.

Although the right to a fair trial (and to full disclosure) applies to adoption proceedings, the Family Procedure (Adoption) Rules 2005, SI 2005/2795 enable certain information to be withheld from birth parents (including the prospective adopters' names and address, and any new surname by which the child will be known, regs. 20 and 21). Regulation 77 allows the court to disclose confidential reports to the parties, with adopter details removed. In principle, disclosure should otherwise be provided to the parties, save where limited exceptions apply or, for example on PII grounds (reg. 81). (Reg. 79 provides for third-party disclosure of information which will support the applicant's case or adversely affect the case of another party and where disclosure is needed to dispose fairly of the proceedings, or to save costs.)

Disclosure of information about proceedings is again restricted (AJA 1960, s.12 and CA 1989, s.97 apply equally to adoption proceedings). FP(A)R, reg. 78, makes similar provision to FPR, rule 10.20A. FP(A)R 2005, reg. 83

additionally confirms that no document or order relating to adoption proceedings should be open to inspection, or copies taken and given to any person. This is subject to regulation 84, which enables the adopted person to receive the application and orders made in the proceedings (with certain information identifying, for example, birth parents) removed (see further **10.7.3**).

10.7 CHILDREN'S AND PARENTS' ACCESS RIGHTS

10.7.1 Parents' rights

Parents have an independent right to access their child's education records, provided the child would not themselves be prevented from accessing that information (for example because they disclose third-party data, disclosure might cause serious harm to the pupil's or another's health, or disclosure would result in early release of exam marks, Education (Pupil Information) (England) Regulations 2005, SI 2005/1437). (Since these Regulations do not apply to children attending further education college or similar establishments, the issue of consent to disclosure to parents is often addressed when the child enrols by asking the child whether they consent to disclosure to parents, and if they do not wish parents to view all records, to indicate what information they would wish to be withheld.) Parents will be provided with certain information prior to and post assessment of a child's special educational needs.

Personal data may in other circumstances be disclosed to parents where the data protection principles are satisfied. Disclosure to a parent of medical information could, for example, be lawful, where a hospital seeks parental consent to treat a child for serious injuries, information sharing being necessary to protect the vital interests of the child.

Since many children are not sufficiently mature to exercise access rights themselves, the ICO recognises that a person with parental responsibility may also exercise rights on a child's behalf (ICO 2000 *Data Protection Act 1998: Compliance Advice – Subject Access to Social Services Records*). However, DPA 1998, s.7 affords rights not to parents, but to their children. As a matter of good practice, it should not be assumed it is appropriate to disclose information to a child's parent. The child might object strongly to such disclosure being made, or following the child's removal into local authority care, it may simply not be in the child's best interests for disclosure to be made to that parent.

10.7.2 DPA 1998, s.7

Primarily information will be provided to children under DPA 1998, s.7. However, information need not be provided under section 7:

- Where other legislative provisions restrict disclosure and take precedence, for example where the information relates to adoption or assisted conception (see below and Data Protection (Miscellaneous Subject Access Exemptions) Order 2000, SI 2000/419). (Information about whether an individual was born following fertility treatment may be obtained from the Human Fertilisation and Embryology Authority under Human Fertilisation and Embryology Act 1990, ss.31 and 33, by adults and by minors engaged to marry or disclosure may be ordered by the court to determine paternity, s.34.)

- Where court rules would allow personal data contained in certain reports or evidence received by Family Proceedings Courts or Youth Courts to be withheld.
- Where personal data has been processed for social work purposes, personal data consists of information as to the physical or mental health of the child, or personal data is held within education records; and
  - disclosure would be likely to cause serious harm to the physical or mental health or condition of the child or another person; or
  - the request is made by someone legally able to make the request on behalf of the child (i.e. a parent with parental responsibility for a child aged below 16) and (a) providing such information is contrary to the child's express wishes, (b) the child disclosed information in the expectation it would not be disclosed to the requester, (c) the information was obtained as a result of an examination or investigation to which the child consented in the expectation that the information would not be disclosed to the requester, or (d) in the case of education records, the personal data reveals information about whether the child has been subject to, or may be at risk of child abuse and disclosure would not be in the child's best interests (The Data Protection (Subject Access Modification) (Social Work) Order 2000, SI 2000/415; The Data Protection (Subject Access Modification) Health Order, 2000, SI 2000/413; The Data Protection (Subject Access Modifications) (Education) Order 2000, SI 2000/414).
- Where disclosure would reveal third-party personal data and the third party has not consented to the disclosure or it is not reasonable to comply with the request without the third party's consent. This is subject to the caveat that information about a professional (from health, social work, education, etc.) is expected to be disclosed (see ICO 2000 *Data Protection Act 1998: Subject Access and Third Party Rights* and s.7(6)).

10.7.3 Adoption information

The rules governing access to adoption information take precedence over DPA 1998, s.7. The specific provisions applicable depend when the adoption order was made.

If a person adopted before 12 November 1975 applies for a record of his birth, the Registrar General may only disclose that information if the applicant has attended adoption counselling (ACA 2002, s.79(6), Sched. 2, para. 4).

Adults who were adopted between 1975 and 30 December 2005 may ask the Registrar General to provide information (birth name, birth parent(s) name(s) and district of birth) to obtain certified copy birth records (ACA 2002, s.79(6), Sched. 2). Before providing such information the Registrar must inform the adoptee about counselling services. If the adoptee seeks counselling the information will be sent to the counselling service rather than the adoptee. Further information about the circumstances leading to the adoption must be sought from the adoption agency or local authority involved in the adoption (the identity of whom may be obtained from the Registrar General or the court). The Adoption Information and Intermediary Services (Pre-Commencement Adoptions) Regulations 2005, SI 2005/890 make detailed provision for intermediary agencies to be used by adoptees to contact blood relatives.

Those adopted after 30 December 2005 can access information about their adoption under the Adoption and Children Act 2002 and Disclosure of Adoption Information (Post Commencement Adoptions) Regulations 2005, SI 2005/888 by applying to an adoption agency. The adoption agency must provide information from the individual's birth records unless disclosure would lead to the commission of a serious crime (in which case the High Court may order non-disclosure). It may provide wider information about the birth and adoptive family. The application for and order for adoption (but not supporting documents) may be obtained from the relevant court.

Often background information will reveal third-party information (for example about siblings or birth parents) which it would not be appropriate to disclose to the adoptee. Where an adoptee is particularly vulnerable, disclosures about why the adoptee was adopted require careful consideration. Since strict restrictions are imposed upon disclosure of adoption information to those other than adoptees, adoption agencies/local authorities must have clear procedures to ensure confidentiality: proof of identity by passport or driving licence. The Post Commencement Regulations deal specifically with these issues. Similar considerations must also be taken into account when requests are made under the Pre-Commencement Regulations.

10.8 CONCLUSION

The law recognises children as particularly vulnerable. Accordingly extensive powers are afforded to public authorities to share information to safeguard and promote children's welfare. However, this same vulnerability warrants increased protection for children's information, as evidenced by court and statutory restrictions on disclosure.

Given the wide range of legal provisions that apply in this area it is no easy task for practitioners to determine whether it is appropriate to share information, with particularly difficult issues arising in relation to disclosure of confidential/sensitive personal data.

A structured approach to determining the application of the key legal regimes and identification of further statutory provisions is essential.

Summary

- Why are you sharing information?
- What legal power empowers or requires you to share information?
- Does the DPA 1998 apply and, if so, can sharing be carried out in compliance with the Data Protection principles? If not, do not share.
- Does the duty of confidentiality apply? Can you share information lawfully?
- Does sharing engage the European Convention? Can sharing be justified? Is it proportionate?
- Do any other legal provisions prevention information sharing? If so, do not share.
- Share no more information than absolutely necessary, only with those individuals who need the information to achieve the identified information sharing purpose.
- Ensure information is shared securely and the recipients understand how to keep information, particularly confidential information, secure.
- Record how and why information was shared, with who, and when.

CHAPTER 11

Disclosure of commercial information

Phil Tompkins, Helen Morris and Dean Murray

11.1 INTRODUCTION

Whilst government is often perceived as the driver of information sharing, the private sector has long recognised the benefits of sharing information, sometimes for profit, sometimes for expediency. Both within the private and the public sector, information sharing can generate considerable cost savings. It enables organisations (including public authorities) to offer better and more targeted services, which in turn have the potential to increase revenue and indeed to develop new revenue streams. The public and private sector alike recognise that there is financial value in information, with information collated by one organisation being shared, for a charge.

Notwithstanding the commercial benefits of information sharing, private and public sector organisations must take care, when exploiting information, not to fall foul of the law or of obligations to third parties.

The sharing of commercial information is affected by many aspects of law. This includes contractual rights, rights of confidentiality, intellectual property rights, rights under the DPA 1998, FOIA 2000 and the EIR 2004, and competition law. Organisations need to be aware of the circumstances in which their commercial information will be shared and act appropriately to protect or properly control their information.

11.2 THE DATA PROTECTION ACT 1998

The DPA 1998 applies to all organisations, whatever their size and whether they are private or public sector. Although the obligation to notify may not apply to certain small businesses, all businesses must process (obtain, hold, share) personal data in accordance with the data protection principles.

Much of the personal data held by businesses, whether employee data, supplier data or customer data has commercial value. It is of vital importance to an organisation's ability to function efficiently and to maximise commercial opportunities. Many businesses will not want information to be shared, at least with competitors. However, sharing personal data may provide real benefits (for example, where another business will pay for customer information, in order to market its products). It is vital to understand when such information may be shared lawfully; the detriment to a business that may be caused by sharing information in breach of the DPA 1998 is not inconsequential (from a reputational point of view at least).

11.2.1 How the DPA 1998 applies in the commercial context

As we have seen in previous chapters, the DPA 1998 applies only where personal data is being processed.

Information will be 'data' and the DPA 1998 will apply, if information is:

(a) processed by equipment operating automatically (e.g. by computer) or recorded for the purposes of processing by such equipment; or
(b) held in relevant filing systems (despite the restrictive definition of a relevant filing system in *Durant* v. *Financial Services Authority (Disclosure of Information)* [2003] EWCA Civ 1746, in reality most organisations must treat all manual data they hold as being caught by the definition); or
(c) an accessible record (this includes health records, and would catch a medical report obtained by an insurance company, a pension fund provider, or indeed by an employer in relation to an employee).

(It should be noted that in respect of public authorities, the processing of all personal data is covered by the DPA 1998, in whatever form it is held, although significant exemptions apply to information processed for employment purposes, etc., see **Chapters 2** and **9**).

The data must additionally relate to an identifiable living individual (DPA 1998, s.1(1)). Whilst the definition of personal data is quite narrow, much information relating to, or about individuals is caught. All organisations must take care when sharing data about identifiable individuals whether with a customer, supplier, a public authority or in the case of a limited company, another company within its own group.

11.2.2 Data sharing and the processing of personal data

Undoubtedly the DPA 1998, since it requires all personal data to be processed in accordance with the eight data protection principles, limits the extent to which public and private sector organisations can share personal data they hold. It has a direct impact on the commercialisation of personal data. The principles of primary relevance are considered below.

First principle

The first principle requires personal data to be processed fairly and lawfully, and to be processed only if:

(a) at least one of the conditions in Schedule 2 is met; and
(b) in the case of sensitive personal data, at least one of the conditions set out in Schedule 3 is also met (see **2.6.2**).

Of the six conditions in Schedule 2, the first is consent. Valid consent for the purpose of the Data Protection Directive (Article 2, paragraph (h)) must be a 'freely given specific and informed indication of [the data subject's] wishes'. Accordingly, the individual must know the uses to which those data will be put. Similarly, the fair processing requirements oblige data controllers when obtaining personal information from a data subject (customer, employee, etc.) to inform them how their data will be used (see **2.5.1**). From a commercial information sharing perspective, the difficulty is that whilst it is easiest to obtain consent upon collection, if that is the only time that consent is obtained, the organisation must consider all future uses to which that data can be put at the outset of the relationship. Consent cannot be informed if the individual is unaware of all uses to which the data will be put, yet the wider the consent which is obtained, the less likely it is to be specific and informed. It is this problem which leads the Information Commissioner's Office to consider that data controllers should look at the other Schedule 2 conditions first before seeking to rely on consent.

The second condition (which permits processing necessary for the performance of a contract for which the data subject is a party and the taking of steps at the request of a data subject with a view to entering into a contract) could cover the situation where personal data are shared by the data controller with a third party that is processing it on its behalf, for example for the processing of payroll.

Conditions 3 to 5 may be used to justify sharing commercial information but since their effect in the commercial context is no different to that in any other context they are not considered here (see **2.5** for further information).

The sixth condition is likely to be highly relevant since it enables personal data to be shared where:

> the processing is necessary for the purposes of legitimate interests pursued by the data controller or by the third party or parties to whom the data are disclosed, except where the processing is unwarranted in any particular case by reason of prejudice to the rights and freedoms or legitimate interests of the data subject.

In *Grow With Us* v. *Green Thumb (UK) Ltd* [2006] EWCA Civ 1201 the issue of what was considered a legitimate interest was reviewed obiter. In this case Grow With Us was a franchisee of Green Thumb. Green Thumb refused to renew the franchise on the basis that Grow With Us was in breach of the original franchise. One element of the breach was that it had not disclosed customer details to Green Thumb as the franchise agreement required. Grow With Us argued that the DPA 1998 prohibited it from passing on such details. The court rejecting this pointed out that consent should have been obtained from the customers when customers' details were gained and the fair processing notice was provided to explain how their personal data would be used. In any event, the court considered consent was not needed as it was a legitimate interest of the franchisor to have the information supplied to him. This case seems to break new ground in giving such a wide interpretation to this condition.

Second principle

Since this principle requires personal data to be obtained for specified lawful purposes and not to be processed in a way incompatible with that purpose it clearly restricts how organisations may use customer data which has been obtained solely, for example, to supply goods. Such information could not be shared with an associated organisation, for example, to enable them to market insurance to cover the product sold, unless the customer had been informed of such sharing, and ideally had provided explicit consent.

Third and sixth principles

These principles all have implications for the maintenance of database information. No more personal data than necessary should be retained, the data should be relevant, accurate and kept for no longer than necessary. Organisations must consider carefully whether data needs to continue to be held, and this is again dependent upon the uses for which personal data is held, whether merely to fulfil an order, or to provide continuing services.

Organisations who maintain databases of customer information must take full account of the sixth principle, which will be breached if data subjects are not afforded their right to access information held. A data subject's right to request that information sharing ceases is particularly relevant where an organisation has sold information to a third party to enable that third party to market their own services (again any refusal to cease processing would breach the sixth principle).

Seventh principle

The seventh principle requires organisations to have adequate technical and organisational security to avoid unauthorised or unlawful sharing and to prevent accidental loss or destruction of, or damage to, personal data. Companies must ensure that staff, and third-party processors (which includes organisations with which they share information on the basis that they remain data controller and the third party is a data processor) do not divulge information inappropriately. Where a data processor is used, a data security audit might be useful to confirm whether a data processor provides the necessary guarantees (indeed the DPA 1998, Sched. 1 Part II requires data controllers to use data processors who offer sufficient guarantees regarding data security). Data controllers must take reasonable steps to ensure that the data processor complies with those guarantees, but in any event a written contract must be put in place setting out the terms under which the data processor may process the personal data (see **2.5.7**).

Eighth principle

The eighth principle will have a direct impact on information sharing when the party with which the data controller wishes to share its information is located outside the European Economic Area (EEA). Where this is the case information may not be transferred unless the country ensures an adequate level of protection to the rights and freedoms of data subjects. From a commercial perspective this must be taken account of when considering the transfer of information even if the information to be transferred is between group companies some of which are located within the EEA and some outside (see **2.5.8**).

11.3 COMMERCIAL CONFIDENTIALITY

Overlaps between the DPA 1998 and the duty of confidence will occur in the commercial context as in other areas. The common law action for breach of confidence is often relevant in the commercial context to protect commercially sensitive information of a non-personal nature which is not recorded in a copyright protected form (or where the aim is to protect the information as opposed to the form in which it is recorded). Confidentiality is relevant when considering whether commercial information can be disclosed under FOIA 2000, since the section 41 exemption from disclosure applies only to disclosures which constitute an actionable breach of confidence.

In order for a breach of confidence action to succeed:

(a) the information 'must have the necessary quality of confidence';
(b) the information 'must have been imparted in circumstances importing an obligation of confidence'; and
(c) there must be an unauthorised use of the information to the detriment of the person communicating it (*Coco* v. *A N Clark (Engineers) Ltd* [1968] FSR 415 Megarry J).

These elements are considered below.

11.3.1 The quality of confidence

In practice a lot of information which has some commercial value and which is not readily available is likely to have this quality. Examples include: new product plans, the details of the finances of a business or of the finance behind a particular contract, employee records, customer or service user information or business methods.

Although information cannot be protected if it is in the public domain, the courts are fairly flexible on this point, and may consider that information is confidential even if all its constituent parts are in the public domain (provided the selection of the material involves some skill). Care should however be taken regarding information made available on any organisation's website, which, unarguably being in the public domain, loses its quality of confidence.

11.3.2 Circumstances importing a duty of confidence

In the commercial context it is common for a duty of confidence to be imposed by contract. This enables the parties to specify which information they wish to protect and allows claimants to sue for breach of contract (generally more straightforward than suing for breach of confidence). However, although to a certain extent the courts will take account of the parties' views as to what is confidential, describing information as confidential in a contract does not make it confidential. It is rarely helpful for contractual clauses to declare all information provided is confidential. It could be counter-productive by making it difficult to determine which information is genuinely confidential.

A duty of confidentiality may also arise, independent of contract (see **Chapter 5**). An implied duty of confidence arises in the employment context (although in such situations the employment contract itself will often impose contractual obligations of confidentiality; see **Chapter 9**).

Where information is obtained by a third party who knows (or ought to know) that the information was passed to the original recipient in confidence, then the third party will also be under a duty to treat the information as confidential.

The circumstances in which information is to be treated as confidential arguably extend still further, so that whenever a person comes into possession of information, for example, a company's business plans, that they ought to realise from the context or nature of the information is confidential, they are placed under a duty of confidence in relation to that information. This would therefore apply even where someone obtains material by accident in circumstances which of themselves do not import an obligation of confidence (see *Attorney General* v. *Guardian Newspapers Ltd (Spycatcher)* [1990] 1 AC 109, 281 and *Campbell* v. *MGN Limited* [2004] 2 WLR 1232).

11.3.3 Unauthorised use or disclosure

Disclosures will be unlawful unless:

(a) consent to disclosure is provided; or
(b) disclosure is made to comply with a court order or other statutory obligation; or

(c) disclosure is made in the overriding public interest.

As we saw in **Chapter 9**, particularly difficult issues can arise in the employment context (and often in the commercial context) where employers and employees are subject to implied (and often express) duties of confidence. Whilst employees are free to share information which is so trivial or well known that it cannot be confidential, they are prohibited from ever disclosing trade secrets (even if the disclosure is not detrimental to the organisation). The state of mind of the discloser in such a situation is unimportant. An unlawful disclosure may occur without intention or even knowledge that the information is confidential. Whether employees can share other confidential information depends upon various factors, including whether they remain in employment (*Faccenda Chicken* v. *Fowler* [1986] 3 WLR 288) or whether the disclosure can be justified in the public interest, in which case disclosure will be lawful (*Lion Laboratories Ltd* v. *Evans* [1984] 3 WLR 539).

Preventing inappropriate sharing of confidential/personal data

- Ensure employees are aware when information is confidential or personal, and what restrictions on sharing apply.
- Only share office services with other businesses if security/confidentiality can be ensured.
- Where services such as word processing, telephone call handling or photocopying are outsourced the service provider must be able to ensure the security/confidentiality of information. Confidentiality undertakings should be obtained and regular checks conducted to ensure that confidentiality is not breached. Contractual terms should ensure that data processors adhere to the DPA 1998 principles.

Clients should be informed when outsourced services are used rather than relying on implied consent to share information.

11.4 FOIA 2000, EIR 2004 AND PROCUREMENT

Since both FOIA 2000 and the EIR 2004 oblige public authorities to answer information requests relating to information which they hold, both regimes potentially have a substantial impact on the use and disclosure of commercial information which has been or will be shared by private organisations with public authorities (although where information is personal data, this is explicitly excluded from both regimes). Where public authorities contract with private companies, the Public Contracts Regulations 2006, SI 2006/5 (the Public Contracts Regulations), additionally impose obligations to share information in the procurement context.

The benefits of such information sharing are twofold:

- Individuals can evaluate public authority decision making and scrutinise public authority spending.

- Commercially, information sharing enhances competition, since the more widely available information becomes, the easier it should be for businesses to evaluate risks and benefits, and to enter the market. The healthy competitive environment should enable the public sector to obtain best value services.

Despite these benefits, if too much information (particularly confidential information) is made widely available this may discourage businesses from dealing with public authorities and from providing information to enable the public authority to make informed judgments about bids. It is of concern to many businesses that a public authority is unable to refuse a request under FOIA 2000/the EIR 2004 on grounds of the requester's identity or the recipient's use of the information. Hence one supplier may seek information about another, purely for commercial purposes. By and large, once information has been disclosed under FOIA 2000/the EIR 2004, the recipient is free to use it for its own purposes (save where information is copyright protected, see **11.6**). Specific consideration must be given to the nature of information provided to, and held by public authorities, and whether an exemption from disclosure applies.

11.4.1 Holding information on behalf of a public authority

The EIR 2004 and FOIA 2000 each allow access to information held by a public authority. (The EIR 2004 also covers certain private sector bodies; reference below to public authorities includes such private bodies unless otherwise stated.)

Information is held by a public authority if it is held by another person on behalf of a public authority (FOIA 2000, s.3(2); EIR 2004, reg. 2(b)). These provisions complicate the issue of what information is held by a public authority.

Where a public authority contracts with another body, for example a commercial storage company, to hold information on its behalf, this information is clearly covered by FOIA 2000/the EIR 2004.

It will also cover the situation where a public authority contracts with a third party to provide services on its behalf. In this case, any information which is passed to the third party and processed by it on behalf of the public authority will be held by the public authority for the purposes of the legislation (for example information held by third-party payroll services providers).

It equally covers information created by a third party pursuant to a contract with a public authority whether under outsourcing, PFI or PPP contracts or otherwise. In *Leeds City Council* FS50118044 (2007) market research carried out on behalf of the Council was the subject of an information request. The applicant requested copies of the market research responses carried out by the Council's contractor Swift Research Limited (Swift). The

Council refused to disclose the responses, which it had not received itself. In assessing whether the Council held the information or not, the ICO reviewed the Council's contract with Swift. It found that although the Council had not been sent the responses, it was contractually entitled to them. The ICO concluded the responses were therefore held by Swift on the Council's behalf, and required them to be disclosed to the applicant. This decision suggests that, if a contract between a public authority and a third party allows the public authority to access information produced according to that contract, that information may be held by the third party on behalf of the public authority for FOIA 2000/EIR 2004 purposes. However, this does not mean that a public authority will be able to decline a request for information held by a third party on its behalf if the only reason it cannot access that information is a poorly or negligently drafted contract which gives it inadequate rights to access that information.

Practice point

Neither FOIA 2000 nor the EIR 2004 provide a direct right of access to information held by third parties on behalf of public authorities. If a private sector organisation holds information on a public authority's behalf, the only way the authority can enforce access to that information, if it receives a request for disclosure, is to have a contractual provision in place which allows it to access that information. The public authority must therefore negotiate a contractual right of access detailing the information the authority is entitled to and the timescale in which the third party should provide the information. As information requests must be responded to within 20 working days of receipt (although this period can be extended to 40 working days in the case of requests made under the EIR 2004 which are complex or voluminous), the contractual provision must oblige the private sector organisation to respond promptly to any information request.

From the private sector perspective, companies must make sure that they can comply with contract terms without incurring unreasonable expense.

There is a significant issue from a public sector perspective on legacy contracts, i.e. contracts entered into before the introduction of FOIA 2000 or the EIR 2004. Under such contracts, a private sector organisation may hold substantial information, yet on receipt of a request, the public authority will have no contractual right of access to that information (unless the legacy contract had anticipated the introduction of FOIA 2000 or the EIR 2004). Public authorities should identify where legacy contracts exist and consider renegotiating such contracts to enable them to comply with FOIA 2000/the EIR 2004.

11.4.2 Information held by public authorities about private sector organisations

Any information that a private sector body provides to a public authority and which that authority then holds is potentially discloseable under FOIA

2000/the EIR 2004 unless an exemption applies. As the Scottish Information Commissioner stated in *Sturgeon* v. *Scottish Prison Service* (case 02/04, 24 November 2004):

> . . . companies must be made aware that if they expect to be successful in bidding for contracts paid for by the public purse, then they will operate under reasonable terms of scrutiny and openness provided for by the freedom of information legislation.

Although several exemptions from disclosure may apply, this position must be appreciated by organisations when providing confidential or commercially sensitive information such as information relating to contract prices, levels of performance or methods of working; information relating to a failed tender; or information relating to a proposed development.

FOIA 2000, s.41 provides an absolute exemption where disclosure of information supplied by a third party (not confidential information generated by the public authority itself) would lead to an actionable breach of confidence. The reference to an actionable breach means that the common law tests (see **11.3**) must be applied. Any disclosure must be unlawful. This means that despite section 41 being on the face of it an absolute exemption, it is actually more like a qualified exemption, since consideration must be given to whether disclosure can be justified in the public interest (where the public interest defence succeeds, there is no actionable claim).

Practical example

Section 41 applies only to information which is confidential in nature (not necessarily information designated as confidential). X public authority agrees to a widely drafted contractual clause which protects extensive information provided by a developer. Not all of this information is in fact confidential. X authority could still be required to release the non-confidential information under FOIA 2000, since disclosure would not be an actionable breach of confidence. However, in disclosing that information the public authority would be in breach of its contract with the developer.

When X authority considers whether to disclose the information which is confidential in nature, it must balance the public interest in disclosure against the public interest in maintaining confidentiality to determine whether the disclosure will constitute an actionable breach of confidence (and whether the section 41 exemption therefore applies).

FOIA 2000, s.43 relates to trade secrets and information likely to prejudice the commercial interests of any person holding it (including the public authority). It will apply in relation to any information used in a business which if disclosed to a competitor would be liable to cause real (or significant) harm to the owner of the secret; the owner must limit the dissemination of the information, or at least, not encourage or permit widespread publication. Information about a particular business practice which gives that business a competitive edge would probably be covered.

Under the EIR 2004, reg. 12(5)(e) will also be important, stating that, subject to the public interest test, a public authority may refuse to disclose information which would adversely affect the confidentiality of commercial or industrial information where such confidentiality is provided by law to protect a legitimate economic interest.

Given the importance of issues relating to disclosure of confidential third-party information, we specifically consider public authority consultation with third party suppliers, at **11.4.5**.

11.4.3 Procurement laws

The Public Contracts Regulations govern the procedure for the award of a public works, public supply or public services contract.

When a public authority awards such contracts, it must provide unsuccessful bidders with reasons why their bid is unsuccessful, together with certain information about the winning tender, including the successful bidder's name (Public Contracts Regulations, reg. 32). Such information is available only to other bidders, to enable them to challenge a refusal to award a contract or to challenge any breach of procurement law.

Whilst such disclosures promote information sharing to a limited extent, they do not make the information widely available to the general population or the business community. (Compare the situation under FOIA 2000, which affords a general right of access to information about public contracts and procurement held by a public authority, irrespective of whether the requester is a losing bidder.) However, the authority must also publish a contract award notice in the Official Journal of the European Union (Public Contracts Regulations, regs. 15–18). These contract award notices, which are available online, must contain certain information such as the name of the contracting authority, the type of procedure used, the contract's subject and the value of the contract.

This undoubtedly assists businesses to compete, through identifying their competitors, and determining which tenders have previously been successful. Since the Public Contracts Regulations, reg. 11 require public authorities to notify the European Commission of certain contracts which they propose to award or conclude in the coming financial year (depending on their value, and the procedure by which they will be awarded), businesses are also able to identify new business opportunities.

However, the extent of information that the Public Contract Regulations require to be provided is not unlimited, specifically an authority may keep information confidential if publication would:

(a) impede law enforcement;
(b) be contrary to the public interest;
(c) prejudice the legitimate commercial interest of any person; or
(d) prejudice fair competition between tenderers (regs. 31(2) and 32(13)).

Regulation 43 expressly prohibits an authority (subject to any contrary provision in the Regulations) from disclosing information provided by a tendering organisation, such as technical or trade secrets or confidential aspects of tenders, which that organisation has reasonably designated as confidential.

11.4.4 The OGC Guidance

The OGC Guidance on procurement and FOIA 2000 (FOI (Civil Procurement) Policy and Guidance Version 1.1, Office of Government Commerce (OGC), undated), which can probably be said to apply similarly to the EIR 2004 in the procurement context, aims to assist public authorities to decide whether to release information relating to procurement. It suggests (s.4) that certain guiding principles apply to FOIA 2000 in the procurement context:

(a) transparency in the use of public funds;
(b) demonstrable diligence in managing contractors to ensure best value for money; and
(c) protection of the relationship between the public and the private sector.

Section 5 also details working assumptions to help public authorities decide whether certain classes of information should be disclosed. The assumptions are not meant as absolute rules. Any disclosure decision must take into account the individual factors of the information request. However, the detailed examples of situations in which disclosure might be appropriate and reasons for disclosure or non-disclosure (see OGC Guidance Annex A) are of much practical assistance.

The OGC Guidance envisages that extensive information gathered in the different phases of the procurement process will be discloseable including:

(a) details of bidders and their bids (including their ranking);
(b) information about the successful bid including the total tender price and method of working (unless commercially sensitive);
(c) price breakdown (unless commercially sensitive); and
(d) contract negotiation documents (unless confidential or commercially sensitive).

The timing of information disclosure is very important in the procurement context. If a competitor is able to obtain information about a competitor's bid before the contract is awarded, it will gain obvious advantages. The OGC's guidance makes clear that some information can only be released when the procurement phase to which it relates has finished. The guidance also make clear that whilst most information about successful bidders is discloseable, information about unsuccessful bidders is not.

11.4.5 Informing and consulting the private sector

The OGC Guidance emphasises the need to ensure the private sector understands the impact that FOIA 2000 has on disclosure of information provided to the public authority, particularly given the importance of protecting the relationship between the private and public sectors. Accordingly, the OGC Guidance, s.5, suggests that public authorities:

(a) inform potential bidders of the implications of FOIA 2000, and ask bidders to identify any 'sensitive' information which they consider should be withheld, to justify why it should be withheld and the time period it should be withheld for;
(b) use the contract with the supplier to detail the circumstances in which information can be released;
(c) review legacy contracts for confidentiality agreements which would be unsustainable under the Act (where compliance would result in a breach of FOIA 2000);
(d) consult, where appropriate, with bidders and suppliers before releasing information.

Whether an exemption or exception will apply under FOIA 2000/the EIR 2004 is a matter for the public authority to determine. The Section 45 Code of Practice under FOIA 2000 makes it clear that consultation should normally take place when an information request relates to information provided by a supplier, particularly where that third party's views may help the public authority to determine the appropriate exemption or where the public interest lies. There is no requirement to consult under FOIA 2000 itself.

In the procurement context, numerous information requests may relate to third-party information, placing a considerable burden on the public authority. The OGC recommends a pragmatic approach to consultation. If a supplier has been asked to identify sensitive or confidential information and the request relates to that information, they should be consulted. If the request does not relate to such information, consultation may not be necessary, although this will depend on the particular circumstances of the request.

This contradicts the Section 45 Code and the Information Commissioner's own advice on the matter, which requires consultation on all requests for information, without differentiating on any qualitative basis. Given the case law in which the Information Commissioner has issued practice recommendations to public authorities who failed to consult third-party contractors (see Department of Health Practice Recommendation 31 March 2008), it would seem that the best current advice is to consult. If the supplier has not identified information as sensitive, then consultation may not be necessary, although for good relations and to comply with the section 45 code, it may still be sensible to inform the third party of the information request.

Practice point

The consultation process is designed to identify specific reasons why information should not be released. It gives the supplier an opportunity to advance objections to disclosure. These objections may provide the public authority with grounds to justify non-disclosure. Ultimately, the decision to release or not is one for the public authority to make. Public authorities are not bound to follow the reasons given for non-disclosure by their contractors.

11.4.6 Contracts

It should be evident by now that all contracts issued by or with public authorities should deal with the issue of the information sharing rights created by FOIA 2000 and EIR 2004.

Specific issues that may need addressing include:

- Public authority consultation with the private sector organisation (public authorities are otherwise not legally obliged to consult).
- The view that the supplier (and indeed the authority) takes of the confidential and commercial sensitive information provided to the public authority.
- How information will be dealt with in the event of a request under FOIA 2000/the EIR 2004, or in order to comply with the Public Contract Regulations. (Although, since public authorities cannot contract out of their obligations under either FOIA 2000 or the EIR 2004, a public authority must be careful when conducting contract negotiations, to prevent being faced with the choice of breaching the legislation or breaching the contract.)
- Public authorities must also ensure, where information is held by a private contractor, that the contract provisions require the contractor to disclose information, to again ensure the authority does not breach its FOIA 2000/EIR 2004 obligations.
- Contract dispute resolution procedures to deal with any dispute on the release of information.

The OGC has drafted some standard contract terms to address the issues raised by FOIA 2000 and EIR 2004 in the procurement context.

11.5 INTELLECTUAL PROPERTY RIGHTS

A crucial issue to consider in relation to the disclosure or sharing of commercial material is whether such action might result in infringement of the intellectual property rights of a third party, our focus here being copyright. Copyright protects certain documents. It does not, however, protect the information contained in the document.

Most other intellectual property rights, particularly trademarks and patents, are accessible via public registers and are already in the public domain. Although discussions and documentation leading to an application for a patent or trade mark will be subject to the rules on confidentiality (**11.3**) and copyright, searching the patents register and passing on the results of the search would not infringe any rights of the patent holder.

11.5.1 Subsistence of copyright

In order for a third party to claim copyright infringement, they must show they are the owner of copyright in the item concerned. Copyright subsists in a variety of works including written documents (protected as original literary works), artistic works such as maps, plans, charts and photographs, or databases (Copyright Designs and Patents Act 1988, s.1(1) (CDPA 1988)).

Copyright protects the way in which information is expressed; it does not protect the information as such. Sharing information contained in a copyright document might not amount to infringement of the copyright, as long as it is rewritten and expressed in a different way. However rewriting will not necessarily escape copyright infringement. Liability not only arises from exact copying (e.g. photocopying), but will also arise if the two works contain sufficient similarity that this is more likely to be the result of copying than coincidence, and the defendant had access to the claimant's work (*Designers' Guild* v. *Russell Williams* [2000] 1 WLR 2416). If this is shown, it will be for the defendant to prove they created the work themselves without copying.

11.5.2 Who owns the copyright?

CDPA 1988, s.9(1) defines the 'author' of a work as the person who creates it. The author is the first copyright owner (CDPA 1988, s.11(1)). However, if work is produced by an employee in the course of their employment the copyright will belong to the employer, not the employee, unless there is a contrary agreement (s.11(2)). (Note, there can be issues where it is unclear whether an individual is an employee or an independent contractor/freelance.)

If a work is commissioned, copyright belongs to the person who created it rather than the person who commissioned it, again unless there is an agreement to the contrary. Care is needed when commissioning outside agencies to produce reports, artwork, etc. to ensure that a clear statement of copyright ownership is made in the contract.

Practical example

A company employee writes a newspaper article about his work. Unless he is employed to write articles, or his contract specifically covers the issue, the copyright belongs to him not the company.

Copyright can be assigned or licensed in order to facilitate information sharing. An assignment generally transfers the complete copyright. It must be in writing signed by (or on behalf of) the copyright owner (CDPA 1988, s.90). A licence gives permission to a third party to undertake certain limited activities which would otherwise infringe copyright. An exclusive licence must also be in writing signed as above (CDPA 1988, s.92).

11.5.3 Crown copyright

In general, the public sector body which produces a copyright work is the copyright owner. Central government documents are different.

The copyright in all works created by an officer or servant of the Crown in the course of his duties belongs to the Crown (CDPA 1988, s.163). Crown copyright is held centrally by the Crown as a single entity. Since individual government departments do not hold copyright in works produced by them, no formal licence is required for one government department to use copyright materials produced by another department.

Copyright can also be assigned or transferred to the Crown, for example where a report is commissioned from an outside body by a government department.

11.5.4 Copyright, FOIA 2000 and the EIR 2004

It should be noted that there is no provision in FOIA 2000 specifically exempting information from release on the grounds that it is subject to copyright. Indeed the CDPA 1988 confirms that 'where the doing of a particular act is authorised by an Act of Parliament . . . the doing of that act does not infringe copyright'(CDPA 1988, s.50). Accordingly, a third party which has produced a copyright document held by a public authority cannot prevent the document's disclosure under FOIA 2000, on the basis of copyright alone (unless it could be shown to be a trade secret, and therefore exempt under FOIA 2000, s.43(1), as would be the case with the copyright in the source code of software). However, the release of copyright documents under FOIA 2000 does not entitle the recipient to re-use them in a way which would infringe third-party copyright (see **11.6**).

The position under the EIR 2004 is different in that there is a specific exception for disclosures which would adversely affect intellectual property rights (reg. 12(5)(c)). Like all EIR 2004 exceptions it is subject to the public interest test. The Information Tribunal in *OFCOM* v. *Information Commissioner and T-Mobile (UK) Ltd* [2007] UKIT EA 0078 held that disclosure of information from a database showing details of mobile phone base stations would infringe the intellectual property rights in the database and that this would be an adverse effect.

Sharing documents produced by third parties in circumstances other than those authorised by a statute is likely to infringe copyright.

Practice point

Copyright protected documents which are released pursuant to information requests should always be marked as such, with the release accompanied by appropriate warnings about re-use.

11.6 THE RE-USE OF PUBLIC SECTOR INFORMATION

The Re-Use of Public Sector Information Regulations 2005, SI 2005/1515, (the Re-Use Regulations) implement Directive 2003/98/EC of the European Parliament and Council on the re-use of public sector information.

Although once a document is disclosed under FOIA 2000 and the EIR 2004 the recipient may use it as they wish, this is subject to restrictions upon re-use imposed by copyright. The Re-use Regulations are aimed at people and companies who want to re-use public sector information for commercial purposes, notwithstanding copyright. They provide benefits to private and public sector organisations, by enabling:

(a) businesses to use information (including some copyright information) which they have obtained from public sector bodies, for commercial purposes;
(b) the public sector to obtain income from licensing re-use.

11.6.1 Application of the Re-Use Regulations

The Re-use Regulations apply to public sector bodies. This includes central government departments, local authorities, fire and rescue and police authorities, and companies or groups financed or supervised by public sector bodies (reg. 3). They do not apply to documents held by public service broadcasters, to educational and research establishments, or to cultural establishments (museums, libraries, etc.) (reg. 5(3)).

Regulation 7 simply states that 'a public sector body may permit re-use' in accordance with regulations 11 to 16. Re-use means using a document for a purpose other than the initial purpose for which it was produced, not including transferring it within a public sector body, or between public sector bodies, for the purposes of carrying out their public tasks (reg. 4(4)). A document means any information recorded in any form, including any part of such information, whether in writing or stored in electronic form or as a sound, visual or audio-visual recording, other than a computer program (reg. 2). Re-use will in general cover the use of public sector documents and information for commercial purposes including: the reproduction of statutes in legal textbooks; the inclusion of maps in geography texts and tourist guidebooks; use of planning information in connection with property development; the use of statistics for many different commercial purposes.

> **Practical example**
>
> A publishing company is producing a guidebook to the local area. It can secure the right to use numerous public sector documents via the Re-Use Regulations: maps and plans; statistics; photographs.

The Regulations authorise re-use of information where the document:

(a) has been identified by the public sector body as available for re-use (in other words where it has been included on the Information Asset Register); or

(b) has been accessed or is accessible by virtue of FOIA 2000/the EIR 2004 or of publication under other access regimes (for example under the Water Industry Act 1991, see **Chapter 4**).

Exclusions therefore apply where the document has not been identified by the authority as being available for re-use (i.e. because it is confidential) or where the document has not been provided to the applicant or is not otherwise accessible to the applicant under FOIA 2000 or EIR 2004, for example, because another exemption or exception applies under those regimes.

Documents which are not directly related to a public authority's core responsibilities, but which are, for example, optional commercial products, are also exempted from re-use. Determining whether a document falls within the authority's public tasks is no easy feat, particularly where the value-added service utilises information provided in exercising public tasks (reg. 5).

Public authorities also hold information obtained from the private sector, including where reports have been commissioned, tenders have been submitted, etc. The fact that information derives from a third party does not necessarily prevent its re-use. However, another notable exclusion, under regulation 5(1)(b) applies where a third party owns intellectual property rights in the document. This can be important where work has been commissioned by the public authority from a third party. Care should be taken in the commissioning process to ensure that material which it could be advantageous to re-use is agreed to be the authority's copyright.

> **Practical example**
>
> A local authority has commissioned a report from external consultants into the feasibility of a proposed leisure development. The authority should ensure that it has copyright in the artists' impressions of the finished development, so that these can be re-used in tourist brochures.

11.6.2 Making and responding to a request for re-use

A request for re-use must be made in writing, stating the name and address of the applicant, specifying the document and stating the purpose of the re-use (reg. 6). The public sector body must respond promptly and in any event before the end of 20 working days beginning with the day after receipt, although this can be extended if the documents are extensive or the request raises complex issues (reg. 8).

If the request is refused, the body must notify the applicant in writing of the reason (reg. 9) and notify the requester of the complaints procedure. (The complaints procedure is essentially the same as under FOIA 2000 except that appeal is to OPSI rather than the Information Commissioner.) If the reason for refusal is that the intellectual property rights are owned by a third party, they must identify that person, where known (reg. 9(4)).

11.6.3 Conditions of re-use

The public sector body may impose conditions provided they do not unnecessarily restrict use of the document, or unnecessarily restrict competition (reg. 12). Since the aim is to ensure fair and open competition, conditions must not discriminate between applicants. If the public body intends to use the same material itself, perhaps for commercial purposes, it must apply the same conditions to its own re-use of the document (if it wishes to re-use it for purposes outside its public tasks) as it applies to outside applicants. This will clearly be a difficult issue in many situations. For example, one of the suggestions (*The Re-Use of Public Sector Information: A Guide to the Regulations and Best Practice*, Office of Public Sector Information (June 2005) (the Best Practice Guidance) at **4.19**) is that they should apply the same charges to their own re-use of the information as they do to an outside re-user.

Fair competition also means the public body must not enter into exclusive arrangements with one re-user for re-use (reg. 14), unless service in the public interest makes it necessary to enter an exclusive arrangement. The Best Practice Guidance at **4.21** cites the example of a local authority producing a tourist guide. It produces the content and after a competitive tender process appoints a commercial publisher. The authority must not grant the publisher the exclusive right to publish the material unless, for example, the authority can show that no commercial publisher would publish the document without exclusive rights (in which case service in the public interest requires such exclusivity). The authority should otherwise, for example, grant the publisher the exclusive right to publish the official version of the guidebook on behalf of the authority, but allow others to use the content in other ways, including competing guidebooks. It is clear that dividing lines may be difficult to draw, and that careful drafting of agreements is required.

11.6.4 Licensing and charging

Public bodies will require applicants to enter into a licence agreement regulating the agreed use of the information and detailing any restrictions. OPSI runs a 'Click Licensing' scheme, an online licensing scheme which is now open to a wide range of public sector bodies to make the licensing process simpler.

One of the aims behind the Regulations is to bring economic benefits by enabling public bodies to make commercial use of their assets, and to charge for re-use. Since this is commercial re-use rather than Freedom of Information, the charge can include not only the cost of collecting and copying the documents (which can include staff time) but also a 'reasonable return on investment' (reg. 15). While the Regulations do not state what this can include, some public sector bodies do charge a commercial rate for the re-use of documents, and specifically attempt to recover the commercial value of their intellectual property. The Best Practice Guidance requires the charging structure to be clear and easily available.

11.7 COMPETITION LAW

Article 81(1) of the EC Treaty and Part I, Chapter I of the Competition Act 1998 prohibit agreements which have as their object or effect the prevention, restriction or distortion of competition. This means that any agreement which has the potential to affect competition can be rendered illegal under these provisions. The prohibition applies to all forms of agreement, not solely legally enforceable contracts. The prohibition applies to 'bad faith' or intentional breaches of competition law, e.g. agreements between competitors on things such as price fixing or market sharing (often referred to as cartels). The prohibition also applies to 'ordinary' commercial agreements or arrangements which, when assessed in context, produce such an adverse effect on competition in the market that the law must prohibit them (a classic example being certain exclusive distributorship arrangements).

Information exchange is an essential feature of any cartel. The cartel members must be aware of what the other members are doing if the cartel is to function. Therefore all cartels involve the sharing of information on sales, commercial activity and especially pricing activity. The information sharing therefore underpins the cartel activity, allowing members to ensure that other members are giving effect to their anti-competitive agreement and facilitating retaliatory action against those who are not.

It is too simplistic to conclude that all information sharing between competitors is anti-competitive. Indeed some types of information sharing between competitors are common. One of the primary functions of many trade associations is to gather data from its members and disseminate it to other members. This must be done carefully however in order to ensure there is no suggestion that it is anti-competitive. The more generalised, aggregated and historic the data, the less likely it is to give rise to competition law concerns. Also the greater the degree of existing transparency in the market, the less likely the sharing of additional information is to produce an appreciable effect on competition. Essentially the parties to any information sharing between competitors must ensure that they do not replace the risks and uncertainties of a competitive market with cooperation.

In the context of a supplier/distributor relationship, information sharing can also give rise to competition law concerns. Agreements between distributors on sharing information are essentially agreements between competitors and would be subject to the same analysis as is set out above. An agreement which provides for information sharing between a supplier and a distributor will not usually lead to a breach of competition law. Suppliers have a legitimate interest in obtaining information as to the activity of their distributors, such information can be used to ensure the distributor is fulfilling its obligations under the agreement. However, such information sharing can give rise to competition concerns, for example:

- A supplier might use information on a distributor's pricing in order to put pressure on the distributor to increase prices, if the distributor alters its pricing behaviour as a result of such pressure then this is likely to be an anti-competitive agreement, which has been facilitated by the sharing of information.
- A supplier might also be a competitor to the distributor. If this is the case then the sharing of information could be anti-competitive, as is discussed above.
- A supplier might share the information with its other distributors.

The consequences of breaching competition law are extremely serious. Fines of up to 10 % of group worldwide turnover can be imposed following lengthy investigations by the relevant authorities. Also personal fines and imprisonment for up to five years can be imposed on individuals involved in cartel activity. Anti-competitive agreements are unenforceable and can form the basis for litigation seeking damages and injunctions. At the very least a party accused of anti-competitive activity can expect to suffer significant reputational damage. Therefore, serious consideration of the competition law issues should be undertaken before information is shared in a commercial context.

11.8 CONCLUSION

It is important that private and public sector organisations understand both what information they hold and how it can be used. Any organisation which shares information must be aware that doing so can have commercial implications beyond increased efficiency. Indeed, sharing information can mean that information assets which previously were either not used or used sporadically could become important sources of income.

An information audit should be carried out which will identify assets held and any limits which may exist to their use. By analysing the assets held, an organisation will be in a better position to know how to protect and exploit those assets. Such an audit should for example identify the potential value of the organisation's intellectual property (whilst raising questions of protection and enforcement, and highlighting potential for challenges to the sharing by third-party owners of intellectual property).

Notwithstanding the positive aspects of information sharing, private sector organisations who contract with the public sector may perceive very real threats from information sharing. FOIA 2000, the EIR 2004 and the Public Contracts Regulations facilitate the sharing of a considerable amount of information about the way the public sector conducts business. Commercial organisations may obtain substantial information about their competitors and indeed may be able to re-use competitors' documents, where they have been shared with the public sector. The private sector can, however, take steps to protect the information which is disclosed to the public sector.

Protecting private sector information

The first step any private sector body should take is to raise awareness amongst its own staff of the implications of relevant legislation. This will apply to staff involved in obtaining work from and delivering goods and services to the public sector.

Private sector organisations must know what confidential or commercially sensitive information has been provided to public authorities. In order to get a comprehensive picture of what that information is, the organisation should carry out a full information audit of all information supplied. The audit should also consider what information (not necessarily originating from the organisation itself) is held about the organisation by the public authority. As a result of the audit, policies and procedures should be developed which establish how information is managed. Where confidential or commercially sensitive information is identified, care should be taken to ensure that the public authority holding the information is made aware of the private sector body's view of such information. This process is relatively simple for new contracts but may be time consuming with regard to legacy contracts.

The final strand in any policy to protect information held by the public authority must be to have good channels of communication with the public authority, so that when an information request is made with regard to information held by it, the public authority consults before disclosure. This may take the form of a contractual obligation to consult or an informal understanding or protocol. Private sector bodies should identify specific information which they do not want disclosed and set out clearly why disclosure should not take place. By doing so, they can provide good reasons for use by the public authority in answering the request. The private sector should not simply declare all information provided as confidential (unless of course, it genuinely is). This unhelpful approach will only cause a public authority to disregard or pay limited attention to the representations made by the private sector organisation.

The last resort option for the private sector is to bring an action through the courts to prevent disclosure. Due to the tight timescales involved, this would almost certainly involve the use of an injunction.

CHAPTER 12

Criminal justice

Kevin Kerrigan

12.1 INTRODUCTION

This chapter deals with information sharing in the field of criminal justice, focusing upon the police's role in obtaining and sharing information.

The police gather huge amounts of information in the course of investigating crime. We consider to what extent the resulting data may be shared within the police force, with external agencies and with the suspect or offender. We also consider information sharing, outside specific criminal investigations, to protect the public. The European Convention and the DPA 1998 play an important role in determining how and when information may be shared by and with the police. Since many police bodies are subject to FOIA 2000, we also consider its role in this context.

Note that this chapter focuses on the general criminal law and process. Limited consideration is given to criminal disclosure within court proceedings. Laws relating to terrorism include significant departures from standard procedures and are beyond the parameters of this chapter.

12.2 THE INVESTIGATION OF CRIME

The police obtain information to investigate crime by various means: using existing intelligence, surveillance, CCTV, searches, court orders for disclosure, interviews and fingerprints or samples. The method by which information is gathered, and the nature of the information, often determines what information is shared and with whom.

12.2.1 Police intelligence

'Intelligence-led policing' 'underpins all aspects of policing, from neighbourhood policing and partnership work to the investigation of serious and organised crime and terrorism.' (*Practice Advice, Introduction to Intelligence-led Policing*, Association of Chief Police Officers (ACPO), 2007). Its basis is that:

> the effective and efficient collection, recording, dissemination and retention of information allows for the identification of material which can be assessed for intelligence value and enables decision-making about priorities and tactical options.

The importance of information sharing within the police is made clear.

The Code of Practice on the Management of Police Information, Home Office, 2005 underpins the police's collection, retention and use of intelligence material. All intelligence information gathered, retained or shared should be capable of being applied to one of five broad policing purposes:

(a) protecting life and property;
(b) preserving order;
(c) preventing the commission of offences;
(d) bringing offenders to justice; and
(e) any duty or responsibility of the police arising from common or statute law.

Since these purposes do not correlate entirely to the DPA 1998, s.29 crime and taxation purposes, it should not be assumed that section 29 applies when information is shared for a policing purpose (see **12.3**).

The Police National Computer

The Police National Computer (PNC) is the main repository of data for policing purposes, although some information is held on local intelligence databases. This internal police network aims to provide quick and accurate intelligence for policing purposes. This key tool for gathering intelligence and sharing data within the police service can be accessed by trained personnel in all police forces and other law enforcement agencies.

Examples of its data sharing facilities include:

- QUEST (Querying Using Enhanced Search Techniques): this searches the 'names database' and facilitates suspect identification through use of information including physical description and personal features.
- VODS (Vehicle Online Descriptive Search): this searches the vehicles database by search criteria such as registration, postcode and colour details. It enables the police to identify suspect vehicles, e.g. potentially stolen cars.
- ANPR (Automatic Number Plate Recognition): the video image of a number plate (from motorway and CCTV cameras linked to the PNC) can be recognised and mapped against the vehicles database, alerting police to suspect vehicles.
- Property: searches against the property database to identify lost, found or abandoned items.
- Person: searches against the names database to find information about convicted persons, missing persons, suspects, individuals who are unlawfully at large, etc.

- CRIMELINK: this enables searches against intelligence from serious serial-type crimes to look for similarities in incidents and help identify patterns and links.

Searches which reveal personal data should be assumed to engage the DPA 1998 (see further **12.3**).

> **Practice point**
>
> The police are encouraged to consider information held on the PNC about actual or suspected crime as a tool for managing police resources, targeting offenders, etc. Accordingly, information gathered for one of the five policing purposes is often later used for different purposes. For example, information relating to a suspect's arrest for burglary (obtained to bring the offender to justice) may be used subsequently for crime prevention purposes, being fed into an intelligence system addressing the reduction of burglary offences.
>
> On the face of it this appears to breach the first and second data protection principles, however, such action may not in fact breach the DPA 1998 if a DPA 1998, s.29 exemption applies.

Perhaps surprisingly, information held by one force is often still not available to other forces via the PNC. Through the IMPACT Programme the police are seeking to improve their ability to manage and share information. The Impact Nominal Index will enhance information sharing between police forces by enabling one force to systematically establish whether any other force holds information on a suspected person. The IMPACT programme is also developing a Police National Database, phase 1 of which is to be implemented in 2010, as a single access point for searching information held in police forces' main local operational information systems and national police systems.

PNC – access by non-police organisations

In addition to national police forces, a long list of law enforcement agencies, government departments and other public bodies (43 in total) have full or partial access to the PNC. Prison Service Order PSO 09/05 Operation of the Police National Computer, for example, enables PNC terminals to be installed in prisons to facilitate direct access to information about prisoners (subject to detailed procedures regarding training, data protection, etc.). Further bodies with access to the PNC include:

> Security Service; Secret Intelligence Service; Serious and Organised Crime Agency; Driver and Vehicle Licensing Agency; Royal Mail Consignia Security and Investigation Service; Department for Transport; Department for Business Enterprise and Regulatory Reform; Criminal Cases Review Commission; The Office of Fair Trading; Department for Environment, Food and Rural Affairs; Border and Immigration Agency; Department of Works and Pensions Solicitors; Financial Services Authority; Health and Safety Executive; Charity Commission; Assets Recovery Agency; NHS Counter Fraud Services; The Pensions Regulator;

H.M. Inspectorate of Constabulary; The Environment Agency; Independent Police Complaints Commission; NPIA National DNA Database Custodian.

per Tony McNulty, Home Office Minister,
Written Commons Reply, 5 March 2008

PNC – access by defendants, etc.

An individual is entitled, under DPA 1998, s.7, upon payment of £10, to:

(a) obtain their personal data stored on the PNC or other police information systems, e.g. locally held fingerprint record systems; and
(b) be told why the information is being processed, who it has been shared with, and from whom it was obtained.

This is subject to certain exemptions, for example, where disclosure would prejudice investigation of crime (see **12.3**).

12.2.2 Surveillance, etc.

The trend towards intelligence-led policing requires the police to target offending and offenders proactively by gathering large amounts of information about criminal behaviour, antecedents, associations, movements etc. Two principal statutes regulate such information gathering where undertaken by surveillance or interceptions:

- Police Act 1997, ss.91–108, which authorise covert entry into and interference with property or wireless communications technology by the police and other agencies. This includes bugging and vehicle tracking.
- Regulation of Investigatory Powers Act 2000 (RIPA), Part 1, which permits surveillance which does not involve interference with property. Such surveillance includes:

  - Directed surveillance: covert surveillance carried out for a specific investigation or operation and likely to result in obtaining private information about a person. For example, following a person in a public place or photographing persons entering and exiting premises.
  - Intrusive surveillance: covert surveillance in relation to activities taking place in residential premises or a private vehicle. For example surveillance into a private home from premises across the street.
  - Covert human intelligence sources: where an informant or undercover officer establishes or maintains a personal relationship with a person for the covert purpose of using this relationship to obtain information, provide access to information or covertly disclose information.
  - Interception of letters, telephone communications, e-mail, text messages etc., normally authorised by warrant issued by the Secretary of State.

- Obtaining information from public and private telecommunications providers about communications usage – for example the police may obtain authority to require an Internet Service Provider to provide information about sites accessed by a customer.

Given the extent to which surveillance interferes with human rights, surveillance must be necessary in the public interest, for example, to prevent or detect serious crime. Action taken must be proportionate to these aims. Surveillance must comply with the RIPA (Covert Human Intelligence Sources Code of Practice) Order 2002, SI 2002/1932 and the RIPA (Covert Surveillance: Code of Practice) Order 2002, SI 2002/1933. It will be overseen by the Interception of Communications Commissioner and the Surveillance Commissioners. This is particularly important given the limited rights individuals have to obtain information about surveillance activities affecting them.

Information relating to surveillance activities, the resulting intelligence information, and other products of police investigations, will be routinely shared within the police force via the PNC. However, it will rarely be shared with offenders, even in court proceedings.

Court disclosure and surveillance

Ordinarily, the prosecution must disclose:

(a) evidence on which they intend to rely; and
(b) material not being relied upon, but which has been obtained or inspected by the police during their investigations and might reasonably undermine their case or support the defence case (Criminal Procedure and Investigations Act 1996, s.3).

The prosecution can, however, ask the court, in a Public Interest Immunity (PII) hearing, to withhold disclosure of 'sensitive' information from the defence that the prosecution would otherwise be required to disclose. PII in principle attaches to intelligence gathering techniques such as surveillance and interception. Disclosure may prejudice further information gathering activities, for example, by undercover officers. The courts appreciate the need to protect the identity of informers for their own safety (see *R* v. *Hennessey* (1978) 68 Cr App R 419, 425 per Lawton LJ).

Practical example

Inspector Walton is giving evidence in a drug supply trial. The evidence is that the drug squad raided Kenneth's home and found a substantial amount of heroin, scales, bags and other supply paraphernalia. Kenneth denies knowledge of the material and says it must have been stored there by Gary who had been lodging there recently, and that he is being set up. Kenneth's barrister asks Inspector Walton to reveal who reported the matter to the police.

> As a general rule, the courts will protect the identity of informants who wish to remain anonymous: 'If their identity were liable to be disclosed in a court of law, these sources of information would dry up and the police would be hindered in their duty of preventing and detecting crime.' (*D* v. *NSPCC* [1978] AC 71). Nevertheless, where disclosure 'could help to show that the defendant was innocent of the offence . . . the balance falls upon the side of disclosure' (*ibid.*) It may therefore depend on who is the informer. If it was a neighbour who wished to keep his identity secret the court would not permit his identity to be disclosed. If Gary was the informant, this may need to be disclosed, particularly in light of Kenneth's allegations about Gary.

Chapter 7 explores PII as a justification for withholding information from defendants.

12.2.3 CCTV

Criminal Justice and Public Order Act 1994, s.163 provides local authorities with legal authority to use closed circuit television systems (CCTV) to promote crime prevention and the welfare of victims of crime, provided they first consult the relevant chief police officer.

Once images are captured they may be seized and used by the police in criminal investigations or prosecutions.

In theory a defendant may also use CCTV footage in her defence, although there are often difficulties securing access to the relevant material. This is because defendants do not have the police's resources or powers and cannot expect the same level of cooperation from the public, commercial organisations or public authorities.

If material has already been seized or inspected by the police it potentially falls to be disclosed under court disclosure rules (see **12.2.2** and **Chapter 7**). The defence may alternatively request the police to obtain the footage, referring to the police's obligation under sections 3.5 and 3.6 of the Disclosure Code of Practice (made under the Criminal Procedure and Investigations Act 1996). Section 3.5 requires the police to pursue all reasonable lines of inquiry, whether these point towards or away from the suspect. Section 3.6 applies where the officer in charge of an investigation believes another person possesses material that may be relevant to the investigation, which has not been obtained. The third party should be informed of the investigation and asked to retain the material in case they receive a disclosure request.

Since the collection, retention and use of CCTV images of people is covered by the DPA 1998, the defendant, or their solicitor on their behalf, may also make a section 7 request. However, not all relevant CCTV footage will be recoverable. Much material might not show the defendant – indeed this may be the reason why the video is valuable to the defence – because it suggests the defendant was not at the scene of the crime. Since the ICO 2008 *Data Protection: CCTV Code of Practice,* Appendix 2 suggests CCTV controllers do not disclose images to third parties other than law enforcement bodies, where footage reveals third-party images and it is not possible to remove the third party image, access under section 7 might legitimately be refused.

If it proves otherwise impossible to secure access to CCTV footage, a defendant can seek a court order for disclosure where the CCTV operator will not voluntarily produce the footage and the defendant can establish that the unseen footage is likely to be material evidence (Criminal Procedure (Attendance of Witnesses) Act 1965).

12.2.4 Searches and access to information held by third parties

One way for the police to access information is to enter and search premises and, if they find what they are looking for, seize it. Alternatively, the police may ask the courts to exercise their extensive powers to order a person to provide information or access to documentation, etc. (see also **Chapter 7**).

This section provides a basic overview of key police and court powers of particular relevance. Information obtained by virtue of such searches must be disclosed to the defence in subsequent criminal proceedings under normal court rules (see **12.2.2**).

Search warrants

The police may apply to a justice of the peace under Police and Criminal Evidence Act 1984 (PACE), s.8 for a warrant to enter and search premises for evidence relating to an indictable offence. If granted, a warrant permits access to premises in accordance with its terms, strictly construed. The police may seize and retain anything for which the search is authorised (s.8(2)) and may still seize material not specified in the warrant if PACE, s.19 applies (see below). A warrant may grant entry on one or several occasions and may relate to one set of premises or all premises occupied by an individual.

Practical example

The police and customs officials are investigating a possible excise duty fraud. They suspect that alcohol ostensibly destined for the overseas market is being diverted to the domestic market to avoid alcohol excise duty. They believe the fraud is being perpetrated by staff at Markson's Wines, which has four sets of premises in London. The fraud is thought to be committed by altering computer logs at the head office and changing certificates and paperwork at the bonded warehouse. The police information comes from an informant who used to work at the company.

The police are likely to apply for an all premises warrant given that the criminal activity is thought to take place at different locations. They must show reasonable grounds for believing that:

- an indictable offence has been committed – as suggested from the informant's intelligence;

- there is material on the premises likely to be of substantial value to investigating the offence. The police must identify potentially valuable material, e.g. the computer records and paperwork.
- the material is likely to be relevant evidence. The court must be persuaded that the material may help to prove whether a fraud has been committed.
- the material does not consist of or include items subject to legal privilege, excluded material or special procedure material (considered further below).
- a specified reason exists for justifying a search warrant (e.g. that entry will not be granted unless a warrant is produced, or that the purpose of the search may be frustrated or seriously prejudiced unless an officer can effect immediate entry). The police will need to show a reasonable fear that relevant evidence would be deleted or destroyed if they attempted to gain entry by consent.

PACE, ss.15 and 16 and Code of Practice B set out safeguards for the execution of search warrants. For example, the constable executing the warrant must provide the occupier, or person in charge of premises, with a copy of the warrant, and endorse on the warrant whether any articles sought were found and whether articles were seized which were not specifically sought under the warrant. The warrant must be returned to the issuing court and retained for 12 months.

Police authorised entry and search of premises

In certain situations the police may authorise a search of premises without seeking a court warrant:

- PACE, s.18 provides general power to enter and search premises occupied or controlled by a person who has been arrested for an indictable offence.
- PACE, s.32 authorises searches of arrested persons and, if the offence is indictable, permits the search of premises in which the arrested person was immediately before arrest.

Power of seizure

Where a police officer is lawfully on any premises (exercising any of the above powers or other powers, or with the consent of the occupier) PACE, s.19 grants a general power of seizure. It applies whenever the officer has reasonable grounds for believing anything on the premises is evidence relating to an offence or may have been obtained in consequence of the commission of an offence, and it is necessary to seize it in order to prevent it from being concealed, lost, damaged, altered or destroyed. This power has been significantly extended by sections 50–52 of the Criminal Justice and Police Act 2001, creating a seize now, sort later power whereby the police can take large amounts of material which may contain items they can search for but where it is not reasonably practicable to ascertain their relevance *in situ*. They can even take items they have no power to seize if they cannot reasonably be separated from other items. Information which has been shared with a suspect by a third party may clearly be seized, without the information provider's knowledge or consent (subject to limitations considered below).

Legal privilege, excluded material and special procedure material

Special protection is afforded to material subject to legal privilege or which is excluded or special procedure material (see PACE, ss.10–14).

Legally privileged material may never be the subject of a court order or search warrant (although *McE* v. *Prison Service of Northern Ireland* [2009] UKHL 15 confirms that covert surveillance of lawyer client communications (and privileged communications between doctor and patient) may be permissible under the Regulation of Investigatory Powers Act 2000).

Excluded or special procedure material may be secured only by an order for production or a search warrant under the special procedure set out in PACE, s.9 and Sched. 1. Excluded material includes certain personal records and similar material held in confidence. Special procedure material includes non-personal material held in confidence.

Practical example

Meera is a journalist. She has been investigating a story relating to suspected large-scale pensions fraud in a major bank. She has conducted audio and videotaped interviews with a number of whistleblowers to whom she has promised confidentiality. Concerned about the possibility of being sued by the bank she also sought a legal opinion from her solicitor who provided written advice relating to her investigation, the potential offences being committed by the bank personnel and the proper limits of her own investigation.

She publishes her first story on her internet news blog. This leads to the police commencing their own investigation into the scandal. They request that Meera hand over her file of papers and other relevant material.

In the absence of a court order, Meera can refuse to give the police any information. There is no legal duty to assist the police in investigating criminal offences.

The police may apply to a circuit judge for a production order requiring Meera to hand over her files. The judge may not make any order covering legally privileged material (which includes the letter from her solicitor since it is a communication between a lawyer and client for the provision of legal advice). The interviews with whistleblowers are likely to amount to special procedure material as they are journalistic material held in confidence. The judge must be satisfied on the balance of probabilities: that there are reasonable grounds for believing an indictable offence has been committed (fraud is an indictable offence); that the special procedure material is likely to be on Meera's premises; that it is likely to be of substantial value to the investigation; that it is likely to be relevant evidence and that other methods of obtaining the material have been tried without success or have not been tried because they are bound to fail. Meera's refusal to hand over the material voluntarily may provide evidence in this regard. Finally, it must be in the public interest to order disclosure having regard to the likely benefit to accrue to the investigation and the circumstances in which Meera holds information.

12.2.5 Interviews

One of the police's key evidence-gathering tools is interviews with suspects. Indeed detention in the police station may be authorised for the explicit purpose of obtaining evidence by questioning the suspect. A large amount of personal information may be obtained from a suspect during a police interview. Indeed some interviewing models focus whole interviews on exploring the suspect's background, antecedents, associations, ties, appearance, etc. without discussing the allegations.

Although there is no legal duty to answer police questions, and a suspect has a privilege against self-incrimination, statute has to an extent abrogated the right to remain silent. Criminal Justice and Public Order Act 1994, ss.34–7 enable a court to draw inferences from a suspect's failure to mention facts during interview which are later relied on at court, or from his failure to account for suspicious objects, substances, marks or suspicious presence at the time of arrest. The standard caution given prior to interview explains the current law:

> You do not have to say anything. But it may harm your defence if you do not mention when questioned something you later rely on in court. Anything you do say may be given in evidence.
>
> PACE Code of Practice C, para. 10

In relation to suspicious objects, substances, marks or presence, a special warning requires a detailed English language explanation of the reasons for requesting the suspect to account for the matter and the consequences of not doing so.

The courts have struggled to provide a settled interpretation of the situations where inferences will be permitted and the directions that should be given to juries. Nevertheless, it is clear that permitting inferences from silence does not on its own lead to a violation of Article 6 of the Convention (see for example, *Murray* v. *United Kingdom* (1996) 22 EHRR 29 and *Condron* v. *United Kingdom* [2000] Crim LR 679).

Following the reform of the right to silence, police stations have become negotiation zones with defence lawyers trying to use their client's residual right to silence as a tool to force the police to share information about allegations and evidence they hold. The police duty to disclose in the police station is extremely limited. The suspect is permitted to see a copy of the custody record and the first description by a witness prior to an identification procedure. However, in reality a significant amount of material is often disclosed in the police station, in part due to police recognition that without this the lawyer is likely to advise the suspect not to answer questions. If there is wholly inadequate disclosure, the court is likely to rule no adverse inference may be drawn in the circumstances (*R* v. *Argent* [1997] 2 All ER 27; *R* v. *Roble* [1997] Crim LR 449). The interview therefore provides the defence with an opportunity to gain a fuller understanding of the strength of the case that might be presented at trial if charges are brought.

12.2.6 Samples: DNA, fingerprints, photographs, etc.

PACE, ss.61–4 provide the police with extensive powers to gather substantial personal information from a suspect through taking and retaining samples. The DPA 1998 must be considered when sharing such information (including through the PNC) since information is likely to be personal data.

PACE, ss.61, 61A and 63

Fingerprints and non-intimate samples (including hair samples, samples from or under nails, certain swabs, saliva and skin impressions such as palm or footprints) may be, and are, routinely taken when a detainee is cautioned, warned, reprimanded, arrested or convicted for a recordable offence. Fingerprints and non-intimate samples may also be taken with the detainee's written consent, provided such samples have not been taken in the course of the investigation. Fingerprints may also be taken to confirm identity if a constable reasonably suspects the detainee is guilty of an offence and the detainee refuses to identify himself or their identity is thought to be false.

Fingerprints and palm prints are stored on the National Fingerprint Database on the PNC.

PACE, s.64A

The police have wide powers to take and retain photographs of any person detained at a police station (or who is not detained but, for example, has received a fixed penalty notice under Criminal Justice and Police Act 2001, Chapter 1, Part 1 or has been directed to leave an area under Violent Crime Reduction Act 2006, s.27).

Photographs may be retained, used or disclosed for purposes related to the prevention or detection of crime, the investigation of offences or the conduct of prosecutions inside and outside the United Kingdom, or the enforcement of any sentence or order made by a court dealing with an offence.

Detainees' photographs are stored on the Police National Computer linked to their fingerprint records.

PACE, s.62

An intimate sample is a dental impression or sample of blood, semen or any other tissue fluid, urine, or pubic hair, or a swab taken from any part of a person's genitals or from a person's body orifice other than the mouth (PACE Code of Practice D para. 6.1). PACE, s.62(1) enables taking intimate samples from a detainee to be authorised by an inspector or above where there are reasonable grounds to believe the sample may confirm or disprove the suspect's involvement in a recordable offence. The suspect must provide written consent but will be warned that a court may draw an inference from refusal to consent.

Retention and use of fingerprints, samples, etc.

PACE, s.64 permits the retention of fingerprints, impressions and samples, after they have fulfilled the purposes for which they were taken, to be used 'for purposes related to the prevention or detection of crime, the investigation of an offence or the conduct of a prosecution'. This applies whether or not the individual is subsequently charged, prosecuted, convicted or acquitted of the offence.

Accordingly, a detainee's fingerprints, intimate or non-intimate samples may be checked and matched against the National Fingerprint Database and the National DNA Database (PACE, s.63A). If any positive match arises against an unsolved crime, as a result of this speculative search they may be arrested and investigated for those crimes. Any person who provides fingerprints or samples outside PACE (for example suspects who have not been arrested) can only be subject to a speculative search if they consent in writing to this occurring (PACE Code D Note for Guidance 6E).

Normally fingerprints and samples taken in the course of investigations, from persons who were not suspects, must be destroyed. However, they may still be retained if another person was convicted of the offence investigated and samples were also taken from the convicted person. In this case samples should not be used in evidence against the non-suspect nor should they be used to investigate any offence.

The police's ability to use the PNC to share information such as DNA, fingerprints, etc. with each other is undoubtedly important to identify the perpetrator of many crimes. However, the current law has recently been found by the European Court to violate Article 8:

> the blanket and indiscriminate nature of the powers of retention of the fingerprints, cellular samples and DNA profiles of persons suspected but not convicted of offences . . . fails to strike a fair balance between the competing public and private interests and that the respondent State has overstepped any acceptable margin of appreciation in this regard.
>
> *S and Marper* v. *the United Kingdom* [2008] All ER (D) 56 (Dec)

The future of the UK's National DNA Database and the National Fingerprint Database is therefore currently unclear.

12.3 DATA PROTECTION AND INFORMATION SHARING

Where the police process personal data (for example, when an offender's fingerprints, etc. are recorded on the PNC or retrieved) the police must comply with the DPA 1998. The data protection principles apply whenever the police share information internally, or with other agencies (subject to any exemptions).

12.3.1 Police information sharing

Much information shared by the police will be sensitive personal data (defined at DPA 1998, s.2). Information is sensitive personal data if it relates to the individual's commission or alleged commission of any offence, and to proceedings for any offence committed or alleged to have been committed by him, the disposal of such proceedings or the sentence of any court in such proceedings. Alternatively, information relating to physical or mental health or condition shared for detention and risk assessment purposes, is sensitive personal data.

When sensitive personal information is shared, a relevant Schedule 2 and a Schedule 3 condition must be satisfied. Under Schedule 2, obvious justifications are administration of justice, statutory functions, and public interest functions (paragraph 5). In relation to police investigations, Schedule 3 justifications might include: paragraph 3, vital interests of a victim or potential victim of crime; paragraph 6, actual or potential legal proceedings and legal rights; and paragraph 7, the administration of justice and statutory powers, e.g. the detention of a suspect in police custody.

Practical example

Calum is arrested and detained by the police for being drunk and disorderly. The custody officer books him into the police station and explains his rights. A search on the PNC reveals that Calum is subject to a bench warrant from the magistrates' court for failure to surrender for trial following an offence of theft. It also reveals Calum seriously assaulted a police constable during detention at another police station.

This information is sensitive personal data. Storing and accessing this information is justified under Schedule 2, paragraph 5 (administration of justice) and paragraph 6 (legitimate interests). Information about the warrant is necessary for the purposes of legal proceedings (Sched. 3, para. 6) and for the administration of justice or exercise of statutory powers (Sched. 3, para. 7). Calum's failure to surrender to court amounts to a criminal offence and compromised the progress of the earlier proceedings. Information about previous criminal convictions is necessary since it records the outcome of previous legal proceedings and will affect future proceedings (the previous convictions may be aggravating factors in any future sentencing). It also affects the exercise of statutory detention powers.

The custody officer will be justified in sharing Calum's information (for example with the Crown Prosecution Service and with the court, notifying them of Calum's arrest and his previous convictions, and notifying those responsible for Calum's detention about risks he poses). In addition to the justifications considered above, Schedule 2, paragraph 4 and Schedule 3, paragraph 3 may also be relied upon, justifying sharing as necessary to protect the vital interests of fellow officers (although it must be shown that Calum poses a serious threat to life and limb).

12.3.2 Police requests for information

The police often request information from third parties. For example, victims and witnesses of crimes are asked to make statements for potential use in criminal proceedings.

There is no general common law duty to respond to such police requests, although a small number of statutes do require people to provide information (for example, Terrorism Act 2000, s.19 obliges disclosure of information concerning certain terrorist offences). Assisting the police with their enquiries has been described as a social or moral duty (*Rice* v. *Connolly* [1966] 2 QB 414).

The principle in *Rice* v. *Connolly* applies equally to suspects and potential witnesses (although see **12.2.5** regarding the defendant's right to silence). A person does not commit the offence of obstructing an officer in the execution of duty merely by refusing to supply information. However, if a person makes a statement to the police then, if criminal proceedings are subsequently pursued, the court may compel a witness (but not a defendant) to give evidence.

If the information giver is another public authority, before information is shared, consideration must be given to the DPA 1998, HRA 1998 and any duty of confidentiality.

12.3.3 Statutes permitting information sharing with the police

Information may only be shared by, or with the police, in accordance with the law (first Data Protection principle). Public authorities (the police, local authorities, health, etc.) must have statutory power to share information. Crime and Disorder Act 1998, s.115 is an important provision, providing that:

> Any person who [apart from this section] would not have power to disclose information to a relevant authority or to a person acting on behalf of such an authority, shall have power to do so in any case where the disclosure is necessary or expedient for the purposes of any provision of this Act.

This confers on any person a power to share information with certain authorities (including police, probation, health and local authorities) if necessary, to further the Act's provisions. These include local strategies to reduce crime and disorder. Section 115 does not oblige information to be disclosed and does not itself justify disclosure. The information holder must consider statutory and common law constraints on disclosure, including data protection, human rights and the law of confidence. As the Guidance on Statutory Crime and Disorder Partnerships, Home Office, 2000 states:

> 5.14 Although section 115 ensures that lawful powers are available to all agencies for the disclosure of information to relevant authorities for the purposes of the Act, the law of confidence still applies. This means that anyone proposing to disclose information not publicly available and obtained in circumstances giving rise to a duty of confidence will need to establish whether there is an

> overriding justification for doing so. If not, it is still necessary to obtain the informed consent of the person who supplied the information. This will need to be assessed on a case-by-case basis, and legal advice should be sought in any case of doubt.

In the absence of case law the scope of section 115 remains somewhat obscure. It does not provide carte blanche permission to disclose information to the police in all circumstances. Arguably it is limited to those organisations that participate in statutory crime and disorder partnerships.

Practical example

Dr Sharma is a consultant psychiatrist at a Mental Health NHS Trust. He has been treating Marvin for mental health problems.

Detective Sergeant McBride contacts Dr Sharma. He is investigating a stabbing at a nightclub. Marvin is the prime suspect. DS McBride informs Dr Sharma that the victim is seriously injured and may not survive. Marvin is currently in police custody awaiting interview. DS McBride asks Dr Sharma to provide information about Marvin's symptoms, diagnosis and medication which may be relevant to the commission of the offence by Marvin.

Dr Sharma is under no common law duty to assist the police with their enquiries. No statutory duty appears to apply.

This information is clearly sensitive personal data (s.2(e) physical or mental health or condition). Although Dr Sharma may have implied, and possibly, explicit consent to process this information for medical purposes (see Sched. 2, para. 1, and Sched. 3, paras. 1 and 8) he is now asked to disclose this information for criminal investigation purposes. It might be argued that Schedule 2, paragraph 6 (legitimate interests) and The Data Protection (Processing of Sensitive Data) Order 2000 SI 2000/417, Sched., para. 10 (processing to enable police constables to exercise their functions) would justify sharing. It is unclear whether disclosure is necessary for the purpose of legal proceedings, administration of justice or statutory powers (Sched. 3, paras. 6 and 7). In any event, the police could, if necessary, seek a court order compelling Dr Sharma to provide the medical information sought (Sched. 2, para. 3 and Sched. 3, para. 6 would be satisfied).

Crime and Disorder Act, s.115 is unlikely to assist Dr Sharma or the police. Although drafted broadly, the context is limited to participants in crime and disorder partnerships.

Dr Sharma must also have regard to his legal duty to Marvin under the law of confidentiality and his ethical duties as a doctor (see **Chapter 5**). He must decide whether it is necessary to disclose in the overriding public interest.

Chapter 4 highlights various alternative statutory gateways to information sharing. We consider Criminal Justice Act 2003, s.325(4) at **12.5.2** in the context of Multi Agency Public Protection Arrangements.

12.3.4 DPA 1998 exemptions

There are important qualifications and exemptions to personal data processing for crime and taxation purposes, including (a) the prevention or detection or crime and (b) the apprehension or prosecution of offenders (DPA 1998, s.29(1)).

Section 29(1) provides an exemption from section 7 and the first principle (except for the requirement to comply with a Schedule 2 and/or Schedule 3 condition) where compliance would be likely to prejudice one of the crime and taxation purposes.

An exemption to the subject information provisions (s.7 and the first principle's fair processing requirement) applies where processing is to discharge a statutory function, information was obtained from someone who held it for a crime and taxation purpose, and compliance with a subject information provision would be likely to prejudice the crime and taxation purposes (s.29(2)).

An exemption to the non-disclosure provisions applies where disclosure is for a crime and taxation purpose and applying the provisions would be likely to prejudice any of those purposes (s.29(3)).

Practical example

A social worker proposes to tell the police about his client's threats to murder his wife. If section 29(3) applies he is not required to inform his client that he is sharing information for such purposes. He may disclose information to the police even though the information was obtained to provide social care. He must, however, demonstrate compliance with Schedule 2 and 3 (relevant conditions including Sched. 2, para. 4 (vital interests) and para. 6 (legitimate interests) and Sched. 3, para. 3 (vital interests) and Data Protection (Processing of Sensitive Data) Order 2000 (for detection or prevention of crime).

Section 29 significantly reduces an individual's rights to access information held by the police, although exemptions must not be used as a blanket to withhold everything the police hold on an applicant. They must be used on a case-by-case basis and only to the extent required (ACPO 2006 *Data Protection Manual of Guidance* (the ACPO manual)).

Examples

It may be justifiable to refuse to comply with a subject access request (or to provide only a partial response to a subject access request) where:

- A suspect seeks access to personal data held on intelligence systems in order to determine the level and nature of police interest in, or intelligence held on, her.
- The information requested reveals details of a surveillance operation against the subject during which a bugging device was secretly installed in his home in accordance with the Regulation of Investigatory Powers Act 2000. The police would be justified in refusing to include some or all of this information in their response.
- A defendant in a forthcoming trial seeks access to personal data associated with those ongoing proceedings.
- Compliance with the request is likely to diminish future assistance to the police by the public
- Compliance with the request would reveal confidential police techniques (see ACPO Manual).

There are also extensive exceptions for national security matters under section 28 of the Act. These may be relevant to police investigation and intelligence material.

12.4 THE POLICE AND FREEDOM OF INFORMATION

The following bodies are all public authorities subject to the Freedom of Information Act 2000:

- a police authority;
- the Metropolitan Police Authority;
- a chief officer of police of a police force in England or Wales;
- the British Transport Police;
- the Ministry of Defence Police;
- any person with statutory power to nominate individuals to be appointed as special constables by justices of the peace.

The Serious Organised Crime Agency (SOCA) is exempt from FOIA 2000 despite its officers having the powers of police constables. The Association of Chief Police Officers, the highly influential coordinating and policy making body, is not subject to FOIA 2000. Since the individual Chief Officers that make up ACPO are not exempt, it is possible to make a FOIA 2000 request to the Chief Constable responsible for a particular ACPO area.

Although FOIA 2000, in theory, provides opportunities for the police to share, and the public to access, much information, several exemptions from disclosure apply to police information, particularly limiting access to information about investigations and proceedings:

- Section 23 provides an absolute exemption from disclosure of information directly or indirectly supplied to a public authority by: the security services, National Crime Intelligence Service and the Serious Organised Crime Agency. This significantly compromises applicants' ability to access information about various policing matters relating to national security or organised crime. Similarly, section 24 provides an exemption from disclosure on the basis of national security.
- The section 30 exemptions apply to investigations to ascertain whether a person should be charged with an offence, investigations into whether a person charged with an offence is guilty of it, and criminal proceedings. These provisions enable disclosure of information relating to particular inquiries or prosecutions to be withheld in the public interest. (Section 30(2) applies to information provided in confidence, and will be particularly relevant to covert human intelligence sources.)
- Section 32 (another absolute exemption) exempts information filed with or created by a court for the purposes of particular proceedings, or served

by or on a public authority for the purposes of particular proceedings. This exempts much police and other criminal justice material from disclosure where it relates to specific criminal proceedings.

- The data protection exemption applies where information relates to a particular individual (s.40).
- Sections 41 and 42 apply to information provided in confidence or subject to legal professional privilege.
- Further qualified exemptions apply where disclosure would be likely to prejudice:
  - law enforcement, meaning prevention or detection of crime, apprehension or prosecution of offenders and administration of justice (s.31);
  - the effective conduct of public affairs (s.36); or
  - health and safety, including the health and safety of the public, the police and particularly informants (s.38).

12.5 PUBLIC PROTECTION

Often the police possess information about individuals which indicates they present a threat to the public. Whilst disclosure of an individual's private information may have an adverse impact on her life, it can be justified to disclose information, to protect other individuals, or the wider public. Any disclosure (whether made to an individual or a public authority) must be undertaken in accordance with the DPA 1998, the HRA 1998 and, where relevant, the duty of confidentiality.

12.5.1 Police disclosures for the purposes of public protection

R v. *Chief Constable of North Wales* ex parte *AB & CD* [1997] 4 All ER 691 provides guidance on disclosures to the public for their own protection. In this case, the police disclosed to a caravan site owner that certain persons who had been convicted and served sentences for sexual offences against children were living on the site. When the site owner required these individuals to leave they challenged the police decision to disclose, by judicial review. The Court of Appeal held that as a general rule the police should not disclose information acquired in the course of their public duties, which was not generally available, and where disclosure was potentially damaging to that person. However, where the police considered in the exercise of a careful and bona fide judgment that it was desirable or necessary in the public interest to disclose information for the purpose of preventing crime or alerting members of the public to an apprehended danger, they were entitled to make such limited disclosure as was judged necessary to achieve that purpose. The police had performed the task adequately and the court did not interfere with the decision.

12.5.2 MAPPA

Multi-Agency Public Protection Arrangements (MAPPA) are designed to provide national coordination for assessing and managing risks posed by serious sexual and violent offenders. The arrangements impose statutory requirements on the police, probation and other agencies to arrange for the management of these offenders in the community. This necessitates information sharing between MAPPA agencies and by agencies with the public.

MAPPA Guidance 2007 Version 2.0, National Offender Management Service, Public Protection Unit, 2007 (the MAPPA Guidance), section 3 highlights the importance of information sharing to MAPPA:

> The quality of risk assessments and risk management plans are influenced by the effectiveness of information sharing arrangements. Unless all relevant information is available, in good time, to those making the assessments and drawing up the risk management plans, public protection may be compromised. The Responsible Authority (RA) must have robust arrangements in place for practicable information sharing across the MAPPA agencies.
>
> MAPPA Guidance, Section 3.1

The police's dangerous persons database (ViSOR) is intended to aid MAPPA agencies by assisting cooperative working and information sharing between the police, probation and prison services. The database, which is accessible only by specially trained and security-cleared public protection professionals, contains a national search facility enabling information about dangerous individuals to be accessed from a central point. It also permits transfer of records between agencies across the country.

Lawful information sharing between MAPPA agencies

The MAPPA guidance stipulates that information sharing must:

- have lawful authority;
- be necessary;
- be proportionate and done in ways which ensure the safety and security of the information shared; and
- be accountable.

LAWFUL AUTHORITY TO SHARE

Crime and Disorder Act 1998, s.115 provides lawful authority for sharing information for the purpose of developing local strategies to reduce crime and disorder.

The Criminal Justice Act 2003, s.325(3) further encourages information sharing by imposing a duty to cooperate upon certain Multi Agency Public Protection agencies (including police, probation, prison services, youth offending, local education and housing authorities, registered social landlords and certain health bodies). Section 325(4) makes clear such cooperation may include the exchange of information, thus providing additional legal authorisation for data sharing between these bodies.

NECESSARY

The Guidance details three specific purposes for sharing information within MAPPA:

- to identify those offenders who present a serious risk of harm to the public;
- to ensure the assessment of the risks they present are accurate; and
- to enable the most appropriate plans to be drawn up and implemented to manage assessed risks and thereby protect victims and the public.

If information is shared for these purposes it seems a strong case will have been made for the information sharing being necessary. It will also be relevant to DPA 1998 compliance, since the fourth DPA 1998 principle requires information to be accurate and up to date.

PROPORTIONALITY

Proportionality requires the relevant agencies to show the assessment and management of the risk(s) presented by the offender could not effectively be achieved other than by sharing the information in question. It also requires information to be shared with no more individuals than is absolutely necessary. The MAPPA Guidance puts great store in the value of secure handling and storage of information:

> it must be kept and shared safely and securely and it should only be available to, and shared with those, who have a legitimate interest in knowing it; that is, agencies and individuals involved in the MAPPA processes.

Again this has overlaps with the DPA 1998 requirements that information shared is relevant and not excessive and is protected by appropriate technological and organisational measures (third and seventh principles).

ACCOUNTABILITY

The relevant agencies must ensure the administrative procedures underpinning the efficient operation of MAPPA meetings and case conferences have the confidence of participants. Accurate, clear and timely record keeping is necessary to demonstrate accountable information sharing occurs.

Disclosure by MAPPA agencies

Section 4 of the MAPPA Guidance envisages delicate decisions about whether to disclose information to the public:

> MAPPA requires that the risk assessment of all MAPPA offenders identifies those persons who may be at risk of serious harm from the offender. The risk management plan (RMP) must identify how those risks will be managed. As part of this process, consideration must be given in each case as to whether disclosure of information about an offender to others should take place to protect victims, potential victims, staff and other persons in the community. This applies to all Categories and levels of MAPPA cases.

When disclosure should be considered (from the MAPPA Guidance):

- When there is evidence that grooming behaviours may take place, for example, through leisure clubs, churches, employment, schools or colleges; in the case of young offenders, limited and controlled disclosure may be made to school or college staff.
- If there is a condition in a SOPO/licence excluding offenders from a specific location and/or having contact with named persons.
- Where others may be at risk, for example, in supportive accommodation. This may include other service users, but usually it will be staff and managers who are told in order to enable more appropriate placements and for greater vigilance to be exercised.
- Where there is a need to protect past or potential victims, in particular where offenders strike up new relationships with partners who have children or grandchildren. In some cases, this may include friends or neighbours with children.
- Where a person may be in a position to actively assist in the risk management of an offender by being familiarised with risk factors and scenarios.

Normally when disclosures are made the offender is involved in this process. However, the Guidance envisages disclosures without informing the offender, where informing him could increase the potential risks to victims.

More senior officers will need to be involved where there are sensitive disclosure decisions to be taken, e.g. disclosure to the media including photographs. See for further details, ACPO 2007 *Guidance on Protecting the Public: Managing Sexual and Violent Offenders*.

The disclosing authority must handle all disclosure decisions with sensitivity, considering specifically:

- the potential risk to the offender, although this should not outweigh the potential risks to others if disclosure is not made;
- the identified individual(s) to be disclosed to;
- the offender's involvement (where risk factors allow) both in decisions about the need to disclose and the actual disclosure itself. In some cases,

the ideal situation is for the offender to consent to disclosure and to undertake the disclosure themselves either in the presence of their Offender Manager/supervising Police Officer or with the content of the disclosure being confirmed/verified by the Offender Manager/supervising Police Officer subsequently;

- the level of disclosure required, for example, this might include risk factors but not necessarily an offence history;
- discussions with third-party recipients of information. This includes: checking what they already know; that they understand the confidential and sensitive nature of the information; that they know how to make use of the information and what to do in the event of anything occurring which they need to report, and that they know whom to contact. It might also consider the key triggers for offending behaviour and requirements for successful risk management, for example, 'This is what you need to look out for. . .' or 'if you see X, you need to do Y'; and
- mechanisms and procedures for support for victims and offenders in case of breakdown in the processes.

12.5.3 Notification, registration and prohibition

Where offenders have been convicted or cautioned for certain offences, or are subject to certain other orders made for public protection purposes, they must share specified personal information with the police.

The notification requirements of Sexual Offences Act 2003, Part 2 (often known as the Sex Offenders Register) are an automatic requirement on offenders convicted or cautioned for certain sexual offences. The notification requirements aim to ensure the police are informed of offenders' whereabouts. Offenders have a duty to inform the police of their personal details including whereabouts within three days of conviction or caution or release from prison and at least annually thereafter. There is also a duty to notify the police of any change of personal details including whenever they spend seven days or more at another address. A notification order can be made in the UK requiring a person convicted or cautioned overseas to comply with the notification requirements as if they had been convicted in the United Kingdom.

The police are permitted to retain, use and share the information supplied for managing risks posed by the offender while in the community.

The notification requirements also apply to offenders who:

(a) are subject to a sexual offences prevention order made under Sexual Offences Act 2003, s.104 prohibiting specified conduct, where such prohibitions are necessary to protect the public or particular members of the public from serious sexual harm from that person;
(b) have breached a risk of sexual harm order (a civil preventative order made under Sexual Offences Act 2003, s.123 to protect children from

risks posed by individuals who may not necessarily have previous convictions for sexual or violent offences against children but who have, on at least two occasions, engaged in improper sexual conduct or communication with children and who pose a risk of causing further harm).

The Criminal Justice and Immigration Act 2008, Part 7 will also introduce violent offender orders. These orders permit the imposing of prohibitions, restrictions or conditions on serious violent offenders' movement, activities and associations and, similarly to the Sex Offenders Register requirements, impose requirements to disclose personal details, including addresses at which the offender regularly stays.

12.5.4 Criminal records and enhanced criminal records

When seeking employment, an individual may often be asked to disclose unspent criminal convictions. Police Act 1997, s.112 enables a criminal conviction certificate to be obtained, detailing every unspent conviction recorded against an individual or stating no convictions are recorded.

Normally an offender cannot be required to disclose spent convictions, and the courts, police, etc. are prohibited from disclosing information relating to spent convictions (Rehabilitation of Offenders Act 1974, ss.4(2), 9 and 9A). However, the Rehabilitation of Offenders Act 1974 (Exceptions) Order 1975, SI 1975/1023 recognises that it is appropriate to disclose information about spent convictions in order to assess suitability for certain professions (doctors and certain other health professionals, solicitors, barristers, accountants and teachers), and to assess suitability to work with children, to work for the crown or to work for certain other agencies, for example the prison service.

Police Act 1997, s.113 therefore provides for standard disclosure: a criminal record certificate which discloses spent and unspent cautions and spent convictions, to be provided where an application made by a prospective employee is accompanied by a statement from the prospective employer that the certificate is required for the purposes of an exempted question (one which does not permit the job applicant to withhold information relating to spent convictions or cautions).

Police Act 1997, s.115 governs enhanced criminal record certificates. An enhanced certificate must be disclosed to prospective employees where the position 'involves regularly caring for, training, supervising or being in sole charge of persons aged under 18, or certain specified positions which involve regularly caring for, training, supervising or being in sole charge of vulnerable adults. The enhanced criminal record certificate requires disclosure of:

(a) the prescribed details of every relevant matter relating to the applicant which is recorded in central records (including spent and unspent convictions); and additionally

(b) information which, in the chief officer's opinion, might be relevant to the suitability of the applicant for the position and ought to be included in the certificate (s.115(6)).

Enhanced disclosures: practical examples

In *R (X)* v. *Chief Constable of the West Midlands Police* [2004] EWCA Civ 1068; [2005] 1 W.L.R. 65, information about indecent exposure charges that were discontinued when the victim failed to identify the claimant, was disclosed in an enhanced certificate when the claimant applied to become a social worker. The Court of Appeal held that the Chief Constable was obliged to disclose information of potential relevance unless there was good reason not to so. The claimant unsuccessfully argued that there should be an opportunity to make representations prior to the police making a decision as to relevance.

In *R (S)* v. *Chief Constable of West Mercia* [2008] EWHC 2811 (Admin) the claimant had been acquitted of public order offences by a court on the basis of alibi. The police had decided that the allegations (which involved indecent exposure to women) were relevant to suitability to work with children because they might be true. The Administrative Court considering the police's decision to disclose, ruled that it was unreasonable to take such a view in the face of the court decision and without investigating the reason for the claimant's acquittal. The fact that allegations may have arisen due to mistaken identity could be a good reason for not disclosing.

Section 115(8) also enables a chief police officer to disclose information which might be relevant to the applicant's suitability but which ought not to be included in the certificate in the interests of the prevention or detection of crime and which can, without harming those interests, be disclosed to the prospective employer. This provision effectively enables secret information to be given to the prospective employer. The job applicant may never know about the information or the disclosure.

12.6 CONCLUSION

Much of the information which the police obtain and record (whether on the PNC or local databases) is personal data.

Whilst attention must be paid to the DPA 1998, several conditions under Schedules 2 and 3 enable information to be lawfully shared for crime investigation and prosecution purposes. Recognising the public interest in the effective investigation and prosecution of crime, exemptions from the data protection principles apply, which enable police forces to share information with each other, to obtain information from third parties, and to share information for public protection purposes.

The fact that the police, as a public authority, must act in accordance with the European Convention also imposes requirements to carefully consider the necessity and proportionality of information sharing. Again, sharing will, in the majority of instances, be justified, provided it is undertaken in accordance with statutory powers, and complies with the DPA 1998 and any duty of confidentiality.

Whilst individuals (victims or offenders) may wish to access information held by the police, their rights are relatively restricted (under the DPA 1998 and FOIA 2000) where disclosures relate to specific proceedings, might prejudice investigations or prosecution or cause harm to third parties.

Ultimately, whenever information is shared by or with the police, careful consideration needs to be given to how best to achieve a balance between the rights of individuals (including rights to privacy and to a fair trial) and the rights of the wider public.

Index